Hamlet
After Q1

Hamlet
After Q1

An Uncanny History
of the Shakespearean Text

Zachary Lesser

PENN

UNIVERSITY OF PENNSYLVANIA PRESS

PHILADELPHIA

MATERIAL TEXTS

Series Editors
Roger Chartier   Leah Price
Joseph Farrell   Peter Stallybrass
Anthony Grafton   Michael F. Suarez, S.J.

A complete list of books in the series
is available from the publisher.

Copyright © 2015 University of Pennsylvania Press
All rights reserved. Except for brief quotations used for purposes of review or scholarly citation, none of this book may be reproduced in any form by any means without written permission from the publisher.

Published by
University of Pennsylvania Press
Philadelphia, Pennsylvania 19104-4112
www.upenn.edu/pennpress

Printed in the United States of America on acid-free paper
10 9 8 7 6 5 4 3 2 1

Library of Congress Cataloging-in-Publication Data is available.
Lesser, Zachary.
  Hamlet after Q1 : an uncanny history of the Shakespearean text / Zachary Lesser. — 1st ed.
    p. cm. — (Material texts)
  Includes bibliographical references and index.
  ISBN 978-0-8122-4661-2
  1. Shakespeare, William, 1564–1616. Hamlet—Criticism, Textual.
  2. Shakespeare, William, 1564–1616—Bibliography—Quartos.
  3. Transmission of texts—England—History—17th century. I. Title.
  II. Series: Material texts.
  PR2807.L385 2015
  822.3'3—dc23
                                                      2014025092

Frontispiece: Barton Hall, where the first known copy of Q1 was discovered, after it was destroyed by fire in 1914. Reproduced by kind permission of the Suffolk Record Office, Bury St. Edmunds branch, shelf mark HD526/11/9.

For Taije and Raphael Boaz

belated discoveries and endless rarities

The treasures of time lie high, in Urnes, Coynes, and Monuments, scarce below the roots of some vegetables. Time hath endlesse rarities, and shows of all varieties; which reveals old things in heaven, makes new discoveries in earth, and even earth it self a discovery.
  —Thomas Browne, *Hydriotaphia, Urne-Buriall* (1658)

Who shall tell what may be the effect of writing? If it happens to have been cut in stone, though it lie face downmost for ages on a forsaken beach, or "rest quietly under the drums and tramplings of many conquests," it may end by letting us into the secret of usurpations and other scandals gossiped about long empires ago:— this world being apparently a huge whispering-gallery.
  —George Eliot, *Middlemarch* (1874), (mis)quoting *Urne-Buriall*

Genealogy . . . operates on a field of entangled and confused parchments, on documents that have been scratched over and recopied many times.
  —Michel Foucault, "Nietzsche, Genealogy, History" (1971)

CONTENTS

Introduction. The Urn-*Hamlet*   1

Chapter 1. As Originally Written by Shakespeare: Textual Bibliography and Textual Biography   25

Chapter 2. Contrary Matters: The Power of the Gloss and the History of an Obscenity   72

Chapter 3. Enter the Ghost in His Night Gowne: Behind Gertrude's Bed   114

Chapter 4. Conscience Makes Cowards: The Disintegration and Reintegration of Shakespeare   157

Conclusion. Q1 in the Library at Babel   207

Notes   223

Bibliography   259

Index   279

Acknowledgments   291

Introduction

The Urn-*Hamlet*

Two centuries after the death of its author, William Shakespeare's greatest play was changed forever. In 1823, Sir Henry Bunbury found an old book, "a small quarto, barbarously cropped, and very ill-bound," in a closet of the manor house of Great Barton, Suffolk. Or maybe he had found it two years earlier in the library, or in a closet in the library; Sir Henry could never seem to recall. He had recently inherited the manor and was taking an inventory of his new holdings, which fortuitously led him to this book that otherwise might have continued to rest on the shelf unknown and unread. Or maybe he was inspired to scour his shelves for rare books after reading *The Library Companion* by the self-described bibliomaniac Thomas Frognall Dibdin; so Dibdin claimed, anyway, providing a third possibility for the discovery.[1] Since Barton Hall was destroyed by fire in 1914, it is now impossible to know exactly where this remarkable book was found. But the story I will tell deals repeatedly with loss, destruction, and reconstruction.

Bunbury's "small quarto" contained twelve of Shakespeare's plays, nearly all in their first editions, including *Romeo and Juliet*, *The Merchant of Venice*, *A Midsummer Night's Dream*, and several of the histories. Such a compendium would today be worth a fortune, had it not been disbound sometime later in the nineteenth century while in the collection of the Duke of Devonshire, the pages of each play "barbarously cropped" once again to be inlaid in fine paper and rebound.[2] Despite the obvious value of these Shakespearean first editions, however, in an age when antiquarian book collecting was a relatively new gentlemanly pursuit and when numerous Shakespearean playbooks were still in private hands, this "ill-bound" book would not have created such a stir had it not included one oddity (Figure 1).

Figure 1. Title page of Q1 *Hamlet*.

Reproduced by permission of the Huntington Library, San Marino, California, shelf mark 69304

This was a copy of the first quarto of *Hamlet* (Q1), published a year prior to the earliest text of the play then known and, at the time, the unique example of the edition. What Bunbury had found was recognizably *Hamlet*, but it was radically different from the play that was, already by 1823, the most highly prized and revered work of English literature. Bunbury surmised that Q1 and the other plays in his volume had been purchased and bound together by his grandfather, Sir William Bunbury, "who was an ardent collector of old dramas." If so, one wonders how such a collector could have missed the incredible rarity in the group. But Sir William seems to have had no idea what he had on his hands; he drew no special attention to the book, and it lay quietly on that shelf in Barton Hall for two more generations. Nor apparently did Sir Henry value the book highly enough: he exchanged it with the booksellers Payne and Foss "for books to the value of £180," but they quickly sold it to Devonshire at a tidy profit.[3] Before completing this sale, however, Payne and Foss sought to satisfy "the intense curiosity which this book has raised in every literary circle" by issuing a reprint edition from their shop at 81 Pall Mall.[4] The 1825 publication of *The First Edition of the Tragedy of Hamlet, By William Shakespeare* created huge excitement in the press and brought Q1 to general notice (Figure 2).

In what seems to have been the earliest public report of the discovery, the *Literary Gazette* told its readers that Q1 contained "new readings, of infinite interest; sentiments expressed, which greatly alter several of the characters; differences in the names; and many minor points which are extremely curious."[5] This *Hamlet* was about half the length of the familiar version, and to some its poetry seemed only a "poor version" of the speeches they already knew, although others found many new "lines of great beauty."[6] Some of the most famous lines, in fact, were different. Instead of asking, "To be, or not to be, that is the Question," Hamlet pondered, "To be, or not to be, I there's the point," before going on to speak explicitly of God's judgment that consigns us to an afterlife in heaven or hell.[7] Hamlet's last words were likewise transformed: the rest was no longer silence, as Hamlet piously implored "heauen receiue my soule" before dying (sig. I3v). The plot followed broadly the same trajectory, but with a number of "extremely curious" variations: "To be, or not to be" and the ensuing "nunnery scene" with Ophelia (Ofelia in Q1) were transposed to an earlier point in the play; in the so-called closet scene, the Queen (here called Gertred) explicitly denied any knowledge of the murder of Hamlet's father and vowed to assist her son in revenge, shedding new light on a long-standing debate about her character; and in a scene with no parallel in the familiar version of the play, Horatio told the Queen of Hamlet's adventures at sea, and the two proceeded

THE FIRST EDITION

OF THE

TRAGEDY

OF

HAMLET,

BY

WILLIAM SHAKESPEARE.

LONDON.
PRINTED FOR N. L. (NICHOLAS LING)
AND JOHN TRUNDELL
1603.

REPRINTED AT THE SHAKESPEARE PRESS,
BY WILLIAM NICOL,
FOR PAYNE AND FOSS, PALL-MALL.
1825.

Figure 2. Title page of Payne and Foss's 1825 reprint of Q1 *Hamlet*.
Reproduced by permission of the Horace Howard Furness Memorial Library, Kislak Center for Special Collections, Rare Books and Manuscripts, University of Pennsylvania Libraries, shelf mark PR2750.B07 1825.

to conspire against Claudius. Polonius's name had oddly become Corambis, his servant Reynaldo had turned into Montano, and scattered throughout the text were numerous other differences large and small, at the broad level of plot and character and at the narrow level of single word choices. "From these variations," the newspaper confessed, "and the absence of so much of what appeared in the edition of the ensuing year 1604, we hardly know what to infer."[8]

The writer of the report in the *Literary Gazette* expressed not only "gratification that an edition of Hamlet anterior to any hitherto known to the world has just been brought to light." Like many other contemporary commenters on Q1, he also emphasized his "surprise that it should have been so long hidden," for "it is a strange thing that such a volume . . . should have been suffered to be undiscovered or unnoticed among the lumber of any library." He suggested that the book had been previously owned by Bunbury's ancestor Thomas Hanmer, editor of the first Oxford Shakespeare (1743–44), although given Bunbury's own, presumably more reliable, ideas about its provenance, the newspaper may have simply been associating it with Bunbury's famous Shakespearean relative.[9] If in fact Hanmer ever owned the volume, then he too had not understood its importance: had he known that it contained the sole exemplar of a remarkably different text of *Hamlet*, presumably he would have mentioned it in his edition. Like so much else about Q1, exactly how this book made its way into Bunbury's closet remains a mystery. About its history prior to Payne and Foss's 1825 reprint, we have only shadowy guesses.

The entire textual history of *Hamlet* is haunted by bibliographic ghosts. Repeatedly, new archival finds offer tantalizing hints of texts that no longer exist, if they ever did, and of lineages that can no longer be traced. In the middle of the eighteenth century Richard Farmer found the earliest recorded mention of the play, Thomas Nashe's satirical comment in 1589 that "English *Seneca* read by candlelight" helps unlearned dramatists patch together "whole *Hamlets*, I should say handfulls of tragical speeches."[10] Since no *Hamlet* playtext survives from the sixteenth century, and since Shakespeare had no known connection to the London theater in the 1580s, Nashe's comment has engendered fierce debate over the dating of the play, its authorship, and Shakespeare's biography ever since Farmer uncovered it. Farmer first drew attention as well to another allusion that poses similar chronological difficulties, Thomas Lodge's 1596 reference to a devil who "looks as pale as the Visard of the ghost which cried so miserably at the Theator, like an oister wife, *Hamlet, reuenge*." Several early seventeenth-century writers also seem to allude to this phrase, which appears to have become famous, and yet it does not appear in any extant text of *Hamlet*.[11]

From the beginning of *Hamlet*, the time is out of joint, with the play strangely seeming to predate its own existence. Two decades after Farmer's archival finds, Edmond Malone discovered the diary of Philip Henslowe in the Dulwich College Library as he was preparing his monumental variorum edition of 1790. The diary contained another ghost of *Hamlet*: "9 of June 1594, R[eceive]d at hamlet . . . viij s."[12] Is this the *Hamlet* to which Nashe and Lodge refer? What is its connection to Shakespeare's play? And how do these references relate to yet another *Hamlet* text that turned up in Germany in 1779? Published from a manuscript dated 1710 and possibly deriving from an early English troupe touring the Continent, this version of the play is entitled *Der bestrafte Brudermord* (*Fratricide Punished*). It bears some intriguing similarities to the Q1 text, particularly the name of the councillor, who is called Corambus. Unfortunately, the manuscript has since been lost, and so here again we stand at several removes from the "true original copy," with little access to its textual history and provenance.[13] *Der bestrafte Brudermord* is a strangely slapstick and farcical play; it has even been suggested that it is the script of a Punchinello-type puppet show.[14] Partly for this reason, it was largely ignored before the discovery of Q1. It is remarkable how little commentary the German play generated in the decades after its initial publication; Malone, for instance, makes no mention of the text anywhere in his edition, nor does Isaac Reed in his editions (1803, 1813), nor James Boswell in his revision of Malone (1821). By the mid-nineteenth century, however, once scholars could see that it shared some odd features with Q1, *Brudermord* could no longer be so easily dismissed. Whereas these editors had remained completely silent about the German play, a century later entire books were devoted to its relationship to Q1.

Together, these textual traces have conjured up the so-called *Ur-Hamlet*, a pre-Shakespearean drama that survives, if in fact it survives at all, only in the single phrase quoted by Lodge: "*Hamlet, reuenge.*" As Emma Smith remarks, despite the unfortunate detail of its nonexistence, the text of this "phantom play has been variously deduced, discussed and even edited by textual scholars," fabricated from portions of *Der bestrafte Brudermord* and Q1.[15] Again and again, we encounter missing texts, cryptic allusions, and bibliographic shades. Indeed, even Q1 existed as a faint echo before Bunbury found it: Malone noted that the second quarto (Q2) claimed on its title page to be "Newly imprinted and enlarged to almost as much againe as it was, according to the true and perfect Coppie," and he correctly inferred that "from [these] words it is manifest that a former *less perfect* copy had been issued from the press" (Figure 3).[16]

THE
Tragicall Historie of
HAMLET,
Prince of Denmarke.

By William Shakespeare.

Newly imprinted and enlarged to almost as much againe as it was, according to the true and perfect Coppie.

AT LONDON,
Printed by I. R. for N. L. and are to be sold at his shoppe vnder Saint Dunstons Church in Fleetstreet. 1604.

Figure 3. Title page of Q2 *Hamlet*.
Reproduced by permission of the Elizabethan Club, Yale University, shelf mark Eliz 168.

Since the eighteenth century, then, the idea that there was a *Hamlet* before *Hamlet* has haunted Shakespearean editors and critics. If the play predated Shakespeare, just how Shakespearean was it? While we know that some kind of *Hamlet* play was being performed in London as early as 1589, we have very little idea of its content, despite frequent attempts to imagine it. What if this *Ur-Hamlet* looked more like Shakespeare's *Hamlet* than we have generally been willing to admit? Shakespeare's habit of drawing on narrative sources like Holinshed's *Chronicles* and Cinthio's *Gli Hecatommithi* was widely accepted, of course. And even *Hamlet* was acknowledged to have a direct prose source: *The Hystorie of Hamblet*, an English translation of François de Belleforest's French translation of the Hamlet story in Saxo Grammaticus's medieval *Gesta Danorum*. While the *Hystorie* did not appear until 1608 and is now generally understood to postdate the play, eighteenth-century scholarship imagined it as a primary source of Shakespeare's version and inferred that there must have been an earlier, lost edition.[17] The use of sources like these, however, did not pose the same threat to Shakespeare's authority as the ghost of the earlier *Hamlet* play, since the Bard could easily be presented as spinning poetic gold from the dull straw of these bare prose accounts. Similarly, as we shall see in Chapter 1, many scholars believed that Shakespeare began his career by revising the dramas of other playwrights. But revising an earlier play of *Henry VI* was one thing; revising a previous *Hamlet*, Shakespeare's masterpiece, posed far greater concerns. So long as there was no actual text that might be connected to any earlier version of the play, these doubts could be kept at bay, and eighteenth- and early nineteenth-century scholars largely agreed to forget about this pre-Shakespearean *Hamlet* after a routine mention of its existence. When Q1 reemerged from its purgatory in Barton Hall, however, all that changed. This "former *less perfect* copy" was far different from anything that Malone or anyone else had suspected, and it forced a reconfiguration of everything that had previously been known about the play.

Few would have appreciated the belated return of Q1 *Hamlet* more than Thomas Browne, early modern England's greatest writer on the accidents of time and history. Browne's *Hydriotaphia, Urne-Buriall* meditates on precisely the problems raised by Bunbury's find: the sudden emergence of objects from the past provokes a kind of explanatory fever while resisting any easy assimilation into our received orders of knowledge.[18] Browne's narrative begins with the unexpected irruption of the unknown into the mundane countryside of his native Norfolk: "In a Field of old *Walsingham*, not many moneths past, were digged up between fourty and fifty Vrnes, deposited in a dry and sandy soile, not a yard deep, nor farre from one another."[19] In Browne's essay, the urns become emblems "silently expressing . . . the ruines of forgotten times" and symbolizing how little we can hope to know of the past: "What Song the *Syrens* sang, or what name *Achilles* assumed when he hid himself among women, though puzling Questions are not beyond all conjecture. What time the persons of these Ossuaries entred the famous Nations of the dead, and slept with Princes and Counsellours, might admit a wide solution. But who were the proprietaries of these bones, or what bodies these ashes made up, were a question above Antiquarism."[20] And yet despite the difficulty of reconstructing the past, the brute fact of these urns, the miracle of their continuing existence and resurfacing, demands Browne's attention: "Seeing they arose as they lay, almost in silence among us . . . we were very unwilling they should die again, and be buried twice among us." Rather than attempting to know the unknowable, to answer "a question above Antiquarism," Browne is instead "hinted by the occasion" to discourse on time, loss, and eternity. In its encyclopedic catalogue, *Urne-Buriall* speaks of virtually everything to do with death, burial, and immortality—everything, that is, except for "who were the proprietaries of these bones, or what bodies these ashes made up."[21]

What most strikes Browne about the urns is that they lay "not a yard deep" in that field in Walsingham and yet had remained hidden for more than a millennium. This paradox delighted him and led to his brilliant opening meditation: "The treasures of time lie high, in Urnes, Coynes, and Monuments, scarce below the roots of some vegetables. Time hath endlesse rarities, and shows of all varieties; which reveals old things in heaven, makes new discoveries in earth, and even earth it self a discovery. That great Antiquity *America* lay buried for a thousand years; and a large part of the earth is still in the Urne unto us."[22]

A large part of the earth is still in the urn unto us: scarcely a yard deep, waiting to be found . . . or perhaps not. These urns could have remained underground with the vegetable roots for another thousand years, Browne implies. And even when the urn is opened, there is no guarantee that we will be able to make sense of its contents, which do not necessarily yield an increase in knowledge or understanding. The past grows from the accidents of survival, and our histories are written out of such simultaneously ordinary and numinous things as the urns contained: "peeces of small boxes, or combes handsomely wrought, handles of small brasse instruments, brazen nippers, and in one some kind of *Opale*."[23] Time periodically divulges urns, coins, and monuments from the earth—the material texts of human existence—and we struggle to understand the past from these scattered fragments. The same could be said of the copy of Q1 *Hamlet* lying in the closet of Barton Hall. With Browne, therefore, this book begins by turning away from a search for origins that may well be unknowable, and instead, "hinted by the occasion" of the discovery of Q1, traces the reordering of our presumed knowledge after the unearthing of this treasure of time.

The *Gentleman's Magazine* sounds rather like Thomas Browne when it refers to Q1 *Hamlet* as an "exhumated curiosity."[24] So does the *Literary Gazette* when it marvels that the playbook had gone so long "undiscovered or unnoticed among the lumber of any library." When exactly Q1 disappeared from memory is a question above antiquarianism. "Hamlet Prince of Denmark 1603" appears in a manuscript list of plays owned by Henry Oxinden in the 1660s, but we have no public seventeenth-century references to the edition after the blurb on the title page of Q2. Perhaps this advertisement of textual superiority rendered the earlier edition obsolete almost immediately, or perhaps, a bit later, the Folio (F) made copies of Q1 expendable. By the Restoration, it seems, Q1 had already been forgotten. The foundational Shakespearean editors of the eighteenth and early nineteenth centuries—from Nicholas Rowe (1709) to Samuel Johnson (1765) to Malone (1790) to Boswell (1821)—had certainly never seen it. And the great Romantic readers of *Hamlet*—Goethe and Schlegel, Coleridge and Hazlitt—had written their pioneering analyses with no idea that the play had first appeared in this very different form.[25]

The central argument of this book is that Bunbury's discovery, itself a historical accident, has had profound effects on our understanding of *Hamlet*, of Shakespeare as an author, and of the nature of the Shakespearean text. These effects have gone unnoticed, however, because they derive from what I call the "uncanny historicity" of Q1, which does not easily fit our usual modes of historicist scholarship. The *Literary Gazette* perfectly captured the strangeness of Q1 by terming it a "new (old) Play": Q1 is simultaneously a text of 1603 and a text of 1823.[26] Behind Freud's conception of the uncanny lies just the sort of temporal confusion that Q1 embodies: *then* impinges on *now* as the forgotten or concealed past returns to life in the present, producing a disorienting sensation of alterity within familiarity.[27] This "new (old) Play" comes both "before" Q2 and F, published earliest of the three, and "after" them, becoming widely known only after two centuries of editing, performance, and criticism had raised *Hamlet* to the pinnacle of English literature. The immediate reaction to Q1 in the nineteenth century entirely depended on this uncanny temporal oscillation, as does the ongoing and shaping power it has had on twentieth- and twenty-first-century ideas of *Hamlet*. Q1's status as the earliest edition of the play demanded that it be understood as in some way originary, while its belated emergence ensured that this understanding would be rooted in an already extensive tradition of Shakespearean interpretation. Only because readers, performers, and spectators first encountered it in the early nineteenth century has Q1 transformed *Hamlet* and Shakespeare in the particular ways that it has done.[28]

The uncanny sense that, as Freud writes, something "known of old and long familiar" had returned to the Victorians in an unfamiliar form—one perhaps related to that other, mysterious *Hamlet* imagined as pre-Shakespearean both chronologically and aesthetically—produced the imperative to investigate that accompanies the ghostly.[29] For Marjorie Garber a ghost "is a memory trace. It is the sign of something missing, something omitted, something undone. It is itself at once a question, and the sign of putting things in question."[30] What appeared in Bunbury's closet was a ghost in this sense, the trace of the forgotten or repressed memory of a *Hamlet* before *Hamlet*, a sign that something was—is—missing from our understanding of the Shakespearean text. Like the ghost of Hamlet's father, Q1 returns in such a questionable shape that we will speak to it.

Q1 is thus anachronistic in the root senses of that word. The Greek prefix *ana-* can signify not only "against" or "backward"—yielding the common meaning of *anachronism* as misplaced in time—but also "again" or "anew," suggesting the oddity of a belated return that, Rip Van Winkle–like, scrambles our expectations of temporal order and progression. Q1 comes back again in time, in the wrong time, but also *just in time* (inevitably so) for the role it is to play in its "own" time. As Margreta de Grazia has noted, in "the field of literary studies, as presently historicized, nothing could be worse than to be accused of anachronism."[31] But what to do when history itself is unsettlingly anachronistic?

The uncanny nature of Q1 challenges both traditional bibliographic scholarship and the historicist criticism that has recently dominated Shakespeare and early modern studies. Textual critics have long analyzed the three texts of *Hamlet* in terms of their stemmatic relationships, and their study of Q1 has largely involved a search for its origins. Such bibliographic work has illuminated many aspects of Q1 (and of Q2 and F), but because it focuses solely on the moment of creation of these texts, it cannot account for the strange effects of a quarto that is simultaneously first and last. Indeed, one of the foundational achievements of the eighteenth-century editorial tradition culminating in Malone's edition, systematized in the twentieth century by the New Bibliographers, was to establish that only the earliest editions can carry any weight in textual matters. By definition, anything to do with Q1 as a nineteenth-century text can have no textual "authority," and not surprisingly, bibliographers have ignored its reemergence in that period.[32] And yet, as I will argue, we cannot fully understand Q1 without treating it as a text existing simultaneously in two very different historical moments.

The main strands of historicist criticism in early modern studies have likewise sought to root the text in the moment of its coming-into-being. For New Historicism, as I have argued elsewhere, this was generally (if usually only implicitly) the moment of composition, which provides the signal date anchoring the otherwise jarring juxtapositions of that methodology.[33] The assumption of a totalized synchrony, centered on the time of writing, justifies the typically rapid movement among the various aspects of early modern culture.[34] There is thus a hidden investment in the author as a "principle of thrift"—in this case, a temporal thrift—in a movement that sought foundationally to decenter that figure.[35] For it is ultimately the author who allows New Historicism to locate its texts in time, and these texts are rarely allowed to escape "their" time.

More recent historicist criticism affiliated with the history of the material text has shifted the relevant historical context away from the moment of authorial composition and toward other events in the life of the work. Studies of the materiality of the dramatic script have attended to the multistage process of revision (authorial or theatrical), denying any single moment of origin for a play such as *Hamlet* that derives from various sources and that evidently went through numerous changes over the course of its life in repertory.[36] Other scholars, and here I include my own earlier work on the "politics of publication," have focused on the moment of the play's entrance into the marketplace of print, sometimes years removed from its first staging and years after the (literal) death of the author. Still others have attended to the material traces left by readers as they used books, annotating them, compiling them into larger volumes, cutting and pasting them into new textual configurations.[37] But while these critical approaches go some way toward decentering not merely the author but also the moment of authorial composition, they still tend to retain the periodizing framework of more traditional literary history, training their attention on the play's meanings as they are rooted in early modern culture. As Russell Berman writes, the "assertion of the priority of contemporaneity, the celebration of the present, defines the politics of periodization: it is either our present, the vanguard of historical progress, or it is the historical present of the objects of study, presumed to be fully grounded in that single, isolated moment of time."[38] In this way, our literary histories lead us to imagine, on the one hand, an orderly diachronic parade of movements, texts, and authors in a kind of secular typology of supersession, and on the other, a synchronic coherence that ties literary works to the period of their creation.[39] Indeed, the diachronic transformation of one period into the next depends on the synchronic uniformity attributed to each. But Q1 "belongs" as much to the early nineteenth century as to the early seventeenth century, not because we can trace a continuous chronological path from its publication to its later nineteenth-century "reception"—quite the opposite—but rather because Q1 seems to flicker back and forth between 1603 and 1823. Our usual historicism cannot imagine that these two dates might coexist as a single "period," strangely disconnected from the intervening years.

For this reason as well, Q1 has not been amenable to the cultural-studies model that has guided much of the work on the meaning of Shakespeare after "his" time, work focused on appropriation, adaptation, and afterlives. This field has sought to understand, in Michael Bristol's words, "how the value of Shakespeare is sustained and transmitted over time against a background of rapidly shifting cultural frameworks" throughout the "long and significant cultural afterlife" of the plays; or, in Douglas Lanier's words, "how and why popular culture uses Shakespeare, and how those uses bear upon the image and value of Shakespeare in our culture."[40] While I am certainly interested here in showing how the value and meaning of Shakespeare as an author, and of *Hamlet* as a play, was fundamentally reshaped by the discovery of Q1, nonetheless what Bunbury discovered in his closet and what Payne and Foss reprinted was not quite an "afterlife" of *Hamlet*. To the contrary, the importance of Q1 was immediately perceived to derive from the fact that it had existed *prior* to the play that readers had come to know as *Hamlet*.[41] The result was a renewed effort to historicize Shakespeare and a contentious debate over how to locate *Hamlet* properly in biographical, theatrical, literary, and national time. In this sense, Q1 is less an afterlife than a past life, a ghostly voice recovered in a séance. A historicism based on the idea of afterlives or appropriations, which emphasizes the forward chronological movement of Shakespeare as a cultural icon that gets reimagined and repackaged in later periods, cannot fully account for the uncanny historicity of Q1.

A number of critics, in early modern studies and in other fields, have lately begun to call for a less hermetically periodized, less chronologically rigid sense of history: from de Grazia's interest in anachronism and Wai Chee Dimock's theory of the "resonance" of literary texts across time; to Jonathan Gil Harris's work on "untimely matter"; to Peter Stallybrass and Ann Rosalind Jones's study of the memory embedded in clothing; to book-historical work on the multiple temporalities of reprinting; to Hugh Grady and Terence Hawkes's advocacy of "presentist Shakespeares"; to recent work in queer historicism by Carolyn Dinshaw, Carla Freccero, and Heather Love and the queer philology of Jeffrey Masten; to postcolonial critiques of "Western time."[42] My own interests do not quite align with the governing assumptions of any of these critical methodologies, and my study of Q1 has confirmed for me (in a way that Masten and Valerie Traub have also articulated) the ongoing vitality and necessity of the kind of historical and genealogical inquiry that some strands of "unhistoricism" and presentism reject entirely.[43] Nonetheless, I am influenced by their common impulse to break down, in Harris's words, the "idea of the 'moment' as a self-identical unit divided from other moments that come before and after it."[44]

Because the uncanny historicity of Q1 locates it in a blind spot of our usual disciplinary modes of historicism, an odd bifurcation has developed in the scholarship on that edition.[45] The *text* of Q1 has received immense attention over the years, and yet the discovery of the *book* that contained that text has received virtually none. The events that culminated in Nicholas Ling and John Trundle's 1603 publication have been imagined and scrutinized from every possible angle, but the events that followed from Payne and Foss's 1825 republication have been wholly ignored. We have been so busy trying to uncover Q1's *origins*, in other words, that we have neglected its *history*. To write this history, we must conceive of it as a genealogy written, in Foucault's elegant phrase, "on a field of entangled and confused parchments, on documents that have been scratched over and recopied many times." Like Browne's meditation on the urns, genealogy "opposes itself to the search for 'origins.'" Instead, "the genealogist . . . listens to history," thereby discovering "not a timeless and essential secret" but rather "the secret that [things] have no essence or that their essence was fabricated in a piecemeal fashion from alien forms."[46]

Our *Hamlet* is "after Q1" because our very conception of this play depends on a long history, one that rests like a fulcrum on Bunbury's discovery but that does not proceed in any neat chronology. This book therefore does not purport to solve the mystery of Q1's origins. Rather, it explores some of "the accidents, the minute deviations—or conversely, the complete reversals—the errors, the false appraisals, and the faulty calculations that gave birth" to the

Hamlet and the Shakespeare that we know, or think we know.⁴⁷ The history of *Hamlet* after Q1 is one of palimpsestic and piecemeal fabrication. It follows a wandering, echoic path that begins in the nineteenth century, reverberates back into the seventeenth and sixteenth, and returns to haunt the twentieth and twenty-first—"this world," as George Eliot learned from Thomas Browne, "being apparently a huge whispering-gallery."⁴⁸

Bunbury's find may have been a historical accident but it prompted copious theories and narratives, which rival Browne's meditation in their variety and labyrinthine elaboration and which have not ceased ever since. Indeed, as Dover Wilson once observed, Q1 seems to bring forth theory after theory of its origins, out of all proportion to its bibliographic significance in establishing the text of Shakespeare's *Hamlet*.⁴⁹ It is the uncanny historicity of Q1 that produces this explanatory drive: appearing only after the canonization of *Hamlet* as "the chosen representative of the English drama, nay of the English artistic faculty, among the great nations of Europe," Q1 immediately became a text that "would be spoke to" (sig. B1v), in a way that would never have occurred had the book existed continuously since 1603.⁵⁰ As de Grazia has shown, by the late eighteenth century *Hamlet* had come to be understood as fully "modern," in the Romantic sense of the modern as that which "opens itself to the upcoming, ever-advancing future."⁵¹ The sudden appearance of Q1—which seemed rather to open itself to the past, to the same antiquated prehistory as Nashe's and Lodge's satiric gibes about the stale bombast of the earlier *Hamlet*—created a paradox that required unraveling. As Browne understood, accidental loss and recovery cast a mysterious aura over the everyday objects of human life (a comb, a pair of scissors, a book), creating a kind of epistemological vacuum that demands to be filled with historical narrative.

In fact, even the survival of the complete text of Q1 rests on a lucky archival accident. Bunbury's copy lacked the last leaf; it breaks off in a way that seems perfectly to symbolize this strangely recovered play. Hamlet speaks his final line, followed by the stage direction "*Ham. dies.*"—and the last word in the book is the catchword: "*Enter*" (sig. I3v). We have no idea who enters or why. This play about a haunting, which had itself just returned unexpectedly to the world of the living, concludes on a ghostly entrance. But of course none of this is actually symbolic; it is only a habit of the literary critical mind that finds it resonant. Rather, this incongruous "*Enter*" is merely an accidental by-product of the materiality of early playbooks, which required catchwords so that the sheets could be properly assembled, and which were sold as unbound, stitched pamphlets that were particularly liable to lose their first and final pages.[52]

With the loss of the last leaf, we would never have known how the play ends if a second copy had not surfaced a generation after the first. In 1856, the Dublin bookseller M. W. Rooney was approached by a student at Trinity College who wanted to sell an old playbook. According to Rooney's account, which is likely tinted by self-aggrandizement, the student had shopped it around to several booksellers, but no one was interested in an old pamphlet of "insignificant appearance," perhaps because this copy, while it included the final leaf, lacked the title page. Unless one actually read the book, it might seem to be any old edition of *Hamlet*. Rooney decided to buy it—still, like Bunbury's grandfather, having no idea of its true nature. But "when collating it," he tells us, "I discovered a different reading in the last page from that to which I had been accustomed; and, on further examination, I found the 'Old Man, Polonius,' in the character of Corambis."[53]

Rooney apparently first offered the book to the Duke of Devonshire, "thinking by that means that a perfect copy would be in the possession of His Grace," but "received no reply." He then approached the scholar and collector James Orchard Halliwell (later Halliwell-Phillipps), asking a hundred guineas (£105) for it, adding "that, if he did not give me that sum, I would try the British Museum." Halliwell correctly predicted that the museum would never buy an imperfect book at Rooney's asking price, and he offered considerably less. Rooney refused and ultimately sold the copy to the booksellers T. and W. Boone for seventy pounds, still far more than he had paid for it.[54] But Rooney bristled at the arrogance of the Londoners who had taken him for a rube, incapable "(I suppose from being merely an Irish bookseller)" of "trac[ing] this quarto to be the exact one of 1603." It gratified him immensely to learn that the Boones had turned around and sold the book to none other than Halliwell, who had by this point seen his error: the "gem" that, "in the hands of an Irish bookseller, two days before," Halliwell had denigrated as "imperfect, cut down, not worth more than 40*l*.—is purchased as the greatest literary treasure for 120*l*."[55] Halliwell was now was constrained to pay, in "Sybilline fashion," far more than the initial offering price.[56] Finally, the British Museum bought the book in similar "Sybilline fashion" from Halliwell, "as part of a parcel of rare quartos, none individually priced, but costing £1000 in all."[57]

The allusion to the Sibylline books is well chosen, for as in the Roman legend, the value of Q1 *Hamlet* grows paradoxically through destruction, loss, and missed opportunity. According to Lactantius, an old woman (in fact the

Cumaean Sibyl) offered to sell nine rolls of prophecies to Tarquinius Priscus, fifth king of Rome, but he "mocked the huge price and laughed at the woman's madness." When she burned three of the rolls and offered the remaining six at the same price, Tarquin "thought the woman madder still." She burned another three, repeating the initial terms of sale. Finally, recognizing that the prophecies must have great value if the woman persisted in pricing them so highly, Tarquin bought the three surviving rolls, which were placed in the Temple of Jupiter to be consulted in case of emergency.[58] In "Sybilline fashion," it seems, the true worth of Q1 *Hamlet* could be perceived only in retrospect, with each owner in turn appearing unaccountably to misunderstand its true value. But in fact the opposite is the case: that value does not inhere in Q1 but is rather produced through a series of transactions that begin the process of creating meaning from, and for, this strangely recovered text, just as the Sibyl's destruction of some of the rolls produces the value of those that remain.

Again and again in the history of *Hamlet* after Q1 we see this Sibylline progression, in which meaning accrues to the text over time but then is retrospectively imagined to have been there from the beginning. As I show in the ensuing chapters, historicist scholarship repeatedly discovers in archival research, philological inquiry, and bibliographic analysis truths about the Shakespearean text that in fact derive from the very process of "discovering" them. This recursive progression explains another fact about the Rooney copy that would otherwise seem inexplicable. Like the Bunbury copy, it no longer exists in its nineteenth-century state; in the early 1920s, conservators at the British Library removed the leaves of Q1 from the volume in which Rooney originally bought it and rebound them separately.[59] When Rooney first saw his copy of Q1, however, it was interleaved with parts of the 1718 edition of the play, used to compare the received text with this new one. Whoever did the interleaving also underlined and emended the Q1 text, largely following the work of Lewis Theobald in his *Shakespeare Restored* (1726) and his edition of Shakespeare's works (1733). Lacking the title page, this person could only guess at the date of publication: "This Edition of Hamlet must be one of [th]e very first for there is one in *1605* & ano[the]r in *1611*—Both which must allude to this Edition by these Words in the Title Page of each—Newly imprinted and enlarged to almost as much again as it was—&c."[60] Since this owner refers to nothing later than Theobald's 1733 edition, and since therefore the annotations were likely made around this time, what this copy of Q1 in its original (now lost) condition reveals is that someone in the early eighteenth century was aware of the variant text and had hypothesized (correctly, as it turned out) that it preceded all other editions of the play. In other words, whoever he or she was, this person knew what no eighteenth-century Shakespearean knew and had access to a text of *Hamlet* that utterly eluded Theobald himself, along with Johnson, Malone, and the other editorial giants of the century. But the owner of this copy did nothing with this seemingly epochal find, and Q1 disappeared again for a century. How could a play that would revolutionize Shakespeare studies when it appeared in Payne and Foss's reprint in 1825 have been so blithely reconsigned to oblivion around 1733, and by someone who had clearly invested a great amount of effort into understanding its text? Why not make this find known to the world?

Again, the anachronism of Q1 offers an answer. In the early eighteenth century, *Hamlet* was certainly a highly regarded play, but it had not yet become the "chosen representative of the English drama, nay of the English artistic faculty, among the great nations of Europe." The first extended piece of literary criticism on the play, George Stubbes's *Some Remarks on the Tragedy of Hamlet*, appeared only in 1736, and it took an even-handed view, faulting Shakespeare for various "injudicious" decisions and accusing him of having "fallen into an Absurdity; for there appears no Reason at all in Nature, why the young Prince did not put the Usurper to Death as soon as possible."[61] By the time Bunbury found his copy in 1823, on the other hand—after the Romantic paeans of Goethe and Coleridge and the theatrical successes of David Garrick and others—*Hamlet* had been transformed into a work of such centrality to Shakespeare's oeuvre and to English literature as a whole that the discovery of a "new (old)" text of the play was an event of seemingly world-historical importance.

For this reason, before Halliwell could put his Sibylline book into his collection, it was left on display for three months at the Boones' shop at 29 New Bond Street so that it could be examined by "Shakspearian and other students," like the antediluvian giants' bones displayed in some churches around early modern London.[62] And while Payne and Foss hadn't worried much about the missing final leaf in the copy they reprinted—"as the play is perfect to the death of Hamlet, the loss is of comparatively small importance"[63]—no doubt many people went to the Boones' shop to see this literary curiosity. They had waited thirty years to learn who entered after that mysteriously incomplete stage direction in the catchword at the end of the Bunbury copy. (It was Voltemar and the English ambassadors.)

More important for the genealogy of *Hamlet* after Q1, the discovery of this second copy elicited renewed attempts to unravel the mystery of that text.

Early in 1857 the German scholar Tycho Mommsen published a landmark article in the *Athenaeum* precisely because the "discovery of the last leaf of the earliest 'Hamlet' [had] . . . some months ago, excited great interest on both sides of the water, and again directed the public attention to that curious edition."[64] And in the same year, again responding to the new discovery, another German scholar was the first to suggest tentatively that *Der bestrafte Brudermord* and Q1 shared a common ancestor: "We are tempted to assume that Hamlet must have appeared on the English stage in an earlier form than that of the Quarto of 1603, and that the German piece is a weak copy of the earlier form."[65] The *Ur-Hamlet* was being summoned back to life; the pre-Shakespearean *Hamlet* was assuming a more defined shape, and the challenging questions it raised about Shakespeare's "artistic faculty" were becoming increasingly unavoidable.

All of this might not have happened. The strangely mirrored supplementarity of the two copies of Q1—one with the title page but lacking the final leaf, the other with the final leaf but lacking the title page—suggests how easily this text might have been lost forever, just as it was lost throughout the eighteenth century, that Golden Age of Shakespearean research. The discovery of the Rooney copy, completing the imperfect Bunbury copy, seems an almost impossible gift. And yet, while it told us who entered at the play's finale, and while it inspired further theories of Q1's origins, the Rooney copy did nothing to resolve any of the most important questions about Q1 and its relationship to *Hamlet*. The archive holds out the hope of solving mysteries, but it also conceals their solutions or creates new obscurities.

Reading the editorial apparatus and textual studies written both before and immediately following Bunbury's discovery, one is struck by the immense power of new archival knowledge to reshape our understanding of Shakespeare and the English Renaissance stage. When Malone got a look at Henslowe's diary, for example, he understood immediately how crucial it was to any narrative of the Elizabethan theater. He attempted frantically, at the last moment, to revise much of the material surrounding his long-gestating edition. Where time or energy failed him, he simply thrust massive excerpts from the diary into his own text. But one is struck as well by the power of the archival unknown, and by the power of false knowledge, the *pseudodoxia epidemica* that also fascinated Thomas Browne. It was commonly "known," for example, that the Globe had been built around 1594 and that the Chamberlain's Men had been playing at the Blackfriars since the early 1590s.[66] A forged document showing Shakespeare's name on a theatrical petition from 1589 resulted in decades of problems in the writing of his biography.[67] Other errors were more purely accidental, but no less persistent: Malone saw "N. L." in the imprint of Q2 *Hamlet* and invented an early modern stationer named "N. Landure" in place of Nicholas Ling. Half a century later the error continued to crop up in textual accounts, even when editors correctly listed Ling as the publisher of Q1.[68]

After the ensuing centuries of Shakespearean scholarship, such pseudodoxia may now seem merely laughable; they may make us wonder at the credulousness of otherwise rigorous scholars who could fall for a seemingly obvious forgery, at the sloppiness of otherwise careful editors who could dutifully repeat the errors of their predecessors. But in fact this is a trick of perspective; we have our own historicist blind spots that will amaze and amuse what Browne called "the curiosity of future ages."[69] Returning to the discovery of Q1 *Hamlet* and tracing its far-reaching effects reminds us of just how much is still missing in our understanding of Shakespeare and his texts, even as it undermines the persistent fantasy that the next miraculous archival find will resolve these mysteries.[70] Our Shakespearean narratives emerge from a series of gaps in the historical record. We see these gaps best in relief, retrospectively and counterfactually, only as they are disappearing. Behind my interest in Q1 lies just such a counterfactual question, impossible to answer by its very nature but revelatory in its demands. If this play had never been lost and found, what would *Hamlet* be, who would Shakespeare be?[71]

If Bunbury's accidental and belated discovery continues to shape our ideas about *Hamlet*, then in order to perceive that influence we need to learn to forget a host of ingrained "facts" about the play. "Knowledge," Browne wrote, "is made by oblivion; and to purchase a clear and warrantable body of Truth, we must forget and part with much wee know."[72] Just as that field in old Walsingham is a stratified accretion of matter that gets significantly rearranged when the urns, which should be below in "their" historical stratum, suddenly rise to the surface or the layer of the "now," so too our understanding of *Hamlet* is made up of a deep field of critical commentary that can be productively disordered by the anachronistic emergence of Q1—if we attend to it. In each of the chapters that follow, therefore, I begin with something that we think we already know about *Hamlet*. Each is a widespread and frequently repeated bit of critical wisdom; indeed, I have passed along all of them to my own students at one time or another. Each concerns a local textual issue—a title-page advertisement; a possible pun; a stage direction and prop; a key word in a soliloquy—that has large implications for how we read *Hamlet* and, more broadly, for how we interpret Shakespeare through bibliographic analysis, biographical narrative, marginal glossing, stage performance, philological research, and close reading. These seeming bits of knowledge are not quite wrong, but they are not quite right either; they have become so entrenched that we can no longer see alternatives. I show how these contingent "truths" about *Hamlet* have become true only through a long process of critical, editorial, and theatrical engagement with the uncanny historicity of Q1. The genealogy of these pseudodoxia challenges the historicist methods of reading that have long dominated Shakespeare studies and prompts a rethinking of our critical and editorial practices. For this reason, at the end of each chapter I return to the three early texts of *Hamlet* to reexamine what they might tell us if we can "forget and part with much wee know."

The first chapter addresses the novel ideas of Shakespearean authorship and the transmission of his texts that emerged immediately in the wake of Bunbury's discovery, Romantic ideas that ultimately lie behind our modern bibliographic theories about Shakespeare's quartos and folios. This history prompts a reconsideration of entrenched narratives about the relationship between the printing of Q1 and Q2, and in particular of the long-standing belief that the blurb on the title page of Q2 tells us something about Shakespeare and his textual desires. Chapter 2 shows how these ideas of authorship play out at the local level through an extended microhistory of a single variant phrase and its glossing by editors over the centuries: instead of asking Ophelia about *country matters*, which our annotations have long told us carries a highly obscene pun, Q1 Hamlet asks about *contrary matters*.[73] Returning to the three early versions of this exchange after this meditation on the "power of the gloss" reveals the internal contradictions in our editorial accounts of Hamlet's putative vulgarity. Chapter 3 turns to performance history, and to another ubiquitous bit of historicist wisdom: we are repeatedly informed that there must be no bed in the closet scene because this prop is thoroughly anachronistic, emerging out of the Oedipal reading of the play developed by Freud and his disciple Ernest Jones. But like the reading of *country matters* as an obscene pun, this pseudodoxos hides from us its origins in an aspect of Q1 that was widely remarked after the publication of Payne and Foss's reprint: the new stage direction in this scene, "*Enter the ghost in his night-gowne*" (sig. G2v). Tracing an alternate history of the closet scene across nineteenth-century performance, editing, and criticism, I return at the end to a remarkable, but oddly unremarked, fact about Q1: there is no closet scene in that version of *Hamlet*, because the word *closet* appears nowhere in that text. As I show in Chapter 4, close readings of the most famous speech in *Hamlet* similarly hinge on a piece of historicist wisdom that demarcates "expert" or scholarly readers from the lay person. The keyword *conscience* in "To be, or not to be" vacillates in meaning—from the familiar moral-religious sense to something like "philosophical speculation" or "consciousness," and back again—according to prevailing understandings of Q1's relation to the other texts of *Hamlet* and to Shakespeare. This process has obscured a real strangeness about "To be, or not to be," one that we can only see by returning to Q1 after forgetting this accreted history: Hamlet's thought about conscience and cowardice makes far more sense in Q1 than it does in the familiar version.

Together, these chapters trace the genealogy of *Hamlet* after Q1, the genealogy of *our Hamlet*, from the earliest reactions to Bunbury's discovery through our ongoing attempts to grapple with its challenges. Along the way, the book illuminates the changing theoretical assumptions that organize the study of Shakespeare's texts and that underlie these particular glosses, readings, and emendations.[74] I show how the discovery of Q1 has affected all aspects of both scholarly and nonscholarly engagement with *Hamlet*, from questions of biography, authorship, and the bibliographic relationships among the texts associated with Shakespeare (Chapters 1 and 4), to textual studies and the establishment of the authoritative text (Chapter 2), to theatrical and performance histories (Chapter 3), to editorial glossing and its attempt to shape reader response (Chapters 2, 3, and 4). In conclusion, I discuss the dominant tendency in studies of the Shakespearean text in recent years, after the New Bibliographic theory of memorial reconstruction could no longer be taken for granted. Culminating in and epitomized by the two-volume Arden *Hamlet* (2006), this "unediting" movement has attempted to sidestep all the traditional problems posed by Q1—its genesis, its relationship to the received text—and instead to study that text on its own terms. This approach has served us well in many respects, and I often follow it when I return to the early texts of *Hamlet* at the end of each chapter. There I generally begin with the texts as we have them, and my rereadings do not fundamentally depend on any particular narrative of their origins or relationship. Bracketing the question of their bibliographic relationship enables us to see aspects of these texts that we have tended to miss while we have been busy searching for their textual origins. And yet, it turns out to be exceedingly difficult to bracket these issues completely; as soon as we compare the "same" passage in multiple versions, the question of how they are related begins to impinge on interpretation. If the seemingly endless quest for the origins of Q1 has been part of why we have failed to grasp the significance of its history, then precisely for this reason a methodology based on "unediting," if applied too strictly, risks fundamentally misunderstanding the play. As I hope the ensuing chapters amply demonstrate, our very conception of *Hamlet*, of Shakespeare as an author, and of Shakespeare as *the* author of *Hamlet*, depends on the sedimented history of critical engagement with the problem of Q1, with its origins and its relationship to the received text of the play. To attempt to escape these questions is therefore to attempt to escape our own past. And as Henry Bunbury learned in his manor house in Great Barton one day in 1823 (or was it 1821?), the past has a habit of returning unexpectedly.

CHAPTER 1

As Originally Written by Shakespeare

Textual Bibliography and Textual Biography

As soon as Henry Bunbury's discovery became public, its importance "to every English gentleman and scholar" led to calls for a reprint edition, "for the sake of the immortal author, and for that of society."[1] Payne and Foss promptly obliged, and later that same year, their reprint was itself reprinted in Leipzig, demonstrating its importance beyond England and, as I discuss further in Chapter 3, drawing the attention of no less a Shakespearean commentator than Goethe. Payne and Foss included a brief introductory note on the origins of the text, the only editorial apparatus in the book. Spare as it is, this note, which also appeared in the Leipzig edition, set the agenda for much of the discussion that followed, influencing not only Goethe but numerous others as well:

> The present Edition of Hamlet is an accurate reprint from the only known copy of this Tragedy as originally written by Shakespeare, which he afterwards altered and enlarged. It is given to the world under the impression of rendering an acceptable service to literature. Some variations in the plot, as compared with the received Text, will be perceived; but its chief value consists in bringing to light several lines of great beauty subsequently omitted, and in many new readings of passages which have been the subject of much controversy among the critics. The typographical errors and even negligent omissions in the Text are common to all the Editions published during the life time of Shakespeare, who, it is believed, never superintended the publication of any of his works, excepting the Poems of Venus and Adonis, and Tarquin and Lucrece.

The last leaf is wanting; but as the Play is perfect to the death of Hamlet, the loss is of comparatively small importance.[2]

Like this note to the reader, journalistic accounts throughout 1825, and in the following years, focused on the intersection of bibliography and biography, detailing the intriguing variants in the Q1 text and speculating on what they could tell modern readers about Shakespeare's writing process. Most of them agreed with Payne and Foss that Q1 represented the play "as originally written by Shakespeare."

Over the ensuing decades, this "exhumated curiosity" pushed critics and editors to develop new theories of the origins of Shakespearean texts, which implied new conceptions of Shakespearean authorship.[3] What kind of an author was Shakespeare? Clearly he was a genius—indeed, the paradigm of poetic genius—but what exactly *was* a genius? How did he work? The stakes of Q1 were high, according to one contemporary writer nothing less than "the most interesting and instructive subject of philosophical inquiry in the annals of intellect."[4] Did Shakespeare write his plays in a poetic fury of inspiration, as John Heminges and Henry Condell seemed to claim when they told readers of the First Folio that Shakespeare's "mind and hand went together: And what he thought, he vttered with that easinesse, that we haue scarse receiued from him a blot in his papers" (sig. A3r)? Or did he persistently return to old material, polishing individual lines and reframing the action of a play until it perfectly expressed his meaning? So Ben Jonson apparently thought, for he wrote in his commendatory poem in the same volume that "*he, / Who casts to write a liuing line, must sweat, / (such as thine are) and strike the second heat / Vpon the Muses anuile*" (sig. A4v). While Jonson saw exhausting artisanal labor behind Shakespeare's lines, John Milton's commendatory poem in the Second Folio followed Heminges and Condell, praising Shakespeare's natural creativity: "*to th' shame of slow-endevouring Art / Thy easie numbers flow*" (sig. A5r). As these lines make clear, the debate over whether Shakespeare revised—and whether, if he did, this was a good thing—goes all the way back to 1623. But the uncanny historicity of Q1, its belated appearance at the height of the Romantic engagement with *Hamlet*, ensured that this "new (old) Play" would become the key to understanding Shakespeare's textual biography.

The editorial indifference of Payne and Foss to the lack of the final leaf in their copy of Q1 may now seem amusing. But stage productions of the play throughout the eighteenth and nineteenth centuries usually concluded with the death of Hamlet, treating the rest of the finale as "of comparatively small importance": since Fortinbras was routinely omitted entirely, the curtain often dropped on "the rest is silence" or Horatio's elegiac "flights of angels sing thee to thy rest."[5] More telling, in historical context, is Payne and Foss's blithe assurance about the nature of the text they were reprinting. Even shortly after the reprint appeared, Shakespeare scholars would no longer feel quite so comfortable describing most of the textual variation between Q1 and the received text as the kind of "typographical errors" and "negligent omissions" prevalent in the quartos generally. And it would of course be impossible today, after the twentieth-century revolution in textual bibliography, to state simply that Q1 gives us the "Tragedy as originally written by Shakespeare," not only without providing evidence but indeed without providing any specific reference to the text at all. But in fact this transformation in bibliographic theory and evidentiary standards derives in part from the emergence of Q1 at this moment.

To the New Bibliographers of the early twentieth century, the lack of attention to the processes of scribal and print transmission made nineteenth-century assertions like these seem unscientific and impressionistic. And indeed, the theories of authorship and the text that developed in response to the reprint of Q1 largely predate the episteme of New Bibliography, with its polemical emphasis on the scientific assessment of bibliographic evidence. Instead, these theories were firmly rooted in late eighteenth- and early nineteenth-century critical concerns about the nature of poetic genius and authorial development, in questions of taste and propriety more than paleography and stemmatics. As both this chapter and Chapter 4 show, however, the New Bibliographic narrative of its predecessors' premodernity obscures its own continuities with that earlier scholarship. For the New Bibliographers, as for their Victorian predecessors, Q1 *Hamlet* was a foundation stone in the construction of Shakespeare's textual biography and the consolidation of his authorship, serving as a key text in the related theories of "bad quartos" and memorial reconstruction. Much of this work has depended on the blurb on the title page of Q2—"Newly imprinted and enlarged to almost as much againe as it was, according to the true and perfect Coppie"—which has long prompted the biographical imagination (see Figure 3). As I show at the end of this chapter, the New Bibliographers in particular read a Shakespearean romance into these words. After tracing the history of responses to Q1, which have consistently sought to understand the bibliography of *Hamlet* through the biography of Shakespeare, I therefore return to this title-page advertisement in an effort to reread the relationship between Q1 and Q2 *Hamlet* without this biographical imperative.

The claim by Payne and Foss that Shakespeare "afterwards altered and *enlarged*" the play suggests that they were influenced by the title page of Q2, with its promotion of that text as enlarged. Thirty-five years earlier, Edmond Malone had similarly noted Q2's claim to be printed "according to the true and perfect Coppie" and guessed that Shakespeare must have revised his own "rude sketch of that which we now possess; for from the title page of the first edition, in 1604, we learn, that (like *Romeo and Juliet*, and the *Merry Wives of Windsor*) it had been enlarged to almost twice its original size."[6] Malone's "star was not propitious": he died in 1812, and Q1 was found "too late, alas!" for him to see it.[7] But after Bunbury's find, Malone was seen to have been posthumously justified in his inference. Writing in 1832, Thomas Caldecott likewise quoted the Q2 blurb and concluded that "the lately discovered copy" provided "full confirmation" that Shakespeare's plays "must have undergone considerable alteration," with Q1 "exhibiting, in that which was afterwards wrought into a splendid drama, the first conception, and comparatively feeble expression, of a great mind."[8]

The immediate assessment in the newspapers was largely the same: "The author himself elaborated and augmented it after it had been for some time on the stage"; it is "the first rude sketch of *Hamlet*."[9] In comments like these, the rough quality of the text of Q1 is itself taken as evidence that it preserves Shakespeare's preliminary draft. Few doubted that Q1 also contained numerous textual corruptions, but at the outset, as in Payne and Foss's introductory note, these were largely assigned to the same sources of corruption that editors throughout the eighteenth century had seen as plaguing all of Shakespeare's quartos.[10] The *Gentleman's Magazine*, for instance, complained of the "vicious and incorrect mode of editing the play in 1603," but nonetheless believed that the edition "shew[ed] that the great beauties of our immortal Bard have been the results of much contemplation, and of laboured revision and correction, at moments most favourable for inspiration."[11] Here the inferior text of Q1 reveals that Jonson rather than Milton had correctly perceived the genius of Shakespeare's art, a poetics based in "laboured revision and correction." But there was not even universal agreement that the text of Q1 *was* inferior. Some thought that chronological priority simply implied textual superiority: "*Hamlet* first appeared [on stage], according to Malone's calculation, in 1600 . . .

therefore, [Q1] was published only three years after the tragedy was produced. Hence it may be, in many respects, a more exact copy of the original than any subsequently printed."[12]

This reaction is surprising only when viewed retrospectively through the lens of later bibliographic developments. *Hamlet* was not the only play to exist in multiple texts, and before the discovery of Q1, the earlier versions of plays such as *Romeo and Juliet* and *The Merry Wives of Windsor* were matter-of-factly assumed to be Shakespearean drafts. Chronology in printing, that is, was imagined to align smoothly with chronology in writing: first published, first written. The New Bibliographers considered these plays as much as *Hamlet* to be bad quartos; indeed, *Merry Wives* served as a primary locus for the development of their theory of memorial reconstruction, in W. W. Greg's 1910 edition of the play.[13] But George Steevens reprinted them and others in his edition of *Twenty of the Plays of Shakespeare* (1766) for a very different reason:

> There are many persons, who not contented with the possession of a finished picture of some great master, are desirous to procure the first sketch that was made for it, that they may have the pleasure of tracing the progress of the artist from the first light colouring to the finishing stroke. To such the earlier editions of KING JOHN, HENRY THE FIFTH, HENRY THE SIXTH, THE MERRY WIVES OF WINDSOR, and ROMEO AND JULIET, will, I apprehend, not be unwelcome; since in these we may discern as much as will be found in the hasty outlines of the pencil, with a fair prospect of that perfection to which He brought every performance He took the pains to retouch.[14]

It is easy enough to spot the Bardolatry in Steevens's capitalization of the third-person pronoun. More important is that, for Steevens and indeed for all the great eighteenth-century editors without exception, this deification of Shakespeare is completely compatible with the notion that His plays were created through a long process of revision from "first sketch" to "finishing stroke."

Despite their often vitriolic disagreements over particular emendations and textual theories, the early editors all agreed on this point, and largely without argumentation. *The Merry Wives of Windsor* was "entirely new writ" (Alexander Pope) following "the first imperfect Sketch of this Comedy" (Theobald); the quarto reproduced "the first sketch of this play" (Johnson), a "first draft" that was "but the skeleton of the true one" (Edward Capell), and it was "revised and enlarged by the authour, after its first production" (Malone).¹⁵ *Romeo and Juliet* was altered "since the first edition; but probably by *Shakespear*" (Pope); "the play was alter'd" in "a revision, at the time of enlarging it" (Capell), and Q1 was "apparently a rough draught" (Malone).¹⁶ Shakespeare made revisions throughout *King Lear*, from "two lines . . . added in the authour's revision" to longer passages and entire scenes (Johnson).¹⁷ *Henry V* had been "extremely improved" (Pope) and "much enlarged and improved after the first edition," with the folio being "the second draught of the same design" (Johnson); "the Chorus's . . . (with many other noble Improvements) were since added by the Author, not above 8 Years before his Death" (William Warburton).¹⁸

With the *Henry VI* plays, *The Taming of a/the Shrew*, and *King John*, editorial opinion was more varied, although revision typically remained central. Editors sometimes suspected that these early plays were not completely Shakespeare's but rather had "been brought to him as a Director of the *Stage*; and so to have receiv'd some finishing Beauties at his hand" (Theobald on *Henry VI*).¹⁹ Others saw them as fully Shakespearean, with the early quartos representing "the first Sketch only" (Warburton) or the "first draught" (Capell).²⁰ And even in plays without such wide divergences between quarto and folio, editors saw evidence of Shakespearean revision: a few lines in *Richard II*, "expunged in the revision by the authour" (Johnson);²¹ various passages in *2 Henry IV*, "inserted after the first edition" and "plainly by *Shakespear* himself" (Pope);²² an altered metaphor in *Troilus and Cressida*, an "improvement . . . of the Poet's after his first edition" (Capell);²³ the passage about the boy players in *Hamlet* (Capell), or even a single variant—"o'er-offices" (F) or "o'er-reaches" (Q2) in the graveyard scene—resulting from the "authour . . . revising his work" (Johnson);²⁴ repeatedly in *Othello* in the choice of single words, "which the authour substituted in his revisal" (Johnson).²⁵

When Q1 *Hamlet* appeared, then, authorial revision had long been taken for granted. This theory persisted after the discovery of Q1, but, as we shall see, it was significantly transformed by the belated appearance of that edition at the height of the play's Romantic canonization. This is not to say that these early texts—or any Shakespearean texts—were imagined to represent the author's intentions clearly or unproblematically. The folio was constantly condemned for the blunders of its printers and its "player editors," and editors had to be always alert for "the Players trash," later stage accretions.²⁶ Meanwhile, Heminges and Condell themselves had claimed that the earlier editions were "stolen and surreptitious," and eighteenth-century editors believed they had been subject to every conceivable form of corrupt transmission. Johnson inveighed that the quartos

> were immediately copied for the actors, and multiplied by transcript after transcript, vitiated by the blunders of the penman, or changed by the affectation of the player; perhaps enlarged to introduce a jest, or mutilated to shorten the representation; and printed at last without the concurrence of the authour . . . from compilations made by chance or by stealth out of the separate parts written for the theatre; and thus thrust into the world surreptitiously and hastily, they suffered another depravation from the ignorance and negligence of the printers. . . . It is not easy for invention to bring together so many causes concurring to vitiate a text.[27]

Theobald similarly thought that the "train of Blemishes" in Shakespeare's texts resulted from their having been "printed from piece-meal Parts surreptitiously obtain'd from the Theatres, uncorrect, and without the Poet's Knowledge" or "taken down in Short-hand, and imperfectly copied by Ear, from a *Representation*."[28] In Theobald's remarks we can see a glimmer of the crucial development in Shakespearean bibliography after the discovery of Q1 *Hamlet*, one that would overturn the dominant eighteenth-century assumption that first printed meant first written: John Payne Collier's theory of stenographic reporting (Figure 4). But Theobald here mentions stenographers alongside other nonauthorial agents only as a general explanation for the state of Shakespeare's texts: any word in any play might need emendation because of this pervasive corruption. It was never specified exactly which plays were stenographic reports (or indeed otherwise corrupted), nor exactly how stenography affected the text.[29]

Indeed, prior to Bunbury's discovery, there appears to be only one instance in which a major Shakespearean editor linked a specific edition to a shorthand report, and the same editor later withdrew the claim. This was Malone's discussion of the first quarto of *Henry V*, which itself developed from his rejection of Johnson's earlier theory of both *Henry V* and the latter two parts of *Henry VI*.[30] Johnson was the most forceful proponent of authorial revision among the eighteenth-century editors, pointing out more "revised" lines in a wider range of plays than anyone else, but he was also the first to suggest that a specific early Shakespeare edition was taken down by someone

Figure 4. John Payne Collier (1789–1883), Shakespearean editor. Engraving in the *Illustrated London News* (29 September 1883).
Reproduced by permission of the Horace Howard Furness Memorial Library, Kislak Center for Special Collections, Rare Books and Manuscripts, University of Pennsylvania Libraries, shelf mark AP4.I29.

listening in the theater—although not in shorthand. At the end of the *Henry VI* plays, Johnson argued that they were indeed wholly by Shakespeare, but he continued: "The old copies of the two latter parts of *Henry* VI. and of *Henry* V. are so apparently imperfect and mutilated, that there is no reason for supposing them the first draughts of *Shakespeare*. I am inclined to believe them copies taken by some auditor who wrote down, during the representation, what the time would permit, then perhaps filled up some of his omissions at a second or third hearing, and when he had by this method formed something like a play, sent it to the printer."[31] More crucial than the particular mode of transcription, however, is that, as shown by his discussion of the folio version of *Henry V* as "a second draught," Johnson is still thinking of the early texts of these plays as different versions, later revised by Shakespeare into their folio versions but first mangled in their transmission by an auditor.

Malone rejected Johnson's view of the quartos of *2–3 Henry VI*. While he had "formerly coincided with Dr. Johnson on this subject," he now concluded that "the old plays in quarto . . . are by no means mutilated and imperfect."[32] In a long "Dissertation" on these plays, Malone argued that they were originally by a different author, and that Shakespeare had revised them into his own versions. Only with *Henry V* did Malone consistently deny revision, largely because his efforts to root the plays in their precise historical moments revealed to him that the last chorus, with its reference to the Earl of Essex, must have already been written before the printing of the first quarto, in which it nonetheless does not appear. Furthermore, Malone hoped to rehabilitate the early editions, which to him carried far greater textual authority than they had for any previous editor. Even with *Henry V*, therefore, Malone downplayed the corruption of the quartos and the sort of problematic transmission that had so worried earlier editors. In the first version of his decades-long attempt to write a chronology of Shakespeare's plays, he concluded that the "fair inference to be drawn from the imperfect and mutilated copies of [*Henry V*] . . . is, not that the whole play, as we now have it, did not then exist, but that those copies were surreptitious, (probably taken down in short hand, during the representation;) and that the editor in 1600, not being able to publish the whole, published what he could."[33] Here we have the first clear reference to the production of a particular Shakespearean text by shorthand. When he revised the chronology for his own edition in 1790, however, Malone deleted the parenthetical clause entirely.[34] He gives no reason for the change, but he almost certainly eliminated the mention of shorthand because this kind of corrupt transmission had been taken by earlier editors as license for the sort of freewheeling "speculative emendation" that Malone deplored.

As a result, Malone's final explanation for *Henry V* resembles his explanation of plays such as *2 Henry IV*, in which an entire scene was seemingly missing in the quarto, "not because it was then unwritten . . . but because the editor was not possessed of it."[35] By the time he completed his landmark edition, in other words, Malone's desire to restore Shakespeare's text as preserved in the early quartos, combined with his more optimistic assessment of their textual condition and his belief in Shakespearean revision, all worked to push him toward a rejection of stenography as an explanation for textual corruption.

Up through James Boswell's revision of Malone in 1821, only two years before Bunbury's discovery, the variant quartos were almost unanimously assumed to be rough drafts. Textually corrupt and incomplete, perhaps, but nonetheless witnesses to earlier Shakespearean versions of the plays.

The sudden reemergence of Q1 *Hamlet* quickly changed all this. By the early nineteenth century *Hamlet* had been enshrined as the pinnacle of poetic genius, and the theory of rough drafts, which had previously been taken as a given, now became widely controversial. In the hands of its most enthusiastic Victorian proponent, Charles Knight (Figure 5), Shakespearean revision was a process very different from what it had been for Malone and his fellow eighteenth-century editors. Knight's understanding of revision was deeply infused with Romantic ideas about *Hamlet* and about poetic creativity more broadly, and it was shaped in dialectical opposition to Collier's novel theory of stenographic piracy. Knight and Collier were routinely contrasted in the period, imagined as "mighty opposites" in contemporary reviews of Shakespearean editions and in journalistic accounts surrounding Q1. This opposition divided the Shakespearean world for much of the nineteenth century, but while the two editors did indeed react in very different ways to the revelation of Q1, they also shared a fundamental Romanticism that formed the contours of those reactions.

Whatever the actual practice of the Romantic poets, the ideology of Romantic authorship favored originality, spontaneous creativity, and inner genius over the older values of external inspiration (Jonson's "Muses' anvil") and the studious imitation of traditional models.[36] "I appeal to the greatest Poets of the present day," Shelley wrote in his *Defence of Poetry* two years before Bunbury's discovery, "whether it be not an error to assert that the finest passages of poetry are produced by labour and study."[37] According to Edward Young's hugely influential *Conjectures on Original Composition* (1759), an original work of art "may be said to be of a *vegetable* nature; it rises spontaneously from the vital root of Genius; it *grows*, it is not *made: Imitations* are often a sort of *Manufacture* wrought up by those *Mechanics*, *Art*, and *Labour*, out of pre-existent materials not their own."[38] As Margreta de Grazia has stressed in her study of Malone's influential chronology of Shakespeare's plays, the idea that original art grows organically was paralleled by a new emphasis on the author's career as itself an organic process and "a new mode of viewing the works: as development."[39] It became axiomatic that there were some plays Shakespeare simply could not have written in his youth, and others he could not have written later in life. In the mid-century reaction to Q1 *Hamlet*, all

Figure 5. Charles Knight (1791–1873), Shakespearean editor.
Portrait by Charles H. M. Kerr.

Reproduced by permission of the Guildhall Art Library, City of London.

of these strands—spontaneity, originality, and organic development—played important roles, for that edition raised troubling questions about all three. The paramount work of English literature had to conform with Romantic theories of authorship: we can read this demand in the vehemence with which Collier maintained that Q1 was a stenographic piracy; we can see it in the rapid spread of his stenographic theory to other plays and other critics; and we can read it in Knight's vision of Shakespeare as a supreme reviser. In the end, it was this Romantic consensus, just as much as the very real disagreement between the two editors over the origins of Q1, that shaped discussions of *Hamlet* and of Shakespeare into the twentieth century.

* * *

While most early newspaper and magazine notices agreed with Payne and Foss that Q1 was an early authorial version, a few suggested something more underhanded. A writer in *Drama*, for instance, believed that it was "an imperfect and unauthorised publication, the substance of which has been picked up by some one who attended frequent representations of the play, and perhaps derived some assistance from the actors who performed it." The *London Literary Gazette* thought that the variations from the received text "tend strongly to confirm the suspicion, that the play was picked out by hearing it performed, and getting speeches and parts from some of the actors." As these comments make clear, immediately following Payne and Foss's reprint, and after a century of assuming that other similar quartos were rough drafts, some writers theorized that what Bunbury had discovered was a reported text based on performance, although (like Johnson) they do not mention stenography in particular. Despite being "picked out by hearing it performed," however, Q1 *Hamlet* was "certainly Shakspearian."[40] For these early writers, in other words, as for Johnson on *Henry V* and *2–3 Henry VI*, neither the evident textual corruption of Q1 nor its irregular mode of transmission precluded its being a (garbled) record of Shakespeare's first version of the play.

Collier's theory of Q1 differed from these accounts by specifying shorthand as the method of transmission; it differed from earlier editors' vague invocations of shorthand by clearly linking this method to a specific Shakespearean text—initially Q1 *Hamlet* but later a whole range of editions. And Collier's influential narrative pushed the theory of corrupt transmission much further than ever before by making authorial revision and piratical stenography mutually exclusive: Q1 is essentially nothing but a corrupted stenographic report of the same version of *Hamlet* represented by Q2 and F. Collier first touched on the subject in his *History of English Dramatic Poetry* (1831), interrupting his narrative history for a textual footnote: Q1 *Hamlet* "was demonstrably published in haste from a short-hand copy, taken from the mouths of the players."[41] As he later elaborated this brief, casual aside, Collier revolutionized Shakespearean textual scholarship. He was the first to argue forthrightly that the text of a specific edition was a stenographic piracy not of an earlier version or draft but of the complete and only true text of the play. In this way, he originated a theory that would have profound and lasting effects on Shakespearean scholarship: the earlier editions of some of Shakespeare's plays might in fact represent, in garbled form, the very same texts as are found in later editions.

Collier thus created the "retrograde bibliography" that would undergird the New Bibliographic theories of bad quartos and memorial reconstruction, positing that what seemed earlier was actually later, what was printed first was created last. This crucial innovation developed from Collier's encounter with Q1 *Hamlet*, but it by no means stopped there. Ten years later, in his 1842–44 edition of *The Works of William Shakespeare*, he extended the theory to cover Q1 *Romeo and Juliet*. Indeed, the treatment of that play offers an important reflection of the changes wrought by Q1 *Hamlet*. Before Bunbury's discovery, as we have seen, editors took the first quarto of *Romeo and Juliet* to be "an imperfect sketch by the author himself," later revised into the text found in Q2 and F.[42] The change in attitude toward this preexisting first quarto, however, was as rapid as it was with the newly discovered one of *Hamlet*. While Q1 *Romeo and Juliet* "has generally been treated as an authorised impression from an authentic manuscript," Collier believed it "was made up, partly from portions of the play as it was acted, but unduly obtained, and partly from notes taken at the theatre during representation." With *Romeo and Juliet*, unlike with *Hamlet*, Collier did not "go the length of contending that Shakespeare did not alter and improve the play, subsequent to its earliest production on the stage." But he was confident that the style of the first quarto and the "degree and kind of imperfectness" it displayed testified to its preparation "from defective shorthand notes."[43] Other critics soon followed, claiming to see a large difference in the style between the two versions. "We see that Shakespeare never could have written thus," wrote Richard Grant White, the leading American editor of his day, about Q1 *Romeo and Juliet*, in a locution that turns up repeatedly in later editions of the play.[44] To take just one example, here are the editors of the 1865 Cambridge edition: "It is impossible that Shakespeare should ever have given to the world a composition containing so many instances of imperfect sense, halting metre, bad grammar, and abrupt dialogue." By this time, even the minimal amount of authorial revision for which Collier had allowed was ruled out: "We believe that the play, as at first written, was substantially the same as that given in the later editions," with the only real difference being that the quarto was printed from a manuscript "obtained from notes taken in short-hand during the representation."[45]

It is not merely that this evaluation of the style and quality of Q1 *Romeo and Juliet* had not been entertained before the discovery of Q1 *Hamlet*, when editors had seen nothing that suggested Shakespeare "never could have written thus." Rather, in a very real sense, such opinions *could not* have been entertained before editors were forced to confront Q1 *Hamlet*, because it was through this confrontation that Collier developed the idea of shorthand reporting, previously confined to general statements about the poor quality of all of Shakespeare's texts, into a theory of the origins of particular plays and the interlocking and potentially inverted relationships among the surviving editions of those plays. The case of *Romeo and Juliet* confirms that it was precisely the uncanniness of Q1 *Hamlet*—its reemergence only after the play had already become emblematic of Shakespeare's mature art and the peak of poetic achievement—that led critics to adopt the theory of stenographic piracy. Had Q1 *Hamlet* never been lost, it might well have been treated exactly like the variant edition of *Romeo and Juliet*, or of *Merry Wives*, assumed all along to be a rough draft.

Once Collier's invocation of stenography made this kind of retrograde bibliography possible, it seems to have been hard to resist, and like its later avatar, memorial reconstruction, it spread rapidly to other plays. Perhaps the theory appealed to Collier and his followers because it offered a narrative in which editorial perspicacity sees through chronological appearances to a deeper reality: scholarly detection triumphs over the misinterpretations of the popular critic and the naïve, "common sense" notion that first-published equals first-written. Thus, for Collier, *Henry V* as well was "made up . . . from what could be taken down in short-hand, or could be remembered, while the performance was taking place"; as for the Choruses, these were missing because "the short-hand writer did not think [them] a necessary portion of the performance to be included in the earliest quarto, 1600, which was to be brought out with great speed; and perhaps the length of these and other recitations might somewhat baffle his skill."[46] So too *The Merry Wives of Windsor*: "It has been the custom to look upon this edition as the first sketch of the drama, which Shakespeare afterwards enlarged and improved to the form in which it appears in the folio of 1623. After the most minute examination, we are not of that opinion." Rather, in the now familiar refrain, the first quarto "was made up, for the purpose of sale, partly from notes taken at the theatre, and partly from memory."[47]

Even with *Pericles*, Collier detected a "short-hand writer" where none had been seen before, though in this case not for the 1609 first quarto of the play but rather for the novelization published the year prior: "Nathaniel Butter probably employed some person to attend the performance at the theatre, and with the aid of notes there taken . . . to compose a novel out of the incidents of the play."[48] Thanks to Collier's confrontation with Bunbury's discovery, in other words, stenographic piracy suddenly accounted for an entire range of Shakespearean texts that had previously been simply understood as early drafts. Indeed, Collier's shorthand theory encompassed all five of the plays that would later be famously labeled as bad quartos by A. W. Pollard.[49] The uncanny historicity of Q1 *Hamlet* ultimately lies behind Pollard's influential theory, a foundational intervention of the New Bibliography.

But while *Hamlet* provided the basis for his theory of stenographic piracy, Collier presented little evidence for it in his editorial preface to the play. Instead, he justified his assessment of the quality and nature of the edition mainly by his authority as the preeminent scholar of his day and by his connection with the Duke of Devonshire, who by then owned the unique copy of the edition and who allowed Collier to "take home with me every early edition of Shakespeare in his library."[50] "As an accurate reprint was made in 1825," Collier wrote with gentlemanly *sprezzatura*,

> it will be unnecessary to go in detail into proofs to establish, as we could do without much difficulty, the following points :—1. That great part of the play, as it there stands, was taken down in shorthand. 2. That where mechanical skill failed the short-hand writer, he either filled up the blanks from memory, or employed an inferior writer to assist him. 3. That although some of the scenes were carelessly transposed, and others entirely omitted in the edition of 1603, the drama, as it was acted while the short-hand writer was employed in taking it down, was, in all its main features, the same as the more perfect copy of the tragedy printed with the date of 1604.[51]

We are never told exactly what the details of such a proof might be, and the tone here resonates with the later repeated claim that Shakespeare simply "never could have written thus." All educated readers of good taste and judgment will be able to see the evidence for themselves, and Collier's "unnecessary" demonstration of such a proof, we are meant to understand, would insult the intelligence of his readers.

"Collier had never been keen on explaining what was (to him) obvious," according to his modern biographers, but the rhetoric here is not merely personal idiosyncrasy.[52] In fact, Collier's reticence helps to create a social boundary. On the one side stand those scholarly insiders for whom it is "unnecessary to go in detail into proofs," and on the other side, baffled by this new model of retrograde chronology, is the lay community that lacks the necessary insight gained from years of study. And if other scholars—such as Collier's former friend and now bitter rival Alexander Dyce—likewise failed to see the evidence that Collier held close to his chest, so much the better.[53] Collier's preface to *Hamlet* thereby provides a rhetorical analogue to the social world of Shakespearean scholarship in the 1830s and 1840s. The period saw a craze for founding new scholarly societies, and as the initial director of the Shakespeare Society and a founding member of the Camden and Percy Societies, Collier was adept at navigating the often bitter politics of these gentlemanly groups. Such societies operated through norms of collegiality and competition that mirror Collier's rhetoric on Q1 *Hamlet*, a combination of professional authority, gentlemanly deference, and emulative rivalry.[54] Collier's appeal to his personal authority would ultimately backfire, as it slowly became apparent that he was a compulsive forger of the documentary evidence for his scholarship. Before this downfall, however, his remarks on *Hamlet* and his piracy theory struck the perfect tone of scholarly detachment for his historical moment, one quite different from the scientism of the New Bibliographic moment or, as I show in Chapter 4, of the late nineteenth-century "disintegrationist" movement. The norms of this regime of knowledge production, and the social boundary enforced by these new scholarly societies, contributed to—and embittered—the debate over Q1 *Hamlet*. As the Shakespeare world divided into two camps, the period's foremost Shakespearean stood on one side, assuming that his readers would (as he put it in a letter to the *Athenaeum*) "take my word for it" rather than make him stoop to the workmanlike explication of "unnecessary . . . proofs."[55] On the other side was the self-consciously "popularizing" publisher Charles Knight, who completed his edition of Shakespeare just as Collier was beginning his own.

The son of a Windsor bookman, the publisher-editor Charles Knight was aiming at a very different set of readers from those Collier was addressing, and the gentlemanly norms that governed knowledge production in the period often excluded him and his work from Collier's circles. Knight's *Pictorial Shakespeare* (1838–43), however, reached a far larger audience than Collier's edition, which was probably responsible for some of Collier's animosity toward him, since Collier both scorned and desired this kind of "popular" appeal.[56] But the shared Romanticism of these two major mid-century editions of Shakespeare can be readily seen in their identical choice for the paramount Shakespearean critic: Samuel Taylor Coleridge.

Collier considered Coleridge a "man of genius."[57] In Collier's preface to *Hamlet*, Coleridge is the only critic discussed, and the only interpretive remarks on the play consist of a long quotation from Coleridge that simply "sums up the character of Hamlet."[58] If not for Collier's adoration, in fact, Coleridge's landmark lectures on Shakespeare and Milton in 1811–12 would not have survived at all: published for the first time in 1856, the primary text of these lectures derives—in a neat bit of historical irony—from shorthand notes that Collier had taken forty-five years earlier.[59] In his edition of the lectures, Collier credits Coleridge with opening his "faculties to the comprehension, and enjoyment of poetry, in a degree beyond anything that I had then experienced."[60]

Knight likewise positioned Coleridge at the apex of Shakespearean criticism. He ends his history of Shakespearean criticism in the *Pictorial Shakespeare* by simply printing the critic's name in centered majescules:

We desire to conclude this outline of the opinions of others upon the works of Shakspere, in connexion with the imperfect expression of our own sense of those opinions, with the name of
COLERIDGE.[61]

In the *Pictorial Shakespeare* and his various repackagings of this edition, Knight did more than anyone else in the period to renew the case for authorial revision. As suggested by his fervent admiration for the "new era of critical opinion upon Shakspere . . . [that] may be dated from the delivery of the lectures of Samuel Taylor Coleridge," however, his theory of revision took on a distinctly more Romantic aspect than it had in the eighteenth century, when it was more assumed than argued.[62]

Knight picked up on different strains of this "new era of critical opinion" than Collier, largely because Knight was deeply committed to popularizing the Bard. A pioneer in publishing for the masses, he saw his own work as aiding the movement for moderate social reform.[63] He was the longtime publisher for the Society for the Distribution of Useful Knowledge (SDUK), which provided "improving" texts such as *The British Working-Man's Almanac* and *The Working-Man's Companion* that might "better the Condition of the Manufacturing and Agricultural Classes."[64] He also created some less dour material for the SDUK, including the (at least initially) immensely successful *Penny Magazine*, which apparently sold two hundred thousand copies in 1832 alone. Thirty years later, more highbrow journals such as the *Edinburgh Review* and *Blackwood's* were selling only about ten thousand copies annually;

"even in 1832 Knight was reaching a mass market which remained untapped by respected journals a generation later, despite higher literacy levels."[65]

Knight relied heavily on illustration, even inventing his own method for printing in color.[66] In 1838, he announced not only his *Pictorial Shakespeare* but also the *Pictorial History of Palestine*, the *Pictorial History of Rome*, and the *Pictorial History of Greece*, "each work to be completed in 12 monthly parts" to make them easier to afford.[67] In the prospectus for the *Pictorial Shakespeare*, Knight called for an edition "that should address itself to the popular understanding, in a spirit of enthusiastic love, and not of captious and presumptuous caviling." While the rejection of editorial contention had become a ritualistic self-denying ordinance among Shakespeare's editors, Knight went further by suggesting that such arguments among the scholastic commentators derived from an elitist "desire to parade the stores of useless learning," a serious criticism from the publisher for the Society for the Distribution of *Useful* Knowledge.[68]

Knight's adherence to the text of the First Folio—an "idolatrous" and "almost superstitious veneration" for which he was often criticized[69]—seems to have derived partly from the same desire to free the national Bard from the rarefied realm of the scholars. In the preface to his revised edition, he wrote: "I have been charged with a too exclusive reliance upon the folio of 1623, to the neglect of the authority of the quartos, which the elder commentators generally followed, *valuing them in many cases in proportion to their rarity*."[70] Knight here implies that it is precisely the rarity of the quartos that appeals to scholars like Malone and Steevens, for this enables their continued "fierce and ridiculous controversies" above the "popular understanding."[71] Elsewhere, he writes more explicitly, and satirically, that the text of Shakespeare "possesses this singular advantage for the cultivator, that, if he studies it in an original edition, of which only one or two copies are known to exist (the merit is gone if there is a baker's dozen known), he is immediately pronounced learned, judicious, laborious, acute."[72] In an era when gentlemanly book collecting reached new heights, and when scholarly editing followed Malone and Collier in valuing early over later editions and documentary over aesthetic evidence, the satiric bite in Knight's remarks about Shakespearean scholarship sounds a revolutionary popularizing note.

Knight wanted not only to "popularize" Shakespeare—to make him available to those readers who might have felt intimidated by the thicket of scholarly annotation that had grown up around his text—but also to demonstrate Shakespeare's "popularity." Indeed, the two concepts were deeply interwoven in Knight's thinking. He attempted at great length to show that "the facts connected with the original publication of Shakspere's plays sufficiently prove how eagerly they were for the most part received by the readers of the drama" in his own lifetime.[73] And speaking like the working publisher he was, he argued that the critics had actively hindered Shakespeare's popularity: "A plain reprint of Shakspere without a single note, but with the spelling modernized, would have made him more popular than all the critical editions which the eighteenth century had produced."[74] Shakespeare had always "lived in the hearts of the people, who knew nothing of the English critics. The learned, as they were called, understood him least."[75]

Knight's Romantic belief in the folk, the "hearts of the people," as the embodiment of a nation's culture led him to reject the kind of archival and documentary learning (forged as it sometimes was) that supported Collier's edition. Although Knight was a founding member of the Shakespeare Society, he was never fully accepted by scholars like Collier, the society's director, and James Orchard Halliwell, who seems to have been its initiator.[76] Partly this was because of social status: although Collier and Halliwell came from similarly middle-class backgrounds, they had climbed into more rarefied circles than had Knight.[77] More important, however, was an emergent disciplinary boundary demarcating amateur from professional critic: the notion that in order to understand literature, one needed to immerse oneself in the historical and linguistic context out of which it grew.[78]

Collier and Halliwell saw themselves as far more serious scholars than a "popularizer" like Knight.[79] Both men damned the *Pictorial Shakespeare* with faint praise or ridiculed it outright. In his *Reasons for a New Edition of Shakespeare* (1841), Collier wrote, with condescending approval, that Knight had made many "improvements . . . in the text of previous editions, by restoring some of the readings of the first folio"—not, we are meant to understand, by his own editorial skills. He praised, if it can be called praise, "the originality of some of his views, and . . . the ingenuity and ability with which he has enforced and illustrated them. He has pointed out a line in 'Hamlet,' which was left out by Reed in 1803, but it is restored in Malone's Shakespeare by Boswell."[80] Since Boswell's edition had appeared twenty years prior, Collier's compliments about Knight's "ingenuity" and "originality" appear backhanded, to say the least.

Halliwell was more overt when his journal the *Archaeologist* reviewed Knight's *Pictorial Shakespeare* alongside Collier's *Reasons for a New Edition*. The review begins, as had already become customary, by praising Knight for "restoring many good readings from the first folio." But then the knife comes out: "We miss, however, any original information respecting Shakespeare, or his writings, in this picture-book." In this period of great archival discoveries, Knight's lack of "original information" proved him an amateur. Since his forthcoming revised edition will contain "the same woodcuts and the same text," the reviewer continues, "we can only anticipate the wonted mediocrity from that quarter."[81] In a single brief notice, the review manages to look down haughtily on the material format of Knight's edition (which contains frivolous pictures), its intended audience (which requires picture books for its amusement), and Knight's own social presumption (in thinking that a popular magazine publisher could edit Shakespeare correctly).

Foremost in this critique is the same social snobbery that Wordsworth exhibits in his late (and pedestrian) sonnet "Illustrated Books and Newspapers," which decries "this vile abuse of pictured page": "Now prose and verse sunk into disrepute / Must lacquey a dumb art that best can suit / The taste of this once-intellectual Land."[82] But what seems to have upset Collier and Halliwell most was Knight's audacity in daring to critique his scholarly betters. Knight was no Shakespeare specialist, and he had rather insouciantly jumped into Shakespearean editing without having first spent decades in the archives, as editors since at least Malone had come to consider necessary. (Instead, Knight was simply looking for a "fit successor" to his already thriving line of *Pictorial* books.)[83] At the end of his introduction to the Shakespeare Society's reprint of Robert Armin's *Nest of Ninnies*, Collier took a gratuitous swipe at Knight, critiquing him specifically on a question of editorial method: Knight had made several errors "from not having consulted the earlier editions of the plays" prior to the Folio.[84] Collier took pride in his meticulous collation, which he considered "the most sacred part of the duty of an Editor," and for which he was consistently praised by contemporary reviewers.[85] This collation, furthermore, required editorial ingenuity so that the bibliographic relationships among all the early editions could be properly understood. He saw Knight's scholarly credentials for this task as negligible and his editorial procedure slipshod, since his text was based slavishly on the Folio.

In fact, the same Romantic opposition between ingenuity and mechanism underlies Collier's stenographic theory of Q1 itself. The "mechanical skill" that Collier attributes to the stenographer distinguishes his form of writing from the genius of Shakespeare and thereby allies Q1 with the imitative art that Edward Young described as "a sort of *Manufacture* wrought up by those *Mechanics, Art,* and *Labour,* out of pre-existent materials not their own."[86]

Likewise the working publisher Knight, who wrote and published precisely for "the Manufacturing and Agricultural Classes," lacks the insight necessary for editing Shakespeare and instead simply resorts to the First Folio for all his readings.[87]

In turn, Knight accused scholars like Collier of obfuscation and fetishism. His energies were trained less on establishing the text of Shakespeare by collating all those rare early editions in the Duke of Devonshire's library, to which only Collier had access, and more on the biographical figure of Shakespeare the dramatist. For Knight, the "learned, as they were called," were just beginning to catch up with the folk, thanks to the "translation of Schlegel's work in 1815, in conjunction with the admirable lectures of Coleridge."[88] The popular Shakespeare deserved a popular edition pitched to the popular understanding. And central to this popular edition was Knight's belief in authorial revision, and particularly in the status of Q1 *Hamlet* as an authorial rough draft.

The *Pictorial Shakespeare* is entirely organized around the figure of the author as genius who towers above his critics. Knight's reliance on the Folio text, even after being critiqued by Collier and others for "Foliolatry," derived from his unwavering belief that it recorded the author's final revisions and desired meaning far better than any mere editor could divine. Like the eighteenth-century editors, Knight believed that Q1 "gives us the play as originally written by Shakspere," but he pushed his view of the author as originating genius far beyond anything that earlier editors had ever thought to do.[89] Whereas they had seen revision as an ordinary component of playwriting, like the adaptation of source material or the reworking of earlier plays by other dramatists, Knight imbued revision with the full weight of Romantic theories of poetic composition and originality. Most important of all, he denied the very existence of any pre-Shakespearean *Hamlet* play, which had been widely accepted for generations, ever since Richard Farmer had drawn attention to Nashe's and Lodge's early references to *Hamlet*. Malone, for instance, had emphasized that they alluded not to "Shakespeare's drama, but an elder performance, on which, with the aid of the old prose History of Hamlet, his tragedy was formed."[90] And Collier too accepted that these comments referred to "the old drama, which was in existence long before Shakespeare took up the subject."[91]

Forcefully rejecting this consensus, Knight was working against received wisdom, but then he had never been much in awe of Malone, Farmer, and the other scholarly editors. Denying that Shakespeare's "tragedy was formed" on any "elder performance," Knight thundered: "Not a tittle of distinct evidence exists to show that there was any other play of Hamlet but that of Shakspere;

and all the collateral evidence upon which it is inferred that an earlier play of Hamlet than Shakspere's did exist may, on the other hand, be taken to prove that Shakspere's original sketch of Hamlet was in repute at an earlier period than is commonly assigned to its date."[92] Indeed, he similarly argued—again *pace* Malone and almost all contemporary critics—that the three *Henry VI* plays were entirely Shakespeare's, and more broadly, he denied the "general belief that Shakspere, in the outset of his career, was a mender of the plays of other men; or that, in any part of his career, he was associated with other men in writing plays."[93] This conception of Shakespeare the reviser is thus completely different from Malone's at the end of the eighteenth century: Knight's Shakespeare revises himself *but no one else*.

Knight raises Shakespeare to such heights of genius that virtually all textual variations among the different editions of his plays originate with him. When Payne and Foss wrote that their 1825 reprint of Q1 represented the play "as originally written by Shakespeare," they seem to have meant "as *initially* written by Shakespeare." Knight emphasizes *originally* in both senses of the word: Q1 is Shakespeare's "original sketch," his first draft, but also an *original* composition, since there was no "other play of 'Hamlet' but that of Shakespeare." The two senses of the word are mutually reinforcing: precisely because Knight imagined Q1 as an early effort, rather than a later piracy of the Q2/F text, he could date that "original sketch" to the 1580s and thereby avoid the specter of a non-Shakespearean *Hamlet* that might undermine Shakespeare's originality.

Both here and in his more general claims about Shakespeare's writing process, Knight consistently consolidates the corpus of texts associated with Shakespeare around the figure of the author, denying both source material and collaboration. Shakespeare now seems to have created his plays ex nihilo, first drafting them hastily and then polishing them to perfection. But this extreme emphasis on originality inevitably requires Knight to sacrifice some of Shakespeare's genius: "When he wrote his first copy," Knight says of *Hamlet*, "his power as an artist was not so consummate."[94] Similarly, Knight perceived in the quarto version of *Henry V*—which Malone had singled out as the only variant text that was *not* an early draft—a "first sketch" that "hastily met the demands of [Shakespeare's] audience"; later, as his artistic powers grew, Shakespeare "saw the capacity which the subject presented for being treated in a grand lyrical spirit."[95]

The appearance of Q1 *Hamlet* thus forces a difficult choice upon the Romantic editor: the values of originality (there was no previous *Hamlet*) and spontaneous genius (Shakespeare did not revise) cannot fully cohere. Knight chose the former, Collier the latter. It is almost as if the two editors divide Wordsworth's dicta on poetic composition between them: Collier adheres to the famous definition of poetry as "the spontaneous overflow of powerful feelings," while Knight remembers the qualifier that "it is frequently true of second words as of second thoughts, that they are the best."[96] Both editors stress original composition, rather than poetic tradition or exemplary models, and both view the author in Romantic terms as the genius from which originality springs. But their different Romanticisms lead them in opposite directions on the origins of *Hamlet*.

To temper his critique of Shakespeare's weaker "power as an artist," Knight ironically relied on Collier's recent "discovery"—viz., forgery—of a document that "distinctly proved . . . that [Shakespeare] was a sharer in the Blackfriars Theatre" as early as 1589.[97] Collier's invented document allowed Knight to argue that Shakespeare was working in the London theater early enough to have written the *Hamlet* to which Lodge and Nashe refer. He could thereby fold this play and other early productions into the organic development of Shakespeare's poetic career. As one of his earliest efforts, Q1 *Hamlet*, like Q1 *Henry V*, naturally lacks the "consummate" power that enabled Shakespeare to treat the subject later "in a grand lyrical spirit."

As we have seen, Collier differed from Knight in accepting the existence of an earlier, non-Shakespearean *Hamlet*, but like Knight he wove his evidence into a narrative of authorial development. Despite Collier's own forgery that showed him at Blackfriars in the 1580s, Shakespeare could not have been the author of the earlier *Hamlet* because, while he "had by this time given clear indications of powers superior to those of any of his rivals, he could not have written any of his greater works until some years afterwards." The earlier version existed "in all probability before Shakespeare had written any play, much less 'Hamlet.'"[98] While both Collier's and Knight's positions hinge on their assessments of Shakespeare's development as a playwright and his career trajectory, Collier's precisely inverts Knight's: since Collier denied that Q1 *Hamlet* represented a rough sketch of the play and instead saw it only as a garbled version of the received text, he had no "rough" text available that the immature Shakespeare could have written. He could hardly imagine Shakespeare writing his full-blown masterpiece as early as Nashe's reference.

The problem for Collier was that this rejection of Shakespearean revision meant sacrificing some of Shakespeare's originality by acknowledging the existence of the earlier *Hamlet*. And Collier's choice, like Knight's, had implications beyond *Hamlet*. Collier too saw Shakespeare's early years as an apprenticeship marked by revision, but not of his own work: "Shakespeare in the first instance confined himself to alterations and improvements of the plays of predecessors" and only later "found himself capable of inventing and constructing a great original drama."[99] Collier would not go so far as to deny that, in these early years, Shakespeare had ever "ventured upon original composition," but he saw him largely as the very "mender of the plays of other men" that Knight had rejected.[100] The phrasing here echoes the title of Young's *Conjectures on Original Composition*: Collier imagines Shakespeare progressing from an early apprenticeship in which he was dependent on the labors of others to a mature period in which he wrote, like a Romantic genius, entirely original dramas. The problem, of course, is that according to Collier's own theory Shakespeare's greatest and most Romantic play had not in fact been an "original composition."

To deal with this seeming contradiction, Collier subtly altered the meaning of originality. If Shakespeare was a reviser of others' work early in his career, then by opposition Collier could represent Shakespeare's mature *Hamlet* as "original" since it was not a "mending" of the earlier play but rather one newly written on the same subject. He refers to the earlier *Hamlet* as a "lost play upon similar incidents" and a "drama, of which Hamlet was the hero"—as if both the earlier author and Shakespeare were merely drawing on the same historical events and personages—but carefully avoids any speculation about the extent to which the language and details of the earlier play might actually lie behind Shakespeare's *Hamlet*.[101] Those kinds of "alterations and improvements of the plays of his predecessors" were confined to Shakespeare's early career. Compared to working over another dramatist's actual text, simply drawing on the same subject matter could easily be represented as original composition, and Collier's rhetoric subtly enables us to imagine *Hamlet* as a new work: "The 'Hamlet' which has come down to us in at least six quarto impressions, in the folio of 1623, and in the later impressions in that form, was not written until the winter of 1601, or the spring of 1602"—at the height of Shakespeare's powers. Much ideological labor is packed into Collier's definition of "the 'Hamlet' which has come down to us," a definition that allows him to assert that *Hamlet* "was not written until the winter of 1601" at the earliest, despite knowing at the same time that *Hamlet* had been performed in the 1580s.[102]

The two great Shakespearean editors of the mid-nineteenth century thus offer opposed but dialectically related responses to the problems of literary authorship posed by the discovery of Q1 *Hamlet*. For Knight, Shakespeare begins with original but rough sketches and then proceeds carefully, in intricate detail, to perfect them into the masterpieces of his mature period. For Collier, Shakespeare begins by revising the work of others, but as his powers wax, he writes his "great original drama[s]" in a burst of inspiration. Both are models of a writing life, and both derive ultimately from the Romantic notion of organic development. Regardless of Collier's attempts to dismiss Knight from the realm of serious scholarship, in other words, the two are playing on the same literary field, and for that very reason the differences between their two models would help to shape the modern discipline of Shakespeare studies.

Crucially for the history of Shakespearean textual studies in particular, these two models emerge from different approaches to the project of editing Shakespeare. Knight's entire *Pictorial Edition*, not merely the Life of Shakespeare that he incorporated, is ultimately a heroic biography: all textual variation is referred to the arc of the author's triumphant career. Picking up on this hagiographic aspect of the edition, one moderately favorable reviewer advised Knight to "endeavour to believe that Shakspeare was human."[103] Collier's *Works*, by contrast, focuses on the bibliographic interrelations among the editions of Shakespeare, which do not necessarily bear any direct relation to the author's writing process. Knight's evidence is almost entirely literary critical: repeatedly, he compares a passage in Q1 *Hamlet* (or in another variant text) with the Folio version, pointing out poetic and dramatic improvements that "are so manifestly those of the author working upon his first sketch."[104] By contrast, Collier looks for his evidence mainly to printers, publishers, stenographers, and other nonauthorial agents; he confines himself largely to documentary history, and even where (as in the case of his "proof" of Q1's piracy) the argument would seem to call for some literary critical analysis, he generally refuses to engage in the kind of comparative reading that is Knight's forte. Again, Collier's reluctance here is not simply an idiosyncrasy: he is rejecting what he saw as an outdated, belletristic mode of editing that involved pointing out to the reader the "beauties" and "faults" of the author. The denial of this kind of literary criticism is constitutive of the scholarly appearance of Collier's edition—just as it was constitutive of the Shakespeare Society he helped to create, which had as its goal not the appreciation of Shakespeare's art but "the discovery of much curious and valuable information . . . that will throw light on our early Dramatic Literature and Stage."[105] It is no accident that this passage is echoed in the critique in Halliwell's *Archaeologist* of the lack of "any original information respecting Shakespeare" in Knight's "picture-book."

And, indeed, this denial is constitutive of modern Shakespearean editing as a whole, even though the sordid revelations of Collier's forgeries led the New Bibliographers essentially to expunge him from their own history. In his groundbreaking edition of *Merry Wives*, for instance, Greg avoids all mention of Collier, instead stating that the first person seriously to claim that Q *Merry Wives* was a stenographic piracy instead of a rough draft was P. A. Daniel in the introduction to his 1888 edition, more than forty years after Collier.[106] Nonetheless, Collier's approach to Shakespearean editing is far closer to the New Bibliographers' than is Knight's, for Greg and his colleagues similarly tended to define their "scientific" project over against what they saw as the belletrism and subjective impressionism of literary criticism.[107]

Furthermore, the twentieth-century theory of memorial reconstruction rests on the same foundation of retrograde bibliography as Collier's innovative theory about Q1 *Hamlet*. When the New Bibliographers traced the history of this theory, however, they generally began not with Collier, who had become anathema, but with Tycho Mommsen's 1857 *Athenaeum* article on *Hamlet* and *Romeo and Juliet*.[108] But Collier and Mommsen were in fact broadly in agreement. They were friends who frequently corresponded, and Collier even provided the introduction to Mommsen's edition of *Pericles*. In his *Athenaeum* article, Mommsen followed Collier in arguing that the first editions of both plays "seem to be no first sketches, as some have imagined, but mere misrepresentations of the genuine text."[109] He traced these texts not principally to stenography but to the process of memorial reconstruction that would come to dominate twentieth-century Shakespearean bibliography: "An actor . . . put down" the play "from memory . . . as it was acted" but "wrote very illegibly," and then "a bad poet, most probably 'a bookseller's hack' . . . without any personal intercourse with the writer of the notes, availed himself of them to make up this early copy of 'Hamlet.'"[110] But we should not be distracted by the difference in the *method* of reporting, however much the New Bibliographers might have relied on this difference to make Collier disappear from their own critical genealogy. For one thing, as we have seen, Collier himself had allowed that his stenographer might have "filled up the blanks [in his notes] from memory"; the difference between the two critics on the question of memorial reconstruction is one of degree, not kind. More important for our modern view of Shakespeare as an author, the crucial distinction lies not between Collier's stenographer and Mommsen's forgetful actor but rather, as Mommsen himself notes, between the view of these editions as Shakespeare's "first sketches" and the view of them as "mere misrepresentations of the genuine text." Mommsen's argument clearly derives from Collier's revolutionary idea that *books* printed earlier might contain *texts* composed later.[111]

Before his forgeries were thoroughly revealed, Collier's theory persuaded many, perhaps most, Shakespeare scholars. By the mid-1860s, for instance, it had become obvious to William George Clark and William Aldis Wright, editors of the highly influential Cambridge Shakespeare, that Q1 *Hamlet* was "a very imperfect reproduction of the play," "printed from a manuscript surreptitiously obtained . . . in the first instance from short hand notes taken during the representation."[112] They thought that *Romeo and Juliet* as well was "obtained from notes taken in short-hand during the representation," although they attributed this position only to "the high authority of M. Tycho Mommsen," perhaps because Collier's forgeries had begun to be exposed by then, and his own "high authority" was suffering.[113] As mentioned above, the Cambridge editors' evidence in this case was stylistic: Shakespeare could never have written "so many instances of imperfect sense, halting metre, bad grammar, and abrupt dialogue" as were apparent in Q1 *Romeo and Juliet*. But when we consider the evident fact that prior to 1823 no one—not Pope or Johnson or Steevens or Malone or any other sensitive reader of Shakespeare—had ever objected to anything of the sort in that version of the play, this claim seems more editorial fiat than literary analysis.

Comments like these show that the mid-century appeal of Collier's theory may have had less to do with matters of bibliography than with larger questions of poetic composition and creativity. Richard Grant White condescendingly wrote about Knight's theory that "this notion—it is the merest notion—" nevertheless holds "a great fascination for those who cannot be easy without pulling their Shakespeare to pieces, to see how he goes." His explanation for this fascination reveals that Collier's form of Romanticism had won out over Knight's: "They think that by comparing the two Hamlets, first and second, they can trace the growth of his mind and the development of his thought; although they might as well undertake to trace the development of lightning from a thunder cloud."[114] A play of genius like *Hamlet* emerges in a flash, not by a long process of patient development.

But not all critics accepted the analogy of poetic genius to "lightning from a thunder cloud." An article in Charles Dickens's journal *All the Year Round*, for example, denied the common view that "the great poet's works were poured forth as if by inspiration, without any need for recasting or revision, perfect as we now peruse them."[115] The author of this popularizing article, which seeks to explain the textual situation to novices, went so far as to accept Knight's radical denial of any pre-Shakespearean *Hamlet*. As in Knight's editions, the emphasis is on Romantic heroic biography rather than textual relationships: "Our own opinion . . . is that the idea of Hamlet as the subject of a play . . . was from his youth a favourite one with Shakespeare; that he loved it, and had probably drawn out the draft of it as early as when he roved the fields about Charlecote with Anne Hathaway; that it influenced him in giving his son the remarkable name of Hamnet (if that is not a clerical error for Hamlet); and that he gradually worked on the idea as Goethe did on Faust."[116] These lines could easily have been poached from Knight's own biography of Shakespeare, which had become something of a byword for flights of imaginative fancy. Knight rambled through the countryside around Charlecote himself, inviting readers to imagine Shakespeare, the poet of nature, being inspired by the Avon and its environs:

> Islands of sedge here and there render the channel unnavigable, except to the smallest boat. A willow thrusting its trunk over the stream reminds us of Ophelia:—
> "There is a willow grows askaunt the brook
> That shows his hoar leaves in the glassy stream." . . .
> We open the volume of Shakspere's own poems; and we bethink us what of these he may have composed, or partly shadowed out, wandering on this river-side, or drifting under its green banks, when his happy and genial nature instinctively shaped itself into song, as the expression of his sympathy with the beautiful world around him.

To professional Shakespeareans, such remarks were absurd. Contemporary reviews of the biographies in the two editions—and most did deal with the two comparatively—consistently saw Collier's as the more scholarly. Collier's "sober and sensible account of Shakespeare, has strained our information quite as far as it will go," wrote one reviewer, disparaging the "fanciful and elaborate theories" of Knight's "attempt to guess at the life of a man whose life is unknown."[117] Sounding rather like Dickens's Gradgrind, but perfectly in keeping with the mission of the Shakespeare Society, another reviewer declaimed: "We do not want either fine writing or new theories about Shakespeare: we have had plenty of both already: we want facts."[118] Numerous critics saw the debate in these terms: Collier's rigorous facticity on the one side, and Knight's imaginative biography on the other. But as we have seen, Collier's own theory of Q1 was every bit as biographical as Knight's; it simply relied on a different strand of Romanticism for its model of authorship.

Despite this attempt by some scholars to cast Knight as an amateur who was out of his depth, his revision theory by no means disappeared. Nor, in fact, was it confined only to popular magazine accounts: Collier's great rival Alexander Dyce, for instance, likewise saw Q1 as "Shakespeare's first conception of the play."[119] And indeed, several odd features of Q1 *Hamlet* seemed difficult to explain purely as accidents of stenography, including Q1's use of the names Corambis and Montano instead of Polonius and Reynaldo; the earlier appearance of "To be, or not to be" and the nunnery scene; the Q1 Queen's explicit avowal of her innocence of the murder; and the entirely new scene in which Horatio and the Queen conspire to help Hamlet in his revenge. In addition to Dyce, major critics such as Joseph Hunter, Georg Gottfried Gervinus, and Nicolaus Delius argued from these details that Collier's theory could not account for all the variation between Q1 and the received text.[120]

More important than which side won this debate over the origins of Q1, however, is that it seemingly could have only two sides. The stark opposition of Knight and Collier in virtually all mid-Victorian discussions of Q1 suppressed any alternative possibilities. This narrowing of textual possibility—Knight *or* Collier—served to foreground Shakespeare's authorial genius, since both imagined Shakespeare's authorship along Romantic lines. Only when these underlying Romantic assumptions began to fade could the debate about Q1 move past the question of whether Knight or Collier was correct. In the late nineteenth century, a new generation of critics could suddenly see beyond this dichotomy. These critics reinvigorated the idea of revision, but without Knight's image of the heroically revising Shakespeare; they built on Collier's innovative retrograde bibliography, but in creating their own textual stemmata, they rejected his derivation of Q1 entirely from Shakespeare's finished *Hamlet*.

Collier himself had admitted that the names Corambis and Montano could not be explained by his stenography theory, and he suggested that "they were names in the older play on the same story, or names which Shakespeare first introduced, and subsequently thought fit to reject."[121] He thus confined any revision by Shakespeare—either of himself or of the earlier play—to these two name changes, but nonetheless he had to acknowledge that stenography could not *fully* explain all the features of Q1. The Cambridge editors likewise (but again without citing Collier) argued that—even though Shakespeare had changed the names of the councillor and his servant and "may also have changed the order of one or two scenes, and here and there erased or inserted a few lines"—nonetheless "no substantial change was made," and the "chief differences" between Q1 and Q2 were "only such as might be expected between a bona fide, and a mala fide, transcription."[122] Despite the additional reference to the transposed nunnery scene, in the end they too simply ignore these differences, which do not add up to any "substantial change" and can be largely explained by the inevitable corruptions of textual transmission.

But these nagging variations would not disappear, and they ultimately precipitated the first major break with the Romantic dialectic of Collier and Knight. Only six years after their Cambridge edition, Clark and Wright re-edited the play for the Clarendon Shakespeare (1872), and by then these differences (and perhaps Collier's tarnished reputation) had led them to change their assessment of Q1 completely. They still maintained that Q1 was "printed from a copy which was hastily taken down and perhaps surreptitiously obtained, either from short-hand notes made during the representation, or privately from the actors themselves," but they had made an epochal shift in their view of what version of *Hamlet* lay behind this surreptitious copy. Now the differences that they had earlier dismissed as insubstantial seemed to be "important modifications" that "cannot be explained by the carelessness of short-hand writer, copyist, or printer."[123] Such modifications, however, did not point toward the kind of Shakespearean revision that Knight advocated, both because there was "no evidence for Shakespeare's connexion with the play before 1602" and because in parts of Q1 "we find very great unlikeness and very great inferiority to the later play."[124]

Clark and Wright's dismissal of Knight's revision theory thus turned not only on the kind of documentary evidence that Collier favored—the absence of *Hamlet* in Francis Meres's 1598 list of Shakespeare's plays, for instance—but also on the aesthetic evaluation of Shakespeare's style that had been an important outgrowth of his stenography argument, the idea that "Shakespeare never could have written thus." At the same time, their new belief that "important modifications" had occurred between Q1 and Q2—a rejection of Collier's and Mommsen's theory—depended on the kind of literary analysis of the variation between the texts that had underpinned Knight's revision argument. The editors synthesized the methodologies of Collier and Knight, but now each side of the great mid-Victorian debate over Q1 seemed to rule out the other in an insoluble dilemma.

Clark and Wright's Clarendon edition thus reveals that the dialectical opposition of Knight and Collier that had driven assessments of Q1 since its discovery was running out of steam. The Clarendon editors also offered, tentatively, the first articulation of the new synthesis that emerged from the obsolescence of this debate. As I show in Chapter 4, their new theory would dominate studies of *Hamlet* from the 1880s through the 1940s, completely transforming our understanding of Shakespeare's authorship. By the mid-twentieth century a new paradigm, exemplified in a series of landmark editions of the play, would replace the Clarendon "solution" to the problem of Q1 and become widely taken for granted. But, in dialectical progression, this paradigm too eventually broke down as, pushed to its limit, it opened itself to critique by the "New Textualists." In my Conclusion, I suggest that we have now reached another such moment of exhaustion in our own New Textualist approach to Shakespeare, epitomized by the Arden third series *Hamlet*.[125] In order to understand our current textual situation fully, however, we need to go beyond our by now familiar critique of the New Bibliography to see how that movement itself emerged out of the earlier, nineteenth-century revolution in textual analysis elaborated by the Clarendon edition.

"After a careful examination of the quarto of 1603, and a comparison of the play as there exhibited with its later form," the Clarendon editors wrote,

> we have arrived at a conclusion which, inasmuch as it is conjectural and based to a large extent upon subjective considerations, we state with some diffidence. It is this:—That there was an old play on the story of Hamlet, some portions of which are still preserved in the quarto of 1603; that about the year 1602 Shakespeare took this and began to remodel it for the stage, as he had done with other plays; that the quarto of 1603 represents the play after it had been retouched by him to a certain extent, but before his alterations were complete: and that in the quarto of 1604 we have for the first time the Hamlet of Shakespeare.... A close examination of the quarto of 1603 will convince any one that it contains some of Shakespeare's undoubted work, mixed with a great deal that is not his, and will confirm our theory that the text, imperfect as it is, represents an older play in a transition state, while it was undergoing a remodelling but had not received more than the first rough touches of the great master's hand.[126]

Although the existence of an earlier *Hamlet* had been known for a century, in this passage we can see the true birth of the *Ur-Hamlet*. What is crucially new about Clark and Wright's theory is its integration of the pre-Shakespearean *Hamlet* into Shakespeare's own texts. Previous editors had known about this earlier *Hamlet* but had never imagined they could construct a textual stemma that would explain in any detail its relationship to Shakespeare's play. Collier wrote in his 1843 edition, for example, that "how far that lost play might be an improvement upon the old translated 'Historie' we have no means of deciding, nor to what extent Shakespeare availed himself of such an improvement."[127]

For Collier, there was no real connection between the pre-Shakespearean play and Q1, which derived from Q2/F in any case. He thought of Shakespeare's play as essentially a new creation. For Knight, too, Shakespeare's *Hamlet* was an original creation, but this was because there was no pre-Shakespearean play at all. Before the last decades of the nineteenth century, the Romantic dialectic that bound together Collier and Knight as seemingly the only theories capable of explaining Q1 thereby ensured that the lost play was always cordoned off from Q1 and hence ultimately from Shakespeare's *Hamlet*. The Clarendon edition changed all that, sparking a new interest in the relation of the three extant texts of Shakespeare's play to the earlier version, which now truly took its place as the *Ur-*, or foundational, *Hamlet*.[128]

In opposing the entire mid-Victorian dichotomy of authorial revision or piratical stenography, Clark and Wright also moved beyond the Romantic consensus that underlay that surface opposition. It hardly seems a great imaginative leap to posit that Q1 might preserve something of the pre-Shakespearean *Hamlet*. But so long as Romantic ideas of poetic creation remained dominant, this seemingly obvious theory was, apparently, virtually impossible to conceive. As those ideas waned, and the *Ur-Hamlet* was no longer so rigorously quarantined from Q1 and Shakespeare's *Hamlet*, that ghostly text immediately threatened the idea that Shakespeare's greatest work had appeared like "lightning from a thunder cloud." Rather than being an original composition, as both Collier and Knight had maintained in their different ways, *Hamlet* was now seen to emerge directly out of Shakespeare's engagement with the earlier play. Indeed, in Clark and Wright's theory, Shakespeare seems literally to have overwritten the pages of the *Ur-Hamlet*, resulting in the "transition state" of Q1.[129] The Clarendon Shakespeare does not create spontaneously but rather creates through a process of punctuated revision over time. Perhaps most important, Clark and Wright's theory threatened the organic unity of Shakespeare's play, the central underpinning of Romantic aesthetics.[130] If the received text of *Hamlet* was simply the endpoint in a process of multiple revision, from the *Ur-Hamlet* through Q1 through Q2 and F, could the play still be understood as a single, harmonious work of art?

The unsettling effect of this new theory can be seen in the contradictions evident in Halliwell's *Memoranda on the Tragedy of Hamlet*, published in 1879 but itself a layered text composed over many years, which Halliwell made little effort to unify. At the outset Halliwell—who had helped Collier to found the Shakespeare Society and continued to defend his old friend's reputation—frames the question of Q1 in traditional terms by asking "whether the first edition of Hamlet is a first sketch or a surreptitious copy of the tragedy," the familiar dichotomy of Knight and Collier.[131] But when he advances his own theory, this simple opposition is revealed as insufficient: Q1 is "an abridged jumble compiled partly from the playhouse copy, the use of which may have been surreptitiously obtained and progress arrested by discovery, partly from short-hand notes taken at the theatre and from actors' parts, and partly either by new and clumsy writing, or, as Mr. Aldis Wright conjectures, by the use of the older play."

Likewise, Halliwell initially imagines, conventionally, that "no genius but that of Shakespeare" could have reworked his "rude original" sources into such a "harmonious composition" as *Hamlet*.[132] But by the end of the *Memoranda*, he advances a far more radical theory of the effect of revision on Shakespeare's play: "Unless we bear in mind that Shakespeare's treatment of the story of Hamlet was influenced by the succession of events in the older tragedy, and that the construction of his own drama was to some extent fettered by the circumstances under which he wrote, there can never be an aesthetic criticism on Hamlet which will be other than one that involves an unsuccessful attempt to reconcile inconsistencies that are not explicable on any other hypothesis."[133] Whereas earlier Shakespeare's "genius" had been revealed by his ability to rework sources and mold them to his own purposes, now "the older tragedy" stubbornly resists assimilation into "his own drama." And what was earlier seen as a "harmonious composition" is now riddled with "inconsistencies" that cannot be reconciled by the ingenuities of literary interpretation. Only an attention to the textual history of the play can explain those problematic aspects that had led critics into "an almost impenetrable mass of conflicting opinions, wild conjectures and leaden contemplations."[134]

In his *Memoranda*, Halliwell struggles to assimilate Clark and Wright's new theory of Q1 into the older framework that had organized studies of *Hamlet* in the half century following Bunbury's discovery, a framework that he could not completely escape. A younger generation of scholars, however, would soon sweep away this Romantic consensus entirely. As I show in Chapter 4, to these critics *Hamlet* was riven by multiple strata of writing and rewriting that did not always align and that accidentally resulted in the play's famous "problems." One of the leaders of this group, John Mackinnon Robertson (Figure 6), drew his inspiration from Halliwell's remark that Shakespeare was "fettered" by "the older tragedy," quoting the passage at key moments in several of his works.[135]

In Robertson's view, Halliwell was essentially arguing that, because of these fetters, *Hamlet* "as a whole is unintelligible and inexplicable."[136] Throughout his career, Robertson was fascinated by this idea, which he would return to explore in several books. One of them, *The Problem of "Hamlet,"* in turn fascinated T. S. Eliot, whose famous essay "Hamlet and His Problems" evolved out of a review of the book. Eliot declared the play "most certainly an artistic failure" because it was a "stratification" that "represents the efforts of a series of men, each making what he could out of the work of his predecessors."[137]

From Collier to his friend Halliwell to Robertson to Eliot: in a few short jumps of scholarly citation and influence, we have moved from the Victorian Romantic understanding of *Hamlet* to a modernist movement that utterly rejected Romanticism. While both Knight and Collier had venerated Coleridge as the greatest interpreter of *Hamlet*, Eliot believed that "the kind of criticism that Goethe and Coleridge produced, in writing of Hamlet, is the most misleading kind possible."[138] In Chapter 4, I take up the new ideas of Shakespearean authorship and of *Hamlet* that emerged from the ashes of the Romantic dialectic of Knight's revision and Collier's stenography. What I want to stress here, however, is what unites all of these critics, and what has persisted through the twentieth century and into the twenty-first: their shared belief that Q1 *Hamlet* offers the key to understanding Shakespeare's authorship, his writing process, and even, given his paramount place in the literary canon, the nature of poetic genius itself. Such has been the power of the "small quarto, barbarously cropped, and very ill-bound" that Sir Henry Bunbury found in his closet.

As we have seen, Bunbury's discovery forced an epochal reevaluation of Shakespeare's "textual biography." In so doing, Q1 transformed critical narratives about the textual relationships among the early editions of *Hamlet*; more particularly, it has encouraged us to read a biographical drama into the bibliographic histories of these books. Such readings have focused on the advertising blurb on the title page of Q2: "Newly imprinted and enlarged to almost as much againe as it

Figure 6. John Mackinnon Robertson (1856–1933), Shakespearean critic, politician, freethinker. © National Portrait Gallery, London.

was, according to the true and perfect Coppie." I return here to that brief statement, showing how the history of *Hamlet* after Q1 has affected our interpretations of it and suggesting how we might reinterpret it without the biographical reading that has seemed increasingly imperative since the ghostly return of Q1.

Even before 1823, bibliography had implied biography: Malone read the blurb and inferred that Shakespeare had previously written a "rude sketch" of the play. For Knight, too, it was Shakespeare who "enlarged" the play, and the "Coppie" was a "true and perfect" representation of the play in its finished, authorially "perfected" form. By contrast, nineteenth-century adherents of Collier's theory emphasized the blurb's final clause: Richard Grant White thought the Q2 title page had "done much to mislead those critics . . . who have adopted and ingeniously advocated the alluring theory of a revision, an enlargement, and an elaboration by Shakespeare of his first work," whereas in fact the "enlargement was due to the printing of the play 'according to the true and perfect copy.'"[139] Such comments prefigure the dominant twentieth-century reading of the title page. Like White, most editors after the New Bibliography have interpreted the advertisement as a comment on the different textual authority of the manuscripts behind the two editions. The "true and perfect Coppie" replaces an imperfect, pirated one. And Q2 is "enlarged to almost as much againe as it was" because the process of memorially reconstructing Q1 led to numerous corruptions and omissions that drastically shortened the play.

At first this reading of Q2's title page was less rooted in Shakespearean biography. Collier thought that "the edition of 1604 was probably intended, by some parties connected with the theatre, to supersede the garbled and fraudulent edition of 1603," but who exactly these "parties" were remained unclear, and he seems to have thought of them as acting illicitly, since he added: "We do not believe that Shakespeare, individually, had anything to do with this second and more correct impression, and we doubt much whether it was authorized by the company, which seems at all times to have done its utmost to prevent the appearance of plays in print, lest to a certain extent the public curiosity should thereby be satisfied."[140] While the copy for Q2 was not stenographic or otherwise reported, in other words, it nonetheless arrived at the printing house through the usual underhanded means that most eighteenth- and nineteenth-century editors saw behind all the quartos. Collier's stenographic theory of Q1 did not yet imply that the author himself had anything to do with the publication of Q2 in its "true and perfect" form. But that would soon change.

Beginning with A. W. Pollard's *Shakespeare's Folios and Quartos* (1909) and *Shakespeare's Fight with the Pirates and the Problem of the Transmission of His Texts* (1919), Collier's vague "parties connected with the theatre" began to coalesce more definitively around Shakespeare himself, or at the very least around his theatrical troupe. As Dover Wilson later wrote, by distinguishing between "good" and "bad" quartos, Pollard's landmark texts of New Bibliography "restored confidence in the 'ancient copies.'" Now the "irreparable 'depravations'" of these printed texts, "if rightly interpreted, might often afford us glimpses of Shakespeare's own manuscripts."[141] The blurb on the title page of Q2 could therefore more easily be read as biography in miniature. Pollard argued that "the players seem to have condoned the attack" on their rights that Ling and Trundle had launched by publishing Q1, "and Ling was allowed to publish a revised edition"; in this way, as with Q2 *Romeo and Juliet*, the King's Men "asserted their rights after a piracy by putting out better texts."[142] Like Collier, Pollard denied that "Shakespeare himself had anything to do with the quartos," again largely because of their numerous errors, which seemed to rule out any close involvement by the author.[143] But by dividing the quartos into "good" and "bad," depending on whether they were authorized by the players, Pollard had begun the process of identifying Shakespeare with the agency behind the publication of Q2.

Dover Wilson picked up on Pollard's argument in *The Manuscript of Shakespeare's Hamlet* (1934), which attempted to prove that Q2 had been "printed direct from Shakespeare's manuscript," and which thereby set the editorial agenda for most twentieth-century editions of the play.[144] Like Pollard, he believed that "the copy delivered to James Roberts at the beginning of the seventeenth century" was handed over "by the Globe company" itself, and that Roberts was "commissioned to print it as a rejoinder to the publication of the pirated *Hamlet* of 1603."[145] Wilson's insistence that Shakespeare's own manuscript lay behind Q2 led many scholars to the belief that the author himself had provided the "true and perfect Coppie" to the printers. A few years later, W. W. Greg was "pretty sure" that Shakespeare "must have had a part, if only as a leading member of the company, in placing copy at the disposal of the publishers," especially in "superseding the 'bad' quartos of *Hamlet, Romeo and Juliet*, and probably *Love's Labour's Lost*."[146] In his Oxford edition, G. R. Hibbard writes similarly that the copy for Q2 "must have come from the Globe or from the hands of Shakespeare himself."[147] So too Ann Thompson and Neil Taylor, editors of the third series Arden edition: Q2 was printed "apparently as a deliberate attempt on the part of Shakespeare's company, and presumably with his consent, to correct and displace Q1."[148] And

E. A. J. Honigmann offers an inventive narrative that would not seem out of place in Charles Knight's biography: "The replacement of bad [quartos] by good ones . . . surely points to the author rather than to the actors," because a "bad text did less damage to the players, the soundness of whose commodity would re-emerge when next they put on their production, than to the author, whose literary reputation might suffer permanently." And didn't Shakespeare "rate reputation as the immortal part of a man? Would he have felt less bitter than Achilles when he found that his fame was 'shrewdly gored' . . . by a scarecrow press?"[149]

In the New Bibliographic tradition and after, we thus see the Q2 blurb reinterpreted, within the larger context of bad quartos and memorial reconstruction, to create a narrative about the textual transmission of the play from the King's Men, even from Shakespeare himself, to the stationers. Whereas Collier and his nineteenth-century followers had been content with a vague suggestion that a more "perfect" manuscript had somehow made its way to the printing house, now Shakespeare and the King's Men *desire* to replace the "inferior first quarto with its outrageous claim to be the play that Shakespeare wrote."[150] This dominant twentieth-century approach to the blurb thus strongly reinforces the broader tendency, ever since Bunbury's discovery, to read the bibliography of *Hamlet* through the biography of Shakespeare.

And yet, nowhere on the title page of Q2 is it specified that Shakespeare or his theatrical company provided the copy for the edition, nor that they intended thereby to make the earlier, inferior edition disappear. Reading the advertisement in this way has led to a remarkable blindness in our understanding of the early publication of *Hamlet*. None of the existing narratives can actually explain the most fundamental bibliographic question about Q2: why it was ever published in the first place. To answer this question, we need to rethink the bibliographic situation from the perspective of the stationers, and especially the publisher Nicholas Ling, rather than the players or the author. Doing so will not offer any neat solutions to the textual problem of *Hamlet*, nor solve the mystery of how exactly the copy behind Q1 or Q2 reached the stationers. But thinking bibliographically rather than biographically can help us to understand better the publisher's motives for bringing out Q2. In turn, this understanding will reveal important new meanings to the famous claim that *Hamlet* had been "Newly imprinted and enlarged to almost as much againe as it was, according to the true and perfect Coppie."

The basic facts of the early editions are well known. On July 26, 1602, James Roberts entered in the Stationers' Register "a booke called *'the Revenge of*

Hamlett Prince [of] Denmarke' as yt was latelie Acted by the Lord Chamberleyne his servants.'"[151] In the imprint of Q1 no printer is named, but we know from bibliographic evidence that the edition was actually printed not by Roberts but by Valentine Simmes. Simmes printed the edition "for N. L. and Iohn Trundell": Ling's elaborate personal device (including a ling fish) appears on the title page and makes clear to whom the initials refer. But Roberts became involved again with Q2, which he printed "for N. L. . . . to be sold at his shoppe vnder Saint Dunstons Church in Fleetstreet"; the shop address is Ling's, and once again his device appears on the title page.

Several scenarios have been proposed to account for these bibliographic facts, but even when scholars have addressed the blurb from Ling's perspective, they have tended to take for granted that its appeal to an improved text would justify the publication. The New Bibliographers generally imagined that Ling "brought out the *Hamlet* of 1603 in the teeth of Roberts's entry in the Stationers' Register," but that his piratical publication of the memorially reconstructed text nevertheless "gave him rights in the play." Trundle's role in Q1, and his "disappearance when the bad quarto was succeeded by the better, has sometimes led to a guess—it can be no more—that it was he who secured the unauthorized copy."[152] Therefore, when the King's Men and Shakespeare decided to "supersede" Q1, Ling and Roberts grudgingly put the piracy (and Trundle) behind them for the sake of the improved text. The New Bibliographic narrative thus depends on the belief that, in Pollard's words, "Ling was allowed to publish a revised edition," with the text provided by the players. No consideration is given to whether Ling would agree after being so generously allowed to do so. The commercial appeal of a new edition is simply taken for granted.

Recent scholars have significantly revised this traditional narrative, but again largely without attending to Ling's own financial interests. In his important study of Ling's career, Gerald Johnson downplays piracy, showing instead that "Ling often . . . financed the publication of copy that had been procured by other stationers"; Trundle disappears from the imprint of Q2 not because he acquired that copy by underhanded means but simply because "the agreement between the two" was that "Ling, as usual, would claim the copyright." Since Roberts was Ling's favorite printer, both before and after *Hamlet*, Johnson sees no animosity between the two; instead they "may have reached a private agreement" to produce Q2, since "both could hope to profit from the publication of a new edition that could correctly be advertised" as enlarged and improved.[153] David Scott Kastan fills in another part of the story: Roberts entered the manuscript behind Q1, but because 1603 was a particularly busy time in his shop, he farmed out the printing to Simmes while allowing Ling and Trundle to publish it for a fee. But Roberts maintained his rights in the play, and so when Q2 became available, he jointly published it with Ling.[154] Lukas Erne's interpretation differs somewhat but, like these others, stresses "normal book-trade practice: Ling and Trundle seem to have licensed but not entered their manuscript and had it printed without anyone realizing that Roberts had once entered a different version." When Roberts discovered "Ling and Trundle's unintentional breach" of his rights, he "could have caused them trouble but preferred to negotiate an advantageous deal with his neighbors in Fleet Street, selling to Ling and Trundle his longer and better manuscript and having them pay him to print it."[155]

All of these narratives, like the New Bibliographic narrative they revise, depend on the idea that Ling would be interested in publishing Q2. But simply because a "true and perfect Coppie" had somehow become available to him did not mean Ling was under any obligation to publish it. Even if the King's Men, or Shakespeare himself, came to him with the manuscript and urged him to redress the wrong to their reputation caused by the existence of Q1, why would Ling agree? Not much time had elapsed since the publication of Q1, after all—at most around eighteen months.[156] Why would Ling want to publish a second edition of a play so quickly after he had published the first? If Q2 was meant to supersede Q1, this hardly seems to have been in Ling's economic interest. While Roberts would be paid immediately to print the book, it is difficult to understand how Ling could easily expect to profit from a new edition that would make his previous one obsolete. As Thompson and Taylor pointedly note, if "the wish to drive Q1 off the bookstalls" lay behind the publication of Q2, "Ling would seem to have been in competition with himself."[157] One of the earliest critics to respond to Q1's discovery made essentially the same point in 1825: "Whether the mention of the true and perfect copy was intended to depreciate the first as well as to recommend the subsequent editions, is at best doubtful," since it is not "very likely that these parties would censure their own former work for faults which reflect discredit on themselves."[158]

To sum up: the various publishing arrangements imagined in the existing narratives all seem like a good deal for Shakespeare (who secures his authorial reputation), for the King's Men (who protect their repertoire), and for Roberts (who profits twice from the same play)—for everyone, that is, except the person who had the most at stake in a new edition of *Hamlet*: Nicholas

Ling. Something is wrong with our narratives. To rethink this paradox, we need to return to the early title pages of *Hamlet*, which testify far more to Ling's decisions about how to market his editions of *Hamlet* than they do to Shakespeare's or the King's Men's desires. Instead of seeing Q2 as Shakespeare's intervention into the book trade, in other words, we need to consider how the book trade handled Shakespeare.

Two explanations for Ling's decision could dissolve the paradox, although neither of them has, to the best of my knowledge, ever been seriously entertained. One possibility is that Ling did not actually publish Q2, although he appears in the imprint as the publisher. Stationers sometimes served in the publishing role—securing the right to copy, wholesaling the book to other booksellers—without financing the edition themselves, as editions were subsidized by religious groups, the London livery companies, authors, and others. If the King's Men offered to pay Ling and Roberts to produce the edition, or if they covered the printing costs while Ling sold the edition for them in exchange for a portion of the profits, Ling might have been willing to bring out Q2 even at the risk of decreasing sales of Q1. If so, perhaps the King's Men also agreed to buy up the remaining stock of Q1, which might just explain why only two copies of the edition have survived, since otherwise Ling would have had little incentive to agree to a deal that would still leave him with numerous unsold and presumably unsalable copies of that edition. This is purely speculation, of course, but a subsidized edition would explain what has never been explained by critics who simply assume that Ling would have helped the King's Men and Shakespeare supersede his edition of *Hamlet*.

A second possibility is that Q1 had already sold out, or was well on its way to doing so, and that Ling was therefore happy to bring out a new edition. This is what we would typically assume with any other book: a reprint can generally be taken to indicate that the previous edition had proved popular with book buyers.[159] If so, *Hamlet* was more successful than most first editions of professional plays: from 1590 to 1603, only about 8 percent of such playbooks were reprinted within a year, and around 13 percent within two years.[160] If Q1 did indeed sell out this rapidly, it was clearly not a "bad quarto" for the stationers, and early modern book buyers too must have seen little wrong with it: would a bad reported text that bore only a moderate resemblance to the play as it then appeared on stage really have sold out so quickly? In fact, by this logic, the biggest risk Ling took was his decision *not* to reprint the Q1 text that had already proven itself in the book stalls as a very "good" quarto for him, and instead to publish the untested text of

Q2. This choice likely also made the edition more expensive to produce, not only because Q2 is a considerably longer book but also because it is far easier and faster to set type from printed copy than from manuscript. Even in this scenario, if Shakespeare or the King's Men wanted Ling to reprint *Hamlet* using their "perfect" text rather than the "bad" one he already had, they may have had some persuading to do.

And yet, the title pages of Q1 and Q2 themselves suggest, subtly, that Q1 had not sold out and that copies of the edition were still available in bookshops. Ever since Malone, critics have focused on the part of Q2's title page that most *distinguishes* it from Q1, the blurb about its textual superiority. But Ling does not simply bifurcate his *Hamlet* into opposing "good" and "bad" editions. Indeed, when viewed from the stationer's perspective instead of the author's or playing company's, the title pages of the two editions do far more to align than to distinguish them.[161] The plays' titles are identical and virtually identically set (with the exception of Roberts's swash italic "*THE*" in Q2). Ling's device dominates the page in both, unusually for a publisher who was not a printer: perhaps the lack of a printer's device on Q1 is less surprising since no printer is named in the imprint, but since Roberts both entered the play and printed Q2, the use of Ling's device on that edition as well seems like a deliberate effort to mirror Q1. Most tellingly, Roberts's compositors followed the unusual "hanging indent" format used for the performance attribution in Q1 in order to set Q2's blurb about the "true and perfect Coppie" (see Figures 1 and 3). It has long been noticed that, when the compositors set the opening scene of Q2, they seem to have had a copy of Q1 in front of them.[162] What has not been noticed is that the same is true of the title page. When they set the title page of Q2, Roberts's compositors were copying the distinctive visual features of Q1.

We can be fairly certain that the direction to copy the layout of the Q1 title page came from Ling, and not simply because, as the publisher, he had the most to gain from this parallel design. The clue that points to Ling's hand in the title-page design of Q2 is the hanging indent. The original impetus for the use of this format in Q1 seems to have come from Simmes. The format was rare in general, and when used, it typically served to set biblical quotations that appeared on the title pages of religious books. But Simmes used the hanging indent for secular books far more frequently than other printers did: one in five of his editions (forty out of 198) used the format for something other than a biblical verse. By contrast, Roberts was more typical: less than 4 percent of all his title pages (eight of 205) used the hanging indent in this way.¹⁶³ On the title pages of professional plays, the format was even rarer: only ten editions through 1640 included a hanging indent (1.8 percent of all play title pages), and Simmes himself printed fully half of these.¹⁶⁴ Since Simmes habitually used the format, and Roberts did not, it seems safe to conclude that Ling directed Roberts to follow the layout of Q1 closely, including in this unusual aspect. Ling himself did not use the format with any regularity in his publications: excluding those books printed by Simmes, only three of his sixty-three editions include a hanging indent for something other than a biblical verse. Only because Simmes had already happened to use the format for Q1, it appears, did Ling instruct Roberts to use it in Q2.

What these printing habits strongly suggest is that the similarity between the two title pages was a deliberate decision on Ling's part.¹⁶⁵ And this decision implies that he still had copies of Q1 on his shelves. For a browser in his shop, or in any other bookshop with copies of both editions, the immediate visual impact of the two title pages would have been strikingly similar, and in mirroring their design, Ling manages to have it both ways. A book buyer with enough interest in *Hamlet* to notice the textual differences between the two title pages, despite their visual similarity, will be alerted to the ways in which Q2 differentiates itself from the older edition—which, after all, such an interested reader might well already have bought in 1603. This reader will thus be urged to buy the new version as well. A more casual browser, on the other hand, might miss the distinction altogether, giving Ling a chance to sell off copies of Q1 while still asserting the "new and improved" status of Q2. Rather than being a modern editorial statement about the origins of the two texts, Ling's title page for Q2 seems an ideal solution to a particular, local problem: how should a stationer market a new version of a text he had only recently published, enticing customers to buy the new edition without driving them away from the old? At a moment when Shakespeare's plays were selling extremely well in the book trade, Ling seems to have figured out a way to have more Shakespeare without threatening his previous investment.¹⁶⁶

This double gesture extends beyond the mise-en-page. The actual wording of the Q2 blurb is more ambiguous than the traditional narratives have acknowledged, and this ambiguity again allows Ling to appeal to a variety of potential customers. Here too Ling's publishing strategy slyly differentiates the two editions without necessarily setting one above the other. Modern critics have overwhelmingly understood the claim that Q2 is printed "according to the true and perfect Coppie" to mean that Q1 was printed according to a false or imperfect copy that will now be superseded. But in fact this reading goes beyond the words of the title page, which does not correlate the "true and perfect Coppie" behind Q2 with any explicit claim about the textual condition of Q1; at its most literal level, Q2 simply touts the "true and perfect Coppie" behind its own text. This is not to say that the comparison between the two editions that modern editors have routinely read into the blurb is completely absent. On the contrary, implicit in the blurb is the suggestion that the text of Q1 is "bad" and in need of correction. But it is crucial to Ling's publishing strategy, I think, that this suggestion be *only* implicit. For Ling thereby enables two divergent interpretations of the advertisement, which, like the design of the title page more broadly, allow him to continue selling copies of his first edition alongside his second.

If some customers, like most modern critics, saw Q2 as a corrected text of Q1—and purchased it for that reason—they may have been encouraged in that reading by an important, but overlooked, aspect of Shakespeare's reputation in the book trade. As Alan Farmer has shown, contrary to the frequent assertion that title-page claims of revised or corrected dramatic texts were a common publishing puff, they were actually quite unusual.[167] And not only do very few plays advertise corrected texts, but before 1604 most of these were either by Shakespeare or attributed to him on their title pages: *Locrine* (1595; "Newly set foorth, ouerseene and corrected / By *W. S.*"), *Love's Labour's Lost* (1598; "Newly corrected and augmented"), *Romeo and Juliet* (1599; "*Newly corrected, augmented, and amended*"), and *1 Henry IV* (1599; "Newly corrected by *W. Shake-speare*"). Only two other plays carried similar title-page advertisements: *The Spanish Tragedy* (1592, 1594, 1599; "Newly corrected and amended of such grosse faults as passed in the first impression") and *Solimon and Perseda* (1599; "Newly corrected and amended").[168] When Ling chose the blurb for Q2, he was working within an established mode, but one that was largely associated with Shakespeare. In this context, the appeal to the "true and perfect Coppie" suggests that, as Farmer argues, despite the long-standing critical consensus that Shakespeare was uninterested in the publication of his plays, in the book trade Shakespeare more than anyone else was being marketed as a playwright who not only revised but was interested in publishing corrected versions of his texts.

If this were all the blurb were telling customers, however, it is hard to see how Ling could hope to sell his remaining copies of Q1, since the appeal to a corrected text would seem to obviate any desire for the earlier, uncorrected version. And this is the reason, I think, that Q2 stops short of explicitly claiming to be a corrected text. Indeed, every previous "corrected" playbook had actually included that word on its title page. Even though relatively few editions advertised a corrected text in the 1590s and early 1600s, then, the wording used to do so seems to have become conventional by the time Ling published Q2 *Hamlet*. This convention may have derived from printed sermons, which were sometimes published from notes taken down by audience members; when preachers later printed more authoritative versions, they sometimes advertised this "correction" on the title page. One such example is Henry Smith's *The Affinitie of the Faithfull*, which appeared in two editions in 1591, the second one labeled "corrected, and augmented" on the title page. Both editions were published by none other than Nicholas Ling.[169] The absence of the specific and expected word "corrected" from the title page of Q2 *Hamlet*, therefore, suggests Ling's desire to leave open an alternative interpretation, one that allowed Q1 to stand side by side with Q2 rather than being superseded by it.[170]

The first part of the Q2 blurb, after all, makes a different appeal: "Newly imprinted and enlarged to almost as much againe as it was." The emphasis here is on the enlarged text, not the corrected text. As with title-page advertisements of correction, so too Shakespearean works were prominent among the few plays that claim to include "additions" or to have been "enlarged" or "augmented": *Love's Labour's Lost* (1598), *Romeo and Juliet* (1599), and *Richard III* (1603) account for three of the four such plays before 1604.[171] Like those customers who thought Q2 corrected the text of Q1, those who thought the blurb mainly concerned additions to the play would thus have been primed for this interpretation by the history of Shakespearean printed drama. But Q2 *Hamlet* stands out even within this trend identified by Farmer. For one thing, its blurb is far more discursive than the norm. While other playbooks claim to have been "Newly corrected and augmented," Ling's title page details precisely the extent of the enlargement ("almost as much againe as it was") as well as the fidelity of its text to the "true and perfect Coppie." In fact, the more extended claim on the title page of Q2 *Hamlet* has only a single precedent, in the only non-Shakespearean play before 1604 to advertise an enlarged text.

This precedent was another revenge tragedy, another play that dated from the 1580s and had been long perceived as moldy, another play that had recently been updated to bring it more in line with contemporary taste, and a play that has long been associated with *Hamlet*: *The Spanish Tragedy*. The fourth and fifth editions of *The Spanish Tragedy*, published by Thomas Pavier in 1602 and 1603, were advertised as "Newly corrected, amended, and enlarged with new additions of the Painters part, and others."[172] No other professional play before

1604 includes such detail about the nature of its additions. Like Q2 *Hamlet*, *The Spanish Tragedy* pairs this appeal to an enlarged text with a claim to textual accuracy. And *The Spanish Tragedy* is the only professional play before *Hamlet* to use the specific word "enlarged" on its title page.[173]

The use of the identical word on these title pages may well be coincidental. But the deeper link between the two plays is crucial to understanding Ling's strategy: both were "enlarged" for the same reason, to revitalize these popular dramas for a changing theatrical environment that threatened to render them obsolete. In the Praeludium to Ben Jonson's *Cynthia's Revels* (1601), one of the boy actors offers a satirical character of a mustachioed gallant "with more Beard, then Brayne" who swears that "the olde Hieronimo, (as it was first acted) was the onely best, and Iudiciously-pend Play, of Europe."[174] The parenthetical qualifier—"(as it was first acted)"—emphasizes the gallant's anachronistic taste and the antiquated style of the play. Henslowe would soon pay Jonson to update the play with additions, although it seems unlikely that the new passages appearing in Q4 *The Spanish Tragedy* are his; they may in fact be by Shakespeare himself (but their authorship is not crucial here).[175] Similarly, both Nashe's 1589 comment about the unlearned playwright who has cribbed from "English *Seneca*" and will "affoord you whole *Hamlets*, I should say handfulls of tragical speaches," and Lodge's 1596 reference to the "ghost which cried so miserally at the Theator, like an oister wife, *Hamlet, reuenge*," satirize the apparently bombastic character of the play as it appeared on stage in the sixteenth century. By the time Ling published Q2 *Hamlet*, then, both of these revenge tragedies had been recently revised from their earlier, outdated version to bring them in line with contemporary taste.

By offering the play "enlarged to almost as much againe as it was," Ling of course appeals to customers who want the most current rendition of the play. But he does so without necessarily suggesting that the earlier version is undesirable. Perhaps some customers, like Jonson's fictional gallant, wanted to read the play "as it was first acted"; Ling's blurb might have convinced them that his own earlier edition represented *Hamlet* in that older form. To these readers, in other words, the title page of Q2 may have suggested that Q1—still conveniently available for sale in Ling's shop—offered the play as it had appeared on stage in the 1580s and 1590s, while the newer edition was printed "according to the true and perfect Coppie" of *Hamlet* as it was currently performed in Shakespeare's revised and enlarged version.

If so, the Q2 blurb significantly revises Ling's apparent marketing strategy for Q1: he had originally presented that edition as up-to-date because "acted by his Highnesse seruants," a title that Shakespeare's company had only just acquired.¹⁷⁶ By the time he published Q2, however, Ling could no longer afford to suggest that Q1 was quite so contemporary, since that would leave his customers with little reason to buy it once he had brought out an even newer, even more up-to-date text. Instead, Ling manages to suggest both that Q2 is a corrected text of Q1 and, paradoxically, that Q1 is not a faulty text but rather a version of the play dating to an earlier moment in its ongoing history, before it was enlarged "to almost as much againe as it was."

Indeed, much of this double gesture is packed into that single word "againe," which carries two meanings. It may mean "once more": in Q2, the faulty text of Q1 has been corrected and thereby enlarged *once more* to almost its original length, returned to its "true and perfect" state. But "againe" may also mean "over again" or "double": Q2 has been enlarged to almost *double* the length of the earlier version published in Q1, and it is now being published according to the true and perfect copy of this enlarged version.¹⁷⁷ Both readings of "againe" are equally available, just as both readings of the relationship of Q2 to Q1—corrected text or enlarged text—are equally available. In this ambiguity, Ling found the solution to a tricky publishing situation. His carefully designed title page for Q2, with its multivalent blurb, allowed him to sell two different editions of *Hamlet* simultaneously by appealing to multiple readerships. Since *Hamlet* reached a third edition in 1611, only eight years after its first—a feat accomplished by fewer than one in ten professional plays—Ling seems to have made a good bet.¹⁷⁸ His publishing strategy certainly depended on Shakespeare's name, which appears on the title pages of both editions, and on Shakespeare's established print reputation as a dramatist who sometimes corrected his texts and sometimes enlarged them. But the famous blurb on the title page of Q2 emerged out of Ling's publishing strategy and not, as it has been read ever since Malone divined the existence of the edition that Henry Bunbury later found in his closet, out of Shakespeare's biography.

CHAPTER 2

Contrary Matters

The Power of the Gloss and the History of an Obscenity

It may be the most famous dirty joke in Shakespeare. As he banters with Ophelia before the performance of *The Mousetrap*, in a passage that varies slightly but importantly between Q2 and F, Hamlet asks:

Ham. Lady shall I lie in your lap?
Ophe. No my Lord.
Ham. Doe you thinke I meant country matters? (Q2, sig. H1r)

Ham. Ladie, shall I lye in your Lap?
Ophe. No my Lord.
Ham. I meane, my Head vpon your Lap?
Ophe. I my Lord.
Ham. Do you thinke I meant Country matters? (F, sig. 2o6r)

For the first century of Shakespearean editing, from Rowe in 1709 through Boswell in 1821, editors had only these two versions of the joke. When Bunbury discovered his copy of Q1, however, a more radical variant suddenly appeared (Figure 7).

Ham. . . . Lady will you giue me leaue, and so forth:
To lay my head in your lappe?

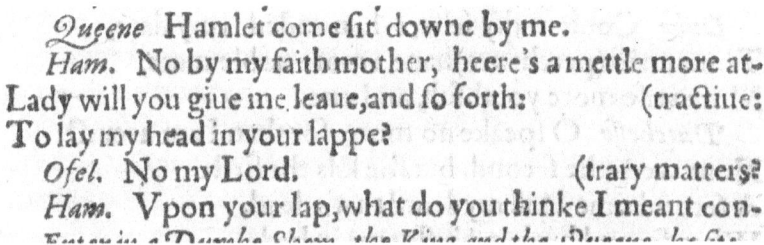

Figure 7. Hamlet's *contrary matters* in Q1.
Reproduced by permission of the Huntington Library, San Marino, California, shelf mark 69304.

Ofel. No my Lord.
Ham. Vpon your lap, what do you thinke I meant contrary matters?
(Q1, sig. F3r)

As we have seen, newspapers and literary reviews in England and abroad reacted energetically to the discovery of a new text of *Hamlet*, and even in short notices they focused particular attention on the variation between *country matters* and *contrary matters*. In this chapter, I move from considering the impact of the belated discovery of Q1 on broader theories of Shakespearean authorship to its effect on readings of the text of the play itself. Here I examine the earliest responses to Q1, all of which dealt in one way or another with this particular variant. These reactions preceded the debate between Knight and Collier that set the terms for much of the Victorian engagement with that text, and they therefore deal with questions of authorship and revision from a more multifarious perspective. Indeed, their responses hinge at least as much on issues of propriety as of bibliography or textual criticism—even in the first edition of Shakespeare to address the newly discovered text, the bookseller-turned-editor Samuel Weller Singer's *Dramatic Works of William Shakspeare* (1826). Singer was the earliest editor to emend the traditional text of *Hamlet* with a reading from Q1, and the rationale behind his decision to print *contrary matters* both exemplifies the initial reaction to this variant and reveals how the discovery of Q1 helped to entrench a particular reading of the familiar *country matters*, one that remains universally accepted among modern editors and critics.

In January, 1825, the *Literary Gazette* commended its readers' attention to "one striking word in the Play Scene, which removes a phrase that has been much objected to," quoting the Q1 passage and italicizing the key word *contrary*.¹ This article was probably the most important account of Q1 in the popular press, since it was rapidly reprinted in numerous papers—including the *Morning Chronicle*, the *Kaleidoscope*, the *Circulator of Useful Knowledge*, and, reaching across the Atlantic, the *United States Literary Gazette*.² The textual variant in this line thereby became one of the best-known attributes of Q1 shortly after the edition's discovery, even before Payne and Foss's reprint.

An article in the *Kaleidoscope* suggests some of the reasoning behind the interest in this variant: "When [Q1] omits passages which reflect no credit on the understanding of their author, we are anxious to believe that it is more faithful to the text of such a man as Shakespeare, than those copies are which impute to him obscenity, without even the apology of wit."³ The *Gentleman's Magazine* explained more precisely how this new variant might be "more faithful" to Shakespeare's intentions. It built a remarkable theory of dramatic authorship on the alteration of this passage and on the omission in Q1 of the subsequent exchange, in which Hamlet tells Ophelia that "Nothing" is "a fayre thought to lye between maydes legs" (Q2, sig. H1r):

> Many striking peculiarities in this edition of *Hamlet* tend strongly to confirm the opinion that no small portion of the ribaldry to be found in the plays of our great dramatic poet, is to be assigned to the actors of his time, who flattered the vulgar taste, and administered to the vicious propensities of their age, by the introduction and constant repetition of many indecent, and not a few stupid jokes, till they came to be considered and then printed as part of the genuine text. Of these the two or three brief but offensive speeches of *Hamlet* to *Ophelia*, in the Play Scene, Act iii. are not to be found in the copy of 1603, and so far we are borne out in our opinion; for it is not to be supposed that Shakespeare would insert them upon cool reflection, and three years after the success of his piece had been determined; still less likely is it that a piratical printer would reject any thing actually belonging to the play, which was pleasing to the great bulk of those who were to become the purchasers of his publication.⁴

Here the New Bibliographic theory of memorial reconstruction is turned on its head. All of the familiar pieces are present: actors' elaborations, piratical publishers, an appeal to less sophisticated playgoers (and readers). But these elements appear in a strangely inverted form, demonstrating that it is Q1, not Q2 or F, that brings us closest to Shakespeare's manuscript.

In reactions like this one, we can see how deeply the uncanny historicity of Q1 has affected readings of its text. The common thread in virtually all of the early responses to this passage—taken to the extreme by the author in the *Gentleman's Magazine*—is relief at the absence of the vulgar phrase in what was largely imagined to be Shakespeare's original draft.[5] Contrary to modern views, these early critics understand Q1 to be a much *better* text of this passage: closer to Shakespeare's hand, further from the corrupting influence of the theater, and free of the vulgarities that appeal to the common people but have no place in Shakespeare's canon. What interests me about this response is not so much the relief that these readers feel at seeing *contrary matters* in Q1, which after all may not be surprising if we think of the stereotypical prudery of the nineteenth century. Rather, I am interested in the idea that underlies that relief as its necessary precondition, one more in keeping with Foucault's revision of our "repressive hypothesis" about the Victorian period.[6] In order to feel relieved that the *contrary matters* of Q1 is not obscene, one must believe that the *country matters* of Q2 and F is. Most of the early writers on Q1 simply take this obscenity for granted. As I will show, however, the earlier reception history of *Hamlet*, both in print and on stage, makes clear that this supposed obscene pun was never simply self-evident, as editors generally imagine. The obscenity was just beginning to be heard when Q1 appeared, and the growing consensus about *country matters* entirely determined the reading of this passage in Q1. In turn this understanding of the newly discovered edition only confirmed and entrenched the idea that the received text contained an obscene joke. The belatedness of the reemergence of Q1 thus prevents any sort of analysis of its text that does not depend on and feed back into an already hardening interpretation of the familiar version.

This dialectic continues to haunt our analyses of *country/contrary matters*. Like these early readers of Q1, modern editors and critics have in general simply assumed they know that *country matters* is obscene and always has been. As Neil Taylor and Ann Thompson have demonstrated, Hamlet's line has long caused problems for editors, readers, and performers, who have subjected *country matters* to a variety of cuts, bowdlerizations, and coy glosses over the years.[7] But while critics and editors often cannot bring themselves to make it explicit, they all seem to agree that we get the joke. In his influential Arden edition, Harold Jenkins glosses *country matters* as "physical love-making (with a popular pun on the first syllable)." The note is indirect not only in refusing to name the pun but also in its unclear usage of *popular*. Was this a widespread pun? A pun that was greatly enjoyed? One used by the lower classes? In fact, Jenkins seems to be using the word mainly to distance himself and his readers from the vulgarity. G. R. Hibbard follows a similar formula in his Oxford edition: "Sexual intercourse (quibbling indecently on the first syllable of *country*)." David Bevington's gloss is virtually identical: "Sexual intercourse. (With a bawdy pun on the first syllable of *country*)."[8] Most twentieth-century editors employ some version of this circumlocution, referring to the "first syllable of *country*" or providing a supposedly analogous passage from a contemporary text without spelling out the word itself.[9] In their own two-volume, multiple-text edition for the third series Arden, Thompson and Taylor reject the periphrasis, glossing the phrase in one instance as "sexual behaviour, with a pun on 'cunt'," and in another as "a vulgar reference, i.e. one suitable for rustics (with a pun on 'cunt' . . .)." The Norton Shakespeare also speaks frankly: "Rustic doings (with an obscene pun on 'cunt')."[10] While conventions governing explicitness in glossing may be changing, the striking unanimity among contemporary editors about the meaning of the phrase itself remains.

Such a double entendre is certainly possible here. The word *cunt* was well established in the lexicon by Shakespeare's day: the earliest reference in the *Oxford English Dictionary* is to a London street in existence around 1230 called "Gropecunt Lane," probably a red-light district.[11] Another early use occurs in the *Proverbs of Hendyng* (before 1325), which offers this bit of advice for prospective brides: "3eue þi cunte to cunni[n]g, And craue affetir wedding" ("Employ your cunt cunningly and press the case for marriage afterward").[12] The frequent claim that Chaucer could still use the word without a strong sense of its vulgarity may be correct, although the form most associated with *The Canterbury Tales* is *queynte* (*quaint*), which may already be a euphemistic or punning evasion of the Middle English *conte*, deemed obscene.[13] In his *Dictionary of Sexual Language and Imagery in Shakespearean and Stuart Literature*, Gordon Williams reports that by the sixteenth century the word was becoming taboo in English, and therefore its "printed use, as with *fuck*, is largely Scottish," as in the anonymous Scottish play *Philotus* (1603): "Put doun thy hand and graip hir cunt." While English usages do appear throughout the early modern period even in print—see the definition of the Italian *potta* as "*a womans priuie parts, a cunt, a quaint*" in Florio's dictionary (1598)—such instances are "exceptional," not the rule.[14]

The increasingly taboo nature of the word is often said to have driven writers to punning glances at it, and the *country* of Hamlet's phrase features prominently in such claims.[15] Numerous contemporary parallels have been suggested, including other possible Shakespearean instances. Williams connects the phrase with Touchstone's reference to the rural couples in *As You Like It* as "country copulatives," and with Donne's "The Good-Morrow," lines that editors often pair with Hamlet's: "I wonder, by my troth, what thou and I / Did, till we lov'd; were we not wean'd till then? / But suck'd on country pleasures, childishly?"[16] Hamlet's entire phrase appears in Sidney's *New Arcadia*, the only other possibly bawdy instance of the collocation *country matters* in pre-Restoration texts in Early English Books Online (admittedly imperfect for full-text searching), where in general the phrase simply means affairs concerning the country or agriculture.[17] After Musidorus/Dorus has recounted his adventures to Zelmane/Pyrocles, including his wooing of Mopsa, Zelmane says to the shepherd Dametas: "I shall grow . . . skilfull in country matters if I haue often conference with your seruaunt." Peggy Knapp argues that a pun on *cunt* here "is intended to further the deception of Musidorus's disguise, while it allows Zelmane/Pyrocles to talk with his cousin about love and pastoral terrains (country-ness)."[18] The trouble with these parallels is that it is hard to know whether "country" simply indicates, with no pun at all, the kind of rustic earthiness, sexual license, or general naïveté that London writers commonly attributed to provincial folk.[19] After all, Touchstone's "copulatives" (those who are joining together, those who are copulating) are literally in the country; the pleasures to which Donne refers are childishly innocent, as the country was often imagined to be in comparison with the city and court; and Zelmane's joke may simply concern the gap between the Musidorus's true identity and his rural disguise. The difficulty of identifying historical puns can be seen in the frequent caveats that editors and critics deploy in footnotes: "Some instances of *country* refer, of course, simply to the terrain or call attention to the rural scene."[20] But discerning the difference between these uses and punning uses is precisely the problem.

Take George Chapman's continuation of Marlowe's *Hero and Leander*, for instance, in which Leander is satirically compared to "an emptie Gallant full of forme." Chapman writes that he "Hath seene the hot Low Countries, not their heat." A. R. Braunmuller may have been thinking of *Hamlet* when he glossed the line as meaning that the gallant "has lived riotously in the Low Countries without suffering from venereal disease," and suggested that "Chapman may have had in mind the common pun on 'low countries.'"[21] Certainly Shakespeare could pun on the "lowness" of the Low Countries. In *Comedy of Errors*, the Syracusan Dromio famously describes the body of Nell the kitchen maid in an extended geographical metaphor. At the end of the exchange, Antipholus asks "Where stood *Belgia*, the *Netherlands*?" and Dromio replies: "Oh sir, I did not looke so low" (F, sig. H4v). And yet, the same problem obtains, since we do not know whether Chapman's "Low Countries" includes a specific pun on *cunt* or merely a reference to the lower parts of the female body. In *Errors* Shakespeare does not use the word *countries* at all: a reference to female genitalia could be conveyed simply by referring to the *Netherlands*. Perhaps Chapman's "Low Countries" is simply another example of this sort of reference, without the syllabic pun.

In all these cases, with a bit of critical ingenuity one could certainly read a pun in *country*, and some readers in the early modern period may well have done so, but there is little inherent in their contexts that demands such a reading. There is, however, at least one instance in the early modern period in which *country* clearly and overtly carries a pun on *cunt*. In an anonymous Restoration burlesque, entitled *Homer Alamode, the Second Part*, we read a description of Calypso,

> who put off Boddis
> And Petticoat, nay, and fine Smock,
> And there she shew'd her dainty Nock,
> Plump Buttocks, Breasts, and trembling Thighs,
> With many other Rarities.
> And so did *Circe*; but I swore,
> Still sight of Count--ry pleas'd me more:
> And rather chose to leave them both
> Than *Ithaca*, I'll take my Oath. . . .[22]

In this pornographic passage, the pun in "Count--ry" seems clear, since that word punningly looks back to the description of Calypso and Circe's naked bodies, and forward to Ithaca, emphasizing Odysseus's choice to return home rather than indulge in sexual pleasure. In this case, however, the reader's attention is drawn to the pun by the typography, which sets off the initial syllable with dashes.[23] In cases such as the one in *Hamlet*, where we do not have typographic cues, would such a pun have been so clear?

The use of the typographic cue in *Homer Alamode*, in other words, indicates not simply that a pun on *cunt* could be gotten across in *country* but, more important for my argument, that the pun had to be *gotten across* to the reader or audience. It was not simply always present in the word but had to be *made* present.[24] Quite apart from the fact that *Homer Alamode* is considerably later than *Hamlet* and may not be the best guide to the original reception of *country matters*, then, the burlesque poem also makes clear that puns are a transactional language use that depends on a particular context and moment. They may be activated in the same word at one time and not another. Perhaps Richard Burbage made this pun present to audiences by the way he pronounced *country matters*, but we do not know; perhaps some spectators heard the pun and others did not. We do know that readers of *Hamlet* in its early editions were given no typographical cues like the dashes in *Homer Alamode* to prompt them to read the word in this way.

Nonetheless, a sexual reference in Hamlet's words would certainly be in keeping with the continuation of the exchange in Q2 and F: the part of the passage that does not appear at all in Q1, to the relief of the *Gentleman's Magazine*. Here Hamlet makes a far more explicit reference to genitalia, although whether male or female is debatable:

Ham. Do you thinke I meant Country matters?
Ophe. I thinke nothing, my Lord.
Ham. That's a faire thought to lye between Maids legs
Ophe. What is my Lord?
Ham. Nothing. (F, sig. 2o6r)

As Thompson and Taylor note, "'Thing' could be a euphemism for a man's penis; alternatively *nothing* (the figure nought) could refer to a woman's vagina."[25] In either case, the double entendre seems certain, given the clear reference to what lies "between maids' legs." We might read the lines as encompassing Hamlet's typically double perspective: it is a "fair thought" both that "no thing"—no penis—will lie "between maids' legs," thereby ensuring their chastity; and, with his usual misogynistic sarcasm falling heavily on the word *fair*, that "nothing"—a vagina—lies "between maids' legs," thereby ensuring their wantonness. Indeed, the entire passage as it stands in Q2 and F lends itself to numerous possible sexual puns, not only these but also *head* and *lap* and even possibly Ophelia's *I / ay / eye*, which (in other contexts, though not usually this one) is often glossed as carrying a pun on *vagina*, and occasionally on *penis* as well.[26]

The sexual banter of the passage as a whole has thus cemented editors' belief in a specific pun on *cunt* in *country matters*. Clearly *country matters* refers generally to sex, imagined to be more freely available and vigorously practiced in rural areas, but does that reference necessarily involve the pun that editors have found in its first syllable? In fact, editors and other readers have not always "known" that the line contained any pun at all, and our own contemporary assurance that we do has blinded us to other possibilities and other histories in this passage—just as it did for the earliest readers of the alternate version in Q1. The genealogy of this particular variant, shaped by the uncanny history of Q1, can therefore illuminate larger issues in how we understand Shakespeare's texts and make that understanding widely available, or inevitable, in editions of those texts.

Underlying the editorial certainty about *country matters* is a largely unexamined idea of glossing. Editorial annotation has been little theorized, especially when compared to the large amount of scholarship devoted to how to edit the text itself. Most contemporary editions of Shakespeare make do with a brief prefatory mention of their principles of glossing, such as Bevington's statement that he has "aimed at explaining difficult passages, not just single words, keeping in mind the questions that readers might ask as to possible meanings."[27] The question left unaddressed here, as Ian Small has written generally of the practice of annotation, is precisely "the one which motivates [the] whole rationale for annotation—namely, what constitutes the understanding of a literary work."[28] For the plays that Bevington is annotating, exactly where do those "possible meanings" reside: In the text itself? In the author's intention? In the minds of the plays' first spectators? In current performance practice?

Overwhelmingly, however unexpressed it may be, editors of Shakespeare rely on a historicist conception of meaning that attempts to bridge the gap between what words and allusions meant *then* and what the reader might not understand *now*. As Martin Battestin, one of the few theorists of glossing, has written: "The editor in annotating a work intends to make the meaning of the text more intelligible to the reader, on the one hand by recovering for him certain information . . . once known to the author's contemporaries but now obscure, and on the other hand by placing the author's ideas and expressions in the context of his own writings and those of his contemporaries."[29] It is true that Shakespearean critics today are usually less interested than Battestin in such an author-centered understanding of meaning: many include notes about cultural context that may not necessarily have been immediately present in the author's mind or literary intentions, alongside occasional references to the interpretations of modern theatrical productions. Nonetheless, in annotating those "difficult passages" and "single words" to which Bevington refers, most editors broadly subscribe to this historicist theory of the gloss, which the editor Ian Jack claims should "enable [the annotator's] contemporaries to read a book as its original audience read it," or should, in Christa Jansohn's formulation, "establish a link between the past and the present."[30]

There is, I am arguing, a theory of historical reception hidden within the glossing practice of most Shakespearean editors—one that plays a large role in shaping the meanings that modern readers will find in the plays but one that also tends to evade the hermeneutic problems at the heart of historicism, problems that more explicitly theoretical discourse subjects to intense debate. When their notes tell us that *country matters* means "sexual intercourse (quibbling indecently on the first syllable of *country*)," editors are not telling us that some twentieth-century productions have staged the scene so as to get that pun across to the audience. Nor are they basing their note on the fact that, as Taylor and Thompson detail, this passage as a whole was routinely cut from nineteenth-century performances due to the discomfort it provoked in directors, and presumably in audiences. Rather, they are telling us (usually without explicitly telling us) that this is how Shakespeare's own audience would have understood the phrase.

Any theory of meaning that depends on the interpretation of Shakespeare's "original audience" will be particularly problematic in the case of puns, and for this reason *country matters* provides an especially good vantage point for critiquing our glossing practice. After all, puns (and indeed jokes in general) often serve to differentiate an audience hierarchically, distinguishing those "in the know" from those outside that privileged community.[31] If part of the point of a pun is to create different audiences (some understanding and some not), then audience understanding alone cannot serve as the ground of meaning, and instead some notion of authorial or theatrical *intention*—the double meaning that the pun was intended to carry, for those quick enough to catch it—will inevitably underlie the gloss.[32] Intention, of course, is a knotty concept, and reception does not always function so smoothly as the neat definitions in our glosses suggest. Shakespeare's audience was hardly monolithic, but glosses tend to homogenize contemporary reception—indeed, depend upon that homogenization.[33] Over time, a repeated and consistent gloss such as *country matters* has received in modern editions can reify the meaning of a word or phrase, as if it were self-evident that the definition in the gloss were what the text simply "meant" in its own time. As I will show, this reification falsifies the sedimented history of the text of *Hamlet* and presents a static idea of a dramatic scene that was, in fact, strikingly fluid in early editions and, apparently, in early performances.[34]

There would seem to be an inherent tension between the stabilizing effect of most glossing and the slippery doubleness of punning. Puns would seem to escape confinement to a gloss, for, as Sheila Delany writes, "every pun is excessive in some way."[35] And yet, such reification in fact seems strongest around puns, especially the supposedly obscene ones. Editors want to make sure readers understand these jokes—and perhaps, given how puns can create distinctions, to demonstrate their own knowingness. With obscene jokes they have also increasingly sought to demonstrate their lack of marginal prudery. Among feminist editors in particular, there has been a movement toward more explicit glossing. In her agenda-setting essay "Feminist Theory and the Editing of Shakespeare," Ann Thompson decries the "coy phrases" that editors use to gloss obscenity, writing that a "modern feminist editor would surely make less of a fuss about printing *fuck* and *cunt*," and adding that were she to redo her edition of *The Taming of the Shrew*, she "might wish to be even more explicit in my commentary about obscenity."[36] Laurie Maguire praises "feminist editions, which reject the euphemisms of Latin which characterized the early twentieth century, but eschew . . . gratuitous slang" as well. Maguire positions herself against both a paternalism that shields readers from discussions of sexuality and a certain laddish pleasure in obscenity about women's sexuality that she detects in some contemporary annotation. Instead, Maguire wants "editions that are not coy nor brash but impudent," where *impudent* signifies "in its etymological sense of 'freedom from shame.'"[37]

The turn toward more explicit glossing, however, may have unintended consequences. Because of the reifying power of the gloss, this movement toward what editors perceive to be more open and liberating annotation may have the paradoxical effect of closing down meaning. The more confident we are that we know what these words "meant"—that is, what they were originally intended to mean in their moment of initial reception—and the more repetitively and uniformly we gloss them, the more we risk homogenizing Shakespeare's audiences and misrepresenting his plays as more static than the early editions suggest they actually were. Since for much of the modern era of Shakespearean editing *country matters* has been perceived as one of the most obscene moments in his plays, this phrase above all has become ossified by repetitive glossing, whether coy, allusive, or explicit.

We can see the power of this glossarial consensus in Stanley Wells's otherwise skeptical exploration of Shakespearean sexual double entendre, *Looking for Sex in Shakespeare*. Wells critiques those who "continue to comb the plays" and "seek out sexuality in previously unsuspected places," and he spends at least as much time debunking what he sees as "over-readings" as he does actually finding sex in Shakespeare. But even Wells accepts without question that the pun editors always find in *country matters* is "authentic." Wells's notion of authenticity here is explicitly historicist: he distinguishes "legitimate readings-between-the-lines" from those "over-readings that are ahistorical and sometimes untheatrical in imposing upon the texts meanings that must originate rather in the minds of the interpreters than of the dramatist." Along with the dramatist himself, Wells does admit one class of interpreters into the circle of legitimacy: authentic "sexual interpretations proceed from . . . the imaginations of the dramatist *and of his early audiences*."[38] But this addition to Shakespeare's intention only underscores the extent to which Wells's theory of interpretation requires a particular kind of historicism, one that depends, in Jonathan Gil Harris's words, on the "idea of the 'moment' as a self-identical unit divided from other moments that come before and after it."[39]

As this chapter will show, however, the bawdy meaning that editors find in Hamlet's phrase cannot be securely rooted in Shakespeare's "moment," for *country matters* is like one of Foucault's documents that have been "scratched over and recopied many times." The phrase accrues its bawdy meaning only *through* time, through the editorial and readerly engagement with the very question of its historical meaning, especially after the discovery of Q1 prompted new theories of how the phrase came to be in the text in the first place. Certainly at times the word *country* might have been construed obscenely in the early modern period, but Hamlet's phrase never had the kind of stable meaning that editors routinely assign it. It had to *become* obscene. In this process of *becoming*, Bunbury's discovery played an important role, as did the very editors who implicitly claim in their glosses to be simply retrieving the phrase's original meaning. Wells's concept of the "authentic" pun turns out to be a hollow shell, for the bawdy joke in *country matters* follows the same Sibylline progression as the monetary value of Bunbury and Rooney's copies of Q1: meaning attaches to the phrase over time but, as the early reactions to Q1's *contrary matters* reveal, that meaning is retrospectively located in the phrase itself and in Shakespeare's own moment (when it was foisted in by the actors to replace the dramatist's "pure" version). The anachronistic nature of Q1, its appearance in Bunbury's closet as both the last and the first text of *Hamlet*, undermines the confidently historicist glossing that would seek quietly to root it in its "own" time.

If *country matters* has become ossified, we have nonetheless known since 1823, but have learned to forget, that the text of *Hamlet* is far from static here. The power of the gloss has caused us to lose a sense of this dramatic moment as both a textual and a performance process that, no doubt imperfectly, resulted in and is embodied by its three extant early versions. As with much of *Hamlet*, this passage oscillates between Q1, Q2, and F like one of those lenticular prints in which the image moves as it tilts back and forth. How we have understood it has depended on our broader understanding of the relationships between the *Hamlet* texts and the nature of Shakespearean authorship. Early responses to Q1 imagined the wholesome *contrary matters* as closer to Shakespeare's hand; in the twentieth century, *contrary matters* was largely ignored because Q1 was conceived as merely a garbled memorial reconstruction of Shakespeare's play. But as I will argue at the end of this chapter, if we read this scene in all its variation—whether we understand Q1 more like Charles Knight did or more like John Payne Collier did—Hamlet could not have meant country matters in quite the ways we have been imagining.

Our contemporary certainty that there is a pun on *cunt* in the familiar version of Hamlet's line has not served us well in making sense of the Q1 variant. What exactly are the *contrary matters* to which Q1 Hamlet alludes? In the vast scholarship devoted to the textual relationships among the three texts of *Hamlet*, this passage has rarely been addressed. So far as I am aware, no critical edition of *Hamlet* (as opposed to an edition of Q1) has chosen to print *contrary* over *country* since the first and last occasion in 1826, immediately following Bunbury's discovery. And when modern editors have discussed the variant, their complete confidence that they have understood the "vulgar reference" in *country matters* has led them into two mutually contradictory arguments about the relationship between the two versions of the phrase, each of them logically contorted.

In the first and more common argument, we are told that the variant word actually makes no difference to the joke. In *Shakespeare's Bawdy*, Eric Partridge matter-of-factly dissolves the distinction: "*Country matters*, or, in Quarto 1, 'contrary matters', where, clearly, the same pun is intended . . . matters concerned with *cunt*."[40] In their edition of Q1, Graham Holderness and Bryan Loughrey are similarly certain that "the same pun is intended." They gloss Q1 Hamlet's question as: "Do you think I meant the opposite of what I said (with a pun on 'cunt')."[41] In his *Rationale of the Dirty Joke*, G. Legman adverts to the variant parenthetically, only to reject the idea that it does vary: "'Country matters' (1st Quarto: 'contrary matters'—the pronunciation hardly matters at all)."[42] While not simply ignoring the variant as many editors have done, these critics make it disappear in another manner, evacuating the difference between the two words by asserting that they carry essentially the same meaning.

In her edition of Q1, Kathleen Irace offers a rare dissent from this view, claiming that *contrary matters* "is simpler, more conventional, and less bawdy than 'country' in the longer texts."[43] We can now see this position as a latter-day variation on the initial responses to Q1, although Irace believes that text to be a memorial reconstruction, not a rough draft. In their Arden edition, Thompson and Taylor concur that "*contrary* . . . could also be evidence of bowdlerization," while taking a middle path overall, noting one stage production in which "Hamlet contrived to say *contrary* in a tone heavy with sexual innuendo."[44]

There are several difficulties with each of these arguments, resulting from circular reasoning. For instance, why should an actor, in Thompson and Taylor's words, have to "contrive" so much harder, "in a tone heavy with sexual innuendo," to make the Q1 version of the pun signify than he would with the Q2 or F text? The reason is that Thompson and Taylor take the pun for granted in the familiar version, which has become reified to such an extent that *country matters* is barely a pun anymore: it is a kind of single entendre. Only with the variant *contrary* do the editors assume that a pun would need to be activated in performance; with *country matters*, the pun is imagined to be present in the text itself, with no reference to particular stage productions or actor's intonation. But a modern theatrical moment like this one, in which an actor manages to project the same pun in *contrary matters* as his audience already "knows" is present in *country matters*, can hardly serve as evidence for the textual origins of the phrase in its three early editions, before such acculturation could have occurred.

Furthermore, if editors are correct that Hamlet is "quibbling indecently on the first syllable" of *country*, then the difference between *country* and *contrary* is exceedingly difficult to perceive. Their initial syllables are quite similar, after all, perhaps even identical, given normal speech variation and our incomplete knowledge of early modern pronunciation.[45] In fact, both spellings of the syllable are present in the Shakespearean passage that most closely approximates this one: the language lesson in *Henry V*. Here a pun is made explicit, since it is remarked by the characters themselves, but what is most important is the variation between the two texts of that play. In the Folio, Katharine exclaims:

> Le Foot, & le Count : O Seigneur Dieu, il sont le mots de son mauvais corruptible grosse & impudique, & non pour les Dames de Honeur d'vser : Ie ne voudray pronouncer ce mots deuant le Seigneurs de France, pour toute le monde, fo le Foot & le Count. . . .
> (F, sig. h6r, emphasis removed)

The Folio spelling of the word *Count*, which has a "bad, corruptible, coarse, and shameful sound," allies it with *country matters*. And there are various other, quite explicit examples in the period of a pun on *count* and *cunt*.[46] In the quarto version of this scene, however, the spelling of Katherine's speech links the word more with the reading in Q1 *Hamlet*, *contrary*:

> Le fot, e le con, ô Iesu! Ie ne vew poinct parle,
> Sie plus deuant le che cheualires de franca,
> Pur one million ma foy.[47]

Alice too consistently says "con" in the quarto, "Count" in the Folio.[48] Given that the boys playing Katharine and Alice at the Globe no doubt affected a stage-French accent, did they pronounce this word more like the first syllable of *country* or of *contrary*? And does it really matter, since Hamlet's line already supposedly involves a sly double entendre, which would naturally lend itself, in order to make the gag clear, to some bending of pronunciation? After all, dictionaries of Shakespeare's sexual puns often gloss other words beginning with *con* as carrying a bawdy meaning derived from the obscene French word. Indeed, Frankie Rubinstein's *Dictionary of Shakespeare's Sexual Puns and Their Significance* defines *contrary* as "Cunt, like constable (P[artridge]), confessor (P[artridge]) and others in this dictionary starting with CON"—though tellingly with no reference to Q1 *Hamlet*.[49]

When Irace writes that *contrary* is "less bawdy" than *country*, therefore, or Thompson and Taylor see it as possible "evidence of bowdlerization," it is hard to know exactly what this might mean. This idea makes sense, strictly, only if we have already been trained to understand that *country* is a bawdy pun *as a word in itself*, rather than as a staged moment of dialogue, since in performance surely an actor could make *contrary* sound obscene just as easily as *country*. But if *country* is taken as an obscene pun in itself, we would have to suspect each of the many other, clearly innocent, uses of the word in Shakespeare of having a sexual meaning. And if it is not the word alone that creates the double entendre but rather that word in its performed context—with particular pronunciation, actor's gestures or mugging, and so on—then if Q2/F can include this reference, it seems clear that Q1 could as well. Irace's annotation, in other words, has been influenced by the very process that I want to challenge here: the ability of repeated glossing to reify a piece of dramatic dialogue into a stable "definition."

The entry on *country* in J. Barry Webb's dictionary of *Shakespeare's Erotic*

Word Usage exemplifies the circularity in which critics often become tangled as a result of this reification. Webb cites several other usages of the word, noting carefully that they are "merely suggestive," adding finally that "the only explicit use is in *Ham.* III.ii.112–4."⁵⁰ The problem is that the very reason Webb found a sexual meaning in the initial "merely suggestive" citations was the supposedly "explicit" usage in *Hamlet*, but those non-Shakespearean usages are then taken as support for the existence of an "explicit" pun in *country matters*. A similar circular reasoning often appears in the passages that editors propose as illustrative analogies to *country matters*. In his New Cambridge edition, Philip Edwards refers readers to "the fifteenth-century *Castle of Perseverance*, when Humanum Genus says to Luxuria: 'Lechery . . . Few men will forsake thee / In any country that I know.'"⁵¹ This passage hardly demands a reading of *country* as punning on *cunt*, and the meaning is completely straightforward without such a pun; Edwards's allusion is clearly based on his preexisting belief in the pun in *Hamlet*. The power of the gloss has reflected the ossified meaning from that instance back onto other instances of the word, even one that predates it by more than a century.

In their edition, Thompson and Taylor similarly refer readers to *Every Man out of His Humor* as a parallel for *country matters*, but again the passage does not seem to me to encourage such a reading.⁵² In Jonson's play, Shift blusteringly resists selling his rapier:

> This Rapier Sir, has trauail'd by my side Sir, the best part of Fraunce and the low Countrey: I have seene *Vlishing*, *Brill*, and the *Haghe* with this Rapier sir, in my Lord of *Leysters* time. . . . I can lend you letters to diuers Officers and Commaunders in the Low Countries, that shall for my cause do you all the good offices that shall pertaine or belong to Gentleman.⁵³

An actor could certainly perform this passage in a manner that conveyed a double entendre in "Low Countries," although the specificity of Dutch cities mentioned seems to militate against that interpretation. But can such a dubious instance serve as proof of the pun in *Hamlet*? Or has it rather been read as a pun in the first place only because of editorial certainty about the very passage it is supposed to illuminate? Indeed, in her edition of *Every Man Out*, Helen Ostovich glosses Shift's speech in this way, but her own confirming parallel passage is—by now there should be no surprise—the same one in *Hamlet* that Thompson and Taylor seek to explain by reference to this passage.⁵⁴

Barbara Mowat has cautioned editors against falling into an "*OED* loop"—in which the *Oxford English Dictionary* is used as evidence for the meaning of a word in a given text even though its definition itself derives from the history of critical commentary on that very text—and the same could be said of this kind of "Shakespeare loop."⁵⁵ The linguistic authority of Shakespeare allows his plays to serve as proof texts for his contemporary writers, whose texts then reflect the weight of that evidence back onto the plays of Shakespeare.

I am not arguing that such a pun could *not* have been active in these instances, but rather that the circularity of these appeals should alert us to the fact that *country matters* has been transformed, by repeated glossing, from what was initially assumed to be a pun in early stage performance into an ossified definition. Only then will the same pun seem so apparent in these other instances, which, as Webb acknowledges, are often "merely suggestive" by comparison with the certainty that has accreted to this moment in *Hamlet*. And only then can *contrary matters* seem somehow "less bawdy" or a "bowdlerization" despite essentially sharing the initial syllable that was the main explanation of the pun in the first place.

On the other hand, the belief of Partridge, Holderness and Loughrey, and Legman that "the same pun is intended" carries its own logical problems. Taylor and Thompson are somewhat skeptical of Holderness and Loughrey's gloss, arguing that it would not "be obvious to a reader unfamiliar with the Folio or the Second Quarto why 'contrary' should suggest this pun."⁵⁶ And they are undoubtedly correct that Holderness and Loughrey, like Partridge before them, would hardly have been likely to make such an instant connection between *contrary* and *cunt* in the Q1 text had they not already been aware of the previous glossing of the familiar text. And yet, by the same token, we can see that Taylor and Thompson's skepticism is itself influenced by the power of the gloss. Only if *country* already does seem "obvious to a reader" as a sexual pun does it make sense to argue that *contrary* would not seem equally bawdy unless the reader was already familiar "with the Folio or the Second Quarto." If we had only *contrary*, we might just as easily point to instances, such as Kate's language lesson in *Henry V*, in which the phoneme *con* carries the bawdy joke.⁵⁷

In other words, both the obvious bawdiness that some editors see in Q1's *contrary matters* and the skepticism with which others view that perception are thoroughly influenced by their preexisting certainty about *country matters*, leading both groups into internal contradictions. At its root, the problem lies in the way that editors have been posing Q1 against Q2/F, a problem that derives ultimately from the uncanny historicity of Q1. Editors have taken the Q2/F reading as stable and always already understood, while the Q1 reading has been understood as a "variant" to be explained by reference to this imagined stability. In so doing, however, they not only render the Q1 reading inexplicable but also falsely remove *country matters* from its own complex history.

As we have seen, something very similar happened immediately after Bunbury's discovery of Q1, as readers for the first time grappled with Hamlet's *contrary matters*. Like Irace and other proponents of the bowdlerization theory, these readers were relieved to find *contrary* in the new text because they assumed a vulgarity in *country*. That assumption depended on Q1's absence from the conversation over the previous two centuries. But in fact the conviction that there was a vulgar pun in *country matters* was relatively new in 1823; before Q1 returned from its purgatory, there seems to have been no widespread consensus that *country matters* was obscene. The discovery of Q1 did not create this interpretation of the phrase, but by presenting a seemingly innocent alternative, it reinforced the perceived vulgarity of Q2/F and thereby ensured the dominance of this reading.

The early reception history of Hamlet's *country matters* by readers, performers, and editors offers a striking contrast to the confidence of our modern editorial glossing. In a remarkable copy of the Second Folio currently at the Folger Library, we can read this passage alongside one near contemporary of Shakespeare.[58] This reader was unusually invested in searching out sexual puns, among other indecencies, because he was leafing through Shakespeare's plays in his official capacity as a censor. Located at the English Jesuit College

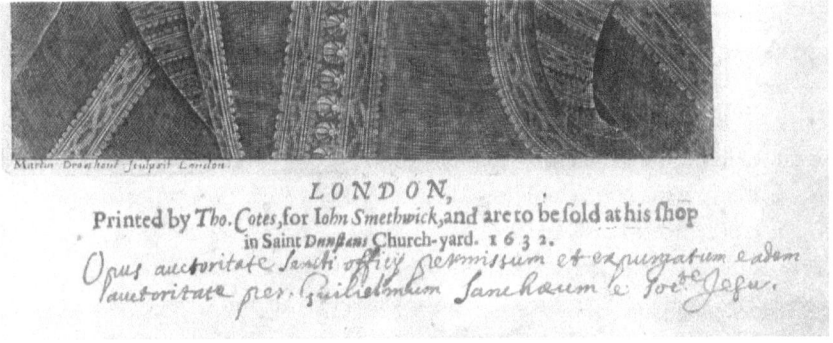

Figure 8. The censor's license on the title page of a copy of the Second Folio.
Reproduced by permission of the Folger Shakespeare Library, shelf mark STC 22274 Fo.2 no.07.

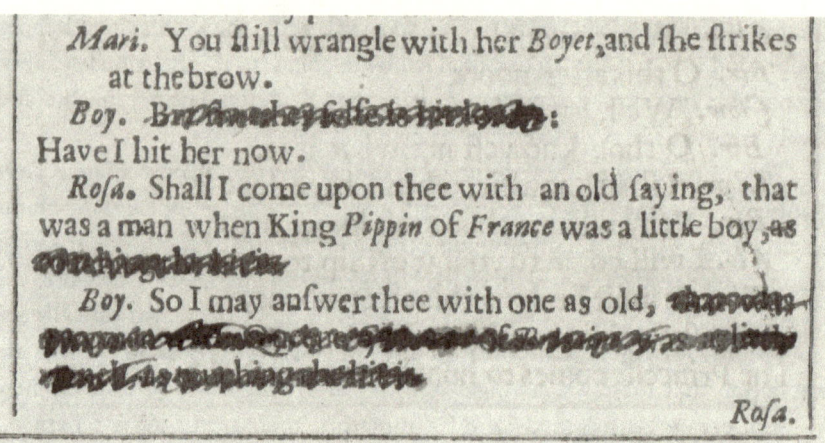

Figure 9. The licenser's censorship of *Love's Labour's Lost*.
Reproduced by permission of the Folger Shakespeare Library, shelf mark STC 22274 Fo.2 no.07, sig. L5v.

in Valladolid, Spain, the censor added his name on the title page of the Folio as part of his license: "per Guilielmum Sanchæum" (Figure 8).

The Latinized name, which appears on other editions held in the college library during the 1640s, may refer to a Spaniard named Guillermo Sánchez (otherwise unknown), but seems more likely, given the censor's subtle knowledge of English innuendo, to have been an English Jesuit named William Sankey who arrived at the college around 1640.[59] Sankey went through the Second Folio, or at least fifteen of the plays in it, looking not only for anti-Catholic material but also for sexual indecency.[60] The former clearly lay behind the numerous expurgations in *King John* and *Henry VIII*. Perhaps a mixture of both reasons led Sankey to cut *Measure for Measure* entirely out of the book, the only play he treated in this way. But in several plays, including *Hamlet*, Sankey blotted out words, phrases, and entire lines of dialogue solely because he deemed them too bawdy.

Sankey was on the lookout for certain keywords: he eradicated *codpiece*, for instance, from both *Love's Labour's Lost* (F2, sig. L5r) and *King Lear* (sig. ss6v), and he deleted Pandarus's question "how goe maiden-heads?" in *Troilus and Cressida* (sig. bb4r). But this censor was a careful and creative reader, not a mechanistic one, and he attempted specifically to root out punning sexual references of exactly the kind that editors have been telling us we should find in *country matters*. In a long passage in *Love's Labour's Lost* 4.1 (sigs. L5v–L6r), Sankey

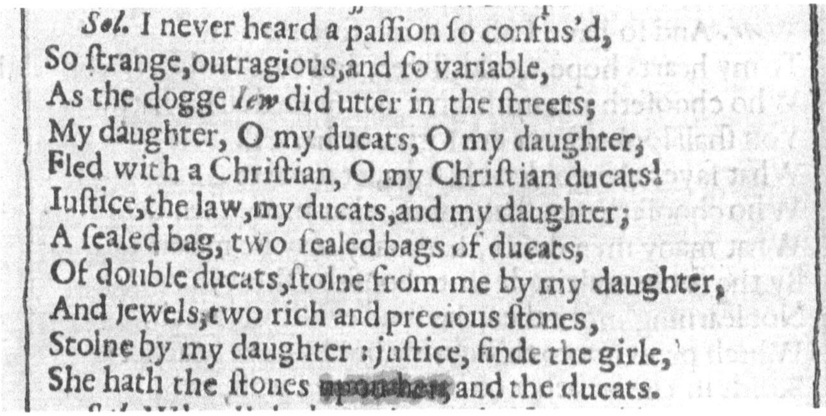

> *Sol.* I never heard a paſſion ſo confus'd,
> So ſtrange, outragious, and ſo variable,
> As the dogge *Iew* did utter in the ſtreets;
> My daughter, O my ducats, O my daughter,
> Fled with a Chriſtian, O my Chriſtian ducats!
> Iuſtice, the law, my ducats, and my daughter;
> A ſealed bag, two ſealed bags of ducats,
> Of double ducats, ſtolne from me by my daughter,
> And jewels, two rich and precious ſtones,
> Stolne by my daughter : juſtice, finde the girle,
> She hath the ſtones ~~upon her~~ and the ducats.

Figure 10. The licenser's censorship of *The Merchant of Venice*.
Reproduced by permission of the Folger Shakespeare Library, shelf mark STC 22274 Fo.2 no.07, sig. P2r.

had no trouble picking up on the double entendres traded by Maria, Boyet, and Rosaline (Figure 9). And in *Merchant of Venice* (sig. P2r), he carefully crossed out two small words, "upon her," to transform a bawdy pun about Jessica's sexuality into a mundane statement about her theft of Shylock's jewels (Figure 10). We can be sure, then, that Sankey was perfectly capable of the kind of "strong" reading that brings possible sexual puns to the fore, and that when he found them in a play he was working on, he tended to deploy his ink.

All the more telling, therefore, is his handling of the *country matters* dialogue. Although he was hardly methodical in going through the Second Folio as a whole, Sankey clearly read this passage, for he expurgated it with the only mark he made in *Hamlet*. But he apparently found nothing objectionable about the famous "bawdy pun on the first syllable of *country*" (Figure 11, F2, sig. 2q4r). Sankey blotted only the more obviously sexual comment on what lies between maids' legs, leaving uncensored not only *country matters* but indeed all of the supposedly sexual puns in this passage. (Nor, for that matter, did he see any pun in Touchstone's supposedly parallel *country copulatives*.) Nonetheless, we know he was looking for just such double entendres. Perhaps "lye in your lap" did not rise to the same necessary level of vulgarity as the comments about Jessica's having "stones upon her" or Rosaline's being hit "lower" and her "mark" having "a pricke in't." Perhaps Hamlet's immediate clarification of his meaning rendered the initial lines innocuous. In any case, if the editorial consensus about *country matters* is correct, it is as vulgar a pun

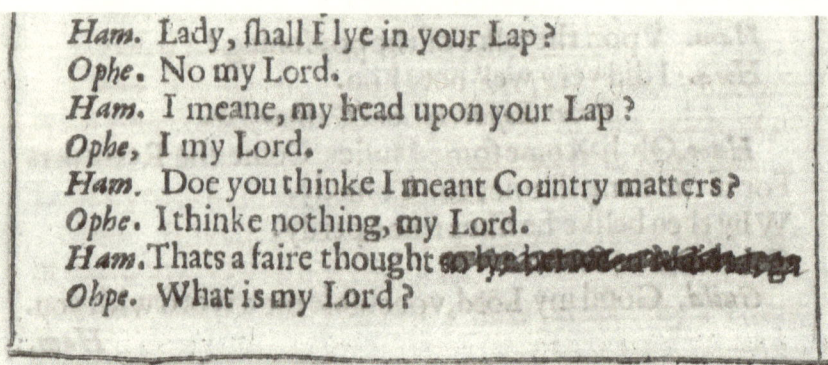

Figure 11. The licenser did not censor *Country matters*.
Reproduced by permission of the Folger Shakespeare Library, shelf mark STC 22274 Fo.2 no.07, sig. 2q4r.

as exists in Shakespeare, and one that we would expect Sankey to have expurgated, given his other blottings. But he did not.

Did the censor nod and simply miss the joke here, even though he was otherwise attentive while reading this passage? Or did he not censor *country matters* because there was simply no pun to censor in the phrase? From our historical distance, it may be impossible to know the answer, and indeed the difference between the two questions is a subtle philosophical one. In either case, the evidence of the Inquisition Folio should make us more cautious about what would be "obvious to a reader" in this phrase, and therefore also about the kinds of contrasts we draw with Q1's alternate reading. Whether he was the Spanish Guillermo Sánchez or the English William Sankey, "Guilielmus Sanchæus" was an actual, historical reader of Shakespeare's plays, roughly contemporary with their author and reading with the specific agenda of finding sexual language. But he found none in this famously bawdy pun.

We can see a theatrical parallel to this censor's reading in early promptbooks. In eighteenth- and nineteenth-century productions, Hamlet and Ophelia's entire exchange was routinely cut, with Hamlet asking, "Lady, shall I lie in your lap?" and Ophelia immediately responding, "You are merry, my lord." But the initial impetus for this bowdlerization seems to have come not from *country matters* but rather from the same part of the exchange that Sankey found objectionable. The Restoration "Smock Alley" promptbook, which dates to the late 1670s, was made by marking up a copy of the play from the Third Folio. Cuts to the dialogue and action were indicated by circling

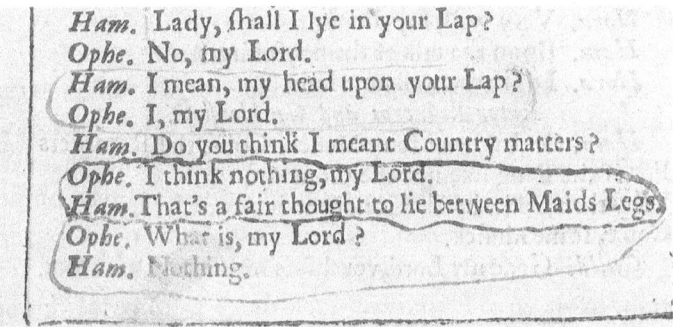

Figure 12. In the Smock Alley promptbook, *Country matters* is not censored.
Reproduced by permission of the University of Edinburgh Library, shelf mark JY 442, sig. 3R4r.

or boxing the text, as well as by crossing out lines.[61] This part of the dialogue between Hamlet and Ophelia before *The Mousetrap* is heavily cut (Figure 12).

Whoever was responsible for the promptbook has circled Hamlet's line "I mean, my head upon your Lap?" and Ophelia's response "I, my Lord," possibly not because of obscenity but rather to bring the passage in line with the shorter Q2 version. But the exchange about "nothing" lying "between Maids Legs" was surely cut for obscenity. Someone initially circled only Ophelia's "I think nothing, my Lord," and Hamlet's "That's a fair thought to lie between Maids Legs." But he went back and added the ensuing two lines as well— Ophelia's question, "What is, my Lord?" and Hamlet's clinching of the pun, "Nothing"— as if he realized only on second thought that these lines were part of the same obscene joke.

Hamlet's question, "Do you think I meant Country matters?" is thus surrounded by material intended to be cut in this performance. But that line itself remains uncircled. Whoever marked up the Smock Alley promptbook saw nothing problematic about Hamlet asking Ophelia about *country matters* onstage. The line also survives all the cuts made to the text in the "Players' Quartos" of the late seventeenth century, which give the play "As it is now Acted at his Highness the Duke of *York*'s Theatre." These editions mark lines that were omitted onstage by means of marginal inverted commas.[62] The four lines about "nothing" are accompanied by these inverted commas, but again *country matters* remains intact.[63] In the Restoration theater, as in the Inquisition Folio, it was only the end of the passage, with Hamlet's explicit reference to what lies "between maids' legs," that seemed to require expurgation for obscenity. Our modern editorial certainty thus runs counter to the early reception history of the phrase both in print and on stage.

One eighteenth-century reader of Shakespeare, who was rather more famous than Sankey and had a far larger impact on the history of Shakespearean criticism and editing, similarly seems to have missed the joke that we are sure is there. In the gloss on this line in his 1765 edition, Samuel Johnson, who might be considered the greatest reader of Shakespeare of his era, writes: "I think we must read, *Do you think, I meant country* manners? Do you imagine that I meant to sit in your lap, with such rough gallantry as clowns use to their lasses?"[64] For Johnson, the word *country* simply indicates the vulgarity of rural men, their lack of courtliness in wooing. Rather than merely placing their heads in the laps of "their lasses," these "clowns" would actually sit in their laps.

If we take the obscenity of *country matters* for granted, if we reify it into a straightforward definition, we will imagine that Johnson is simply embarrassed by the pun that is "actually" present. But Johnson is not being coy here. He genuinely does not see any pun. After all, he suggests emending the text from *country matters* to *country manners* so that it better accords with his interpretation, but this change hardly serves to hide any supposed syllabic pun on *cunt*. He has left the offending word intact in his emendation because he has not understood it as offensive. Indeed, the very inclusion of a note confirms this, since the note only draws attention to the passage. By contrast, when Johnson encounters explicit jokes about vaginas in Shakespeare's texts, he tends to leave them discreetly unglossed. He is silent on Hamlet's ensuing lines about "nothing," which we know had been understood as obscene since at least the 1640s, when the Jesuit inquisitor blotted them in his Second Folio. And he likewise offers no commentary on Katherine's bawdy language lesson in *Henry V*, which the play itself explicitly marks as including "words with a naughty sound, corruptible, coarse, and obscene words that honorable ladies should not use," and which had long been understood as obscene by editors.[65] So too with the passage in *Love's Labour's Lost* that troubled Sankey, Johnson offers no glosses, although it is clear that he understood the puns; as the Princess and her ladies leave the stage before this exchange, Johnson notes laconically that the "rest of the scene deserves no care." He similarly handled Mercutio's jokes on the "old hare hoar," calling them "a series of quibbles unworthy of explanation, which he who does not understand, needs not lament his ignorance."[66] Johnson's treatment of *country matters* in no way resembles his handling of these other scenes that involve far more obvious sexual puns.

It is not that Johnson was too prudish to notice these puns, or that he took Shakespeare too seriously to imagine that he would joke in this way. He simply read no such pun in *country matters*.[67]

In his 1790 edition, Edmond Malone understood Johnson's gloss in precisely this way. He thought that Johnson had missed the joke: "Dr. Johnson, from a casual inadvertence, proposed to read—country *manners*. The old reading is certainly right. What Shakespeare meant to allude to, must be too obvious to every reader, to require any explanation."[68] By "casual inadvertence," Malone means that despite Johnson's usual acuity, he failed to see the intended bawdy reference because of a momentary inattention. From Malone's perspective, Johnson's note can only have been an error, for Shakespeare clearly "meant to allude" to something too vulgar to mention in the polite company of the gloss. Johnson's reading, however, is perfectly plausible: he has only "missed" the allusion if we assume it is always there in the text—put there, according to Malone, by Shakespeare—rather than activated through performance and editorial practices.

Oddly enough, at virtually the same moment that the greatest Shakespearean critic of his day was suffering from this "casual inadvertence," the greatest Shakespearean actor of his day was revising another famously bawdy play in a strikingly similar, and similarly revealing, manner. It is often taken for granted that the title of Wycherley's *The Country Wife* (1675) involves the same pun as Hamlet's *country matters*, and given the abundance of sexual jokes in that play, the assumption seems perfectly reasonable.[69] Indeed, in the eighteenth century, the play was perceived as so bawdy that it was unplayable: in 1766, David Garrick rewrote Wycherley's text to remove much of the vulgarity and make it suitable for his stage. And yet the title that Garrick gave to his revision—like Johnson's emendation of *Hamlet*—strangely alters the "wrong" word, if our assumptions about this pun are correct. Instead of *The Country Wife*, he called his version *The Country Girl*. Changing the Margery character from a wife to a fiancée suited Garrick's revised plot, but he apparently saw no need to alter the other key word in the title. In a play renowned for its bawdy puns, surely audiences were on the lookout for any and all possible double entendres, the same kind of strong reading that Sankey the censor brought to his Shakespeare. Like Johnson's "country *manners*," therefore, Garrick's "incorrectly" revised title suggests that the pun we have found so obvious in *country* was not always so obvious.

Before Malone, in fact, no major edition of Shakespeare had ever glossed the phrase as involving a pun at all, much less a vulgar one. Indeed, part of the reason for Johnson's "casual inadvertence" may be that no previous edition had ever glossed this line at all.⁷⁰ Silence surrounding what we take to be obscenity is always difficult to interpret, of course: did editors see no pun in the line that needed explaining, or were they simply reluctant to discuss an obscene pun? We may incline toward the latter explanation, conditioned as we have been by decades of glossing in modern editions. But in fact the early reception history of the line suggests the former explanation for editorial silence, as indeed does the first gloss on the line, Johnson's "innocent" suggestion.

One early editor, Lewis Theobald, clearly understood a vulgar reference in the passage as a whole, although it is unclear whether he saw a specific syllabic pun in *country matters*. In his *Shakespeare Restored* (1726), after quoting the exchange from "shall I lie in your lap?" to "country matters," he wrote: "If ever the Poet deserved Whipping for low and indecent Ribaldry, it was for this Passage; ill-tim'd in all its Circumstances, and unbefitting the Dignity of his Characters, as well as of his Audience." Theobald is discussing the entire passage, not drawing any particular attention to the phrase *country matters*; indeed, he is specifically objecting to Pope's omission of the additional two lines from the Folio text: "Certainly, HAMLET's Answer is more natural, and less abrupt, if we restore this Passage."⁷¹ Did the "indecent Ribaldry" to which he is objecting here include a pun on *cunt*, rather than simply Hamlet's joke about lying "in" or "upon" Ophelia's "lap," and perhaps the subsequent remarks (not included in his quotation) about what lies "between maids' legs"? Since his comments come in the context of arguing for the inclusion of the extended question-and-response, they seem directed more toward the passage as a whole than *country matters* in particular.⁷² Good editor that he was, Theobald included the lines when he produced his own edition of Shakespeare (1733), despite his aversion to them. But perhaps to avoid lingering here, he did not (as he often did) extract his discussion from *Shakespeare Restored* in a gloss: in his edition, the lines stand without a note. Nor is there any note in the editions of Rowe (1709), Pope (1725), Hanmer (1743–44), or Warburton (1747).

When Johnson proposed emending the line to *country manners*, therefore, and wrote his note—which now seems so amusingly dull-witted, after our history of glossing the phrase—he had no previous model from which to work. Every editor of Shakespeare, both in the eighteenth century and today, "borrows" a great deal from other editions. Despite his stated intention to prepare his text from a fresh collation of the original editions, Johnson in fact produced a variorum based mainly on his predecessors.⁷³ If he had ever read Theobald's comment in *Shakespeare Restored*, he seems not to have remembered it, and it did not influence his edition. In fact, nowhere in his edition of *Hamlet* does Johnson cite *Shakespeare Restored*; rather, his notes to Theobald consistently derive from his edition of the plays.[74] I suspect, therefore, that seeing no previous notes on the line in the editions he had in front of him, Johnson guessed at its meaning with no real guide. And not having been told by generations of editors that the phrase contained an obscene pun, he simply did not see one. The power of the gloss to reify meaning is here revealed by its absence.

Until the 1780s, then, there was nothing in any edition of *Hamlet* to help readers see any pun in *country matters*. Just the opposite: the only gloss on the phrase would have steered them toward a relatively innocent reference to the crude manners of country folk. This is not to say that no one in Johnson's day would have gotten the joke here, simply because he himself seems not to have done so. Theobald may have—or he may not have. And only a few years before Johnson's edition, the anonymous author of *Yorick's Meditations upon Various Interesting and Important Subjects* (1760), written in the style of Sterne's *Tristram Shandy*, used the phrase *country matters* in a sexual sense. But here again it is hard to know whether a specific pun is involved. One of the essays, "A Meditation upon the Thing," alludes to the use of "the thing" to indicate something fashionable or suitable to the times, but the author fears "some lady" will misunderstand him in a more prurient sense and "interrupt me with a lord, sir, what do you mean? why no modest woman will read you—oh! fie the thing. So, madam, you think I mean country-matters, but I had no such stuff in my thoughts."[75] Five years before Johnson's "casual inadvertence," then, we have a clear reference to *country matters* as relating not only to sex but to sexual parts, "the thing," although as in Hamlet's subsequent remarks, it is not clear whether male or female genitalia are alluded to here. Nor is it certain that "Yorick" intends a specific pun on *cunt*. But he clearly expects his readers to understand the allusion to *Hamlet* and to see the phrase as having a sexual reference.

It is more than a little odd, then, that this use of *country matters* to connote sex is so exceedingly rare in the eighteenth century; *Yorick's Meditations* is the only clear instance I can find in Eighteenth Century Collections Online prior to the 1780s. All of the other usages of *country matters* refer simply to rural affairs—and in this sense they are fully in line with Johnson's understanding and with earlier, seventeenth-century usage. In the *Spectator* 269, for example, which was easily the most widely disseminated eighteenth-century text containing the phrase other than *Hamlet*, Sir Roger de Coverley recounts the news of the Christmas season in his rural seat and then, "having dispatched all our

Country Matters," moves on to London affairs.[76] The numerous ordinary uses of the phrase indicate that it had not yet ossified as an obscene pun. When Johnson published his edition, the meaning of Hamlet's words was still open. In his editions of 1773 and 1778, George Steevens simply retained Johnson's commentary, suggesting that he too did not see anything obscene in *country matters*, nor perceive any "casual inadvertence" in Johnson's note. While the tendency to find a vulgar reference in the phrase was clearly emerging, and while Malone's gloss would only encourage that tendency, this reading had not yet crowded out more innocent meanings. By the time of Payne and Foss's reprint of Q1 in 1825, however, the situation had begun to change.

It seems to have been Steevens's 1778 edition that sparked new attention to the sexual pun in the phrase, which may in turn have influenced Malone's landmark gloss. In 1785, two critics of that edition added new information on *country matters* to supplement what they saw as Johnson's and Steevens's failure to understand its implications. John Monck Mason wrote that *country matters* "is a vulgar expression still used in common life, and means, 'Do you think I have any indecent allusion?' The reason why it bears this sense cannot be so decently explained."[77] Mason's remark is the closest anyone had yet come to clarifying that the phrase involved a pun on *cunt*, since he notes specifically that the "reason why it bears this sense" is indecent. Also in 1785, John Pinkerton more directly challenged Johnson's gloss: "The commentator is so chaste, that he seems not to know that both of these words are dissyllables. Tho I should be sorry to claim the prize of Agnolo Poliziano, of finding obscenities where the meaning was possibly innocent, yet such *matters* should either not be understood, or understood aright."[78] Pinkerton somewhat oddly focuses his reader's attention on the other word in the phrase by italicizing *matters* (perhaps imagining a pun on *mater* and *womb*?), but his comment about "finding obscenities" in "both of these words" suggests that he also heard a double entendre in *country*.[79]

In the mid-1780s, then, we begin to see references that explicitly mark *country matters* as a sexual pun.[80] It is unclear why these references emerge at this time, but the changing understanding of the line is reinforced by Malone's 1790 gloss, the first in an edition of the play to suggest such a pun. Malone's coy remark that "what Shakespeare meant to allude to, must be too obvious to every reader, to require any explanation" masks a real historical change. "What Shakespeare meant to allude to" seems not to have been obvious to Johnson, nor to Sankey before him, and there is no reason to assume it would have always been apparent to other readers of *Hamlet* in the eighteenth century—at least not until editions of the play began to guide them to such a reading. As usual, Malone casts his scholarship as historical discovery—here, of Shakespeare's intentions—but in fact his gloss helps to create the inevitability of readers' finding an allusion here, which then gets recoded as obviousness.

Steevens inserted Malone's note in his 1793 edition while removing Johnson's, probably to save space, since Malone effectively subsumes Johnson's note into his own, rendering its inclusion redundant. Isaac Reed's variorum edition of 1803 likewise included only Malone's note.[81] By 1821, in Boswell's second edition of Malone, the passage stands unglossed—but now with a difference. As I argued above, given Johnson's own note and the reception history of the phrase, we should be wary of assuming that the editorial silence over *country matters* before Johnson's 1765 edition merely indicates a prudish reluctance to discuss such things. But Boswell obviously knew Malone's note, as well as Steevens's and Reed's reiteration of it, and he knew how Malone read *country matters*. His lack of a gloss therefore almost certainly indicates that he wanted to avoid drawing attention to the possible obscenity. He admits in his preface that he has, uncharacteristically, omitted some notes from Malone's edition "where Shakespeare has, I think, most perversely and injuriously been charged with an irreverent allusion to Scripture," and the annotational accusation of indecency seems to have been handled similarly here.[82] While the editorial silence on this line may be the same as before Johnson's edition, therefore, the meaning of that silence has been transformed. With Malone's landmark edition, which has since been read and consulted by every later editor of Shakespeare, the power of the gloss begins its work, and the idea that *country matters* contains an obscene pun begins to harden into historical fact.

Just at this moment, as Malone's reading was becoming stabilized in editions in the early nineteenth century, Henry Bunbury discovered his copy of Q1 *Hamlet*. By positioning the Q1 passage as the innocent predecessor of the received text, early reviews of Payne and Foss's reprint helped to cement the idea that *country matters* involves an obscenity. This mutually reinforcing relationship can be best understood in relief, by turning to contexts in which the familiar text of *Hamlet* was not quite so familiar. In France, too, readers could quickly learn about the discovery of Q1 and its variant reading. The *Bibliothèque Universelle des Sciences, Belles-Lettres, et Arts* based its translated account on the *London Literary Gazette*, and although it greatly abbreviated the essay, the passage about *contrary matters* was retained. But the French version reveals that the stabilization of *country matters* as an obscene pun had not yet spread across the Channel. Perhaps due to cultural or linguistic distance, the French translator seems to have been confused by the *Literary Gazette*'s original remark about "a phrase that has been much objected to," which he rendered: "Une variante que nous citerons ici éclaircit un passage qui, jusqu'à présent avoit paru très-obscur."[83] This writer simply believes that *contrary matters* "sheds light on a passage that until now had seemed very *obscure*," rather than objectionable, apparently because he did not understand why *country matters* should be "much objected to" except in the literal sense of textual obscurity. The idea that the phrase was vulgar or obscene seems never to have occurred to him. At least this one reader across the Channel clearly failed to appreciate the allusion that Malone felt was "too obvious to every reader, to require any explanation," and that seems indeed to have been becoming more obvious to many English readers just when Q1 was discovered.

The same distancing effect of language and culture is evident in the mid-nineteenth-century German editions of *Hamlet* by the esteemed philologists Karl Elze and Jacob Heussi. Here too we can see the work required to make Malone's "obvious" allusion obvious to English readers. Despite their excellent philological training, neither Elze nor Heussi saw anything obscene about the word *country*. Indeed, both read the phrase exactly as Johnson did, as referring to the crude manners of rural folk. Elze muses: "What Hamlet means cannot be in doubt; but where does the term 'country matters' come from? Such 'edifying things,' to use Schlegel's translation, occur just as frequently in the city as in the country. Johnson hazarded 'country manners,' and see in comparison K. John I, 1. The Dutch translation helped in the most naive manner, where it reads: 'Did you think that I, as a farmer, wanted to sit on your lap?' We are inclined to see in 'country' a corruption for whose correction [Q1] points the way."[84] Elze recognizes that Hamlet refers to sex, but he sees no syllabic pun in *country*. And since sexual acts—the "edifying things" of Schlegel's ironic translation—are by no means restricted to the country, he cannot understand the import of the term. While he considers Johnson's emendation, and the Dutch translation that accords with it, Elze ultimately thinks that it is the word *country* that is the problem, and that *contrary* in some way (although he does not tell us precisely how) suggests the correct emendation.

Heussi disagreed about the value of Q1's *contrary*, but otherwise his note is similar: "What Hamlet means is not hard to guess, but how that can be signified either through *country* or *contrary* is not to be found. If *country matters* is the correct reading, then we would have to interpret: coarse, clodhopping matters, such as are typical among uncivilized country folk. But is it really any better in cities on this point? Likely a copyist's or printer's mistake gives the explanation. *Contrary* does not make sense."[85] As with Elze and Johnson before him, the only meaning Heussi can find in *country matters* is a reference to the crude behavior of farmers and villagers—although, like his compatriot Elze, he demurs from such an uncouth attack on rural folk. And while he ultimately throws up his hands about the passage—he cannot specify exactly what explanation a typographical or scribal error might provide—nonetheless Heussi reads the phrase basically as Johnson did, oblivious to any "obvious" pun on the first syllable.

As a result, both these German editors handle Q1's variant in a manner strikingly different from that of the early English periodical writers. More important than their varying takes on the bibliographic value of *contrary*—whether it is indicative of the true reading or merely nonsensical—is the complete absence in their analyses of any of the relief at the apparent innocence of the word that dominated in the English press. As we have seen, this relief continues to structure one of the major critical responses to the variant even today. Nor are the German editors intent on determining whether *contrary* carries the same pun as *country*, as the other current editorial argument would have it, because they do not already understand *country* as an obscene pun. Elze and Heussi, in other words, are completely removed from the organizing binary of *vulgar/innocent* that has determined the response to this variant in the English-speaking world from virtually the moment of Bunbury's discovery until today.

For English readers who were already deeply acquainted with *Hamlet*, who already valued it as the greatest work of literature their language had produced, and who were already coming to believe that they got the joke in *country matters*, the reaction to Q1 could not be understood except by opposition to the received text. Had Q1 never disappeared, had it been known all along like Q2 and F, perhaps this variant could have been analyzed in a more dialectical fashion, retaining a sense both of this dramatic moment and of punning itself as dynamic processes rather than static objects. As it was, the uncanny historicity of Q1 meant that its "innocent" variant could only reinforce the increasingly fixed reception of *country matters*.

In his *Dramatic Works of William Shakspeare* (1826), known as the "Chiswick" edition from its place of publication, Samuel Weller Singer became the first editor of *Hamlet* to incorporate a reading from Q1 into his text. The Chiswick edition also seems to be the only conflated edition of Shakespeare's *Hamlet* ever to print *contrary matters* as part of its text. Oddly enough, due to an accident of printing, even here the passage remains obstinately unstable: Hamlet

> *Ham.* Lady, shall I lie in your lap?
>   [*Lying down at* OPHELIA'S *Feet.*
> *Oph.* No, my lord.
> *Ham.* I mean, my head upon your lap?
> *Oph.* Ay, my lord.
> *Ham.* Do you think, I meant contray[15] matters?
> *Oph.* I think nothing, my lord.

Figure 13. Samuel Weller Singer printed *contray matters* in his 1826 Chiswick edition. Reproduced by permission of the Horace Howard Furness Memorial Library, Kislak Center for Special Collections, Rare Books and Manuscripts, University of Pennsylvania Libraries, shelf mark 90 1826S.

asks Ophelia, "Do you think, I meant contray matters?" (Figure 13).[86] Singer's *contray* is no doubt merely a typo for *contrary*, since he adds a note: "This is the reading of the quarto 1603. The quarto 1604 and the folio read *country*." While Singer clearly meant to print *contrary*, the actual appearance of *contray* in his text offers a neat example of the inevitable and multifarious problems of textual transmission that must somehow lie behind the variation in this passage.

Singer gives no rationale for his choice of *contrary* over *country*, but his edition as a whole suggests one. Like numerous editors before him, Singer took a jaundiced view of the editorial tradition: he advocated returning to the early editions to correct the text of Steevens and Malone that was the basis for his edition, "and the satisfaction arising from a rejection of modern unwarranted deviations from the old copies has not unfrequently been the reward of this labour."[87] In fact these rejections were more "unfrequent" than Singer admitted, and he largely followed the traditional text throughout the *Dramatic Works*. But he did include numerous notes about early editions, indicating divergences in the first quarto of *Romeo and Juliet*, for instance. Only occasionally do these readings make their way into the text, however: Singer's inclusion of *contrary matters*—or *contray matters*, anyway—is a rare and hence telling exception.

Upon close inspection, Singer's handling of variants in Q1 *Hamlet* is even more remarkable. The newly discovered text came to his attention in Payne and Foss's 1825 reprint while his edition was in process; Singer's imagination was taken by Q1, and he hastily updated notes that he had already written so as to engage with its readings before completing this volume of the *Dramatic Works*. More than fifty notes draw attention to variant readings in Q1, and yet he regretted not having the time to include more, writing at one point: "I suffer the following note to stand as I had written it previous to the discovery of that copy." And a number of notes fail to take account of Q1 when they should, indicating incomplete revision. For instance, in Voltemand's speech in 2.2, Singer's text reads, "old Norway, overcome with joy, / Gives him three thousand crowns in annual fee," and his note reports that the "quartos read *three score* thousand." But here the plural "quartos" means not Q1 and Q2 but rather the quarto tradition beginning with Q2, since Q1 like F reads "three thousand." Likewise, Singer's note to the line in Ophelia's song, "Which bewept to the grave did go," reads: "Quarto—ground."[88] Q1, however, has "grave," and so, again, Singer's note is comparing the Folio reading only to Q2. In these notes Singer acts as if Q1 did not exist, no doubt because they were written before he saw Payne and Foss's reprint. Since there are none of these unrevised notes in the first act, and since they increase as the text progresses, one gets the sense that Singer began by trying to be more comprehensive in his references to Q1 but ended up by alerting readers only to those variants that particularly interested him.

More than fifty times, however, Singer did manage to update his edition with notes about Q1 variants, including the Ghost's nightgown, Gertrude's declaration of innocence, Q1's *trapically* instead of *tropically* in Hamlet's announcement of the title of *The Mousetrap*, and Q1's *the ignorant* instead of *the groundlings* in Hamlet's speech to the players. But only three times did he promote a Q1 reading to the text. Two of these dealt with traditional cruxes that editors had variously explained but for which Q1 offered a new reading. The first occurs in 1.2, when the King gives the ambassadors "no further personall power / To businesse with the King, more then the scope / Of these *dilated* Articles allow" (F, sig. 2N5r, emphasis added; Q2 reads *delated*). The difficult syntax of the passage, and strange relation of the adjective *dilated* or *delated* to its noun, had begged explanation for some time. Johnson thought the ambassadors were warned not to do "more than is comprised in the general design of these articles, which you may explain in a more diffuse and dilated stile," while Caldecott thought they were limited by what the "tenor of these articles, set out at large, authorizes."[89] Singer evidently found Q1's alternate reading less obscure, and he printed its variant in his text, breezily explaining: "I have not scrupled to read *related*, upon the authority of the first quarto, as more intelligible."[90]

The other crux was even more famous. In Q2, Hamlet tells Rosencrantz and Guildenstern that the King "keepes them *like an apple* in the corner of his iaw, first mouth'd to be last swallowed" (sig. K1v, emphasis added), while in F he "keepes them *like an Ape* in the corner of his iaw" instead (sig. 2P2v, emphasis added). Richard Farmer's conjectural emendation, "keeps them like an ape an apple," won many adherents, although Malone thought emendation of the Folio was unnecessary. He agreed that "the particular food in Shakespeare's contemplation was an *apple*," and produced a parallel passage from Beaumont and Fletcher's *The Captain* to prove it, but he thought the food was simply implied in the Folio's version of the simile. Q1 revealed another option for this "particular food": "For hee doth keep you as an Ape doth nuttes, / In the corner of his Iaw, first mouthes you, / Then swallowes you" (sig. G1r). Singer thought Q1 cleared up the matter entirely: "The omission of the words '*doth nuts*,' in the old copies, had obscured this passage. . . . The words are now supplied from the newly discovered quarto of 1603."[91]

Do these two examples form a pattern that can explain Singer's emendation of *country matters* with Q1's *contrary matters*? In other words, did Singer see this phrase as a crux as well? If so, then like Johnson, Elze, and Heussi, he must have seen no vulgar pun in *country matters* and, because he could not fully explain the phrase, concluded like Elze that Q1 "points the way" to the true reading. As I have been arguing, we should not assume that any particular reader would have read *country matters* as a pun, particularly before that pun had become stabilized by one editorial gloss after another. In the early nineteenth century, as we have seen, the vulgar reading of the phrase seems not yet to have completely eclipsed the more innocent one. And yet, Singer was not just any reader, and it is highly unlikely that he saw no pun in *country matters*. Malone's edition formed the basis of the Chiswick edition and is discussed at length in its preface, and so Singer had surely read the earlier editor's "correction" of Johnson, with its vulgar reading of the phrase. And given his intense interest in Q1, Singer would certainly have read some of the journalistic accounts of its discovery that emphasized the obscenity of *country matters* and the welcome innocence of *contrary matters*.

It therefore seems safe to conclude that Singer emended his text with this Q1 variant for reasons completely different from those in the other two instances. The promotion of *contrary matters* to the text represents the only time that Singer adopted a reading from Q1 when the text in Q2 and F was not obscure to him. Singer's general understanding of the origins of Q1 explains both his unique adoption of *contrary matters* and his overwhelming preference for leaving other readings from Q1 in his notes, despite his obvious fascination with that text: "As in the case of the earliest impressions of Romeo and Juliet, and The Merry Wives of Windsor, this edition of Hamlet appears to have been either printed from an imperfect manuscript of the prompt books, or the playhouse copy, or stolen from the author's papers. . . . The variations of this early copy from the play of Hamlet, in its improved state, are too numerous and striking to admit a doubt of the play having been subsequently revised, amplified, and altered by the poet."[92] Because of this revisionist position, Singer left most of the Q1 readings in his notes so as to present Shakespeare's play in its final version, after the master had "revised, amplified, and altered" it.

All the more striking, then, is his emendation of *country matters*. Singer seems to have been unable to believe that Shakespeare would have revised the Q1 reading into the vulgar pun represented by *country matters*. Like Irace and some other modern editors, and like the early journalistic responses to the discovery of Q1, he apparently saw *contrary matters* as obviously less bawdy than *country matters*, a testament to the increasing reification of the latter phrase as a vulgar pun. But given his belief that Q1 was an early Shakespearean draft that preceded the received text of the play, he could not have believed, as some modern editors do, that Q1's reading was a "bowdlerization" of the Shakespearean text. Instead, he likely agreed with the article in the *Gentleman's Magazine* that saw *contrary* as the true Shakespearean reading and "assigned [*country matters*] to the actors of his time, who flattered the vulgar taste . . . by the introduction and constant repetition of many indecent, and not a few stupid jokes." Since the two cruxes that Singer used Q1 to resolve were imagined as merely recovering the true Shakespearean reading, *contrary matters* is the only instance in which Singer deviates from his straightforward belief that Shakespeare revised the text of Q1 into the Q2/F version of the play in order to adopt a more complex theory of textual transmission, one that (probably) involved rogue actors introducing extra jokes into Shakespeare's script. Unfortunately, Singer offers no explanation for his emendation, but in context it seems clear that, as with the article in the *Gentleman's Magazine*, Singer's relief at finding a supposedly innocent variant generated much of the impetus behind this exception.

Over the course of the nineteenth century, however, the more flexible story of textual transmission evident in both Singer's edition and the early journalistic accounts—in which Q1 may be a first draft but may also preserve Shakespearean final thoughts later altered by the actors—began to harden into the binary opposition of the theories of Knight and Collier. As the text became framed as *either* a rough draft *or* a stenographic piracy, the more hybrid narratives told about the edition in the years immediately following its discovery faded. By 1875, the theory expounded in the *Gentleman's Magazine* (and, I argue, taken up by Singer) seemed unfortunately impossible, as Frank Marshall wrote in *A Study of Hamlet*: "I should like to be able to prove that some of the most offensive lines were inserted by the players to suit the depraved taste of their audience, but I am afraid that they must be acknowledged to have been permitted, if not approved, by Shakespeare, in common with some equally repulsive passages in other plays." Marshall followed Knight in seeing Q1 as Shakespeare's "original bald sketch," and for this reason he seems to have been pushed into taking *country matters* and the exchange about "nothing" as, sadly, part of Shakespeare's revision of his rough draft into the completed *Hamlet*.[93]

In the critical framework established by the 1840s, either the received text was Shakespeare's final version or it was his only version, and so, while Knight and Collier were commonly opposed in editions and reviews as the only two options, both of their theories only reinforced the centrality of the traditional Q2/F text. As I discuss in the next chapter, something of an exception was made for the indications of early performance seemingly preserved in Q1—such as *Enter the ghost in his night gowne*—since staging matters were always considered extra-Shakespearean anyway. But emending Shakespeare's text with Q1 variants grew ever more rare, generally confined to obscure cruxes where the traditional text could not be satisfactorily explained, as in Singer's other two emendations. For this reason, Singer's landmark emendation of *country matters* with *contrary matters* received no support among subsequent editors. Despite the evident relief that greeted the Q1 variant, and despite what we may think of Victorian prudery, the power of the binary opposition of Knight's and Collier's narratives of textual transmission superseded Shakespearean decorum. Nineteenth-century editors could not omit *country matters* from the text because, on either theory, it had the full weight of Shakespeare's authorship behind it.

Instead, editors seem to have come to a communal decision not to discuss the matter. The phrase went without any annotation in all of the major nineteenth-century editions, including those of Knight (1839), Collier (1842–44), G. C. Verplank (1847), Dyce (1857), A. J. Valpy (1857), Howard Staunton (1858–60), and even Horace Howard Furness's Variorum (1877). Again, this editorial silence differs from that of the earlier eighteenth century, since all of these editors were familiar with Malone's note and hence the phrase's putative obscenity. In his 1856 revised edition, even Singer himself rejected the reading without comment. He now followed all other editors in letting the traditional text stand unglossed.[94] With the discovery of Q1's "innocent" alternative reading, the modern consensus was firmly in place. *Country matters* had become, simply, "a bawdy pun on the first syllable of *country*." And it had become, lamentably, an authentically Shakespearean pun.

How might we reassess this variant reading without starting from the automatic assumption that Shakespeare is, in Hibbard's words, "quibbling indecently on the first syllable of *country*"? Underlying the glossing of *country matters* in modern editions, I have suggested, is the assumption that readers and spectators *then* would have gotten this obscene joke, that readers *now* will not get it without editorial help to bridge this historical divide, and that such a joke was intended when Shakespeare wrote and Richard Burbage first spoke the phrase. The genealogy I have traced here, by contrast, suggests that this obscenity only became obscene over time through a process of annotation and commentary, one that pivots around the discovery of Q1. Furthermore, the reading of Q1's *contrary matters* as a more innocent variant rests on the historical accident of its belated discovery just as the consensus was hardening about the pun in the received text. The textual history of this phrase, or these phrases, thus reveals a fluidity that by now seems surprising, but that can suggest new ways of reading not only *country* or *contrary matters* but also the variant passage more broadly as it stands in the three texts of *Hamlet*.

As I have argued, editorial explanations of the relationship between the three texts of *Hamlet* at this point are logically tangled. The bowdlerization theory relies, in an unexamined way, on the editorial reification of meaning that began in the late eighteenth century and was cemented by the discovery of Q1. Furthermore, the text of Q1 would display a very strange method of bowdlerization. If *country matters* were simply too vulgar to be allowed to stand in the text, the entire question—or the entire exchange—could have simply been removed, rather than subtly changing one word to such a similar-sounding one. Indeed, wholesale cutting is precisely how the text was bowdlerized in the Bowdlers' *Family Shakespeare* and, as Taylor and Thompson show, in a large number of other nineteenth- and twentieth-century editions.[95] Finally, as I will show, the dialogue between Hamlet and Ofelia as it stands in Q1 still contains language that, like Q2/F Hamlet's joke about "Nothing," is more clearly sexual than *country matters*. For all these reasons, the change from *country* to *contrary* cannot have been made to bowdlerize the text. And for precisely the same reasons the story does not make much sense in reverse, as the early respondents to Q1 imagined, with the actors replacing Shakespeare's innocent *contrary* with the obscene *country* to amuse the groundlings.

On the other hand, if the two words convey "the same pun," as Partridge, Holderness and Loughrey, and others believe, why is there a variant at all at this point? How did *contrary* come to appear in the text? If there is truly no difference in meaning, the change seems unlikely to have been intentional. Possibly *contrary* is simply a compositor's misreading of *country* as it stood in his copy. Or if (as Collier believed) Q1 derives from a shorthand report of performance, then perhaps what appear to be two different words are in fact the same word pronounced and written diversely. *Country* might well be spoken so as to resemble *contrary*, or *contr'ry*. Whoever wrote the manuscript copy that lies behind Q1 might have heard *contrary* even though *country* was spoken. In any of these cases, we are dealing with accidental variation rather than bowdlerization or revision.

The dominant twentieth-century theory of "bad quartos" might suggest that the reporter simply misremembered the word here, unconsciously substituting one that sounded similar.[96] But if *country matters* really were a vulgar pun intended by Shakespeare, and if this pun had been spoken and understood in early performances of *Hamlet*, wouldn't a reporter be most likely to recall the key word in this exchange? Such an obscene joke would seem highly memorable. Nor would this instance of faulty memory accord with one of the major tendencies of memorial reconstruction as it has been theorized: "What happens [in the genuine text] is often made crudely explicit" in these texts, according to Harold Jenkins.[97] As Laurie Maguire shows, "vulgarization" and "lapsing into looser and more commonplace phraseology, merging into paraphrase" have been widely agreed to be characteristics of reported texts.[98] But if we imagine *country matters* to be an obvious pun—one that, to judge by editors' citation of parallel passages, was broadly understood in the period—the reporter's substitution of *contrary* hardly seems like either "vulgarization" or "more commonplace phraseology."

Interestingly, if Q1 is indeed a reported text, what apparently stuck in the reporter's mind was rather the opposition between lying "in your lap" and "upon your lap"—which mirrors F perfectly well—and the fact that Hamlet then asked Ophelia a question about whether, as a result of his initial choice of preposition, she might have had some other, more vulgar understanding of his meaning. On this reading, in other words, there is indeed a sexual pun in this exchange, but it lies in the distinction between *in* and *upon*. And the accidental alteration of *country* to *contrary* therefore suggests not that they conveyed the same pun on *cunt* but rather that the reporter unconsciously tidied up Hamlet's question, remembering its gist while making it more clearly mean, "Did you think I had the opposite meaning to the one I actually intended?" or possibly, given some historical uses of *contrary* attested in the *OED*, "Did you think I meant wrong or improper things?"[99] I am not arguing that Q1 is in fact a memorial reconstruction, merely that existing theories of this Q1 variant are incoherent under this common hypothesis about the origins of that text. Regardless of how Q1 was created, however, its agreement with F against Q2 on the opposition between lying *in* or *on* Ophelia's lap suggests that perhaps our attention has been misplaced all along. Perhaps the interest in Shakespeare's day was less on *country* or *contrary matters* than we have thought. Indeed, other aspects of the passage show Q1 elaborating Hamlet's aggressively sexual innuendo in a different way altogether.

Q2 presents the sparsest version of the exchange, while the texts of Q1 and F are more expansive.[100] Here are the three passages again, regrouped to emphasize these similarities between Q1 and F:

Ham. Lady shall I lie in your lap?
Ophe. No my Lord.
Ham. Doe you thinke I meant country matters?   (Q2)

Ham. . . . Lady will you giue me leaue, and so forth:
To lay my head in your lappe?
Ofel. No my Lord.
Ham. Vpon your lap, what do you thinke I meant contrary matters?   (Q1)

Ham. Ladie, shall I lye in your Lap?
Ophe. No my Lord.
Ham. I meane, my Head vpon your Lap?
Ophe. I my Lord.
Ham. Do you thinke I meant Country matters?   (F)

In Q2, Hamlet asks only a single question and follows Ophelia's negative response with his line about *country matters*. In F, by contrast, the exchange continues with a second question before Hamlet comes to *country matters*. Q1 incorporates a version of the Folio Hamlet's second question, both in Q1 Hamlet's clarification "Vpon your lap" and in his initial question, "To lay *my head* in your lappe?"

The emphasis on Hamlet's *head* and the underscored distinction between *in* and *upon* make more of a difference than we have noticed.¹⁰¹ Hamlet's additional question in F heightens his cruelty. In both Q2 and F he places Ophelia in a double bind, since if she responds affirmatively to his initial request, she might seem to accede to a sexual encounter, whereas if she denies him, she might seem unchaste by assuming he meant something sexual. But in the Folio, Hamlet's second question makes this double bind more apparent by focusing attention on the potentially ambiguous meaning of the word *lap*. Laying his head *upon* Ophelia's lap carries an innocent meaning, while lying *in* her lap suggests entering her sexually, hence her initial negative response followed by her assent when Hamlet clarifies. In F, it is this distinction between *in* and *upon* that leads to the question about *country matters*, which then crystallizes Ophelia's double bind by suggesting that she had thought unchastely in response to Hamlet's initial question. The same ambiguity may be present in the more spare Q2 version, but F's second question, which varies only slightly from the first and hence highlights the crucial change in preposition, brings that ambiguity to the fore.¹⁰²

The text of Q1 likewise focuses on the difference in prepositions emphasized in F. But from this perspective, far from being a bowdlerization of the other texts, Q1 seems to elaborate the joke even further. In both Q2 and F, Hamlet merely asks to "lie in your lap," with F Hamlet adding that he meant only to place his head upon Ophelia's lap. By contrast, as Q1 condenses F's two questions into one, Hamlet asks to "lay *my head in* your lap." Hamlet's request now may easily suggest cunnilingus, especially if tries to put his head beneath Ophelia's skirts.¹⁰³ *Head* could also indicate the glans of the penis, as Gordon Williams has extensively shown, citing several clear examples, including the satirist William Goddard's comment on a man who contracted syphilis from prostitutes: "Lost'es haire from's head? loste th'ead [the head] of you know what"; and Marlowe's translation of an Ovidian elegy describing impotence: "It mocked me, hung downe the head and sunke."¹⁰⁴ In a more debatable instance, Shakespeare himself may make the same pun in Italian. In *Troilus and Cressida*, after the lovers have spent the night together, Pandarus jokes: "a poore *chipochia*, hast not slept to night? would hee not (a naughty man) let it sleepe."¹⁰⁵ Editors have questioned which Italian word was intended, but it likely relates to the Italian *capo* (head). Since Theobald, some have emended it to *capocchio* (dullard), or imagined the feminine form *capocchia* (not otherwise attested in this sense) for application to Cressida. But Florio's *World of Words* straightforwardly defines *capocchia* as "*the foreskin or prepuce of a mans priuie member.*"¹⁰⁶

Q1 thus puts an even finer point on Hamlet's remark than the Folio. F forces the audience to focus on the difference between lying *in* and lying *on* a lap; Q1 not only includes this prepositional distinction but adds a further bawdy ambiguity on the particular part of the body (whether *head* or *penis* or both) that Hamlet wants to "lay" in Ophelia's lap. Note that in F Hamlet specifies, *I mean, my head upon your lap*, precisely to show that his meaning is innocent. Clarifying the part of the body *removes* any potentially bawdy double entendre: Hamlet means only gallantly to lie down with his head resting on Ophelia's lap. Q1 works in exactly the opposite manner: by moving *my head* from Hamlet's second line (*upon*) to his first (*in*), Q1 suggests a sexual double entendre in the very phrase that serves, in F, to remove the implication of bawdry.[107]

But while Q1 pushes even harder than F on the sexual banter about Ophelia's lap, it lacks what has been read as the most vulgar sexual reference in the entire passage. Since neither the theory that Q1 bowdlerizes *country matters* nor that *contrary matters* involves "the same pun" holds up to scrutiny, this variation remains mysterious. I have tried above to bracket questions of textual origins by simply analyzing each text as it stands, but trying to explain this mystery almost inevitably necessitates invoking some story of their coming into being. For instance, if we assume with most twentieth-century scholars that Q2 represents Shakespeare's manuscript while both F and Q1 testify somehow to the performance history of the play, then we might imagine the variation among the three texts as a fairly natural process of theatrical elaboration and revision, as experience showed what was working on stage and what was not. At each step along the way, the joke becomes more explicit. In Q2 only the phrase *lie in your lap* indicates anything untoward that could prompt Hamlet's teasing question about *country matters* (with or without a pun on the first syllable). In F the original innuendo is underscored by opposition to *upon your lap*. Finally, in Q1 the difference made by the two prepositions is intensified by relocating *my head*, thereby overtly suggesting cunnilingus while making the word pun on *penis*.

In this scenario, F might also make a sexual pun in *country matters* more apparent by drawing attention to what is "in" as opposed to "upon" Ophelia's lap. In other words, the shift from Q2 to F as part of a history of performance might allow us to watch as Shakespeare's company struggled to get across a pun on *cunt*. But if so, what is revealed is not that this pun was always there, but rather the very work that had to be done to make such a pun signify. And the substitution of *contrary* in Q1 would then suggest that the actors were never able successfully to perform this double entendre. At least temporarily, the phrase was therefore abandoned in favor of one that allowed Hamlet more clearly to ask whether Ophelia had some different (and perhaps naughty) interpretation in mind. On this reading, rather than pointing to any "popular pun on the first syllable" of *country matters*, the textual history of the passage reveals precisely its *un*popularity: the phrase was no longer wanted; it failed to signify to the people gathered at the theater. This is not bowdlerization but its opposite: the removal of *country* because it did *not* seem obscene to audiences, only obscure.

Of course, this narrative depends on one particular theory of the history of the three texts of *Hamlet*, one much closer to Collier than to Knight. Other ways of imagining the relationship of Q1 to Q2 and F would yield different understandings of this variant, such as the theory in early responses to Q1 that the actors only later foisted in the obscene *country matters*. Our interpretations of individual variants, indeed the very meanings we ascribe to individual words like *country*, are thoroughly intertwined with our larger beliefs about the origins of Q1. The belated appearance of that text in the early nineteenth century helped to fix the meaning of *country matters* in a way that is at odds with its earlier reception history, and editorial practice has since reified this interpretation into a simple definition. But the implicit theory of meaning underlying most contemporary glossing practice—that readers now need to be told the meanings of words and allusions that Shakespeare's own audience would have simply understood—is in fact belied by a "lenticular" reading of this moment in *Hamlet*.

In this way, the uncanny historicity of Q1 reveals the necessity of a theory and practice of glossing Shakespeare that is less confident in its belief that we can disclose to readers the historical "definition" of key words, as if such meaning were monolithic. An explicitly genealogical annotational practice, by contrast, would seek to incorporate into its glosses some of the historical process that has helped to shape our conception of those meanings, disclosing them as "documents that have been scratched over and recopied many times." Such glossing would not only acknowledge, along with recent studies in the history of reading, the variability and unpredictability of contemporary interpretations of a text, whether in Shakespeare's day or our own. It would also acknowledge that particular readings of the text have predominated over time, have been *made* to predominate over time, first because not all contemporary interpretations carry equal weight (as with jokes that demarcate those in the know from those excluded due to lack of wit), and second because the long history of editorial, bibliographic, and literary critical engagement with Shakespeare has itself made some readings seem obvious while ruling out others. Of course, all of this theorizing and research cannot fit into the small margins or footnotes of an edition, but then neither can the largely unstated and untheorized historicism that subtends our current glossing practice. Shifting toward a more genealogical perspective on glossing will change the annotations that are, in miniature, the end result of the underlying theory.

The power of the gloss to make certain interpretations obvious and inevitable has structured virtually all responses to Q1's *contrary* reading from the moment that Bunbury's discovery was first publicized. But the three versions of *Hamlet* are remarkably fluid here, suggesting that, whatever the textual stemma behind them, the meaning of this passage was by no means fixed in Shakespeare's own day. Some of that fluidity can productively return to our understanding of the play—if we can only forget, briefly, what we have already learned from our glosses.

CHAPTER 3

Enter the Ghost in His Night Gowne

Behind Gertrude's Bed

Hamlet's advice to the players famously expresses the potential for conflict, inherent in the nature of drama, between the play as text and the play as performance. "Let not your Clowne speake / More then is set downe," Hamlet instructs the players, urging them to stick to the script. In Q1, Hamlet himself speaks more than is set down for him in the texts of Q2 and F, elaborating on the sins of the improvisatory clown:

> And then you haue some agen, that keeps one sute
> Of ieasts, as a man is knowne by one sute of
> Apparell, and Gentlemen quotes his ieasts downe
> In their tables, before they come to the play, as thus:
> Cannot you stay till I eate my porridge? and, you owe me
> A quarters wages: and, my coate wants a cullison:
> And, your beere is sowre: and, blabbering with his lips,
> And thus keeping in his cinkapase of ieasts,
> When, God knows, the warme Clowne cannot make a iest
> Vnlesse by chance, as the blinde man catcheth a hare. . . .
> (sigs. F2r–F2v)

In Q1 the tension between text and performance is oddly encapsulated in this one speech. Hamlet begins, like his Q2 and F doppelgängers, by telling the players to keep their clown in check, but then he strangely concludes by criticizing the clown who cannot improvise, whose jests are so stale that the spectators can quote them before they are spoken. The problem with this clown is precisely that his jests have become *scripted*.¹ In the opening lines of Q1 Hamlet's address to the players, the improvisatory, occasional, and adaptive potential of performance is disparaged, and drama as text is elevated. By the end, the positions have reversed: "The latter end of his Common-wealth forgets the beginning" (*The Tempest*, F, sig. A4r). The odd vacillation in the Q1 version of this famous speech about acting highlights what is often a productive tension between the two modalities of drama.²

This tension has long shaped Shakespearean criticism and editing. Among the eighteenth-century editors, it was taken as an article of faith that the players had added to and altered Shakespeare's text as they saw fit—and always for the worse. Pope "degraded to the bottom of the page" some passages that he thought had been inserted by the players, and he placed daggers beside others as a "mark of reprobation."³ Hanmer excised the language lesson in *Henry V* because, like *country matters* after the discovery of the *contrary* reading, "that wretched piece of ribaldry . . . was foisted in by the Players . . . to please the vulgar audiences."⁴ Theobald, probably the most textually astute and sensitive Shakespearean editor before Malone, assumed that much of the textual corruption in the early editions derived from their theatrical provenance: they had "gone thro' as many Changes as Performers, either from Mutilations or Additions made to them. . . . Scenes were frequently transposed, and shuffled out of their true Place, to humour the Caprice or suppos'd Convenience of some particular Actor."⁵

If the eighteenth-century editors blamed the players for corrupting Shakespeare's text, the Romantic critics went further, viewing Shakespeare's plays as almost purely literary texts that could only suffer when materialized on stage. Coleridge "never saw any of Shakespear's plays performed, but with a degree of pain, disgust, and indignation"; Shakespeare's "proper place" was "in the heart and in the closet." Hazlitt concurred: "We do not like to see our author's plays acted, and least of all *Hamlet*. There is no play that suffers so much from being transferred to the stage."⁶ Despite the continuous popularity of *Hamlet* and other Shakespearean plays in performance from the seventeenth century on, for many editors and critics of the eighteenth and nineteenth centuries, the plays were best appreciated in print.

In the twentieth century, by contrast, scholarship has increasingly viewed Shakespeare as a man of the theater, a working playwright. What J. L. Styan called the "Shakespeare revolution" involved the intertwined principles that "the play on the stage expanding before an audience is the source of all valid discovery," that the printed texts are "blueprints for performance," and that Shakespeare himself was "a self-conscious artist working out immediate structural problems of stage communication."[7] Gary Taylor and Stanley Wells's landmark Oxford *Complete Works* can be taken as the editorial analogue of this critical movement. Based on their belief that "it is in performance that the plays lived and had their being," Taylor and Wells sought to reconstruct the plays not as they stood in Shakespeare's authorial manuscripts but "as they were acted in the London playhouses which stood at the centre of his professional life." Such an approach reverses the dominant eighteenth-century mode of editing, viewing performance as the inherent telos of drama, "the end to which they were created."[8]

And yet in many ways Shakespearean performance continues to be viewed skeptically by scholars, because the field's dominant impulse toward historicism coexists uneasily with the plays as they are realized on stage. One particular story about stage productions of *Hamlet* exemplifies this awkward relationship. The story recurs in criticism and in editions often enough to seem a scholarly tic or trope. While it is usually told as an aside or an offhand remark, this story is nonetheless central to our understandings of *Hamlet* both in Shakespeare's day and in our own. It addresses what was by far the most important interpretation of the play in the twentieth century, the Oedipal reading initiated by Freud in a brief discussion in *The Interpretation of Dreams* (1899) but only fully developed and made available to the Anglophone world by Ernest Jones, first in a 1910 article and then in 1923 as a book chapter.[9] The story has been recounted so often because it embodies a mini-drama, with its own cast of characters, that encodes a particular approach to the structural tension between dramatic text and performance. In this story, Shakespeare critics present themselves as rigorously historicist, rising above the shifting cultural trends that have influenced stage productions over the years, to inform us of Shakespeare's original intentions. Meanwhile the players, as in Hamlet's famous comment, persist in speaking more than is set down for them.

The story concerns the bed in Gertrude's closet. This stage property has become inextricably associated with the Oedipal interpretation of *Hamlet*, and scholars often digress from the main line of their argument, or include an extra annotation in their editions, to denounce its use on stage or screen as a presentist error. In what may be the archetypal version of the story, Maurice Charney claims that Shakespeare's original meaning can be discerned in his carefully precise word choice: "By the way, the Elizabethan word 'closet' means simply a private apartment, especially of a king or queen, which would distinguish it from the public rooms of the castle. It does not mean 'bed chamber,' and the ponderous marriage bed that usually dominates this scene is entirely out of place."[10] Following Charney, Hibbard includes a note in his Oxford edition: "A closet was not, it seems worth emphasizing, a bedroom. The bed, which has been so prominent in many productions over the last fifty years, made its first appearance in Gielgud's *Hamlet* as it was staged in New York in 1936."[11] Michael Cameron Andrews also emphasizes the modern assumptions behind the choice, and its infidelity to Shakespeare's intentions: he is not surprised that "an assumption which so strikingly heightens the sexual element in the play should prove congenial in an age to the Freudian manner born," but quickly adds that "the bedroom setting, however appealing, is not what Shakespeare gives us. Hamlet does not go to his mother's bedroom, but to her closet."[12] Even Jenkins, who generally avoids discussion of staging in his Arden edition, writes (with a purely rhetorical confession of ignorance): "It is hard to know why producers nowadays put this scene—so incongruously—in the Queen's bedroom."[13]

One might expect performance-oriented critics to be more amenable to changing representations of the scene, but this critical nugget is remarkably irresistible. In his book on *Hamlet* in the *Shakespeare in Performance* series, Anthony Dawson links the prop to "Laurence Olivier's flirtations with Freudianism on both stage and screen," and notes that "Oedipal interpretations of *Hamlet* have become so commonplace in our century that we now routinely expect a bed to be present in the Closet Scene, a bit of furniture that would have shocked Garrick."[14] In *Understanding Shakespeare's Plays in Performance*, Jay Halio goes further, finding Olivier's 1948 film version not just out of step with earlier performance tradition but simply incorrect: the film "erred in focusing insistently on Hamlet's attitude toward his mother, wrestling with her on a bed in the Closet Scene, for example, where no bed belongs (this is the Queen's dressing chamber, not her bedroom)."[15] Without some unspoken assumption that Shakespeare's intentions control the meaning of *Hamlet* even in twentieth-century productions, Halio's language of *erring* and *not belonging* makes no sense.[16] In a study of Shakespearean stage and screen performance, Pascale Aebischer praises a 1984 Royal Shakespeare Company production that "had the merit of not featuring a bed in the closet scene, and therefore of steering clear of the implications of incest that have been hanging like a Freudian curse over the play's performance history ever since Olivier's 1948 film."[17] And in his book on *Shakespeare in the Cinema: Ocular Proof*, Stephen M. Buhler likewise is careful to clarify that the scene takes place "in Gertrude's private room (the actual meaning of the term 'closet')," even though "the twentieth-century tradition of a very Freudian reading" instead makes "the setting not only Gertrude's bedroom but especially her bed."[18] Like Halio's remarks, Buhler's comment about the "actual meaning" of *closet* anchors the scene in Shakespeare's historical period and in his intentions for the location of the encounter between Hamlet and Gertrude. And like Charney, these performance critics appeal to the apparently self-evident nature of linguistic history: "Gertrude's closet is not her bedchamber, and the large bed we have got used to seeing in it does not belong there (see OED)"—as if reference to the *Oxford English Dictionary* could simply invalidate a contemporary performance choice.[19]

As part of these efforts to root the appearance of the bed in a modernist, Freudian moment, scholars repeatedly trace the first use of the prop, although, tellingly, they do not always agree on the specific production. Many, like Hibbard, identify Gielgud's 1936 New York production as the origin of this bit of stage business. Stanley Wells writes in *Shakespeare for All Time* that "a bed appeared on stage, apparently for the first but by no means for the last time in a New York production starring Gielgud."[20] Styan adds that, while "there never had been a bed on the London stage in the scene between Hamlet and his mother," one year after Gielgud's American *Hamlet*, Tyrone Guthrie's production starring Laurence Olivier finally brought the bed to London. But there are other candidates: Gielgud's earlier, 1930 production at the Old Vic had already "used centre curtains for the closet scene, suggesting a hidden bed," according to Styan, a detail that Gielgud's own recollections confirm.[21] In their Arden edition, Thompson and Taylor point to John Barrymore's 1922 New York production: "This scene . . . takes place in the Queen's *closet*—a private room but not a bedroom, which would have been referred to as her 'chamber'. . . . Since Barrymore gave the scene an Oedipal reading in 1922 . . . modern productions have often included a bed."[22] More recently, scholars have discovered an earlier Czech production that featured a large bed apparently used for this scene: Gary Taylor and Marvin Rosenberg both drew attention to this 1927 production in Prague, and Wells duly updated his claim for this "first" a few years after *Shakespeare for All Time*.[23] The difficulty of reconstructing the details of stage performances explains the varied claims for the origin of the bed, but the impulse to locate this "first" is central to the periodizing efforts of this scholarly narrative.

The search for the first bed onstage is accompanied by a search for the first "bedroom" in print: the moment when the "closet scene" becomes transformed in Shakespearean criticism into the "bedroom scene." Styan, Hibbard, and Wells all trace the critical currency of the "bedroom" to the influence of Ernest Jones on Dover Wilson's *What Happens in Hamlet* (1935). While Wilson himself objected to this sort of character psychoanalysis, "it was a fine testimony to the influence of Dr Jones that what had traditionally been referred to as the closet scene . . . suddenly became 'the bedroom scene' in Wilson's seventh chapter."[24] Others go back further: "No doubt A. C. Bradley, who [in *Shakespearean Tragedy* (1904)] imagined Hamlet 'in his mother's chamber beside his father's marriage bed,' helped to give this idea currency. Repeated by such distinguished Shakespeareans as E. E. Stoll and J. Dover Wilson, the 'bedroom scene' or 'bedchamber interview' . . . has become part of the accepted critical vocabulary."[25]

My point is not that this critical story is wrong in its historicizing of Gertrude's closet: in early modern aristocratic houses, the closet seems generally to have been a significantly different space from the bedroom and was unlikely to contain a bed. Indeed, as Alan Stewart has shown, the bedroom could be a far more public space than the closet.[26] In her extensive study of wills, diaries, and other documents, Lena Cowen Orlin has found some closets that contained beds, although these are a decided minority: "'my lady's closet' at Syon House in 1633," for instance, contained "a gilded couch bed, a table, a chair, and stools."[27] I am less concerned, however, with the historical facts about early modern closets than with the critical repetition of this particular critique of the bed. The insistence on this point of historical information—when numerous other anachronistic performance choices, such as modern dress, go unsanctioned—suggests that there is more at stake here than the definition of the early modern closet. Rather, the critique of the bed in the closet polices the border between text and performance, between scholarship and theatricality, between Shakespeare and the players. It is not mere prudery, I am suggesting, that leads to disavowals of the Freudian bed; far more important is that, unlike with obvious anachronisms such as modern dress, the critic imagines that the general reader or spectator will not be aware of "the actual meaning of the term 'closet'" or of the fact that "no bed belongs" there. The historicist impulse that drives this repetition enables the professional Shakespearean to "debunk" performance choices with an expertise unavailable to the masses, thereby reinscribing the authority of Shakespeare and the scholar over actors and their dramaturgy.

This critical debunking is marked by two fantasies of origin. On the one hand, the scholar returns us to Shakespeare's original intentions for this scene, conjuring a moment of purity before the players began their erring process of transforming the play on the stage, as if that process only began in the eighteenth century, or in the Restoration, or at some other moment after Shakespeare lost control of the meaning of his text. At the same time, by identifying the first use of the bed in this scene and the first critical discussion of the "bedroom scene," the scholar isolates the twentieth-century origin of this particularly errant bit of stage business. Even after the "Shakespeare revolution," the story of the bed in the closet bears a striking similarity to those early comments of Pope, Theobald, and other eighteenth-century editors about "the Players trash."

Despite its professed historicism, however, the critique falters precisely on historicist grounds. Most basically, none of the supposed "firsts" hold up to scrutiny. Well before Dover Wilson discussed the "bedroom scene," even before Bradley put Hamlet's "father's marriage bed" in "his mother's chamber," nineteenth-century writers could refer to the scene in exactly these terms. As early as 1835, a writer in *Blackwood's* referred to "the famous dialogue between Hamlet and his mother . . . in the bedroom of the Queen."[28] And in 1875, the German critic Karl Werder imagined the scene as occurring "close by the bed where [Hamlet] himself was begotten."[29]

Nor was Gielgud's 1936 stage production the first to include a bed; neither was the Prague *Hamlet* of 1927; and Styan is wrong to say that, before the Guthrie/Olivier production, "there never had been a bed on the London stage in the scene between Hamlet and his mother." In fact, when Sarah Bernhardt played Hamlet at the Adelphi Theatre in June 1899, in one of the most important and controversial productions of its day, there was a bed in Gertrude's closet (Figure 14).[30] The French translation used by Bernhardt specified the setting explicitly: "La chambre *à coucher* de la reine. . . . Vers la droite, préparé pour la nuit, le lit de la reine, drapé de courtines" ("The queen's *bedroom*. . . . To the right, made up for the night, the queen's bed, draped with curtains").[31]

Several English reviewers noted the presence of the bed, but their comments suggest that they were hardly shocked by it; indeed, it barely registered. One reviewer was far more upset by Bernhardt's decision to retain the business of Hamlet's lugging the corpse of Polonius offstage: "When Hamlet has killed Polonius in the Queen's bedroom . . . this wag of a son drags his victim away by the legs in arrant mockery." The bedroom is mentioned, but only in passing. The review in the *Times* was similarly nonchalant, admiring the stagecraft but for pragmatic reasons that had little to do with the bed: "[Gertrude's] scene with Hamlet and the preceding one in which the King is at prayer, and

The Queen, Mlle. Marcya.   *Hamlet*, Mme. Sarah Bernhardt.

Figure 14. The closet scene in Sarah Bernhardt's 1899 production featured a bed, which can be glimpsed in this contemporary image on the left behind the armchair and bed curtains (Huret, *Sarah*, 181).

Reproduced by permission of the Horace Howard Furness Memorial Library, Kislak Center for Special Collections, Rare Books and Manuscripts, University of Pennsylvania Libraries, shelf mark PN2638.B5 H8 1899.

which usually takes place in an oratory, are both played in the Royal bedchamber. This saves time and is quite as appropriate as the usual plan."[32]

These underwhelmed reactions, along with the early and mid-nineteenth-century comments, all suggest that Bernhardt's production itself may not have been the first to include a bed in this scene. In fact, the search for a theatrical "first" like this one is doomed; we lack sufficient records of stage performance to know when the prop was first used. By pointing to the bed in Bernhardt's production, then, I do not intend merely to substitute a new candidate for the old ones. Nonetheless, that bed in Gertrude's closet—there on the London stage in June 1899—is telling us something important. It cannot have been prompted by Freud's comment in *Die Traumdeutung*, which was not published until November of the same year; Ernest Jones's dissemination of the theory to the English-speaking world lay more than a decade in the future, as did the translation of Freud into English (1913) and French (1926).³³ Bernhardt's bed, in other words, is pointing us to an alternative theatrical and textual history of *Hamlet*.

This alternative history also centers on a stage property. Unlike the bed, however, this prop is explicitly called for in the text of *Hamlet*—but only after the discovery of Q1. In the years after 1823, one new (old) stage direction caused considerable controversy, at first rejected out of embarrassment, but ultimately embraced both in editorial and theatrical practice: "*Enter the ghost in his night gowne*" (sig. G2v, Figure 15). This single stage direction transformed *Hamlet* at the intersection of text and performance, leaving a profound imprint on nineteenth-century understandings of the closet scene specifically, and of the relationships among the Ghost, Gertrude, and Hamlet more generally.

If the critical nugget about the Freudian bed implies a before-and-after model of the relationship between text and performance, the uncanny historicity of Q1 *Hamlet* explodes it. Q1 is both before and after the history of *Hamlet* performance; it both predates and postdates the received text of Q2 and F that by the eighteenth century had been adapted for the stage in a series of largely traditional cuts and performance choices. "*Enter the ghost in his night gowne*" stood in the text of *Hamlet* from the very beginning, but the significance of that stage direction in the history of the play's interpretation, both on stage and in print, resulted from its belated discovery. In this pre-Freudian

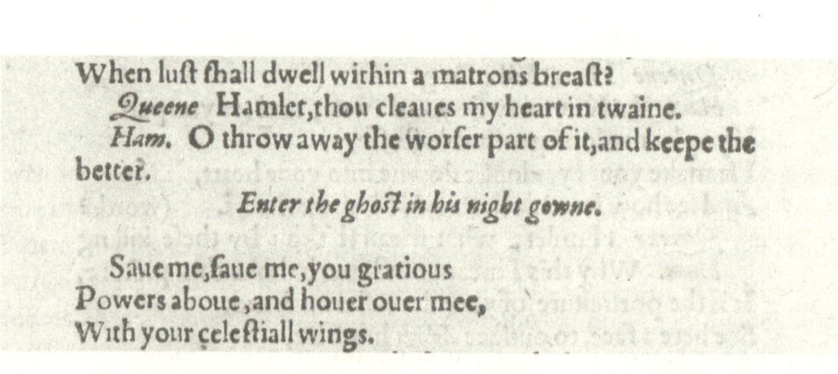

When luft fhall dwell within a matrons breaft?
Queene Hamlet, thou cleaues my heart in twaine.
Ham. O throw away the worfer part of it, and keepe the better.

Enter the ghoſt in his night gowne.

Saue me, faue me, you gratious
Powers aboue, and houer ouer mee,
With your celeftiall wings.

Figure 15. Stage direction in Q1: *Enter the ghost in his night gowne.*
Reproduced by permission of the Huntington Library, San Marino, California, shelf mark 69304.

tradition, the closet scene becomes a domesticized and sexualized encounter between Hamlet, Gertrude, and the Ghost.

I begin with the immediate reaction to this stage direction in the periodical press in London and abroad, including from no less important a Shakespearean than Goethe. The story turns on a later Victorian production, Henry Irving's immensely successful run at the Lyceum in 1874, which was both praised and fiercely criticized for costuming the Ghost in his nightgown (Figure 16). I ultimately return to Bernhardt's 1899 engagement as Hamlet, to the bed that she brought onto the London stage just as Freud was bringing *Die Traumdeutung* to press, and to the work of Bradley and Dover Wilson in disseminating the idea of the "bedroom scene." In this telling, however, that bed is called into existence not by the modern theories of Freud or Ernest Jones but rather by the long history, stretching from 1823 to 1899, of critical and theatrical engagement with this strange new *Hamlet*.

Like *contrary matters*, the Ghost's nightgown stood out immediately as a remarkable feature of this new text. While the earliest notices simply alert the reader to the novel stage direction, the nightgown rapidly became something of an embarrassment.[34] In its account of this "Dramatic Discovery," the journal *Drama* wrote sarcastically that "the *Ghost* is very punctilious with regard to costume; and enters, in the closet scene, habited in a *night-gown!*"[35] The exclamation point begins to suggest the absurdity of such garb for the Ghost, even as the idea that he is "punctilious" acknowledges simultaneously that there is in fact something unduly *appropriate* about the costume. This fitful movement from a bemused tone of mockery toward the growing recognition that the nightgown might be peculiarly fitting characterizes the history of nineteenth-century responses to the stage direction.

For most early writers, "the introduction on the stage of the ghost in Hamlet (*in his nightgown*) as [in] the old play book direction" could only be considered "ludicrous."[36] In "A Running Commentary on the Hamlet of 1603," for example, an anonymous writer who may well have been John Payne Collier foresaw that the Ghost's "night-gown and slippers would be thought too free and easy in these days of fastidious refinement."[37] The addition of slippers to the costume may be a Freudian slip, betraying some anxiety about the bathetic appearance of the Ghost in his sleepwear. If so, it was one that was shared in England's collective unconscious: Thomas Dibdin made the same mistake a few years later, noting that "amongst other oddities [in Q1], the Ghost is made to enter in his *night gown and slippers!*"[38] Dibdin's error was

Figure 16. Henry Irving (1838–1905), Shakespearean actor.
Reproduced by permission of the Philip H. Ward Collection of Theatrical Images, 1856–1910, Kislak Center for Special Collections, Rare Books and Manuscripts, University of Pennsylvania Libraries, shelf mark Ms. Coll. 331, vol. 14, item 506.

pointed out by a writer to *Notes and Queries*, whose mockery nonetheless reveals the concern that lay behind the common mistake: "The philobiblical Doctor must have allowed his imagination to work.... It is true that ... we read 'Enter the ghost in his night-gowne,' but we search in vain for the 'pantaloon'-like addition."[39] The reference to the "leane and slipper'd Pantaloone" (*As You Like It*, F, sig. R1v), a stock character in commedia dell'arte recognizable by his footwear, shows how the Ghost's new costume suddenly threatened to turn him into a figure of low comedy.

Any hint of comedy in the Ghost scenes was intolerable: eighteenth- and nineteenth-century stage tradition had excised all those lines that failed to show proper reverence to Old Hamlet. Hamlet could not be allowed to call him "old Mole," "worthy Pioner," and "this fellow in the selleredge" (F, sig. 2o1v), for example: "Is it not horrible! most repulsive to have such words set down for Hamlet to speak to his dear Father's Spirit?"[40] The closet scene in particular was a site of potential bathos that had to be carefully managed if the Ghost's second appearance was to be handled with the appropriate tone. Voltaire's critique of the play's irregularity haunted English criticism for well over a century, and his mockery of the indecorous moment in this scene when Hamlet "takes the father of his mistress for a rat, runs him throw the body" particularly stung.[41] English critics spent years responding to this French attack on their national poet, an attack that carried over to Old Hamlet as well: "The French wits have often mentioned Hamlet's ghost as an instance of the barbarism of our theatre."[42] Most English critics did agree, however, that while "the coming in of his Father's Ghost once more, adds a certain Weight and Gravity to this Scene," Hamlet's subsequent "*tugging* [Polonius] away into another Room, is unbecoming the Gravity of the rest of the Scene, and is a Circumstance too much calculated to raise a Laugh, which it always does."[43]

The majesty of the Ghost was therefore crucial to staging his scenes with the elevated tone expected of Shakespearean tragedy. And the Ghost's costume was central to his majesty. In *Some Remarks on the Tragedy of Hamlet* (1736), George Stubbes stressed the perfect decorum of bringing the Ghost onstage in armor, in a passage that lays the groundwork for much of the criticism and performance choices dealing with the Ghost through the nineteenth century:

> Many Persons wonder why the Poet should bring in this Ghost in complete Armour.... We are to consider, that he could introduce him in these Dresses only; in his Regal Dress, in a Habit of Interment, in a common Habit, or in some Phantastick one of his own

Invention. . . . The Regal Habit has nothing uncommon in it, nor surprising. . . . The Habit of Interment was something too horrible; for Terror, not Horror, is to be raised in the Spectators. The common Habit (or *Habit de Ville*, as the *French* call it) was by no Means proper for the Occasion.

It remains then, that the Poet should chuse some Habit from his own Brain: But this certainly could not be proper, because Invention in such a Case, would be so much in Danger of falling into the Grotesque, that it was not to be hazarded.

Now as to the Armour, it was very suitable to a King, who is described as a great Warrior, and is very particular, and consequently affects the Spectators, without being phantastick.[44]

Other stage ghosts, Stubbes argued, were either "ridiculous or too horrible"—a failure of decorum in one direction or the other. But the Ghost in *Hamlet* induces reverence in the audience: no other stage "Spectre is introduced with so much Majesty . . . so much Dignity . . . which creates so much Awe, and serious Attention as this does, and which raises such a Multiplicity of the most exalted Sentiments."[45] Only Shakespeare's Ghost struck the perfectly decorous note, and largely thanks to his armor.

Most critics and editors agreed. In his 1773 edition, Steevens wrote that "Shakespeare introduced his ghost in armour, that it might appear more solemn by such a discrimination from the other characters."[46] And even after the discovery of Q1, many critics writing long after 1823 chose simply to ignore the Ghost's nightgown. Across the Atlantic in 1855, for example, the University of Pennsylvania professor Henry Hope Reed discussed the Ghost exclusively as "a kingly soldier" clad in armor, "surely one of the most majestic phantoms that poetic imagination has ever realized," his movements surrounded with an aura "of awe and solemnity . . . an awful dignity brought from the regions of the dead."[47] Indeed, all the major stage productions of the play that I have been able to trace for fifty years after the discovery of Q1 continued to costume the Ghost in armor in the closet scene. Shakespearean stage tradition was extremely conservative, built on a series of traditional "points"—expected staged moments, such as Garrick's famous "start" upon first seeing the Ghost, and Hamlet's tipping over his chair when the Ghost enters in the closet scene, another point for which Garrick was renowned but which may go back to Thomas Betterton and perhaps even to Shakespeare's own day.[48] Illustrations of the closet scene show the Ghost in his armor long after 1823 (Figure 17); in promptbooks the marginal notation

Figure 17. The Ghost appears in armor in the closet scene long after the discovery of Q1, here in an edition of the 1860s. (Bowdler and Bowdler, eds., *Family*, 5.276).

Reproduced by permission of the Horace Howard Furness Memorial Library, Kislak Center for Special Collections, Rare Books and Manuscripts, University of Pennsylvania Libraries, shelf mark 90 1860b.

"truncheon" continues to appear ahead of the scene, indicating that the characteristic prop of the Ghost's armor costume should be gotten ready (Figure 18).

The fact that English theatergoers apparently had to wait so long after 1823 to see the Ghost in his nightgown, however, testifies not merely to the general conservatism of the stage in this period but also to the difficulty that the stage direction posed when it reappeared in Bunbury's closet.[49] John Payne Collier's response exemplifies the problems created by the fact that Q1 was both the first and the last *Hamlet*. Collier naturally had to reckon with this colorful stage direction, since it seemingly represented what his stenographic pirate had actually witnessed. In his 1843 edition, he noted that Q1 cleared up a debate that went back to Malone and Steevens over "whether in this scene the Ghost, as in former scenes, ought to wear armour, or to be dressed in 'his own familiar habit'." Collier thought that Q1 showed "exactly how the poet's intention was carried into effect," and that the nightgown testified "unquestionably

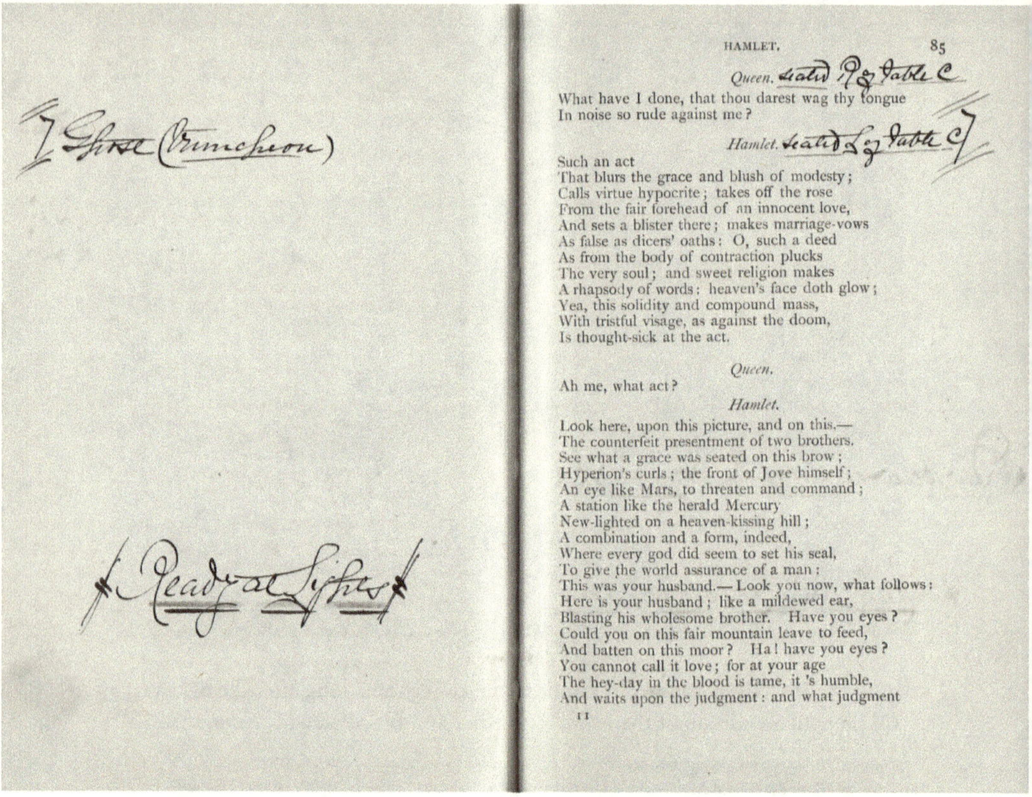
HAMLET. 85

Queen. seated R of table C

What have I done, that thou darest wag thy tongue
In noise so rude against me?

Hamlet. seated L of table C

Such an act
That blurs the grace and blush of modesty;
Calls virtue hypocrite; takes off the rose
From the fair forehead of an innocent love,
And sets a blister there; makes marriage-vows
As false as dicers' oaths: O, such a deed
As from the body of contraction plucks
The very soul; and sweet religion makes
A rhapsody of words: heaven's face doth glow;
Yea, this solidity and compound mass,
With tristful visage, as against the doom,
Is thought-sick at the act.

Queen.

Ah me, what act?

Hamlet.

Look here, upon this picture, and on this,—
The counterfeit presentment of two brothers.
See what a grace was seated on this brow;
Hyperion's curls; the front of Jove himself;
An eye like Mars, to threaten and command;
A station like the herald Mercury
New-lighted on a heaven-kissing hill;
A combination and a form, indeed,
Where every god did seem to set his seal,
To give the world assurance of a man:
This was your husband.—Look you now, what follows:
Here is your husband; like a mildewed ear,
Blasting his wholesome brother. Have you eyes?
Could you on this fair mountain leave to feed,
And batten on this moor? Ha! have you eyes?
You cannot call it love; for at your age
The hey-day in the blood is tame, it 's humble,
And waits upon the judgment: and what judgment

11

Figure 18. Prop call for a truncheon in the promptbook of Edwin Booth's *Hamlet*, from a production after 1879. (Winter, ed., *Edwin*, 85 and facing).

Reproduced by permission of the Horace Howard Furness Memorial Library, Kislak Center for Special Collections, Rare Books and Manuscripts, University of Pennsylvania Libraries, shelf mark PR2807.A2 B6 1879.

[to] the appearance of the performer of the part when the short-hand writer saw the tragedy."[50] Ten years later, however, his attitude toward the nightgown seems to have changed. In the "Perkins folio," a copy of the Second Folio in which he forged numerous supposedly seventeenth-century annotations by an "Old Corrector," Collier invented a marginal note to illuminate—or rather, undermine—the Q1 stage direction (Figure 19):

> When we have *Enter the Ghost* [on his first appearance], the word *armed* is written in parenthesis, to show what was his appearance in this scene; afterwards . . . when the Ghost makes his visit to Hamlet

Figure 19. Collier's forged annotation by his "Old Corrector" on the Ghost's entrance in the closet scene.

Reproduced by permission of the Huntington Library, San Marino, California, shelf mark 56316, sig. 2q6r.

and his mother in the closet scene, he is described in manuscript as *unarmed*, though we are not told, as in the quarto, 1603, that he is "in his night-gown." Perhaps, in consistency with what Hamlet says, he was there supposed to be "in his habit as he lived;" and when the drama was represented before the old corrector it may have been the custom of the theatre that the Ghost should come before the audience, not "in his night gown," but in his ordinary apparel.[51]

Collier's phantom Old Corrector enables him to eliminate the nightgown from early performance—at least as early as the 1630s, when the Corrector supposedly wrote his annotations.

Collier's evasion of the nightgown nonetheless demonstrates the significance that Q1 held for nineteenth-century critics. Whether Q1 was viewed as a stenographic piracy or as a rough Shakespearean sketch, the nightgown could not be completely ignored. Even for those in Collier's camp, stage directions such as this one—and other Q1-only directions about Ophelia's appearance in her mad scenes and Hamlet's leap into Ophelia's grave—retained the authority of early performance, in the days when Shakespeare himself may have acted the role of the Ghost.[52] For those who read Q1 as an authorial rough draft (however garbled in transmission), the nightgown could be traced directly to Shakespeare's hand. Unlike other aspects of the text, therefore, the novel stage directions held the same fascination for both sides of the debate over the origins of Q1. (Modern editors also often include the direction even when they view Q1 as a memorial reconstruction, on the theory that it offers a glimpse of early performance.)[53]

While theatrical tradition could for a time simply ignore the new costume, therefore, critics and editors of all stripes had to grapple with it. One main reaction to the Q1 stage direction involved the reimagination of the Ghost himself: perhaps he was not actually present in the closet scene but merely a figment of Hamlet's tormented mind. This "subjective Ghost" theory was influenced by broader trends in nineteenth-century spiritualism, which emphasized the immateriality of specters. As ideas of spirits changed, Ann Rosalind Jones and Peter Stallybrass write, the Ghost in *Hamlet* risked seeming clunky in his bodily thingness: "The more that theatrical companies attempted to capture [his] spookiness and other-worldliness . . . the more uncomfortably material appeared the Ghost's body, clothes, voice, which no amount of complex lighting or voice-distortion could erase."[54] Within this larger cultural transformation, however, the rise of the subjective Ghost is also linked to the discovery of Q1 and its nightgown. If the Ghost emerges not from his purgatorial prison house but rather from Hamlet's own mind, his costume might seem peculiarly appropriate and hence less embarrassing.

Prior to 1823, no one seems to have thought of the Ghost as any less real in the closet scene than earlier on the battlements. Gertrude's inability to see him, a prime piece of evidence for the proponents of the subjective Ghost, had been explained in various ways: Stubbes thought it "was very proper" that she not be able to see him, "for we could hardly suppose, that a Woman, and a guilty one especially, could be able to bear so terrible a Sight without the Loss of her Reason"; sometimes folk belief was marshaled to show that "this exclusive visibility" to whomever a ghost wished, whether Hamlet here or Macbeth in the banquet scene, "was an acknowledged property of spirits."[55] In the Victorian period, however, the question of whether the Ghost was real or imagined in this scene became something of a minor controversy, debated frequently if not quite on a par with the "problems" of Hamlet's madness or his delay. And belief in the subjective Ghost was often explicitly connected to his nightgown. An anonymous writer in the *Galaxy* found confirmation in the nightgown for his view that the Ghost in this scene "is an optical illusion brought before Hamlet by his excited imagination, and is not the real ghost who is visible to all eyes": for this reason, "the spectral illusion" here appears, "not in the panoply worn by the real ghost, but in the dress in which Hamlet had been in the habit of seeing his father in that very apartment."[56] Richard Grant White, the editor of the first Riverside Shakespeare (1883), similarly thought that this could not have been the Ghost, for "the ghost wore armor; but Hamlet saw his father 'in his night gown'. . . . Hamlet, in his mother's chamber, merely fancied that he saw his father dressed as he had often seen him there in his lifetime."[57]

This line of reasoning had become so familiar by the later nineteenth century that the connection between the new costume and the new theory could be taken for granted: a review of an 1873 production at the Crystal Palace could write that the Ghost's appearance "in royal robes" in the closet scene—both in his portrait and on stage—was "of course" motivated by the idea that he "is purely subjective . . . [and] hence he will appear as Hamlet has last imagined him, that is, as he is painted on the panel." For this reviewer, however, the production did not go far enough, since if the Ghost is subjective, "why introduce [him] at all?"[58] The American editor Henry Norman Hudson likewise wrote that "for this reason I have long thought that the introduction of the Ghost on the stage in this scene ought to be discontinued."[59] For some critics, the subjective ghost theory allowed for the disappearance of the Ghost and his nightgown from Gertrude's closet entirely. But the efforts of these writers to persuade stage managers to convert the Ghost into an ethereal offstage voice were largely unsuccessful, and the majority of critical opinion turned against the subjective theory.[60] Nonetheless, the relocation of the Ghost from the stage to Hamlet's mind, prompted in part by the discovery of this new stage direction in Q1, may have helped to prepare for the Freudian interpretation by rooting this important moment in the play within Hamlet's diseased imagination.

By far the most successful approach to grappling with the nightgown, however, and the one that leads directly to the appearance of a bed in Gertrude's closet, begins with Goethe. Not with *Wilhelm Meister* (1795–96), in which Goethe elaborated his theory of the play that dominated criticism for centuries, but with an obscure, brief article he wrote about Q1 shortly before his death. In *Wilhelm Meister*, published prior to the discovery of Q1, Goethe could only imagine the Ghost's costume in the traditional manner: in the portrait hanging in Gertrude's closet, "the former King must be clad in armour, like the Ghost, and hang at the side where it enters . . . so that it might perfectly resemble the Ghost at the moment when he issues from the door."[61] When Q1 was reprinted in Leipzig in 1825, Goethe had the opportunity to revise his ideas, already hugely influential, and to his credit he did so immediately.

"The first unbiased reading" of Q1, Goethe reported, "has given me a wonderful impression." One of the passages that struck him, as it struck most early readers, was the new stage direction. Goethe initially responds by finding the costume just as ludicrous as most English writers did, but he quickly changes his mind:

> Who, on first hearing this [stage direction], does not find it for a moment incongruous? And yet if we grasp it, if we think it over, we shall find it right and proper. He should—indeed he must—appear first in armor, when he is entering the place where he has rallied his warriors, where he has encouraged them to noble deeds. And now we begin to be less confident of our conviction that it was suitable to see him enter the private closet of the queen in armor, too. How much more private, homelike, terrible, is his entrance here in the form in which he used to appear—in his house apparel, his night robe, harmless and unarmed—a guise which in itself stigmatizes in the most piteous way the treachery which befell him. Let the intelligent reader, as he may, picture this to himself. Let the stage-manager, convinced of this effect, produce it in this way, if Shakespeare is to be staged in his integrity. . . .
>
> If we had been clever enough, we should have already thought of Hamlet's first utterance in this scene, when he sees the Ghost: —"What would your gracious figure?" For we have not words enough to express all that the English mean by the word "gracious,"—everything that is kind and gentle, friendly and benign, tender and attractive, is fused in that word. Certainly it is no term for a hero in armor.[62]

The brilliance of Goethe's analysis—written as a kind of palinode for his earlier "conviction that it was suitable to see him enter the private closet of the queen in armor"—lies in its transformation of a perceived fault into a Shakespearean beauty. Forthrightly eschewing Voltairean neoclassical strictures about tragic decorum, Goethe finds the Ghost's appearance here more powerful precisely because he now appears in a "more private," more domestic or "homelike" (*häuslicher*) guise. Indeed, Goethe chastises himself for not having previously divined this costume from Hamlet's description of his father's "figure" in this scene as "gracious," a word that for Goethe embodies all the tenderness of the domestic, as opposed to the heroic, Ghost.

In the Ghost's prosaic nightgown, in other words, Goethe finds a Romantic beauty that surpasses the dignity he had earlier imagined the Ghost to possess in his armor. Seen from a neoclassical perspective as indecorous, the nightgown is here recoded as the kind of irregularity that Coleridge argued was characteristic of modern or romantic drama. Its quaint domesticity offers the kind of detail that Schlegel praised in Shakespeare, who contained an "inexhaustible supply of what is interesting," and the homely costume thus becomes part of the local and rooted "customs, views, language, national attitudes, traditions and pastimes" from which, according to Herder, organic art springs.[63] Goethe concludes that to stage Shakespeare "in his integrity"—that is, to produce *Hamlet* in its "organic" form rather than with the "mechanical regularity" that Coleridge derided as "impress[ing] a predetermined form, not necessarily arising out of the properties of the material"—one must stage the Ghost in his nightgown.[64] It is not surprising, therefore, that another influential German Romantic Shakespearean, Ludwig Tieck, took Goethe at his word in a Dresden production that may have been the first staging after the discovery of Q1 to show the Ghost in his new costume.[65]

The authority of Goethe's name may have helped to justify the nightgown to English audiences, already familiar with his interpretation of the play in *Wilhelm Meister*, or at least with his famous metaphor of the oak tree growing in a delicate vase. Some English writers certainly knew Goethe's take on the nightgown and disseminated its ideas to their own readers. In 1849, for instance, the *Edinburgh Review* discussed the article and found it "conclusive," before exclaiming in some distress: "But what would Voltaire have said to a Ghost in his night-gown!"[66] By mid-century, the nightgown could occasionally be justified by its fitness for a domestic scene, whether or not the critic had read Goethe's article on Q1: while discussing Hamlet's madness, for instance, John Charles Bucknill wrote in passing that "it seems an error to put the Ghost on the stage clad in armour on this second occasion," since the nightgown "would be suited to the place, even as the *cap-à-pie* armament to the place of warlike guard."[67] It can be difficult to determine whether a comment like this has been influenced by Goethe's lesser-known writing on *Hamlet*. Tieck's German production may have been directly influenced by Goethe, but the first major London production to include the Ghost in his nightgown seems not to have been.[68] Rather, this *Hamlet* and the manager-actor who produced it were heavily invested in the same kind of "homeliness" that Goethe highlights in the nightgown, less for reasons of Romantic philosophy than of Victorian domesticity.

Henry Irving's contemporary biographer defined the actor's approach by opposition to a famous remark Coleridge made about Edmund Kean: "Kean read Shakespeare by flashes of lightning; Mr. Irving reads him by the student's midnight oil. He is great in new glosses and daring in conjectural emendations."[69] Irving's "highly intelligent" and "thoughtful" approach to the play was frequently noted in reviews.[70] And indeed, Irving himself could write the occasional bit of textual criticism: "The text tells us that [Hamlet] knew he was being watched from the first [in 3.1], for in the quartos of 1603 and 1604 (the complete play) Hamlet enters before the *exeunt* words of Polonius to the King."[71] It is not surprising, therefore, that Irving would be drawn to a unique stage direction in Q1.

It has been said that Irving ran the Lyceum Theatre like "the classic Victorian father, patriarchal, authoritarian, relentlessly attentive to the details that shape lives."[72] Certainly his landmark staging of *Hamlet* in 1874 displayed both this attention to detail and this aura of patriarchal domesticity. The production was both lauded and attacked for the unprecedented realism of its décor, even in a theatrical era when realistic scenery was often taken to extremes. Irving's set was a decidedly homey one: many critics praised him for dispensing with "the gloomy grandeur of a conventional atmosphere" and instead bringing the play "within the range of domestic feeling." The design was "regal, but eminently domestic . . . the apartments of the palace all look habitable. . . . The *habitués* move about as if they were at home, and at night they light themselves with torches."[73] Other reviewers objected to these details, especially those torches and "chamber candlesticks": "It may be thought, perhaps, that the scene thus becomes more real; but these details tend to vulgarise poetic tragedy, which should occupy ground removed from the trivialities and the homeliness of ordinary life."[74] Whether praising or blaming, virtually all contemporary writers on Irving's *Hamlet* reacted strongly to the emphasis on "the homeliness of ordinary life." And at the heart of this homeliness were the closet scene and the Ghost's nightgown.

In stressing the domestic aspects of *Hamlet*, Irving was elaborating a trend that, in some ways, went back to Betterton. In most eighteenth- and nineteenth-century productions, a series of cuts had focused attention on the central revenge plot set at Elsinore castle. Fortinbras was often entirely eliminated, as was most of the dialogue involving the ambassadors, as well as Hamlet's recounting of his sea voyage to England. The final curtain usually fell on Hamlet's dying words or on Horatio's eulogy immediately following. Through these choices and others, the *Hamlet* that Victorians encountered in the theater was shorn of much of its political and international context, the better to center the play on Hamlet and his mental deliberations.[75] This domesticating trend thus preceded the discovery of Q1 and the Ghost's nightgown, but Irving "extended the rather cosy domesticity that productions throughout the century had exhibited" in new directions.[76] These production choices turned Irving's *Hamlet* into a blockbuster—it ran for two hundred consecutive performances—and they have had a lasting influence on our understanding of the play.

Like Goethe, Irving revalued as a beauty the perceived fault in the nightgown, its seemingly bathetic evocation of a domestic old gentleman in his sleeping clothes. In the ridiculed stage direction, Irving found the centerpiece of his production. While he may not have read Goethe's essay on Q1, Irving was himself a Romantic actor—his grandson claimed that he embodied the "ideal of the long-awaited romantic actor" of the Victorian age—and he was dedicated to overturning the declamatory style of neoclassical acting. His stagings were "picturesque," emphasizing "the particular, the familiar, the idiosyncratic."[77] Not surprisingly, then, Goethe's remark that the Ghost's nightgown is "much more private, homelike" is echoed by reviewers' praise of Irving for setting *Hamlet* within "the homeliness of ordinary life."

In all of his acting and staging choices, Irving sought to "naturalize" the play, to remove it from what he and many of his contemporaries saw as an encrusted stage tradition. Reviewers stressed "his utter disregard of conventionality": "Mr. Irving's Hamlet is to be regarded as a consistent whole not to be measured by the number or force of his points"; the performance "shows the final abandonment of old traditions of acting and of conventions of declamation."[78] Irving delivered his first soliloquy casually, for instance, "while lounging over the back of a seat," a choice the *Graphic* applauded: "Surely it is much more likely that a man who is supposed to be alone should adopt this unconstrained posture for his broken utterances than that he should stand up like a schoolboy reciting a birthday ode."[79] As a result of his thorough rejection of stage tradition, Irving made Hamlet visible not as a disjointed series of actorly effects but as a real person: "When I reflect on the performance of this evening, the very last things that occur to me are those isolated points. . . . I look upon Mr. Irving's Hamlet as a personage in whose joys and sorrows I can readily participate."[80]

Such comments need to be contextualized, because, as Joseph Roach has stressed, every generation "prides itself . . . on being able to view theatrical exhibitions of human feeling that are more realistic and natural than those of the previous age," and "each acting style and the theories that explain and justify it are right and natural for the historical period in which they are developed and during which they are accepted."[81] Complaints against the tradition of stage points go back as far as the tradition itself. What is important here is not whether Irving discovered a more naturalistic style than Booth or Kean or Garrick before him but rather *why* Irving's contemporaries perceived his acting as naturalistic. A large part of this effect was due to his insistently domestic design. The *Daily News* thought Irving's Hamlet embodied a "bourgeois cordiality," a phrase that goes some way toward explaining why the production struck the late Victorian audience at the Lyceum, which had become England's unofficial national theater, as unprecedentedly realistic.[82] At the Lyceum, Irving's "ideology of the domestic—the Englishman's castle-like home where the father's benevolent rule made possible the private cultivation of every member of the bourgeois family"—was comfortably familiar to the audience.[83] The overwhelming praise of Irving's naturalism, in other words, is merely the flip side of the minority of reviews that saw the "homeliness" of the chamber candlesticks and other "trivialities" in his production as "vulgaris[ing] poetic tragedy."

This domesticity was rooted above all in the closet scene, which used the only box set that Irving constructed for the production, highlighting its central importance. Virtually all reviews discussed this scene, which Irving made the play's emotional climax, and they generally noted the landmark use of the nightgown: "For the first time the *Ghost* entered the *Queen's* closet, not clad in a suit of mail, but with flowing robes, 'his habit as he lived.'"[84] Inspired by this stage direction, Irving extended the domestic tone of the scene far beyond the Ghost's costume. He entered with one of the "chamber candlesticks" to which some critics objected, as if lighting his way through the hallways of a Victorian home, and at the close of the scene, "Hamlet, with real attention, lights [another] and hands [it] to his mother."[85] Not only did the Ghost wear a nightgown, Georgina Pauncefort, who played Gertrude, was also costumed in "night-drapery": she wore a flannel nightgown in the 1874 original production, which was altered to red and yellow robes in the 1878 revival. These robes were apparently meant to be more regal, since critics had objected to "the billowing hither and thither" of Gertrude's nightgown in 1874, but they too were simply read as a "night-gown" by some reviewers.[86] A fire was lit in the room, and there was apparently even more "night-gear, evidently airing at the fire," according to Margaret Oliphant's hostile review of the revival.[87] Despite her scorn, however, Oliphant's sarcastic gibes at the production amply reveal how successful Irving was at suggesting domesticity in this scene: "When, with a rush, a venerable gentleman in familiar domestic costume came on the stage, shaking it with substantial footsteps, the idea of the ghost did not present itself at all to our dull imagination; and it was impossible to avoid the natural idea that the lady's husband, hearing an unaccountable commotion in the next room, had jumped out of bed, seized his dressing-gown, and rushed in to see what was the matter."[88]

Oliphant was in the minority in her judgment of the show, as its unprecedented run and revival attest, but she grasped perfectly the dominant thread of Irving's interpretation. In his preface to the promptbook version of Irving's production, Frank Marshall stressed that the setting for the closet scene was "an ante-room to [Gertrude's] bed chamber," so that the Ghost exited "through the door leading into the bed-chamber, just as he might have done in his life-time; that chamber which has been desecrated by the faithless Queen."[89] Many other spectators similarly inferred that the royal bedchamber was just beyond the door through which the Ghost appeared and exited, an inference that Irving encouraged by restoring a line and a reference to the marriage bed that had traditionally been cut for its vulgarity: "Nay, but to live / In the rank sweat of an enseamed bed."[90]

In Irving's interpretation, which he seems to have been remarkably effective at conveying to spectators, it was Gertrude's desecration of her marriage bed, and of marriage and family more generally, that had caused Hamlet's melancholy.[91] Her betrayal of Hamlet's father led her son to question all women and indeed love itself; Irving wrote that "Hamlet's mother's beauty had been her snare, had tempted her adulterous lover," and this recognition underlay Hamlet's harshness to Ophelia in the nunnery scene.[92] One reviewer was so persuaded by Irving's production choices, that, rather like A. C. Bradley after him, he was led to imagine Hamlet's character before this betrayal and before the play began: at that time, Hamlet "watches with the unmixed enjoyment of a chaste and filial adolescence the conjugal happiness of his parents."[93] The foundation of Hamlet's "problem" was not the traditional Romantic view that his meditative mind was unsuited to the heroic action placed upon him; instead, the violation of familial domesticity had unsettled him.

Consequently, Gertrude was portrayed as a somewhat conventional Victorian "fallen woman," as implied in Irving's own comments about her beauty being her snare. She was a "weak, sensuous, affectionate" woman, "more sinned against than sinning."[94] Irving's choice is part of a long critical tradition in which, in Lisa Jardine's words, "blame for the incestuous marriage entered into by Old Hamlet's brother, Claudius, is passed across to Gertrude as if she were its instigator."[95] Thus Gertrude (or rather, her beauty) is the agent in Irving's comment that she "had tempted her adulterous lover." But in Irving's production we can also see the influence of the other major dramatic genre for which he was famous: melodrama. Indeed, one hostile reviewer believed that

Irving's extensive prior experience in that genre had infected his Hamlet: "The truth is that Mr. Irving's Hamlet . . . is a melodramatic performance."[96] With Gertrude as a fallen woman who had desecrated the family and home, the Ghost's appearance in the closet was now "mainly directed towards the thorough awakening of the Queen's conscience, so as to bring her to repentance," rather than to whet Hamlet's almost blunted purpose.[97] Hamlet's own mission too was the redemption of his mother's feminine virtue: "Hamlet's beseeching of his mother . . . is affecting beyond measure. . . . Here, with a mother to save from sin and destruction, there is nothing left of the son's antic disposition."[98] Irving thus seems to have used the closet scene as the centerpiece of "the conventional melodramatic pattern—the expiation of guilt followed by a kind of secularized apotheosis or revolution of the spirit."[99]

In what now became the denouement of the play, Hamlet redeems his mother, who rejects Claudius and reasserts the superiority of her first husband; with this solace, Hamlet is now prepared to take revenge in the last act.[100] For one reviewer, if grasped "in the full significance of the relations between Hamlet and Gertrude, which Irving helps us to perceive," the scene restored Hamlet's childhood faith in his family: "A son kneeling where he said his first prayers, to implore the mother who taught him to lisp them to forsake her sin, is an incident worthy of the greatest poet, and only to be fitly enacted by the greatest of tragic actors."[101] Now as never before, Gertrude's choice of Old Hamlet over Claudius brought about her redemption and Hamlet's peace. While previous Hamlets had refused their mothers' offered blessing at the close of the scene, Irving's "Hamlet kneels and casts his head upon his mother's lap."[102]

But Irving went even further to emphasize the restored family in this scene, introducing a startlingly original bit of stage business to bring all three family members together.[103] As the Ghost exited, and Hamlet implored, "Look where he goes even now out at the portal," Georgina Pauncefort's Gertrude became "so worked upon by the horror of the situation" that the Ghost briefly became "visible to her as well as to her son," and she gave a "terrific shriek" as she caught a glimpse of her dead husband.[104] This expression of horror and guilt neatly reunited the original, defiled family, gave voice to Gertrude's repentance, and prepared the emotional ground for her blessing of her son. Most earlier critics had followed George Stubbes in explaining the Ghost's invisibility to Gertrude by her guilt: "We could hardly suppose, that a Woman, and a guilty one especially, could be able to bear so terrible a Sight without the Loss of her Reason." Irving had Gertrude momentarily pierce the Ghost's invisibility, expiating that guilt to transform her from the fallen woman led astray by passion to the redeemed mother who has properly recognized her familial duty.

With this familial restoration, Hamlet could at last take action. Irving cut virtually all of act 4—except for Ophelia's mad singing, the report of her death, and parts of the scenes in which Claudius and Laertes plot Hamlet's death—and the entire scene in act 5 in which Hamlet recounts to Horatio his adventures aboard ship. In this way, he pushed the momentum quickly forward toward the graveyard scene and the final duel, thereby urging audiences to understand the closet scene as the play's denouement.[105] Here too he departed from traditional Romantic interpretations of the play. For Goethe, Schlegel, and Coleridge, it was precisely the plot twists that Irving eliminated—Hamlet's journey to England, his inspired decision to alter the commission, and his capture by pirates—that revealed the play's ultimate meaning. Earlier critics had criticized the progression of the action in the latter part of the play: Samuel Johnson complained that Hamlet became "rather an instrument than an agent," and it was widely agreed that the "plot of this [play], is rather irregularly carried on, and the winding up exceeding lame."[106] In keeping with this tradition, Goethe's Serlo tells Wilhelm that the "English themselves have admitted that [the play's] chief interest concludes with the third act; the last two lagging sorrily on, and scarcely uniting with the rest." But Wilhelm pointedly rejects this view: "Poets and historians would willingly persuade us that" man may attain his ends by "acting on his own strength," since this idea "flatters us," but in *Hamlet* "we are taught another lesson: the hero is without a plan, but the piece is full of plan. . . . Neither earthly nor infernal thing may bring about what is reserved for Fate alone."[107] Coleridge argued similarly that "Shakespeare wished to shew how even such a character is at last obliged to be the sport of chance, a salutary moral doctrine"; the twists and turns of the later acts reveal that Hamlet, "after still resolving, and still deferring," finally "give[s] himself up to his destiny." And Schlegel found a profound mystery in the seemingly haphazard events of the last two acts: "The destiny of humanity is there exhibited as a gigantic Sphinx, which threatens to precipitate into the abyss of scepticism all who are unable to solve her dreadful enigmas."[108]

Irving downplayed this kind of Romantic philosophical take on the "enigma" of *Hamlet*. The idea of *Hamlet* as a Sphinx that threatens to plunge us into skepticism was incompatible with the melodramatic Manichaeism typically on display at Irving's Lyceum, the habit of drawing bright lines between good and evil, often embodied within a single divided character who longs "for innocence and absolution."[109] Importantly, Irving also moved away from a common Christianized version of this interpretation that imagined these events as providential, with Hamlet "falling into his proper place in God's great order and government of the world."[110] Instead, drawing on his understanding of the power of melodrama, Irving located the heart of Hamlet's mystery firmly within the domestic family; the drama centered on the Ghost's revelation of domestic secrets and Hamlet's purification of his contaminated family through the reformation of his fallen mother. The Ghost's nightgown both enabled and epitomized this approach for Irving and for many of his reviewers. The effect was to transform the trajectory and meaning of the play, rooting Hamlet's "problem" not in his overactive imagination and underactive will but rather in the psychic effects of his torturous relationship to his family and, in particular, to his mother. "The essential emotion of the play," as T. S. Eliot wrote in 1919, "is the feeling of a son towards a guilty mother."[111] We might call this a shift from Romanticism to Modernism, or from Coleridge to Freud—if not for the odd fact that it predates Freud's interpretation.

In her mockery of the domesticity of Irving's production and particularly of his adoption of the Ghost's nightgown, Margaret Oliphant offered what should by now be a familiar critique: "After all, it is not the queen's bedroom, but only some boudoir *appartenant*."[112] Her invocation of this critical nugget in itself suggests the hidden lineage from the nineteenth-century discovery of Q1 to what has been seen by critics as an exclusively modern, post-Freudian stage property. As we have seen, many reviewers of Irving's *Hamlet* were led by the nightgown and other domestic touches to imagine that the queen's bedroom lay just beyond the door through which the Ghost exited. But some critics went further: they saw the Ghost's nightgown and imagined that the scene was in fact set in the queen's bedroom. In a review of "Shakespeare on the German Stage" published shortly after Irving's 1878 revival, a writer in the *Academy* compared a recent production in Munich to "that of the Lyceum Theatre." He found the German production much inferior: not only did it fail to clothe the Ghost in his nightgown—"the Ghost appears again in full armour"—but "the eye was again offended by the two pictures on the wall of *the Queen's bed-chamber*."[113] While focusing on Irving's choice to have the portraits of Old Hamlet and Claudius exist only in the mind's eye, the reviewer casually refers to the setting as a bedroom.[114] Here we can see clearly how meditation on the Ghost's nightgown could lead spectators and critics into the Queen's bedroom.

Whether they were positive or negative, and wherever exactly they placed the Queen's bedroom in relation to Irving's box set, all of these contemporary reactions show how the heightened domesticity of this scene affected their understanding of its meaning. And that meaning was clearly sexual, although not quite in the Oedipal sense that we have come to associate with the idea of the closet as a bedroom. Irving's quasi-official critic Frank Marshall wrote that the Ghost was clad, "as the stage direction has it in the first Quarto (1603), '*in his night gowne,*' as if he were going to the bed that his wife had so cruelly dishonoured." The appearance at this moment "of the reproachful spirit of his father may well recall to Hamlet the solemn injunction laid upon him at their first meeting:— 'Let not the royal bed of Denmark be / A couch for luxury and damnèd incest.'"[115] Other reviews drew attention to precisely the same lines when commenting on the Ghost's appearance in his nightgown and his exit "through the door of . . . the Queen's bedchamber."[116]

The Ghost's nightgown suggests incest, in other words, but not the Freudian version. Note how close these remarks are, however, to Bradley's *Shakespearean Tragedy*, published six years before Jones's initial essay on *Hamlet* and nine years before Freud's *Interpretation of Dreams* appeared in English translation: "[Hamlet's] whole mind is poisoned. He can never see Ophelia in the same light again: she is a woman, and his mother is a woman. . . . He can do nothing. He must lock in his heart, not any suspicion of his uncle that moves obscurely there, but that horror and loathing; and if his heart ever found relief, it was when those feelings, mingled with the love that never died out in him, poured themselves forth in a flood as he stood in his mother's chamber beside his father's marriage bed."[117] Like Irving, Bradley sees Hamlet's broken family and specifically his disillusion with his mother as the foundation of his despair, infecting his relationship with Ophelia. He views the situation in similarly melodramatic terms: Hamlet's "chief desire . . . is to save [Gertrude's] soul. . . . No father-confessor could be more selflessly set upon his end of redeeming a fellow creature from degradation." Gertrude's role as the fallen woman is overt in Bradley's rhetoric: "Though Hamlet hates his uncle and acknowledges the duty of vengeance, his whole heart is never in this feeling or this task; but his whole heart is in his horror at his mother's fall and in his longing to raise her." And as in Irving's production, Bradley imagines that the Ghost appears in the closet scene not to urge Hamlet to revenge but rather out of "the same tender regard for his weak unfaithful wife" as when, in his first appearance, he urged Hamlet not to contrive against her.[118]

For Bradley too the closet scene is the emotional climax of the play, and it provides the cathartic release and expiation of guilt that enables Hamlet

Figure 20. Sarah Bernhardt (1844–1923) poses as Hamlet for a publicity photo.

Reproduced by permission of the Philip H. Ward Collection of Theatrical Images, 1856–1910, Kislak Center for Special Collections, Rare Books and Manuscripts, University of Pennsylvania Libraries, shelf mark Ms. Coll. 331, vol. 5, item 149.

finally to act. Like many reviewers of Irving's *Hamlet*, Bradley's discussion of this scene leads him to imagine that it takes place "beside his father's marriage bed"—the bed that must not become "a couch for luxury and damned incest" and that is conjured by Irving's crucial restoration of Hamlet's anguished cry about "the rank sweat of an enseamed bed." And like Irving, Bradley moved away from the Romantic idea that Hamlet's meditative, sensitive nature prevents him from acting, arguing instead that Hamlet suffered from a melancholy particular to his situation and deriving from his mother's betrayal.[119]

Shortly before he took up the post at Oxford that would lead to *Shakespearean Tragedy*, Bradley may well have seen the most important production of *Hamlet* to follow Irving's: Bernhardt's hugely discussed and debated 1899 performance at the Adelphi (Figure 20).[120] The royal bed that had been summoned up in the mind's eye in Irving's production, rather like the portraits of Old Hamlet and Claudius, was physically present on stage at the Adelphi. We can now better understand why reviewers of that staging were by no means outraged by the appearance of this bed, as modern critics have been. While this may have been the first time a bed had actually appeared in the closet scene on the London stage—although it also may *not* have been, for all we know—nonetheless the idea that the scene occurs in "the Queen's bedchamber," or at least that the royal bed was just barely beyond the "portal" through which the Ghost disappears, was hardly new.

While it is not clear that Bernhardt ever saw Irving's production of *Hamlet*, there is considerable evidence that she was influenced by him. The two were good friends; their relationship began in 1879 when Bernhardt toured London with the troupe of the Comédie-Française, arriving just after Irving's revival closed, and it "continued over the years, with Sarah Bernhardt's attending performances at the Lyceum whenever she was in London." Since Bernhardt's letters to Irving demonstrate how often she sought his advice about theatrical matters, her biographer Gerda Taranow concludes that it is likely she would have "discussed all aspects of [*Hamlet*] with an actor who had become a close and admired professional friend."[121] In fact, there is some evidence of direct influence on the text, because Bernhardt's production, like Irving's but unlike most other nineteenth-century productions, retained Hamlet's key line about "the rank sweat of an enseamed bed": "Non! mais vivre dans la puante sueur d'un lit gras."[122] Whether or not Irving and Bernhardt discussed the closet scene, however, the bed onstage at the Adelphi was fully in keeping with the domestic emphasis of Irving's production.

If we now reexamine Dover Wilson's comment on this scene in *What Happens in Hamlet*, often erroneously claimed as the first to discuss the "bedroom scene" under the influence of Freud and Jones, we can see more clearly the influence of this alternate lineage: "But though the Ghost comes his 'tardy son to chide', Shakespeare, we can be sure, wished us to see more in his advent than this. The scene is in the Queen's bedchamber; the spirit of King Hamlet appears in his dressing-gown; it is the first and only meeting, since death and worse than death had separated them, of the royal family of Denmark; and the words that follow the rebuke show that the father's visitation is as much on the wife's behalf as on the son's."[123] Here Wilson brings together all of the elements that Irving had highlighted in his production: the Q1 stage direction; the climactic reunion of "the royal family of Denmark"; Gertrude as a "fallen woman" who must be saved from sin; and the Ghost as a loving spirit seeking to effect this salvation, his visitation designed primarily to awaken the conscience of the Queen.[124]

Tracing Wilson's debt to late nineteenth-century Shakespearean productions may clarify his argument more than any reference to Freud, despite how it appears to critics writing in the wake of the twentieth-century dominance of the Oedipal interpretation. In the introduction to *What Happens in Hamlet*, after all, Wilson had explicitly rejected the argument of Jones's early essays, and he reiterated that critique in the third edition (1951) in response to Jones's elaboration of his argument in *Hamlet and Oedipus* (1949). While he admitted that Jones's book was "brilliant," he "remained unshaken" in his critique: "It is entirely misleading to attempt to describe Hamlet's state of mind in terms of modern psychology at all, not merely because Shakespeare did not think in these terms, but because—once again—Hamlet is a character in a play, not in history."[125] But if in Wilson's view Shakespeare could not think like Freud, he could apparently think like Henry Irving. And Henry Irving could think as he did because of the discovery of Q1 and its revelatory stage direction.

After excavating this forgotten lineage for the bed in Gertrude's closet—a genealogy that derives from the discovery of Q1 in 1823—we can return to the Q1 of 1603 without the presuppositions that may have blinded us to evidence that does not fit our conventional wisdom that the bed is a purely modern, post-Freudian invention. In fact, several early texts that constellate around *Hamlet* place a bed in the closet right from the beginning. Bernice Kliman has drawn attention to the engraving of the closet scene in the second edition of Rowe's Shakespeare (1714).[126] The more well-known engraving in the 1709 first edition shows Gertrude seated in a chair, the ghost appearing in full armor, and Hamlet standing in a startled position, with his own chair lying on its side (Figure 21). This image has long been taken as a representation of Betterton's actual stage practice, since the chair-tipping seems to have been one of his "points."[127] The revised version of the illustration that was included in the second edition, however, includes a prominent bed (Figure 22). Kliman does not see any theatrical connection in the 1714 engraving, but we cannot be sure: it *might* represent the engraver's memory of some actual production, after all.

Either way, the bed apparently seemed appropriate enough to the scene for the engraving to be reused (in reverse and slightly altered) four years later as the frontispiece to the "Players' Duodecimo" edition of the play "As it is now Acted by his MAJESTY's Servants" (Figure 23). Since the edition states explicitly that its text reflects performance, it is at least worth considering whether the image might do so as well. And even if the scene is purely imaginary, it nonetheless offers clear evidence that someone familiar with the play, less than a century after Shakespeare's death, thought there was—or perhaps, ought to be—a bed in this scene.

And, in fact, the bed goes back earlier than this, directly to the origin of *Hamlet*. While Polonius hides behind an arras in Shakespeare's version, in Saxo the councillor is concealed under the *stramentum*, which might merely indicate rushes strewn on the floor, but could also mean a quilt or mattress stuffed with straw. Belleforest is less ambiguous: there the councillor hides "sous quelque loudier"; the preposition *sous* almost certainly indicates that the *loudier* or quilt is a bedspread rather than a wall hanging.[128] In a sense, the bed in the closet has been there all along; rather than being dragged on stage by twentieth-century Freudians, it is among the possibilities Shakespeare had before him as he worked through his source materials. Since he made his own councillor hide behind a wall hanging, we might assume that he chose to eliminate the bed from the scene, or that it had already been eliminated by the time he took up the play. And indeed in all the other texts surrounding the *Hamlet* play—including *Der bestrafte Brudermord* and *The Hystorie of Hamblet*—Polonius hides behinds tapestries or hangings; Corambis in Q1 likewise says that he "will stand behind the Arras" (sig. F1v) or "shrowde my selfe behinde the Arras" (sig. G2v). Finally, when playwrights wanted a bed, they generally wrote it into the opening stage direction for the scene (although they rarely indicated how it would "exit"), and no such direction appears in any *Hamlet* text.[129] For all these reasons, it seems clear that a decision was made to revise the sources of the play to eliminate this bed.

Figure 21. Engraving of the closet scene in Rowe, ed., *Works* (1709), 5.2365 facing.
Reproduced by permission of the Horace Howard Furness Memorial Library, Kislak Center for Special Collections, Rare Books and Manuscripts, University of Pennsylvania Libraries, shelf mark PR2752.R8 1709.

Figure 22. Engraving of the closet scene, including a bed, in Rowe, ed., *Works* (1714), 6.301 facing.

Reproduced by permission of the Folger Shakespeare Library, shelf mark PR2752 1714a Copy 2 Sh.Col.

Figure 23. Frontispiece engraving of the closet scene, including a bed, in the "Players' Duodecimo" edition of *Hamlet* (1718).

Reproduced by permission of the Horace Howard Furness Memorial Library, Kislak Center for Special Collections, Rare Books and Manuscripts, University of Pennsylvania Libraries, shelf mark C94.13 1718.

And yet, in other ways, the text of Q1 strongly prompts us to imagine the scene occurring in the Queen's bedroom. Oddly, whether it was Shakespeare or a reporter or someone else, whoever was responsible for writing the text of Q1 writes out the bed with one hand, while writing it back in with the other. As Alan Dessen and Leslie Thomson show, stage directions calling for a nightgown, like the one for the Ghost in Q1, are consistently used to suggest that the character enters "as if" coming from or going to bed.[130] In Webster's *The White Devil* (1612), the stage direction is explicit: "*Enter* Isabella *in her night-gowne as to bed-ward, with lights after her*" (sig. D4v). Precisely because of this association, when in *Macbeth* the knocking begins after the murder of Duncan, Lady Macbeth urges her husband: "Get on your Night-Gowne, least occasion call vs, / And shew vs to be Watchers." The nightgown will signify that Macbeth comes from bed and will thus exculpate him, and when he enters after the Porter scene, he presumably enters in his nightgown, although the stage direction reads simply "*Enter Macbeth*" (F, sig. 2m3r).

But other Shakespearean stage directions do call explicitly for this particular costume: when Brabantio is awoken from sleep by Iago and Roderigo, for example, he enters "*in his night gowne*" (*Othello*, Q 1622, sig. B3r). And other such directions similarly concern "the beast with two backs": in *The Two Maids of More-clacke* (1609), a husband calls his wife from bed—"Wife, wife, rise and come forth"—to accuse her of adultery, and she enters "*in her night gowne, and night attire,*" followed by her lover "*vnready, in his night-cap, garterles*" (sig. E3v); in *A Woman Killed with Kindness* (1607), when Frankford surprises his wife and her lover, he chases Wendoll "*running ouer the stage in a night-gowne,*" and then his wife enters "*in her smocke, night-gowne, and night attire*" (sig. F4r). As these examples and others demonstrate, because it could signify "bed-ward," the nightgown often appears in scenes associated with sex, especially illicit sex. So too in Q1 *Hamlet*, the Ghost's appearance in his nightgown is linked to "the rank sweat" of "the adulterous bed" (sig. G3r).

When a character enters "as if" from bed, of course, the bed may not literally be on stage—indeed, it is very likely not to be, since the nightgown is designed to substitute for it.[131] But unlike later spectators, those watching *Hamlet* at the Globe would have seen a largely unlocalized stage that lacked the kind of scenic details used in eighteenth- and nineteenth-century productions to identify the setting as a closet or oratory or bedroom. Seeing the Ghost in his nightgown would have encouraged Shakespeare's audience to imagine this relatively bare stage as the Queen's bedroom, or (as in Irving's production) a chamber immediately adjacent, to which the old king had hauntingly returned in appropriate costume.

Why might Shakespeare, or the Chamberlain's Men, have written a version of *Hamlet*, attested in some way by Q1, in which the bed is simultaneously excised as a stage prop from the sources (hence Corambis's "Arras") and called up in spectators' minds by another theatrical property, the nightgown? One explanation is that the Chamberlain's Men may not have always had access to a bed. A bed was an expensive prop, large and somewhat difficult to manage, and so it may not have been available at all times and in all venues—on tour, for instance, or perhaps at Newington Butts, where the Chamberlain's Men performed *Hamlet* in 1594.[132] There are several examples of multiple-text plays in which a bed that appears in one version is absent in the other, either because for some reason the prop had become unavailable or undesirable, or because a bed was added to the scene when it became possible to do so.[133] If early performances of *Hamlet* included the Ghost in his nightgown, as the Q1 stage direction strongly suggests, then Shakespeare or the Chamberlain's Men may have wanted to *suggest* a bed without incurring the trouble of actually *staging* one.[134]

Which brings me to the most striking fact about the version of this scene in Q1, something we seem never to have noticed, precisely because we have been too busy chastising modern productions for putting a bed in an early modern closet. There is no closet scene in Q1, because there is no "closet" in Q1. The word *closet* appears nowhere in that text of the play.[135] In Q2 and the Folio the word appears three times in conjunction with this scene: Rosencrantz tells Hamlet that his mother "desires to speak with you in her closet ere you go to bed" (Q2, sig. H3v); Polonius then alerts the King that "hee's going to his mothers closet" (Q2, sig. I1r); and afterward, the King tells Rosencrantz and Guildenstern that "Hamlet in madnes hath *Polonius* slaine / And from his mothers closet hath he dreg'd him" (Q2, sig. K1v; the lines in F are essentially the same). Q2 adds a fourth usage when Ophelia earlier describes how, "as I was sowing in my clossett" (Q2, sig. E2r), Hamlet appeared in a disorderly manner; in F, the scene occurs in Ophelia's "Chamber" (F, sig. 2o2r).

In all four cases, Q1 avoids the word. In that text, Hamlet's encounter with Ophelia occurs as she is "walking in the gallery all alone" (sig. D2v). The variation here among "closset," "Chamber," and "gallery" might have occurred in any number of ways, whether revised by an actor on his part, or by a reporter with faulty memory, or by an author deliberately rewriting. Setting the scene in the "gallery" makes it more public and hence less dangerous to Ofelia's chastity, a trend that seems to run throughout Q1: Ofelia is called a "maiden" at several points exclusively in that text, and only Q1 Ofelia tells her brother that "I . . . doubt not but to keepe my honour firme" (sig. C2r). F's "Chamber," by contrast, signifies a private room and possibly, as Thompson and Taylor suggest, a bedroom; it hardly makes the scene less private than Q2's "closset." Whoever was responsible for F's choice of word may have thought it best, for the sake of clarity on stage, to restrict the word *closet* to Gertrude's private room. In any case, given the triple variant, we should probably exercise restraint in explaining Q1's choice of word at this point.

A more thoroughgoing variation occurs, however, in the scene that we can no longer quite so confidently call the "closet" scene, changes that are unique to Q1. The consistency of these variants, and the fact that they are restricted to that text, points more toward some kind of conscious strategy than toward faulty memory. Here it is Gilderstone instead of his partner who tells Hamlet, "your mother craues to speake with you" (sig. F4v), but without saying where. In Q1, Corambis never alerts the King that Hamlet is "going to his mother's closet"; the exchange is cut entirely, as the text proceeds quickly from Hamlet's resolution to "let ne're the heart of *Nero* enter / This soft bosome" (sig. G1r) to the King's attempted prayer. But interestingly, Q1 makes up for this absence by having Hamlet himself remind the audience, at the beginning of his speech about Nero, that "My mother she hath sent to speake with me" (sig. G1r), a line that does not appear in Q2 or F. And here too, tellingly, the location is unspecified.

The final reference to Gertrude's "closet" in Q2 and F disappears from Q1 in what seems a similarly ingenious manner. The King does not inform Rossencraft and Gilderstone that Hamlet has killed the councillor and dragged him "from his mothers closet," because unlike in Q2 and F these two "Lordes" are onstage the entire time while Gertred recounts the episode. The King then orders the Lords to "inquire the body out," and they quickly return with Hamlet, reporting "we can by no meanes / Know of him where the body is" (sig. G3v).[136] By comparison with this economical dramaturgy, the staging in Q2 and F comes to look somewhat clunky: Claudius and Gertrude enter with Rosencrantz and Guildenstern; Gertrude asks them to "Bestow this place on us a little while," and they exit; Gertrude tells Claudius how Hamlet killed Polonius; Claudius calls for Guildenstern, and he reenters with his partner; Claudius orders them to find out exactly where Hamlet has stowed Polonius after dragging his body "from his mothers closet." The action in Q1 is far more streamlined than the awkward sequence of entrance, exit, and reentrance in the received text—and as part of this simplification, Q1 again does not specify where the encounter occurred.

In every case, Q1 not only refuses to say the word *closet* but indeed avoids localizing the scene between Hamlet and Gertrude in any way—at least in the dialogue. With the setting thus left completely vague, other aspects of performance must have helped to set the scene, and it seems more than coincidence that Q1 also provides the crucial stage direction: *Enter the ghost in his night gowne*. While critics routinely refer to the "closet scene" even when discussing Q1, early audiences at a performance of the Q1 text (if such a performance ever occurred) would have had no idea where the scene was taking place—until the Ghost's appearance. At that point, the unlocalized setting must have started to take shape; the absence of any spoken indication would only have heightened the importance of nonverbal signals like the Ghost's costume. And based on the evidence of other plays with similar stage directions, the audience would have been prompted to imagine a bedroom. Whether a bed was physically on stage in some early performance of *Hamlet* can of course never be known, but what is clear is that by comparison to the received text, Q1 never specifies that the scene takes place in Gertrude's closet and instead suggests that it occurs in, or at least immediately adjacent to, the kind of room where a man or a ghost might appear "*as to bed-ward.*"

There is tantalizingly suggestive evidence for this argument in *Der bestrafte Brudermord*, which has long been recognized to bear a special relationship to Q1. As in Q1, nowhere in *Brudermord* is the nature of the Queen's room made explicit. Immediately before the scene, Horatio announces: "Most gracious Queen, Prince Hamlet is in the antechamber [*Vorgemach*], and desires a private audience." This tells us that the room is private, but in no way helps us decide between a closet, a bedroom, or some other kind of room. The *antechamber* is *ante* to something, but we have no idea what. Before the German play's analogue of the nunnery scene, the King says, "Dearest wife, we beseech you, go to your chamber [*Gemach*]." Is this the same "chamber" that adjoins the "antechamber" in which Hamlet later waits to speak with her? The only other mention in the text of a "chamber" or anything like it comes in the equivalent of 1.2, when we first meet the King and Queen. Here the King closes the scene by telling his wife, leeringly: "You, my dearest consort, shall I follow to your bedchamber [*Schlafgemach*]. Come, let us hand in hand and arm in arm entwine, / Ourselves to the sweet joys of love and rest resign."[137] The progression of references to the "chamber" associated with the Queen in *Brudermord*, in other words, gives that room strongly sexual associations with the bedchamber, exactly what we have long been scolding "erring" twentieth-century performers for doing to Gertrude's closet.

These sexual associations are not Oedipal, of course; neither were they for Irving, Bernhardt, or Bradley. We have here the "damned incest" not of Oedipus but of the widow who marries her dead husband's brother. Interestingly, the incestuous overtones of this scene are increased in both Q1 and *Brudermord*. In the German text, the Queen explicitly says that her second marriage required a papal dispensation; in Q1, instead of exclaiming against "the rank sweat of an enseamed bed," Hamlet urges his mother to shun "the *incestuous* pleasure of [Claudius's] bed" (Q1, sig. G2v, emphasis added). The Hamlet of Q2 and F never speaks the word *incest* to his mother. In Q1, by contrast, Hamlet's presentation of the "portraiture" (sig. G2r) of the two brothers, his attempt to make his mother recognize the proper valuation of his father and uncle—"this was your husband . . . here is your husband" (sig. G2v)—culminates in the explicitly incestuous bed, here in the chamber where the ghost of his dead father walks "*as to bed-ward*."[138]

Given this heightened attention to the incestuous bed in Q1, it is not surprising that the scene in that text leads up to the Queen's most forceful rejection of the one brother in favor of the other and of the son who represents his memory. Only in Q1 does Gertred "sweare by heauen" that she "neuer knew of this most horride murder" and "vow" to God to "assist [Hamlet] in reuenge" (sig. G3r). Like Irving's choice to have Gertrude momentarily see the Ghost, thereby reconstituting her family while confessing her own guilt, Q1 represents Gertred's reformation by invoking the "incestuous pleasure" of "the adulterous bed," while simultaneously conjuring the marital bed that the Ghost seems to be either coming from or searching for. It is as if, in addition to the contrast between the "portraiture" of the two brothers, Q1 presents a parallel contrast between two beds: "this was your bed . . . here is your bed." The Ghost in his nightgown finds adultery and incest in the one bed—the kind of sexual vice typically associated with nightgowns on the early modern stage—but he simultaneously reminds Hamlet and the audience of that other, purer bed.

As Jones and Stallybrass show, the father's bed, like his armor, carried special significance in constructing early modern aristocratic identity: beds "were both extraordinarily costly and symbolically charged as the site of patrilineal inheritance." Part of the scandal in *Hamlet* is "the scandal of his mother still sleeping in his father's bed. For the rules of inheritance . . . increasingly laid down that the bed of the father should become the bed of the eldest son, as the armor of the father became the armor of the son."[139] With its new (old) stage direction, Q1 thus signals a faulty or perverted inheritance, not the Oedipal crisis of the son who wants to inhabit his father's bed, but an early modern crisis in which the son has not properly assumed his father's noble identity, just as the Ghost's armor signifies precisely that Hamlet himself has *not* inherited that armor.

But while the inheritance of the father's armor marks a specifically aristocratic construction of identity, as Jones and Stallybrass detail, the passing of the father's bed to the son was not restricted to the upper ranks. Shakespeare's own will demonstrates that upwardly mobile men of the middling sort could aspire to this same aristocratic patriarchal prestige: Shakespeare may have left his widow his "second-best bed" in the hope that his best bed would ultimately pass to a male heir in future generations, since his own son had already died.[140] More broadly, by costuming the Ghost in his nightgown and by not specifying that the room is Gertrude's closet, Q1 shifts the scene subtly away from the markedly aristocratic ideology of the warrior-king in armor. Numerous critics have noted that Q1 Gertred seems to be characterized in a thoroughly different manner from the Gertrude of Q2 and F. In Q1 the Queen becomes less an "imperiall ioyntresse" (Q2, sig. B3v)—an epithet of royalty used for her only in Q2 and F—and more a mother. As Dorothy Kehler writes, in Q1 "Gertred's rank seems secondary rather than integral to her role," and her behavior "is not entirely appropriate to a queen regnant." Instead, she seems a more "ordinary woman" in her social standing.[141] Q1 stresses Gertred's position within a family: as Lukas Erne suggests, her part becomes more straightforwardly "the loyal mother."[142]

Indeed, this shift occurs at a basic linguistic level in this scene: the terms for familial relations recur insistently in Q1 where they do not appear in Q2 or F. Only in Q1 does Hamlet explicitly use the words *father* and *husband* to describe Claudius's crimes and name the incest Gertred has committed: "can you looke on him / That slew my father, and your deere husband, / To liue in the incestuous pleasure of his bed?" (sig. G2v). And when he implores the Queen to refrain from vice, Hamlet calls her *mother* and again invokes her marital love for Old Hamlet—"O mother, if euer you did my deare father loue, / Forbeare the adulterous bed to night" (sig. G3r)—instead of urging her to do so for "love of grace" as in the received text. This emphasis is paralleled in the Q1-only scene between the Queen and Horatio, in which Gertred invokes her motherhood as a sign of her purified allegiance to Hamlet and his father: "commend me / A mothers care to him" (sig. H2v), she says, and "I take my leaue, / With thowsand mothers blessings to my sonne" (sig. H3r).

Compared to the received text, Q1 thus offers a subtly different image of the violation at the heart of this scene, one we can now trace most clearly in the architecture of the space the audience is led to imagine. If Hamlet goes to Gertrude's closet, then the scene occurs, as Lisa Jardine argues, in "her most private quarters," possibly "the sole place over which she ostensibly exercised total control." The lady's closet is an aristocratic space, allowing the noblewoman some measure of autonomy from the lord's dominion over the estate. Polonius "has no legitimate place within the intimate space of Gertrude's closet; his presence fatally confuses privacy with affairs of state." Hamlet's entry into this private space, "where customarily a woman would only entertain her husband or lover," may carry "intimations of erotic possibility" as well: "The son crosses into the enclosure of his mother's privacy to encounter her as a sexualised subject."[143] The scene is shocking—and was routinely cut down in eighteenth- and nineteenth-century stage productions—precisely because of these multiple, eroticized violations of the Queen's private room. One man hides to observe secretly what goes on in her closet, while another enters the closet to berate her for her sexual license; here in the space of her greatest control and autonomy, the Queen finds herself subjected to surveillance and condemnation by those who ought to be subject to her, the court councillor and her son.

The same basic action occurs in Q1, of course, and some of the same sense of violation must be present. But without the aristocratic "closet," and with the Ghost in his nightgown, the audience is encouraged to imagine the marital bedroom, and the emphasis falls more on the violation of family and home. The domestic architecture becomes more bourgeois than noble.[144] We are now prompted to picture something like the nightgown scenes in *The Two Maids of More-clacke* or *A Woman Killed with Kindness*, the kind of adulterous revelation more typical of city comedy or domestic tragedy than a tragedy of state. A king and queen, after all, do not share one bedroom. Nor was there only one "royal bed of Denmark"—or of England. At Hampton Court, for instance, Henry VIII had two bedchambers on the "King's Side," the formal bedchamber with the bed of state for public occasions and the more private room in which he actually slept. He also had a third bedchamber on the "Queen's Side," where the queen also had her own bedchamber.[145] If the Ghost in his nightgown is just coming from or going to bed, which bed is it? If Gertrude has betrayed the marital bed, in which of the numerous royal bedchambers would we find this bed? In Q1, in other words, the scene seems subtly to migrate from a royal palace to the kind of home in which the husband walks into the marital bedroom in his nightgown only to discover that his bed has been invaded by another man. It is this strand of the play, epitomized by the Ghost's nightgown, that Henry Irving picked up and heightened in his landmark production. Imagining the Ghost exiting "through the door leading into the bed-chamber, just as he might have done in his life-time; that chamber which has been desecrated by the faithless Queen," Irving is not imagining the royal palace of Denmark (or of England). The domesticity that was so remarked in his production is not to be found in the aristocratic lady's closet. Precisely for this reason Margaret Oliphant sneered at the Ghost in Irving's production: "The lady's husband, hearing an unaccountable commotion in the next room, had jumped out of bed, seized his dressing-gown, and rushed in to see what was the matter."

Hamlet's "horror and loathing" at his mother's betrayal, which A. C. Bradley famously diagnosed as the root of his melancholy, is the culmination of this long trajectory. It is a loathing caused by the adulterous betrayal of marriage, family, and home. Freud and Ernest Jones would soon transform this horror into a different kind of incestuous desire, one symbolized in twentieth-century productions by the bed in Gertrude's closet. But their theory is only that, a transformation of an earlier tradition that stretches all the way back to Q1 in 1603, not a radical departure or invention. In this sense, the repeated charge that the bed in the closet is a Freudian anachronism misses the mark. But in another way, anachronism indeed lies at the root of this tradition. For ultimately it was not simply the presence of this stage direction in the *Hamlet* of 1603 that prompted Irving's and Bradley's and Dover Wilson's interpretations of the play. Rather, it was the anachronistic emergence of the Ghost's nightgown in the nineteenth century, and the ensuing efforts of Victorian critics, editors, actors, and spectators to understand that uncanny playbook, that led to the bed in Gertrude's . . . room.

CHAPTER 4

Conscience Makes Cowards

The Disintegration and Reintegration of Shakespeare

No study of *Hamlet* would be complete without some attention to its most famous speech: "To be, or not to be, I there's the point" (Q1, sigs. D4v–E1r). For most of the history of Q1, that attention was overwhelmingly negative. Indeed, as soon as Bunbury's discovery was made public, the soliloquy provided an easy target for ridicule. The *Literary Gazette* quoted the speech and dismissed it with the simple phrase "This is a poor version," before moving on to discuss "contrary matters" and the Ghost's nightgown.[1] The rhetoric soon intensified: a few months later, in April, the *London Magazine* wrote that the passage "reads like a re-translation from the French, or rather like the version of the Negro Roscius at New York, as given by Mr. Matthews in his admirable Trip to America," alluding to a racist bit in Charles Mathews's popular one-man show.[2] In the December 1825 "Running Commentary on the Hamlet of 1603" that may have been written by Collier, the lines were understood to be self-evidently absurd and hence proof of the piratical nature of the edition. The author, "Ambrose Gunthio," argued that Q1 bears "palpable marks of having been surreptitiously taken down piecemeal in the theatre, by a blundering scribe, who contrived to pervert the meaning of every other sentence with surprising ingenuity." After reproducing the first portion of the Q1 soliloquy, Gunthio halts: "To quote more is needless. Can any one for a moment believe that Shakspeare penned this unconnected, unintelligible jargon . . . ?"[3] More than half a century later, Richard Grant White similarly felt that merely quoting the speech was its own conclusion: "There are some things that are past caricature, because they themselves reach the limit of the ridiculous: as, for example, Mr. Barnum's calling his tight-rope woman Queen of the Lofty Wire. The absurdity of incongruity can no further go. And so this misrepresentation of Hamlet's solemn self-communing unites resemblance and distortion with an effect which surpasses that of intentional burlesque."[4]

And yet, as some recent scholars have argued, the speech is not in fact such a monstrosity of nonsense (Figure 24).[5] With some creative editing and punctuating—the sort of work done on all "genuine" Shakespearean texts—the soliloquy makes good enough sense.

> To be, or not to be: ay, there's the point.
> To die, to sleep, is that all? Ay, all . . . No:
> To sleep, to dream—Ay, marry, there it goes.
> For in that dream of death, when we awake
> And, borne before an Everlasting Judge
> From whence no passenger ever returned—
> The undiscovered country, at whose sight
> The happy smile, and the accursed damned—
> But for this, the joyful hope of this,
> Who'd bear the scorns and flatt'ry of the world,
> Scorned by the right rich, the rich cursed of the poor,
> The widow being oppressed, the orphan wronged,
> The taste of hunger, or a tyrant's reign,
> And thousand more calamities besides,
> To grunt and sweat under this weary life,
> When that he may his full quietus make
> With a bare bodkin? Who would this endure,
> But for a hope of something after death?
> Which puzzles the brain and doth confound the sense;
> Which makes us rather bear those evils we have
> Than fly to others that we know not of.
> Ay, that—O, this conscience makes cowards of us all.

As in the familiar version, Hamlet begins with the question of being and nonbeing. He imagines death as a kind of sleep before correcting himself by positing the existence of "dreams" after death. The two versions then diverge; it is not the fear of bad dreams that Hamlet ponders here, as in the famous version. Rather, death itself is a dream, from which we will surely awaken: "*when* we awake," Hamlet says, and that *when* signals his certain faith.

This is not the eschatology of Q2/F "To be, or not to be" but rather of Donne's "Death be not proud": "One short sleepe past, wee wake eternally, / And death shall be no more, death thou shalt die."[6] Death is merely temporary, a "short sleepe" or a "dream," for Christ has conquered death and returned to tell us the good news. Hamlet's faith that death is transitory leads him naturally to the scene of divine judgment. It is the "joyful hope"—not the dread—"of something after death" that gives us the strength to endure a life of suffering. In Q1, what "puzzles the brain" and "makes us rather bear those evils we have / Than fly to others that we know not of" is the fear of the Last Judgment, when we may be among "the accursed" who are "damned." (The "which" that begins Hamlet's final four lines has to be taken here as a sentential relative that refers to the entirety of the preceding idea, rather than to any specific antecedent noun, since otherwise it would refer, incongruously, to "hope.")[7] Suicide condemns the accursed to an eternity of torment in hell, with evils that we cannot even begin to comprehend—that "we know not of"—and so instead we "bear those evils we have" in the joyful hope of being among the happy who smile when borne before the Everlasting Judge.

Q1 "To be, or not to be" thus presents a powerfully traditional Christian understanding of the afterlife, one that is, in Jesse Lander's words, "consumed by the four final things: death, judgment, heaven, and hell."[8] As I will show, the overt religiosity of this passage played a crucial role in its later nineteenth-century reception, helping to promote a reading of the Q2/F soliloquy as far less orthodox, perhaps even atheistic. But regardless of whether the two versions do in fact differ in their theology—itself an important and contested question—it was surely the very familiarity of this most famous passage in English literature that made the Q1 text seem like burlesque. Had Q1 never been lost, had editors throughout the eighteenth century labored over its text as they had over the first quartos of *Romeo and Juliet* and *Merry Wives of Windsor*, would its soliloquy have seemed like "unconnected, unintelligible jargon"?

It is worth remembering that the famous version of the soliloquy has itself been noted for its "unconnected" syntax and sequence of ideas. Samuel Johnson "endeavour[ed] to discover the train [of thought], and to shew how one sentiment produces another," a difficult task since, "bursting from a man distracted with contrariety of desires, and overwhelmed with the magnitude of his own purposes," the speech "is connected rather in the speaker's mind, than on his tongue."[9] Oliver Goldsmith was more bluntly critical: he thought that Hamlet's soliloquy was "a heap of absurdities" because its "whole chain of reasoning . . . seems inconsistent and incongruous."[10] Various of Hamlet's

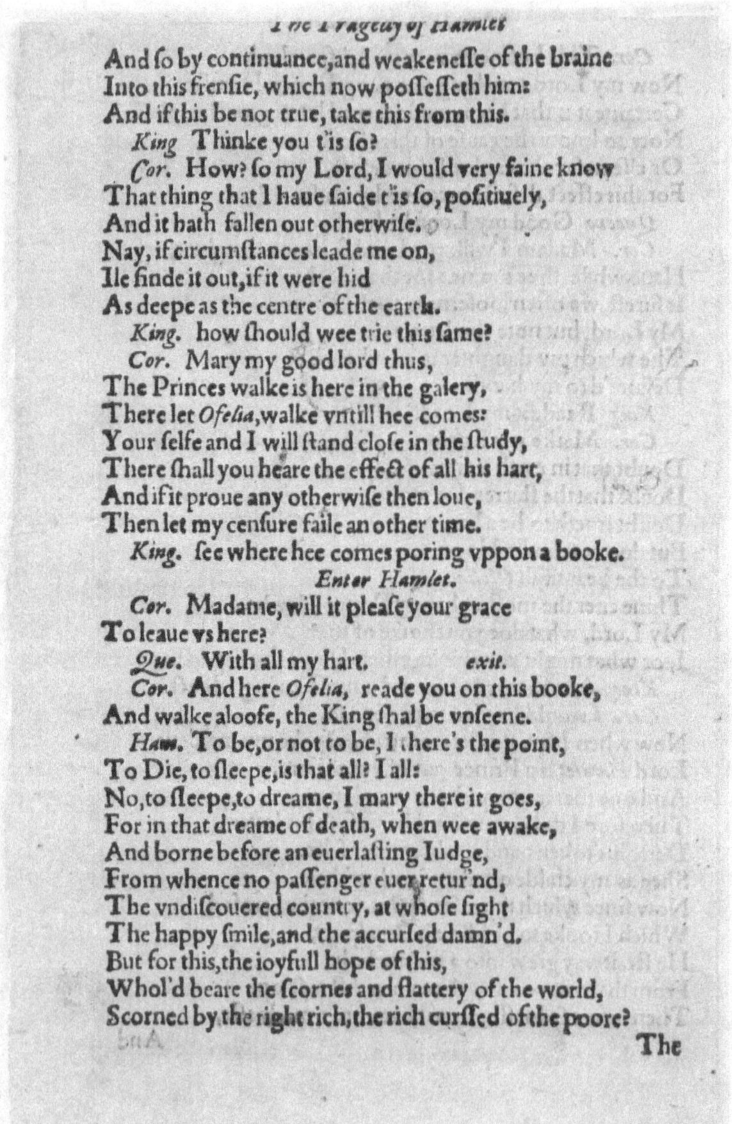

And so by continuance, and weakenesse of the braine
Into this frensie, which now possesseth him:
And if this be not true, take this from this.
  King Thinke you t'is so?
  Cor. How? so my Lord, I would very faine know
That thing that I haue saide t'is so, positiuely,
And it hath fallen out otherwise.
Nay, if circumstances leade me on,
Ile finde it out, if it were hid
As deepe as the centre of the earth.
  King. how should wee trie this same?
  Cor. Mary my good lord thus,
The Princes walke is here in the galery,
There let *Ofelia*, walke vntill hee comes:
Your selfe and I will stand close in the study,
There shall you heare the effect of all his hart,
And if it proue any otherwise then loue,
Then let my censure faile an other time.
  King. see where hee comes poring vppon a booke.

          Enter Hamlet.

  Cor. Madame, will it please your grace
To leaue vs here?
  Que. With all my hart.   *exit.*
  Cor. And here *Ofelia*, reade you on this booke,
And walke aloofe, the King shal be vnseene.
  Ham. To be, or not to be, I there's the point,
To Die, to sleepe, is that all? I all:
No, to sleepe, to dreame, I mary there it goes,
For in that dreame of death, when wee awake,
And borne before an euerlasting Iudge,
From whence no passenger euer retur'nd,
The vndiscouered country, at whose sight
The happy smile, and the accursed damn'd.
But for this, the ioyfull hope of this,
Whol'd beare the scornes and flattery of the world,
Scorned by the right rich, the rich curssed of the poore?
                                                    The

Figure 24. *To be, or not to be* in Q1.

Reproduced by permission of the Huntington Library, San Marino, California, shelf mark 69304.

Prince of Denmarke

The widow being oppressed, the orphan wrong'd,
The taste of hunger, or a tirants raigne,
And thousand more calamities besides,
To grunt and sweate vnder this weary life,
When that he may his full *Quietus* make,
With a bare bodkin, who would this indure,
But for a hope of something after death?
Which pusles the braine, and doth confound the sence,
Which makes vs rather beare those euilles we haue,
Than flie to others that we know not of.
I that, O this conscience makes cowardes of vs all,
Lady in thy orizons, be all my sinnes remembred.

   Ofel. My Lord, I haue sought opportunitie, which now
I haue, to redeliuer to your worthy handes, a small remembrance, such tokens which I haue receiued of you.

   Ham. Are you faire?
   Ofel. My Lord.
   Ham. Are you honest?
   Ofel. What meanes my Lord?
   Ham. That if you be faire and honest,
Your beauty should admit no discourse to your honesty.

   Ofel. My Lord, can beauty haue better priuiledge than
with honesty?

   Ham. Yea mary may it; for Beauty may transforme
Honesty, from what she was into a bawd:
Then Honesty can transforme Beauty:
This was sometimes a Paradox,
But now the time giues it scope.
I neuer gaue you nothing.

   Ofel. My Lord, you know right well you did,
And with them such earnest vowes of loue,
As would haue moou'd the stoniest breast aliue,
But now too true I finde,
Rich giftes waxe poore, when giuers grow vnkinde.

   Ham. I neuer loued you.
   Ofel. You made me beleeue you did.

phrases have, at different times, struck editors as impossible. Most notorious among the cruxes in the speech is the "sea of troubles" that Pope wanted to emend to "siege of troubles" and Warburton to "assail of troubles," due to the apparent mixed metaphor.[11] Editors have also caviled with "whips and scorns of time," which Johnson thought corrupt since "*whips* and *scorns* have no great connection with one another, or with *time*," proposing instead "quips *and scorns of* title."[12] Meanwhile, Theobald, Steevens, Malone, Schlegel, Coleridge, and many others either attacked or defended Shakespeare for making Hamlet incongruously claim that "no traveller returns" from "the undiscovered country" shortly after seeing his father's ghost.[13]

Even the central topic of the soliloquy has never been clear. Johnson denied that Hamlet was contemplating suicide, instead seeing him as deciding whether to kill Claudius:

> *Hamlet,* knowing himself injured in the most enormous and atrocious degree, and seeing no means of redress, but such as must expose him to the extremity of hazard, meditates on his situation in this manner: *Before I can form any rational scheme of action under this pressure of distress,* it is necessary to decide, whether, *after our present state, we are* to be or not to be. That is the question, which, as it shall be answered, will determine, *whether 'tis nobler,* and more suitable to the dignity of reason, *to suffer the outrages of fortune* patiently, or to take arms against *them*, and by opposing end them, *though perhaps* with the loss of life.[14]

Malone responded that "Dr. Johnson's explication of the first five lines of this passage is surely wrong," because Hamlet is in fact "deliberating . . . whether he should continue to live or put an end to his life."[15] The debate has never been resolved, and while it is safe to say that the majority of critics have agreed with Malone that the speech is about suicide, a number of prominent scholars in every generation have upheld variations of Johnson's position.[16]

In all of these ways and many others, the familiar text of the speech, no less than the Q1 text, has often seemed obscure, disjointed, and in places even nonsensical. By the time Bunbury discovered his copy of Q1, however, "To be, or not to be" had become deeply ingrained in English literary culture. Indeed, Hamlet's soliloquy may have become famous immediately: a character in John Fletcher's *The Scornful Lady* (1616) says that "to sleepe to die, to die to sleepe" is "a very Figure," a familiar phrase or metaphor.[17] In the early eighteenth century, the speech was so well known that George Stubbes could "purposely omit taking Notice of the famous Speech, *To be, or not to be, &c.* every *English* Reader knows its Beauties."[18] By the Romantic period, the soliloquy had become central to the character of Hamlet and, in Coleridge's words, "of absolutely universal import."[19] It was not any inherent obscurity in the Q1 "To be, or not to be" that made it seem uniquely "unintelligible" but rather its reemergence only after the more familiar text had been entrenched at the peak of the literary canon.[20] In this sense, Richard Grant White's description of the Q1 speech as "caricature" and "burlesque" was more apt than he realized, since those forms rely for their meaning on the audience's deep familiarity with the original. And so the rhetoric of burlesque, which emerged shortly after the discovery of Q1, continues to be invoked: it "may strike you as comic, almost a parody"; it is "gibberish," "likely to be greeted as parody," "an apparent burlesque," "garbling familiar lines to the edge of parody."[21]

Because for most of the nineteenth century the Q1 speech was read simply as a degradation of the "original" version, individual variants in these lines did not receive the same notice as did *contrary matters* or the Ghost's nightgown. Even Charles Knight did not attempt to read the speech as Shakespeare's initial draft, passing over it quickly: "The soliloquy in the first copy is evidently given with great corruptions, and some of the lines appear transposed by the printer."[22] Indeed, it seems to have taken decades for anyone to perceive the speech as significantly *different from* the received version, rather than merely "a poor version" of it. A striking exception appears in an 1826 article in the French journal *Le Globe*, which notes that the "tendency of the [familiar version] is hardly at all religious," while the "tendency of the speech [in Q1] is completely different. . . . What keeps Hamlet in this world is the joyful hope . . . of another life, where the happy smile. . . . What holds us here is the fear of evils in the other world, and the awareness of having committed sins makes us all cowards, we fear torments new and unknown . . . a very religious sense."[23] But this exception only confirms that it was the familiarity of the received version that rendered the Q1 text absurd: the text initially becomes available for analysis only across the Channel, where the play as a whole was far less ossified through repetition, just as we saw in the French reception of *country/contrary matters*.

For this reason, the Q1 version of the line that I discuss in this chapter has produced essentially no critical commentary, not only in the nineteenth century but afterward as well. Nor does this line vary between the three texts nearly as drastically as those I have discussed in previous chapters. Beginning the final movement of the soliloquy, Hamlet remarks in the Folio text: "Thus Conscience does make Cowards of vs all" (sig. 2o5r). The Q2 version lacks "of us all" (sig. G2v), while Q1 reads: "O this conscience makes cowardes of vs all" (sig. E1r). But while the variation in Q1 is less important in this line than elsewhere, Bunbury's discovery completely transformed how this line was understood *in its familiar version*. The line has often been seen as a key to understanding the play as a whole, cited as a crucial insight into Hamlet's character and into the meaning of his meditation in "To be, or not to be." Yet its precise meaning has been the subject of long debate. As part of these debates, critics and editors have repeatedly claimed that the key word *conscience* has been misunderstood—but they have not all shared the same understanding of its "true" meaning. As with *country matters* and the bed in Gertrude's closet, so too close readings of the most famous speech in *Hamlet* hinge on a piece of historicist wisdom that demarcates "expert" or scholarly readers from the lay person—but that likewise turns out to be a pseudodoxos with a genealogy stretching back to the discovery of Q1.

In this final chapter, I continue the story of authorship that I began in Chapter 1. Here I examine changing notions of Shakespeare's writing process in the late nineteenth and early twentieth centuries, in the wake of the debate between Knight and Collier over the nature of Q1 *Hamlet* and on the cusp of the New Bibliography that inaugurated the modern era of bibliographic and editorial theory. The fin-de-siècle controversy about exactly how Shakespeare wrote his *Hamlet* was deeply interwoven with the meaning of the play as a whole, and with the meaning of Hamlet's line about conscience in particular. And this controversy has continued to influence our understanding of what it means to ask the question, "To be, or not to be."

Around the turn of the twentieth century, numerous scholars suddenly began to insist that *conscience* must be construed not in its familiar moral-religious sense but rather, as the gloss in Arthur Wilson Verity's *Students' Shakespeare* informed readers, as "speculative reflection; from the sense 'consciousness'."[24] Verity was even more emphatic in his revised edition: "*conscience*, speculative reflection; from the sense 'consciousness'; *not* 'the moral sense,' as at V. 2. 58, 67."[25] The added cross-references to Hamlet's remarks about Rosencrantz and Guildenstern ("They are not neere my Conscience") and Claudius ("is't not perfect conscience / To quit him with this arme?"; F, sig. 2p6r) are striking: even though Shakespeare uses the word elsewhere in this very play in "the moral sense," Verity is adamant that it cannot have this meaning in "To be, or not to be." But why not?

Verity was by no means alone in his reading of Hamlet's *conscience*. Similar glosses appear in many contemporary editions, and it is clear that these editors see themselves as fighting for a properly historicized definition against widespread popular misunderstanding. Hence in a predecessor of the Yale Shakespeare, John Livingston Lowes wrote that "the greatest danger in reading Shakespeare is that of giving to familiar words the sense they now have, instead of the meaning which they had in Shakespeare's time. . . . 'Thus conscience doth [*sic*] make cowards of us all' (see note on III, i, 83) does not mean what most readers think it does." The relevant note glosses the word as "consciousness,—i.e., knowledge that this is so," and provides historical context: "This sense of the word is very common in Shakespeare's time (see the examples in the *Oxford Dictionary*, under I, i), and is the only one that fits the context."[26] Likewise, M. R. Ridley's headnote to the glossary in the New Temple *Hamlet* tells us: "Many words and phrases in Shakespeare require glossing, not because they are in themselves unfamiliar, but for the opposite reason, that Shakespeare uses in their Elizabethan and unfamiliar sense a large number of words which seem so familiar that there is no incentive to look for them in the glossary." His list of such dangerously false friends includes *conscience*, which he defines as "habit of reasoning."[27]

These fin-de-siècle editors understood that most readers, and most previous scholars, simply assumed that *conscience* carried its familiar moral-religious sense. In this, they were largely correct: only a few scattered references to this "philosophical" meaning of Hamlet's *conscience* appear before the late nineteenth century. In 1828, for instance, an anonymous writer in *The Crypt, or, Receptacle for Things Past* critiqued Oliver Goldsmith's reading of the soliloquy: "Goldsmith has altogether mistaken the meaning of the word *conscience* in this passage; it alludes to nothing that lay heavy on the speaker's mind, or inspired him with a rational fear of future punishment; it implies simply *consciousness, innate perception, instinct*."[28] The only example I have found in an edition—although not in a gloss on the text itself—comes in Knight's *Pictorial Edition*; in his introduction to the play as well as in his biography, Knight writes in passing of "Hamlet, whose conscience [consciousness] 'puzzles the will'."[29]

But these remarks are quite rare: Goldsmith's reading of *conscience* was in fact the usual one, even if his judgment of the soliloquy as a whole was not. Entirely typical is Edward Strachey's discussion in 1848, which has numerous parallels: "'Thus,' says Hamlet, 'conscience,' which is this sense of moral responsibility, 'does make cowards of us all.'"[30] In early editions of the play, *conscience* is never glossed as speculation or reflection as opposed to the moral faculty, and precisely because the familiar moral reading was taken for granted, in the great eighteenth-century editions the line is simply not glossed at all: Pope, Theobald, Hanmer, Warburton, Capell, Steevens, Malone, and Reed all seemingly thought readers required no assistance in understanding this perfectly ordinary word. In 1821, Boswell cited John Brickdale Blakeway's cross-references to *Richard III*, in which both the Second Murderer and King Richard similarly suggest that conscience makes us cowards, with *conscience* here unmistakably meaning the moral-religious faculty. Following Boswell, some editors reproduced this note, but until the late nineteenth century most remained as silent as their predecessors.[31]

It is not surprising, therefore, that Furness merely printed Blakeway's cross-reference in his 1877 Variorum, for this was about the extent of existing commentary on the line. By 1908, however, when Furness's son edited the Variorum *Richard III*, things had clearly changed. Furness Jr. goes out of his way to discuss the alternative usage of the word in *Hamlet* when glossing one of the very lines in *Richard III* that Blakeway had seen as illustrative of that usage: "With all deference to my betters I suggest that, in *Hamlet*, the context hardly seems to warrant this interpretation. . . . Is there in this any question of *moral sense*? Does not the use of 'thus' rather convey the idea that it is the thinking too precisely on the event, or the speculating thereon too deeply, without any reference to the right or to the wrong, which makes us hesitate. . . . In the present line in *Rich. III.* the Murderer uses 'conscience' not as in Hamlet's use of it, but in the sense of *moral judgement*."[32] In these two Variorum editions, which attempt to summarize more encyclopedically than ever before the history and current state of criticism on the plays, we can see the advent and consolidation of this new meaning. To Furness Sr., as to the eighteenth- and nineteenth-century editors before him, the word seemed unexceptional; thirty years later his son thought it important enough to digress in order to clarify the "true" meaning of Hamlet's *conscience* against previous authorities.

When Charles Knight pointed to the "philosophical" meaning of *conscience* in his *Pictorial Edition*, his reading was so unusual that it failed to catch on. Fifty years later, when another editor promoted this reading, it spread rapidly to nearly all learned editions of the play. The editor who ensured the widespread adoption of this reading was E. K. Chambers. The note in his 1893 Warwick Shakespeare edition reads: "*conscience*, the exercise of conscious thought, speculation on the future. This speech is not merely ironical. Hamlet has become aware of the flaw in his own character, though he attributes it to humanity in general." And the entry in Chambers's glossary carefully assigns only this specific meaning to the use of the word in Hamlet's soliloquy, despite other instances in the play: "*conscience* (1) (iv. 7. 1), the moral consciousness; (2) (v. 2. 67), morality; (3) (iii. 1. 83), consciousness generally, especially self-consciousness, speculation."[33] After Chambers, this meaning proliferates across numerous major editions: "'scrupulousness,' but not in a moral sense" (Riverside Shakespeare, 1897); "speculative reflexion" (C. H. Herford, 1899); "consciousness, thought" (William Allan Neilson, 1906); "introspection, speculation" (Sidney Lee, 1908); "reflection, consciousness" (John Dover Wilson, 1934); among many other lesser-known editions.[34] And in what was by far the period's most influential critical work on the play, A. C. Bradley complained of the "total misinterpretation" of the line: "'Conscience' does not mean moral sense or scrupulosity, but this reflection on the *consequences* of action."[35]

The rapid consensus on this new understanding can also be seen in the revision of several important editions to bring them up to date on this newly contentious question. The New Grant White Shakespeare of 1912, for instance, added a new note to the text of the twelve-volume *Works* that White had published between 1857 and 1866: "*conscience*, reflection upon the facts of *consciousness*."[36] Similarly, Henry Norman Hudson's 1856 edition and his Harvard Shakespeare of 1881 both left the line unglossed; but the New Hudson Shakespeare of 1909 added a note that indicates, even while demurring slightly, that the new meaning had become widespread: "Against the interpretation that 'conscience' here means only 'consciousness' (of such risks) or 'exercise of conscious thought,' common meanings in Middle English, may be cited *Richard III*," with the usual cross-reference.[37]

While Chambers's influence is clear, this reading of the line had been gaining in importance in the late nineteenth century more generally, and some editors may have arrived at the new gloss independently. Only a few years before Furness repeated the traditional cross-reference to *Richard III* in his Variorum, for instance, the German professor Alexander Schmidt published his *Shakespeare-Lexicon* (1874) simultaneously in Berlin and London. Schmidt's definitions for *conscience* include both "the involuntary moral judgment of our own actions" and "consciousness in general, private judgment, inmost thought," but the specific citation to "*thus c. does make cowards of us all*, Hml. III, 1, 83" appears under the latter definition and includes the further gloss, "(= thought, consideration)."[38] Not surprisingly, it is impossible to point to any single, decisive moment when the meaning of the line changed, as if no one had ever previously imagined that it might mean anything other than the moral faculty. Nonetheless, the occasional early references should not lead us astray: before the late nineteenth century, the idea that Hamlet's *conscience* might mean "speculation" or "self-reflection" was practically unheard of, while the moral-religious meaning was almost universally taken for granted. By the first decades of the twentieth century, however, all that had changed: the critical climate had become receptive enough to the new gloss that it rapidly came to dominate.

While this understanding of Hamlet's *conscience* continues to be widely promulgated today, by the second half of the twentieth century, the cutting-edge critical position was precisely the reverse. The meaning that had seemed to fin-de-siècle editors to be "the only one that fits the context" was emphatically ruled out, and the definition that they had considered a false friend was preferred. Now both historical usage generally and Shakespeare's own usage suddenly pointed to the moral-religious meaning of Hamlet's *conscience*. Bertram Joseph may have been the pioneer: in 1953, he wrote that for "many years this soliloquy, with its famous question, has been misinterpreted . . . as a discourse on suicide"; instead the speech was about the legitimacy of killing Claudius. Hamlet's *conscience* is "the faculty in man which warns him not to sin and keeps reminding him of punishment if he does."[39] C. S. Lewis then subtly traced the intertwined linguistic history of the two meanings of *conscience* in his *Studies in Words* (1960): in Hamlet's soliloquy "it means nothing more or less than 'fear of Hell'," despite the editorial impulse "for taking it to mean 'reflection, thought'—an instance of the Middle English sense."[40] Perhaps the most influential work on the subject was Eleanor Prosser's *Hamlet and Revenge* (1968), which argued that to "Shakespeare and his contemporaries, the word rarely meant 'consciousness,' the usual editorial gloss. More commonly it meant the faculty that not only accused a man of past sin but also warned him against future sin."[41] And in a frequently cited and detailed essay, Catherine Belsey concluded that, as opposed to the overingenious glossing of previous editors, the "apparent meaning of the text is fairly straight-forward: the moral sense inhibits action by generating fear (of the consequences)."[42]

While turn-of-the-century editions consistently cautioned readers to beware their commonsense ideas of the meanings of words, three landmark scholarly editions of the late twentieth century took their cue from this mid-century counterrevolution in favor of the familiar and straightforward. In the New Cambridge *Hamlet*, Philip Edwards noted that "conscience here means conscience, the inner knowledge of right and wrong. . . . Many commentators claim it means 'introspection', but Hamlet is talking about one's implanted sense of good and evil, which knows the canon of the Everlasting "gainst self-slaughter'."[43] G. R. Hibbard's Oxford edition glossed the word as "one's sense of right and wrong (the normal meaning of the word in Shakespeare)."[44] And after listing the two options in his Arden *Hamlet*—"(1) as in ordinary modern usage, the inner voice of moral judgment; (2) consciousness, the fact or faculty of knowing and understanding"—Harold Jenkins recorded his own view: "I believe firmly in (1)," not only because of the immediate context but also because of its use elsewhere in Shakespeare and in Belleforest.[45] While various editions still suggest that the word carries some sense of *consciousness*, they now generally supplement that gloss with the moral-religious one as well.[46] The counterrevolution against the philosophical meaning of the word has not been quite as absolute as the original revolution, but the general trend is clear: a rapid collective decision in the late nineteenth century that the word could not have its "ordinary" meaning, followed by a strong mid-twentieth-century reaction in favor of this "normal meaning of the word."

The choice of gloss has major implications: as Prosser rightly perceives, the "crux of the entire soliloquy lies in the word *conscience*." For if *conscience* means the divinely implanted "internal lawgiver that judges the good or evil of a proposed action,"[47] if it means essentially "fear of Hell," then the soliloquy carries a strongly religious message, as shown by Edwards's citation of Hamlet's more explicitly religious first soliloquy about God's "canon 'gainst self-slaughter." If by contrast *conscience* means philosophic speculation, then the soliloquy lacks any overt religious discourse and will be more readily understood as a skeptical interrogation of the nature and even the existence of the afterlife. The adoption of the new reading of this line, and its subsequent reversal, thus involve the largest issues of "To be, or not to be" and of *Hamlet* as a whole.

Some of this reversal can be attributed to the usual rhythms of scholarship and the disciplinary need for new interpretations. But the rapid and near universal acceptance (and then rejection) of the new gloss, and the insistence of each side that the other interpretation cannot be maintained, suggest that something more is at work. Belsey argues that the "widespread reading of 'conscience' as 'consciousness' must . . . reflect an understanding of Hamlet's meaning which is determined by a different interpretation of Hamlet's problem. It is, I think, a vestige of the Romantic view of the play, which locates the central problem not in Hamlet's situation but in his character: the tender, delicate, sensitive prince, unequal to the sacred duty of revenge, endlessly inventing excuses to escape from the harsh reality of action."[48] This explanation makes intuitive sense, given the endurance of the Romantic interpretation and its importance in focusing attention on Hamlet's consciousness. Coleridge's famous notion that in Hamlet "we see a great, an almost enormous, intellectual activity, and a proportionate aversion to real action consequent upon it" fits perfectly with the idea that the gloss of *conscience* as *consciousness* is a "vestige of the Romantic view of the play."[49] As we have seen, Charles Knight understood Hamlet's character and Shakespeare's authorship of *Hamlet* in a thoroughly Romantic manner, and he was also exceptionally early in writing that Hamlet's "conscience—(consciousness)—'sicklied o'er' his 'native hue of resolution'."[50] And this interpretation has likewise encouraged Romantic readings of the line among recent critics unswayed by the counterrevolution in favor of the moral sense. In *Hamlet in Purgatory*, for instance, Stephen Greenblatt writes that Hamlet "famously complain[s] that conscience—here consciousness itself—'does make cowards of us all'," and that this "corrosive inwardness" is "the hallmark of the entire play and the principal cause of its astonishing, worldwide renown."[51]

And yet, fitting as it seems, this explanation is one of the pseudodoxia of *Hamlet* after Q1; it is not quite wrong, but it cannot quite be right either. What appears to be an "unbroken continuity" from the Romantic critics to seemingly Romantic interpretations of Hamlet's *conscience* turns out to involve all of the "the accidents, the minute deviations—or conversely, the complete reversals," that Foucault identifies with the work of genealogy.[52] For one thing, the Romantic critics themselves never read the line in this way. Indeed, in their discussions of *Hamlet*, neither Goethe, Schlegel, Coleridge, nor Hazlitt seems ever to have cited this line at all.[53] When Coleridge refers to it in an unrelated context, he quite clearly understands *conscience* in the moral-religious sense: the reason that tyrants do not fear regicide, he writes, is "the spirit-quelling thought: the Laws of God and of my Country have made his Life sacred! I dare not touch a hair of his Head!—'Tis Conscience that makes Cowards of us all'."[54] Schlegel does quote the soliloquy as the key proof text for his view that the play "is intended to show that a consideration which would exhaust all the relations and possible consequences of a deed to the very limits of human foresight, cripples the power of acting." But he begins his quotation only with the lines immediately following this one: "And thus the native hue of resolution / Is sicklied o'er with the pale cast of thought."[55] If his interpretation of *conscience* adhered to Belsey's "Romantic view of the play," Schlegel would surely have included the line in his discussion. Indeed, in his critique of Schlegel, Hermann Ulrici wrote that it is Hamlet's "regard for the eternal salvation of his soul"—his moral conscience—that "forces him to halt and consider," as shown by the very "passage which Schlegel quotes (but mutilates to support his view)." Ulrici then italicizes *Thus conscience does make cowards of us all* in his own quotation, believing that he has caught Schlegel fudging the evidence and omitting this line precisely because Schlegel too understood it as referring to the moral-religious faculty. Indeed, it seems clear from their failure to discuss the line that none of the famous Romantic critics took *conscience* to have much to do with Coleridge's "overbalance of the imaginative power" or Hazlitt's "prince of philosophical speculators."[56] The gloss is not, in any direct way at least, a lingering remnant of the Romantic interpretation of *Hamlet*.

Belsey's explanation thus does not quite fit either the textual evidence—none of the foundational Romantic critics discusses the line—nor the critical history: it is an odd "vestige of the Romantic view of the play" that first becomes widely known nearly a century after the Romantic view from which it supposedly remains left over like a useless appendix. And while Chambers's gloss, like Knight's, clearly invokes a generally Romantic view of the play—this *conscience* is "the flaw in [Hamlet's] own character"—many of the critics who gloss the word in this new way are decidedly *anti*-Romantic: the Cornell University professor Hiram Corson, for instance, took *conscience* to mean "consciousness in general" and also thought that "Coleridge and Goethe . . . contributed more . . . toward shutting off a sound criticism of the play, than any other critics or any other cause."[57] Rather than a vestige of Romanticism, in fact, this understanding of the word is just the reverse, a *development* out of that critical heritage, but not in any clean or necessary line. True, this meaning would almost certainly never have emerged had not the famous Romantic interpretation preceded it, and, as shown by Knight and Chambers, this meaning could easily be conjoined to a Romantic reading of Hamlet's character. But the Romantic interpretation neither ensured its emergence nor completed it. Only at the end of the nineteenth century do we see a scholarly consensus that Hamlet's *conscience* had been consistently misinterpreted, and that this misinterpretation needed emphatic correction.

This fin-de-siècle consensus was driven by the accidental discovery of Q1—and indeed the equally accidental discovery in 1856 of the second copy of Q1. As the Romantic dialectic of Knight and Collier ebbed, continued scholarly engagement with Q1 sparked a critical and editorial movement that for convenience I call "disintegrationism," although the label was given by its detractors. The disintegrationist movement offered a completely new idea of Shakespeare the author, and of the writing of *Hamlet* especially, which provided the foundations for the understanding of Hamlet's *conscience* as "speculation." But this was no Romantic movement; its theory of Shakespearean authorship was totally antithetical to Romantic presuppositions. And in its overturning of Romanticism, disintegrationism helped to usher in modern Shakespearean editing, interpretation, and textual studies.

The news that another copy of Q1 had turned up in M. W. Rooney's Dublin bookshop reinvigorated the study of the origins and development of *Hamlet*. The following year, Tycho Mommsen was prompted to write his influential essay on the memorial reconstruction of Q1 *Hamlet* and *Romeo and Juliet* because the "discovery of the last leaf of the earliest 'Hamlet' . . . excited great interest on both sides of the water, and again directed the public attention to that curious edition."[58] Also in 1857, the German philologist William Bernhardy published a series of articles that linked Q1 to *Der bestrafte Brudermord*, for the first time suggesting that the German play was a debased rendition of the pre-Shakespearean *Ur-Hamlet*.[59] As interest in this theory grew, Albert Cohn published the text of *Brudermord*, with an English translation, in his *Shakespeare in Germany* (1865). And in his widely read Variorum, Furness provided editions of both Q1 and *Brudermord* (in translation), bringing together all of the relevant texts alongside extensive critical commentary.

With these texts now more readily available to them, English critics and editors intensified their efforts to find a unified narrative that could account for Q1, the received Q2/F text, and *Brudermord*. In their Clarendon edition, W. G. Clark and W. A. Wright agreed with Cohn that "the German text . . . may contain something of the older English play upon which Shakespeare worked." They then put forward their new theory that was to transform understandings of *Hamlet* and Shakespeare for generations: Q1 gives us access to the *Ur-Hamlet* "in a transition state, while it was undergoing a remodelling but had not received more than the first rough touches of the great master's hand."[60] As I discussed in Chapter 1, Clark and Wright thus rejected the quarantining of the earlier, non-Shakespearean *Hamlet* that both sides in the debate between Knight and Collier had rigorously enforced. Suddenly it became possible to imagine this earlier play as intimately linked to and indeed the foundation of Shakespeare's work.

Clark and Wright themselves did not imagine that the received Q2/F text of Shakespeare's *Hamlet* contained anything substantial "that is not his," only that Q1 did. And yet, once Q1 was understood as neither an early Shakespearean draft (Knight's view) nor merely a botched report of Q2/F (Collier's view), the damage was done. Q1 simply includes too much of *Hamlet* to resist the contamination of Shakespeare's play by the pre-Shakespearean version. F. J. Furnivall quickly recognized the epochal shift that this theory embodied, and its danger:

> Till 1871, all critics were, I believe, agreed that, except as to the incidents named above [i.e., the basic plot as derived from Belleforest, and the Ghost from "the old fore-Shakspere play of *Hamlet*"], Shakspere was indebted to no one for his *Hamlet*, and especially to no one for his conception of the man Hamlet. But in 1872 the Cambridge editors of the Clarendon Press *Hamlet* . . . propounded a new theory of the First Quarto of the play (1603); and this theory, when carefully examined and worked out, just robs Shakspere of about four-fifths of the conception of the characters of Hamlet, Claudius, Getrude, Ophelia, and Laertes: "Flat burglary as ever was committed!"

Furnivall himself reasserted that Q1 was the "the first sketch of Shakspere's play," even if filled with "mangled speeches and broken phrases" thanks to the reporter's ignorance; everything important "in the misreputing First Quarto as well as the Second" was "no old-play writer's, but in all essentials Shakspere's own."[61] But this rearguard action in defense of what was essentially Knight's old view was soon overwhelmed by the new disintegrationist theories. As Furnivall essentially predicts, the disintegrationists would go well beyond Clark and Wright, finding other hands even in the Q2/F text of the play. In their work, beginning in the 1870s with the "scientific" metrical tests of F. G. Fleay and flourishing from the 1890s through the 1920s in studies by scholars such as J. M. Robertson, E. E. Stoll, and L. L. Schücking, *Hamlet* would become a layered text resulting from a multistep process of revision, with Shakespeare altering and incorporating the work of several other playwrights.[62] Indeed, the disintegrationists based their interpretation of the entire play, and their solution to the traditional "problems" of *Hamlet*, on this very idea.

The disintegrationist movement now seems antiquated, partly because the New Bibliographers developed their own "scientific" bibliography by denouncing their predecessors as impressionistic amateurs.[63] But in fact it was a thoroughly modernist theory, itself relying on a "scientific" methodology, rejecting its predecessors as unduly subjective and decrying older "aesthetic" modes of reading, especially the Romantic triumvirate of Goethe, Schlegel, and Coleridge. And yet, the upshot of this modernist movement, as it analyzed *Hamlet*, was to pave the way for a new understanding of *conscience* that could easily be mistaken for a Romantic interpretation of the play—a striking example of Foucault's "complete reversals."

Disintegrationism has usually been discussed solely in the context of authorship studies; the statistical studies of verse forms by the distintegrationists provide an early example of stylometrics.[64] But their work went well beyond the identification of authorship, and their influence on modern Shakespeare studies is far broader than has been recognized. In their attempts to place Shakespeare's writing in historical context, the disintegrationists prefigure one of the main strands of twentieth-century literary criticism. All of these critics insisted in their own ways that only "historical literary research" could avoid the "anachronistic point of view" of most criticism and arrive at a true understanding of the text.[65] On this view, Shakespeare was "to be judged as a man writing for the stage (and for a particular kind of stage) and as an Elizabethan poet writing for Elizabethan audiences. To interpret him in terms which would not come off on the stage, or could not be understood by an Elizabethan audience, is, strictly speaking, not to interpret Shakespeare's work at all, but our own superfluity of sophistication."[66] The disintegrationists here laid the foundations for much of the important Shakespeare scholarship of the twentieth century.

Hamlet was at the center of this movement, and the disintegrationist analysis of the play hinged on Q1 and its relation to *Brudermord* and the *Ur-Hamlet*.[67] By linking all of these *Hamlet* texts, the disintegrationists rooted the play firmly in the dramaturgical trends of its moment and in the sedimented history of its transformation into the final form of Shakespeare's drama. Compared to this "scientific" and "historical" method, older analyses were now seen as merely subjective. The evidence for their subjectivity and consequent inadequacy lay in the very fact that critics had been disagreeing over the central questions of *Hamlet* for well over a century. In this sense, Furness's Variorum edition provided much of the impetus for disintegrationism, not merely by making widely available the texts of Q1 and of *Brudermord*, but also by collating the vast history of divergent critical opinion about the play. Fleay read this critical history as a "weltering mass of chaotic half animate protoplasm" that had completely neglected "the facts that we do know of the play and its author."[68]

The Variorum also spurred the thinking of the most important and (in)famous of the disintegrationists, J. M. Robertson, who concluded in 1885 that the "almost impenetrable mass of conflicting opinions, wild conjectures, and leaden contemplations" in the Variorum offered no hope of resolving the mysteries of the play.[69] A self-educated man who had worked as a telegraph operator, legal clerk, insurance agent, and journalist, Robertson rose to become one of the most prominent freethinkers of his day. His anti-authoritarian streak was amply on display in his anti-imperialist opposition to the Second Boer War and to British policies in Egypt and India, as well as in the atheistic magazine he founded, the *Free Review*.[70] His comments on the critical history of *Hamlet* similarly resonate with his writings against religious doctrine: "Fallacious 'subjective' solutions, ably expounded, have held the ground since . . . Goethe, that of Coleridge and Schlegel having coloured the bulk of English criticism . . . and for such solutions men fight as they do for dogmas."[71] For Robertson, the "only way to get a sound common ground" was to understand not only the historical context of the plays but also the historical process of their construction. In this way, he hoped to "bring to bear to some extent on the study of Shakspere the method of science proper, emancipated alike from metaphysics and idolatry."[72]

In *The Genesis of Hamlet* (1907), Charlton Lewis similarly favored a new objectivity, "a sound method of investigation" that would work "by comparison of Shakespeare's Hamlet with the German play, and of both with Belleforest's novel."[73] The "ultimate purpose" of this method was "to learn something about the missing link between Belleforest and Shakespeare; and that missing link is the lost play," the *Ur-Hamlet*.[74] The term *missing link* had recently been widely popularized by the discovery of *Pithecanthropus erectus* in 1891, and references to evolution recur constantly in disintegrationist writing: "The solution, once more, is to be found only in the study of the evolution of the play"; "Shakespeare had laboured wonderfully to evolve a Hamlet whose apparent abstinence from a possible and eagerly proposed revenge should be as it were emotionally intelligible"; "evolving a Hamlet of the highest mental lucidity."[75] The disintegrationists saw Shakespeare's *Hamlet* as an evolved organism, a higher form than the *Ur-Hamlet* but one nevertheless fundamentally derived from it and hence displaying certain vestigial traits that would remain inexplicable unless properly located in the descent of the play.

According to Robertson, one of the major errors of aesthetic criticism, and of Romantic criticism above all, was to "consider Hamlet as a real person," a fatal conflation of art and life.[76] Stoll argued vehemently against this error, urging critics not to write biographies of fictional characters but rather to "discover, if possible, something of the dramatist's intention."[77] There were two complementary paths to this goal: "One is by studying the technique, construction, situations, characters, and sentiments of the play in the light of other plays" of the era; the other is to examine "the modifications which Shakespeare made in his material."[78] Schücking followed the same method: only "the investigation of the genetic connexions" of the play could form the basis of a sound literary interpretation.[79] This characteristic rejection of any interpretation that could not be rooted in the history of Shakespeare's adaptation of sources and in the context of Elizabethan drama more broadly led Dover Wilson and many others regularly to group Robertson, Stoll, and Schücking under the label of "historical critics."[80]

For the disintegrationists, the "essential fact" about *Hamlet* was, in Robertson's words, that it was "an adaptation of an older play, which laid down the main action, embodying a counter-sense which the adaptation could not transmute."[81] Through a historicism that placed Shakespeare's writing in a complex stemmatic relation to all of the other *Hamlet* texts, criticism could deduce exactly what Shakespeare inherited from others, what he transformed into his own, and what remained as recalcitrant vestiges unable to be "transmuted" into his own work. Frederick Boas summed up this perspective in his edition of Thomas Kyd, a project clearly inspired by disintegrationism, since by the turn of the century Kyd was commonly understood to be the author of the *Ur-Hamlet*: "Generations of critics have sought to find a completely satisfying interpretation of [*Hamlet*]. They have failed to do so—even the greatest of them—and failed inevitably. For the *Hamlet* that we know is not a homogeneous product of genius. It is . . . a fusion, with the intermediate stages in the process still partly recognizable, of the inventive dramatic craftsmanship of Thomas Kyd, and the majestic imagination, penetrating psychology, and rich verbal music of William Shakespeare."[82] Boas was more positive about this "fusion" than another famous critic. When T.S. Eliot reviewed Robertson's *The Problem of "Hamlet"* in 1919 and famously declared that the play was an "artistic failure" resulting from the "'intractable' material of the old play," Furnivall's fears about the ultimate implications of Clark and Wright's theory had been fully realized.[83]

At the turn of the century, a spate of disintegrationist books proposed to solve all of the famous "problems" of the play—Hamlet's madness, his delay, Gertrude's questionable knowledge of the murder, and so forth—by recourse to this new understanding of Shakespeare's "genetic connexions" to his sources. With the ascription of the *Ur-Hamlet* to Kyd now well established, critics supplemented their reading of Q1 and *Brudermord* with *The Spanish Tragedy* to infer the nature of this "missing link."[84] The *Ur-Hamlet*, these critics concluded, must have been a "crude play" conceived around a "barbaric action," "a primitive tale of lust, blood-feuds, and revenge," a "crude tragedy of blood."[85] The goal of disintegrating *Hamlet* into its component parts was thus to identify the higher values that Shakespeare brought to the drama, which raised "the tone of his play above all other versions of the story" and set his tragedy "above the many others of personal revenge . . . in a class entirely by itself."[86] If Shakespeare could not quite succeed in his task without leaving insoluble problems in the play, that was only because the task was impossible: "The master is performing a miracle of transmutation," Robertson wrote, "vitalizing, elevating and irradiating a crude creation into a world's wonder, and finally missing artistic consistency simply because consistency was absolutely excluded by the material."[87]

For these critics, what Shakespeare added to the old tale was, above all, the philosophical side of Hamlet's character. Charlton Lewis pithily summed up the difference between the two versions: "Kyd's Hamlet does most of the deeds of the play, and Shakespeare's Hamlet thinks most of the thoughts."[88] John Corbin wrote similarly that when "Hamlet is in action his character dates back to the lost play: the Shaksperean element has to do almost exclusively with the reflective, imaginative, humane traits of his portraiture."[89] This view became dominant, even among critics not associated with disintegrationism such as A. C. Bradley, who thought that Shakespeare revised "one of those early tragedies of blood and horror from which he is said to have redeemed the stage" into his masterpiece through his "new conception of Hamlet's character and so of the cause of his delay."[90]

For the disintegrationists, the "problems" of *Hamlet* arise because Shakespeare has transformed the main character without fully transforming the plot in which he appears: the Elizabethan audience, already familiar with the play from its earlier version, would have balked "at any excision of the Ghost, the mock madness, the 'ragging' scenes, the railing at Ophelia, the killing of Polonius, the 'lugging the guts into the neighbour room,' the doom of Rosencrantz and Guildenstern, the leaping into Ophelia's grave, and all the rest of it." Elevating Hamlet's character while retaining "all the archaic machinery" of the crude plot of the *Ur-Hamlet* ensured that inconsistencies would appear.[91]

According to Lewis, for instance, the long-standing question of whether Hamlet's madness is feigned or real derives from Kyd's introduction of the Ghost into the *Ur-Hamlet*. Dragging in one of his favorite Senecan devices, Kyd inadvertently caused a problem: the murder is now secret, revealed by the Ghost only to Hamlet, rather than openly known to the entire court as in the source text. Hamlet's fake madness now "ceased to be very reasonable," since Claudius does not know of the Ghost's revelation of the crime and hence has no reason to suspect Hamlet of seeking revenge. Whereas in the sources Hamlet insulates himself from the king's suspicion by playing mad, now he only arouses it. Faced with this puzzle inherited from Kyd, but unable to write the popular Ghost out of the plot, Shakespeare asks himself: "What kind of man, with such a task thrust upon him, would go off on so impracticable a side-track? What is the meaning of this absurd pretence of madness?" The answer was to imagine this madness "as a safety-valve for the ebullitions of Hamlet's own passion," for the "hysterical intensity of his agony when his cherished ideals are shattered." Lewis thus arrives at an explanation for Hamlet's madness quite similar to Bradley's in *Shakespearean Tragedy*, but not by imagining Hamlet as a real person, as in Bradley's character criticism. His hermeneutic, and the modernist approach of disintegrationism more broadly, rejects subjective analysis rooted in character: "The composite Hamlet is not an entity at all, and therefore not a subject for psychological analysis."[92] Instead, Lewis works "objectively" by tracing the textual history of the play from Belleforest to Kyd to Shakespeare.

While Lewis's main subject was Hamlet's madness, Robertson focused on the problem of delay. He begins with Shakespeare's decision to remove the guards who, in *Brudermord* and the *Ur-Hamlet*, constantly surround the king and hence prevent Hamlet's revenge. In Shakespeare's play, commensurate with the elevation of Hamlet into a meditative Elizabethan, the "barbaric feudal court" of the sources becomes a Renaissance court, "with no guards normally about the throne.... Thus at the very outset of Shakespeare's transmutation the plain reason for Hamlet's delay ... has absolutely disappeared."[93] Now faced with a character who seems to have every opportunity to take revenge, and yet does not do so, Shakespeare undertook a "masterly effort to hint a psychological solution of the acted mystery." He did so, brilliantly and counterintuitively, by heightening the mystery, adding Hamlet's speeches of self-condemnation for his delay, and thereby elaborating "that aspect of the hero as he did every other." If Shakespeare inserted any reason for this delay—and Robertson is not sure he did—it is Hamlet's sense of "his mother's degradation." Whereas the Q1 Queen had avowed her innocence of the murder, in Q2 "these passages disappear," and Gertrude's guilt leads to Hamlet's inaction: "The guilt of a mother is an almost intolerable motive for drama, but it had to be maintained and emphasized to supply a psychological solution, or rather a hint of one." Hamlet's existential pessimism makes us feel "that for a heart so crushed revenge *is no remedy*." There is something of Bradley in this as well, and perhaps something of Freud and Jones. But Robertson too specifically rejects character analysis: all the previous, psychological explanations for Hamlet's delay cannot account for the fact that he does act, confidently and decisively, when he kills Polonius and Rosencrantz and Guildenstern. Ultimately, neither can Robertson's own theory, he admits: a character who would kill those people and yet "recoil from vengeance on a villain is not finally thinkable," because Shakespeare "left standing matter which conflicts with the solution of pessimism" but which had to be included to gratify audience expectations. In the end, "Shakespeare *could not* make a psychologically or otherwise consistent play out of a plot which retained a strictly barbaric action while the hero was transformed into a supersubtle Elizabethan."[94]

Stoll and Schücking probably went the furthest in shifting the study of *Hamlet* from aesthetics to historicism. According to Stoll, the Romantics erred in imagining the poet as a "genius omnipotent as a god, self-taught and self-impelled," when in reality poetic genius was "utterly dependent, potent only as it absorbed all the living thoughts and sentiments of the period and was initiated into the newest mysteries of the craft."[95] For this reason, while he notes Shakespeare's "unrivalled art," Stoll at times comes close to characterizing even Shakespeare's *Hamlet* as a fairly generic revenge tragedy: a "tragedy . . . (though so much else besides that) of intrigue, fate, and blood." Hamlet was an Elizabethan hero through and through, and Stoll rejected any fatal psychological weakness in him as anachronistic, not only "the diseased spirit and limping will" of the Romantic critics but also the Bradleian "pessimism" that even Robertson allowed.[96] Schücking did find a psychological disorder in Hamlet, but it was a thoroughly Elizabethan one, melancholy, and the prince was primarily a "type" who could be found in a host of other contemporary plays. The lack of historical understanding of this stock character had led to "the error of a great many critics" and "caused the whole problem of the play to be regarded from a wrong point of view."[97] For both critics, as always, it was Shakespeare's adaptation of an earlier plot that led to difficulties. While Shakespeare made "a more compact, a more vividly interesting play," wrote Stoll, nonetheless "an element of confusion and obscurity is produced as a result of shifting and omitting scenes and of toning down Kyd's crudities."[98] Schücking rehearsed the problem of madness analyzed by Lewis but rejected even his "safety-valve" solution as too character based: "The true explanation is that Shakespeare, here as in other instances, after fixing upon the plot as a whole, takes over the inherent faults into the bargain without examining them too closely."[99]

In seeking a historicized understanding of *Hamlet* that located the play "objectively" in stemmatic relation to Q1, *Brudermord*, and the *Ur-Hamlet*, the disintegrationists were far more the allies and progenitors of the New Bibliography than that later movement wanted to acknowledge.[100] Early in his career, W. W. Greg himself was something of a fellow traveler in the disintegrationist movement. In 1906, he praised Robertson's work on *Titus Andronicus* as a "most welcome and refreshing contrast to that of the traditionalists," worthy of "the deepest respect," although he already found him "too fond of supposing a divided authorship."[101] Only later, as the New Bibliography gained confidence in its own "scientific" methodology and Robertson's excesses in author attribution made disintegrationism an easy target for ridicule, did Greg come to reject what he called the previously "orthodox view that Shakespeare more than once revived and rewrote an earlier play."[102]

Indeed, when E. K. Chambers coined the label *disintegrationism* in 1924, his two prime suspects were Robertson and a scholar more associated with the New Bibliography: John Dover Wilson. Chambers thought Q1 derived essentially from a bad report of the full text of Q2 and F, and he attacked both Robertson and Wilson for their views of Shakespearean revision.[103] In an early essay on "The Copy for 'Hamlet,' 1603," Wilson had explained Q1 through an elaborate narrative of revision, piracy, and adaptation that in its fracturing of the text rivaled anything Robertson could imagine; he found the *Ur-Hamlet* not only in Q1 ("it exhibits Shakespeare actually in the middle of a revision!") but even in the received text of the play, because some of "the leaves of the Q1 manuscript were to be found in the 'Booke of Hamlet' from which Q2 was taken." Shakespeare's final version was the end result of a continuous process of revision, which Wilson expressed in a horticultural metaphor: "The Q1 manuscript is a sapling, which the gardener is in the act of pruning and grafting, that of Q2 is the full-grown tree, laden with eternal fruit."[104] It is not surprising that Chambers lumped Wilson in with Robertson; all of this is fully concordant with the line of thought leading from the Clarendon edition to Robertson and the disintegrationists. Wilson too later distanced himself from Robertson—and from his own idea of "continuous copy" that had caused Chambers to group him under the label.[105] In the introductory epistle to Greg in *What Happens in Hamlet*, Wilson rejected the disintegrationists' "main conclusion" that *Hamlet* "is dramatically a thing of shreds and patches." While that theory may have been salutary in explaining the play from "a very different standpoint from that of the older, psychological, school," it nonetheless fails for the same reason as Coleridge's psychological one: it misses that "what seems obscure" in the play may in fact be part of "Shakespeare's dramatic purposes."[106]

As this comment makes clear, what Wilson, Greg, and the New Bibliographers ultimately rejected was the disintegrationist vision of Shakespeare's plays as internally divided, inorganic, and not fully intended. It was one of the triumphs of the New Bibliography, and the source of much of its success as a movement, to demonstrate their wholeness. Nonetheless, Wilson fully accepted the disintegrationists' historicist position that "*Hamlet* and the audience for which it was written belong to the beginning of the seventeenth century . . . and these considerations must be allowed due weight."[107] This perspective was widely shared around the turn of the century; it was hardly the sole creation of the disintegrationists. Chambers himself, of course, was both the main opponent of disintegration and a pioneer in early twentieth-century Shakespearean historical investigations. But as Stoll noted, while this kind of historicism went back at least to Steevens and Malone, such work largely "kept to the life of the playwright and the language and external history of the plays," while critical interpretation of the plays themselves proceeded with little attention to historical context: "The scholars have moved heaven and earth to get at the original text, and the critics have done no less to give it a modern meaning."[108]

What was new in the work of the disintegrationists—and what remained centrally important to twentieth-century Shakespeare studies even after Robertson in particular became something of a scholarly joke for finding other hands everywhere in Shakespeare's plays—was how deeply their historicist understanding of the *text* affected their interpretation of the *play*. For the disintegrationists, the history of *Hamlet* completely ruled out all previous interpretations of the play and its main character, while offering solutions to most of their long-standing mysteries. The widespread influence of their method can be seen in much criticism of the period, in landmark editions like Boas's *Works of Thomas Kyd*, and in investigations into the traditional genre of revenge tragedy. The Riverside Shakespeare of 1897, for instance, was entirely typical in addressing key questions of *Hamlet* by beginning with the caveat: "We shall come closest to his probable point of view as a dramatist by examining the dramas of his time. It will be found that the revenge-play was a well-defined and exceedingly popular species."[109] The great Harvard Shakespearean George Lyman Kittredge was himself no disintegrationist, but he owes a great deal to that movement when he explains why Hamlet decides not to kill Claudius at prayer and instead to choose a moment that will damn his soul to hell: "The views in question accord with an old-established convention with regard to adequate revenge. With this convention the Elizabethan audience was familiar, and it made allowance accordingly."[110] By placing Shakespeare's *Hamlet* in stemmatic relation to Q1, *Brudermord*, and the newly imagined *Ur-Hamlet*, the disintegrationists helped to create a critical movement that dominated the early twentieth century and continues to reverberate in the twenty-first. As Percy Houston, who had himself studied under Kittredge, reflected skeptically several decades later: "From romantic dreaming and Victorian sentimentality the pendulum has swung to the hard-boiled realism of modern textual critics and students of the stage who permit a playwright to mean only what the action in a first-class Elizabethan melodrama reveals."[111]

It was in this context that "To be, or not to be," and specifically Hamlet's remark about conscience, began to be reevaluated. Whereas in the initial decades after Bunbury's discovery the Q1 soliloquy had scarcely been perceived as different from the famous version, now critics focused intensely on the gap between the two forms of the speech. Q1 "To be, or not to be" at last began to be read closely, more than half a century after it had first appeared in Payne and Foss's reprint edition. The work of the disintegrating critics had highlighted the "genius" of Shakespeare's more philosophical prince by contrast to the crude "tragedy of blood" that preceded and still lingered vestigially in Shakespeare's own text. Now the most famous lines in the play could be similarly located along this spectrum. The new interpretation of Hamlet's *conscience* succeeded so rapidly at effacing the traditional moral-religious reading of the line because it fulfilled the two crucial requirements for scholarly criticism emerging out of the disintegrationist movement, even for criticism antipathetic to that movement: the new gloss both *historicized* Shakespeare's play and *elevated* it above its sources and its genre.

The historicist impulse of the disintegrationists tended toward an evolutionary periodization in which Shakespeare's *Hamlet* surpasses its sources and previous versions as the civilized surpasses the barbaric, the Renaissance the medieval, and the Protestant the Catholic. For Robertson, the *Ur-Hamlet* "was a tragedy of blood, of physical horror"; the work of Shakespeare's revision was "to overlay and transform the physical with moral perception," ensuring that the characters were "purified of that taint of their barbaric birth."[112] Even Stoll and Schücking, the critics in this circle who most aggressively assert Shakespeare's similarity to other contemporary dramatists, nonetheless suggest that "the point of view of a new age is expressed, with cautious scepticism in 'To be or not to be,' or, in the conversations in the graveyard, with a unique mixture of sober, rational, almost scientific thought."[113]

Lewis was more explicit about this "point of view of a new age." He discovered "a curious complexity in the religious assumptions" of the finished play. Sometimes Hamlet "is moving in a world bounded by the narrowest superstition of medieval catholicism": hence the "real Ghost and his talk of purgatorial fires," Hamlet's first soliloquy on the Everlasting's canon against self-slaughter, and so forth. And yet, "in another familiar passage this same man is querying whether there can be any life beyond the grave. To die is to sleep; but whether in that sleep dreams may come, who knows?" As usual, Lewis thought "the circumstances of composition were chiefly responsible" for the contradiction. Through a detailed reading of "To be, or not to be" in Q1 and the final version, he showed that Shakespeare had partially but not fully brought the medieval superstition of the *Ur-Hamlet* into the modern age: "The Hamlet who uttered the soliloquy [in Q1] was the same medieval man that heard the Ghost's revelation, suspected the agency of the devil, and would not send a villain's soul to heaven. It was only later, as Hamlet became the mouthpiece for some of Shakespeare's own maturer reflections, that the agnosticism of the Second Quarto crept in."[114]

The agnosticism of "To be, or not to be," in its final version, became a hallmark of scholarly criticism, distinguishing Shakespeare's work from the more orthodox ideology and dramaturgy of the *Ur-Hamlet*. Robertson's *Montaigne and Shakespeare* helped to cement the idea that Montaigne's modern, skeptical philosophy had influenced *Hamlet* and especially this speech: "The concrete perception of the fatality of things, 'the riddle of the painful earth' . . . has emerged in philosophic consciousness as a pure reflection. . . . And this is the secret of the whole transformation which the old play of HAMLET has received at his hands."[115] Lewis similarly saw in Hamlet's soliloquy a philosophical skepticism about "the uncertainty of conditions beyond the grave." In the concluding lines of the speech, beginning with *Thus conscience does make cowards of us all,* Hamlet "seems to say, in effect: 'The uncertainty that unnerves the would-be suicide is the same thing that partly daunts me, the would-be avenger.'"[116] Here Hamlet's comment about *conscience* has been fully assimilated to his ensuing reflections about the *pale cast of thought*—precisely what Schlegel did *not* do—and his hesitation has become a problem of thought itself.

Robertson himself never glossed Hamlet's line about *conscience* so specifically, but he clearly thought of it along the same skeptical, philosophical lines. He rejected any parallel to the traditionally cited passages in *Richard*

III, which Robertson thought was mainly Marlowe's work: "The psychology [in *Richard III*] is simply that of the unsubtle monster of Marlowe, in which Shakespeare had no creative part. There was nothing new in the notion of 'coward conscience': it was not a specialty of phrase . . . but a current formula; and the idea associated with it in HAMLET is not that put here."[117] By contrast, the "idea associated" with *conscience* and *cowards* in *Hamlet*, everything that "is definitely Shakespearean" in the play, concerns "agnosticism on the subject of a future life," rather than those survivals of an earlier stratum when "Hamlet is made repeatedly to express himself, in talk and in soliloquy, as a believer in deity, in prayer, in hell, and in heaven."[118]

By the late nineteenth century, in other words, disintegrationism had provided a theoretical framework in which the differences between the two versions of "To be, or not to be" could be perceived and organized into a coherent set of ideological differences.[119] For most scholars, even those who were not disintegrationists themselves, the familiar version of the soliloquy became a Montaignean questioning of religious orthodoxy, and the new interpretation of *conscience* as philosophical reflection fit easily in this framework. The influence of disintegrationism can be readily seen in C. H. Herford's 1899 edition, for instance, which glosses *conscience* as "speculative reflexion": Herford thought that Q1 "rudely reproduced . . . an earlier version of the story, which underwent a revision by Shakespeare before it became the definitive *Hamlet* we know." He inferred that "the old *Hamlet* was a tragedy of vengeance," going on to elaborate the plot of the lost play at length. And he followed Robertson in his belief that "Montaigne's *Essays*, in Florio's excellent English, may have contributed to the speculative subtlety of [Hamlet's] speech."[120] Like Herford, most scholars and editors around the turn of the century rejected the extreme positions that Robertson ultimately advocated, but they nonetheless accepted most of the historicist premises of the disintegrationist analysis of *Hamlet*.

We have already seen that Chambers, the most famous critic of disintegration, may have been the first to gloss Hamlet's *conscience* in this way in an edition of the play. But what seems a contradiction in fact masks an underlying consensus that accounts for the widespread glossing of *conscience* as "speculation." It was no accident that Chambers and Robertson each accused the other of Bardolatry. Robertson thought traditional critics were "idolatrous in spirit" for thinking that the plays were "systematically conceived, planned, and finished products," and for their refusal to lose even a single word of their Shakespearean scripture. Chambers argued precisely the opposite: Robertson "idealizes" Shakespeare by taking anything not "at the top of his achievement" to be the work of an inferior poet.[121] In fact both critics, and in a broader sense both disintegrationists and their opponents, sought to elevate Shakespeare above the contemporary drama and earlier sources that were newly important to the understanding of *Hamlet*, all while also working to place Shakespeare within the context of the drama of his time. Robertson pleaded "guilty to a reverent admiration of Shakespeare" and his "unmatched power" of "laying the hands of genius upon other men's work and recreating their inferior creations of character."[122] And while Chambers admitted that there were "things in the plays which any other Elizabethan could just as well, or just as badly, have written," he thought that Shakespeare's style ultimately shone through the generic or routine: "Magic of phrase, lyrical impulse . . . a questing philosophy, a firm hold on the ultimate values of life: you are never far from one or the other of these at any turn in Shakespeare."[123] Just this "questing philosophy" was at stake in the glossing of *conscience*, in a way that appealed to both disintegrationists and their critics. Both sides of this debate sought to renegotiate Shakespeare's relation to his contemporaries after the discovery of Q1, after the waning of the Romantic consensus that underlay the opposition of Knight and Collier, and after the subsequent suggestion, which so upset Furnivall, that much of what had been thought to be uniquely Shakespearean may have in fact belonged to the pre-Shakespearean *Ur-Hamlet*.

The historicizing impulse that rooted Shakespeare in his own time and the elevating impulse that raised him above it are thus dialectically linked, as epitomized by Herford's peroration in his introduction to *Hamlet*: "If *Hamlet* is the most individual of all Shakespeare's works, if it is penetrated with the personal accent beyond any other dramatic utterance of man, it probably owes even less than usual—less certainly than *Macbeth* or *Lear*—to inventive construction of plot. But Shakespeare's supreme power of wholly transforming the spiritual complexion of a tale while leaving its material form almost intact, is nowhere so wonderfully seen."[124] If the new view of Q1 meant that Shakespeare's genius now resided less in the invention of plot or character, it could still be found in the "spiritual complexion" of the play. His "personal accent" lay in the questioning philosophy of a "new age" that distinguished the famous soliloquy from its orthodox Q1 doppelgänger. Glossing *conscience* as "speculation" instead of its ordinary religious meaning helped to canonize Shakespeare not as the kind of timeless genius that Stoll attacked as a Romantic fiction but rather within the fin-de-siècle historicist consensus shared by both disintegrationists and their critics. Even though Charles Knight himself had been one of the earliest writers to suggest that Hamlet's *conscience* meant *consciousness*, only after this historicist consensus had replaced the Romantic dialectic structured by the opposition of Knight and Collier could this understanding of *conscience* become dominant.

The older religious understanding of *conscience*, meanwhile, persisted mainly outside scholarly circles, in texts that found Christian meaning in Shakespeare's work.[125] For example, the *Sunday at Home Family Magazine for Sabbath Reading*, published by the Religious Tract Society to compete with secular periodicals, included a section of "Proverb Lore" on "Good and Evil," which told readers: "How many are the advantages and blessings which belong to a good man," but "How different is it with the person who has an evil conscience, for when that is so, 'Conscience doth make cowards of us all.'"[126] Hamlet's *conscience* turns up similarly in "A Sermon from Shakespeare" in *The World of Proverb and Parable* (1885); in the sermons of J. B. Lightfoot, bishop of Durham, published in 1890; in the "Prayer-Meeting Topics" of the *Homiletic Review* (1905); and in *A Guide to Preachers* (1906) by the London theologian Alfred E. Garvie, intended to help Congregationalist lay ministers write their sermons.[127]

Religious writers of this period rarely treat the textual condition of *Hamlet* or address Q1 specifically, but when they do, the difference from contemporary Shakespearean scholarship is stark. The Scottish minister George MacDonald, for instance, understood *conscience* as the righteous fear of punishment for sin; Q1 was simply Shakespeare's rough draft of the play, which therefore carried the identical theological message. He followed Samuel Johnson in denying that Hamlet was contemplating suicide in the speech, paraphrasing the key lines as: "'Who would bear these things if he could, as I can, make his quietus with a bare bodkin'—that is, by slaying the enemy—'who would bear them, but that he fears the future, and the divine judgment upon his life and actions—that conscience makes a coward of him!'" Unlike the majority of Shakespearean scholars and editors who now saw a clear distinction in the theological tenor of two versions, MacDonald uses Q1 as evidence for his reading of the familiar text: "That the Great Judgment was here in Shakspere's thought, will be plain to those who take light from the corresponding passage in the *1st Quarto*." MacDonald is completely uninfluenced by the new stemmatic understanding of the relationship of Shakespeare's *Hamlet* to Q1, which he thinks was "printed from Shakspere's sketch for the play, written with matter crowding upon him too fast for expansion or development, and intended only for a continuous memorandum of things he would take up and work out afterwards."[128]

The Jesuit priest Simon Augustine Blackmore likewise denied that Hamlet ever seriously contemplated the sin of suicide, nor did he accept that the speech was influenced by skeptical philosophy: "The Prince, far from being disposed to self-murder and rationalistic thought, is, on the contrary, very Christian in mind and sentiment." Hamlet's "hand is stayed"—from killing Claudius, not himself—"by the moral pressure of his Christian conscience," a word that "Hamlet employs . . . not as some suppose, as a term synonymous, with thought or speculation, or even consciousness, but as . . . the intellectual faculty of the soul employed in the consideration of an act in relation to moral rectitude or depravity." And, again like MacDonald, Blackmore sees the Q1 version of the speech as fully compatible with the received text, and indeed freely mixes quotations from both in his paraphrase of the soliloquy:

> Supposing then, as Hamlet does, the continued existence of the soul after it has shed its chrysalis of clay, he dwells on the cause of that "dread of something after death," which is common to mankind. It is the passing into that "undiscovered country" of the spirit world . . . where, "borne before an Everlasting Judge," the soul shall hear its sentence of justification or of reprobation.
>
> In that "undiscovered country," of which we know so little, "the happy" are said to "smile," because of their happy reward for a virtuous life; and "the damned" are "accursed," because of their crimes.[129]

For other contemporary Christian writers too the textual and the theological are interwoven. The tendency to read the two versions as fundamentally identical goes hand in hand with a tendency to view Q1 as an early Shakespearean draft.[130]

In the late nineteenth century, then, there arose for the first time a true debate over the meaning of Hamlet's *conscience*. Rather than being a vestige of the Romantic vision of Hamlet's overspeculative nature, the new gloss formed an important part of a very modern contest over the meaning of Shakespeare—as shown by the Catholic writer Henry Bowden's bitter reference to the common representation of him as "a pioneer of 'modern thought' . . . a positivist, a pantheist, a fatalist, in short, a typical agnostic." As Blackmore argued, again relying on Q1 to supplement his reading of the familiar version of the soliloquy, "The Christian view of death as a sleep from which we shall again awaken, is a strong caveat against the Materialist and the Positivist, who fain would see in the dramatist a champion of their anti-Christian principles."[131] The rise of the new gloss of *conscience* as "speculative reflection" reflects this desire for a *modern* Shakespeare, a Shakespeare who—as the progressive reviser of the more barbaric "tragedy of blood" represented by both the *Ur-Hamlet* and the pious orthodoxies of Q1—heralds the dawn of a "new age" in the Renaissance.

What also becomes clear in these Christian readings of *Hamlet* is the role of *conscience* in another cultural contest, not over the religiosity of Shakespeare but over the right to interpret him. The new gloss helped not only to elevate Shakespeare above his contemporary dramatists but also to elevate a professional cadre of Shakespearean scholars above "common" or "popular" understandings of the play. The historicist imperative that led editors like John Livingston Lowes to warn that "the greatest danger in reading Shakespeare is that of giving to familiar words the sense they now have, instead of the meaning which they had in Shakespeare's time" likewise ruled out Blackmore's casual conflation of the texts of the soliloquy and MacDonald's notion that Q1 was purely a Shakespearean rough draft. After the stemmatic innovations of the disintegrationists, most Shakespeare scholars now saw the textual theories of these religious writers as obsolete relics of an earlier, less "scientific" era of criticism. Just like the bed in Gertrude's closet, Hamlet's *conscience* had become a shibboleth that served to demarcate professional historicist Shakespeareans, who sought to root the Bard in his particular linguistic and cultural moment, from writers like Blackmore and Bowden who found more eternal truths in the play. The shibboleth would retain its power for half a century.

If this late nineteenth-century movement to situate Shakespeare's *Hamlet* in stemmatic relationship to Q1, *Brudermord*, and the *Ur-Hamlet* underlies the nearly universal scholarly turn toward reading *conscience* as "speculative reflection," how can we explain the mid-twentieth-century rejection of this gloss? As we have seen, the fin-de-siècle scholars stressed the *difference* between the mundanely pious Q1 version of the speech and the "questing philosophy" of the Q2 version, while contemporary religious writers stressed instead the *continuity* between the two versions. These religious writers found the Christian understanding of life, death, heaven, and hell that is so evident in Q1 in the Q2 soliloquy as well, with *conscience* as the lynchpin of their argument. What is striking is the extent to which the rehabilitation of the religious meaning of *conscience* in the mid-twentieth century was accompanied by—one is tempted to say, required—a new understanding of Q1 that, albeit in a very different way, also stressed its textual continuity with the received text of *Hamlet*.

That new understanding arrived seventy years after the Clarendon editors wrote their revolutionary preface. Rarely does a single critical work transform an entire field the way G. I. Duthie's *The "Bad" Quarto of "Hamlet"* (1941) transformed the scholarly approach to Q1. Elaborating on early twentieth-century New Bibliographic work, Duthie's theory of memorial reconstruction saw in Q1 only the poor attempt of one or more actors to transcribe what they recalled of the full, authoritative text of *Hamlet* that would later appear in Q2 and F. His argument had roots stretching back to Collier's "retrograde bibliography" but also made significant innovations that enabled Shakespeareans in the latter half of the twentieth century to rest easy in the knowledge that *Hamlet* was Shakespeare's and *Hamlet* was unitary.[132] It did so by returning to the origins of the problem and essentially rediscovering Collier's solution, cutting off Q1 from any pre-Shakespearean history of *Hamlet*. After Duthie's novel version of memorial reconstruction, claims that Q1 was linked to either an earlier Shakespearean draft or the *Ur-Hamlet* became virtually forbidden in scholarly circles.[133]

The immediate impact of *The "Bad" Quarto of "Hamlet"* can be vividly seen in the fate of an important monograph published a year prior, Fredson Bowers's *Elizabethan Revenge Tragedy* (1940). Bowers's study clearly emerges out of the earlier critical environment of disintegrationism. Bowers includes a lengthy summary of the *Ur-Hamlet*, which he infers from Q1 and *Brudermord*, admitting to having "written more about the *Ur-Hamlet* than Shakespeare's *Hamlet*." He addresses the problem of delay through the stemmatic relation of all the *Hamlet* texts, including a discussion of the "strict guard kept about Claudius" in the *Ur-Hamlet*, a key element of disintegrationist interpretations. He notes "the logical uselessness of the device" of Hamlet's feigned madness once the murder has become secret, but explains its retention as a concession to audience demands: "To discard it would have been to ruin the play." And he saw Shakespeare's version as "the supreme achievement of the form since he made the issue turn on the character of the revenger and thus gave ample scope for the philosophical consideration of life, death, and human endeavor inherent in the central situation."[134] In all these ways, Bowers's mid-century book strongly resembles the work of Lewis, Robertson, Schücking, and others around 1900.

By 1958, however, when Bowers was preparing a reprint edition, Duthie's argument had become canonical. Bowers felt compelled to include an unusual admonition to the reader just below the table of contents:

Note: When this book was written, George Ian Duthie's *"Bad" Quarto of Hamlet* . . . had not been published to establish the derived nature of the First Quarto *Hamlet* text. As a consequence, that part of my discussion of *Hamlet* that assumes Q1 to be a primary text, as conventionally thought at the time, cannot be taken seriously now: Q1 may not be utilized as an independent witness in such respects to Shakespeare's original intentions and to the development of his play. In an offset reprint like the present, the required rewriting of the argument could not be managed, and hence this note must serve as a warning.[135]

The declarative prohibitions in Bowers's note—"Q1 may not be utilized," "cannot be taken seriously"—demonstrates the nearly unanimous agreement that greeted Duthie's book, which here simply rules out a sizable portion of Bowers's original argument.

Duthie's crucial innovation was recognized immediately by W. W. Greg in his foreword to the book. "The most important section of the work" was Duthie's conclusive proof that those passages in Q1 not corresponding to anything in the received text are not remnants of "an earlier *Hamlet* of which Kyd may or may not have been the author." Rather, they "are built up out of verbal reminiscences, mainly of various and scattered portions of the full text, partly of other Shakespearian and non-Shakespearian plays."[136] In his novel technique of finding parallels for these passages in other parts of *Hamlet*, and in other plays altogether, Duthie had created a powerful machine for making the *Ur-Hamlet* disappear. Suddenly all the aspects of Q1 that had posed a nagging challenge to any theory that it derives from the Q2/F text could be readily explained. The Queen's offer to "conceal, consent, and do my best" to help Hamlet becomes "substantially an importation from another play," *The Spanish Tragedy*. Her explicit avowal of innocence can now be seen as "only putting more directly and crudely what is implicit in Q2 itself. Q1 being a pirated text, and there being ample room for adulteration by the reporter, there is no need to suppose that this denial ever stood in any *Hamlet* play."[137] The dialogue in the unparalleled scene between Horatio and the Queen "is composed of fragments gathered from no less than three separate passages earlier in the play," and so it "is to be attributed to the reporter-versifier. . . . It is not a remnant of the *Ur-Hamlet*, nor a portion of a Shakespearian first draft."[138] The different placement of "To be, or not to be" and the nunnery scene in Q1 does not predate Q2 but is "an alteration [of Q2/F] which has resulted in an inconsistency," for Hamlet enters two consecutive scenes reading a book.[139] The German *Brudermord* is likewise a memorial reconstruction of Shakespeare's final version, cobbled together by actors "driven to try their fortunes abroad by lack of success in England."[140]

In all of these ways, Duthie's methodology has the effect of banishing the *Ur-Hamlet* from Q1 and indeed of making virtually all earlier versions of *Hamlet* irrelevant because irretrievable. We have returned almost to where we began, with Collier's strange insistence that, even though there was an earlier *Hamlet*, Shakespeare's *Hamlet* was still "a great original drama." In Collier's telling circumlocutions, we recall, the pre-Shakespearean play was merely "a lost play upon similar incidents" and "a drama, of which Hamlet was the hero," rather than truly an earlier version of what would become Shakespeare's *Hamlet*.[141] Since Q1 derived from a shorthand report of the full play, the "lost play" was totally unknown and could therefore be safely ignored, as Collier imagined *Hamlet* as a new play written in Shakespeare's mature years. Similarly, Duthie's textual stemma consistently begins with Shakespeare's complete version and explains all other extant texts as derivative. The urgency behind this seemingly dry bibliographic investigation becomes clear when Duthie discusses *Brudermord*: "If in the main the *Brudermord* represented the old *Hamlet*, then the latter resembled Shakespeare's full play very much more than I should be prepared to suppose was the case."[142] Here we have a version of the same fears that had haunted critics since the discovery of Q1, fears that led Collier to his odd periphrases and roused Furnivall's ire at the Clarendon editors' "flat burglary" of Shakespeare's originality. With his new approach to memorial reconstruction, Duthie comes close to consigning all pre-Shakespearean versions of *Hamlet* to oblivion.

Close, but not quite. Duthie still allows a few glimmers of the *Ur-Hamlet* to peer through all the memorial reconstruction. Several phrases in Q1 and *Brudermord* that echo Belleforest but not the "good" texts of Shakespeare's *Hamlet* show that the reporters "remembered material from . . . the old *Hamlet*." These remembrances occur especially around Hamlet's interview with his mother, perhaps indicating "contamination of what is essentially a reported version of Shakespeare's final play by occasional reminiscences of the character-relationships of the old play."[143] Then there was Q1 Horatio's oddly disjointed explanation of how Hamlet changed the commission, sealed the fates of Rossencraft and Gilderstone, and returned to Denmark. Because Horatio's claim that Hamlet's ship was "crossed by the contention of the windes" (sig. H2v) seems to echo a line in *Brudermord* about a "contrary wind," Duthie argues that the reporter "trumped up an incomplete and incoherent account of Hamlet's voyage, drawing details from each of two quite distinct versions of the story—that underlying Q2, and that underlying the German *Hamlet* (or one similar to that)." Since "it would be absurd to suppose that the person responsible for Q1 drew directly upon the *Brudermord* itself," Duthie took both Q1 and *Brudermord* to be independently echoing the *Ur-Hamlet* at this point.[144]

Thanks to the explanatory power of Duthie's methodology, however, in later years the editorial position hardened, and even these moments tended to be explained as faulty remembrances of Shakespeare's play. Philip Edwards's New Cambridge edition remains closest to Duthie, accepting that "the reworking of the news of Hamlet's escape" as well as some aspects of "the new role for the queen" may be "a recollection of the old play of *Hamlet*."[145] But both Jenkins and Hibbard—and a host of less influential editions depending on their work—banish the *Ur-Hamlet* at these points, finding only a "corrupt derivative" of Shakespeare's complete play in both Q1 and *Brudermord*.[146] For the odd echo of *Brudermord* in the account of Hamlet's escape from the ship in Q1, both Jenkins and Hibbard found alternative explanations. According to Hibbard, "an adverse wind is not the same thing as a violent storm"; hence the "similarity between *Der bestrafte Brudermord* and the First Quarto at this point in the play is not a genuine similarity at all, and so there is no need to drag in the *Ur-Hamlet* to account for it."[147]

If Hibbard's declaration that the supposedly parallel phrases simply are not parallel seems a bit like critical fiat, Jenkins's explanation stretches credulity even further. Like Hibbard, he denied the parallelism of the two incidents—"There is no hint of a storm in [*Brudermord*]"—and found the genesis of the Q1 passage elsewhere:

> Q1 gets the hint for [the storm], I believe, not from some presumed original of [*Brudermord*] but from the turbulence in Q2. There Hamlet says
> > Sir in my hart there was a kind of fighting
> > That would not let me sleepe.   (V.ii.4–5)
> and it was because he could not sleep that he got up and, as Q1 puts it, "found the Packet." Hamlet's sleeplessness is not mentioned in Q1, but it is surely that which tacitly connects his being "crossed by the contention of the windes" with his finding of "the Packet." A confused recollection of the Shakespearean text has transferred the disturbance within Hamlet to the elements around him, so that the "fighting" in his heart becomes the "contention" of the winds.[148]

The critical ingenuity of Jenkins's explanation, with its rather strained attempt to find some passage in Q2 that could parallel Q1's "contention of the winds," reveals not only the ideological imperative to eliminate all traces of the *Ur-Hamlet* but also the power of Duthie's methodology to do so. Jenkins's edition presses to its absolute limit the retrograde bibliography that Collier first advocated, that Mommsen advanced, and that Duthie made dominant. Within a decade of Jenkins's edition, the theory of memorial reconstruction, strained here to its breaking point, would be seriously critiqued by revisionist textual critics, and, as I discuss in my Conclusion, a new Arden *Hamlet* would supersede Jenkins's based on entirely different editorial principles.

Before that critique, however, the power of Duthie's *"Bad" Quarto* ensured that "To be, or not to be" and its line about *conscience* could be reevaluated without the specter of Q1 and the *Ur-Hamlet*. Religious understandings of *conscience* returned to the fore as Shakespeare's play no longer had to be elevated above the older version by highlighting Hamlet's philosophical character. Whereas earlier critics like Charlton Lewis had stressed "the agnosticism of the Second Quarto" in contrast to the "medieval" faith of Q1, now the "rub" that prevents suicide, the "dreams" that come with death, were to be understood as hell and damnation. Jenkins quotes the Homily against the Fear of Death, which "sees 'the chief cause' of fear in 'the dread of the miserable state of eternal damnation'." Hamlet's "dread of something after death" becomes, for Jenkins, "the 'dread' of the after-life, which an uneasy conscience will increase."[149] Edwards understands this "dread" in the same manner: "Hamlet . . . calls himself a coward for having a conscience," and so the "sleep of death becomes a nightmare, because of the dread of damnation. What began as a question which was more noble ends as a contest in cowardliness. What is one more afraid of, the possibility of damnation or the certainty of suffering on earth?"[150] So too Belsey, in her influential article on Hamlet's conscience: "If death were no more than sleep . . . it would surely be welcome, but men choose to go on living, however wretchedly, because of the fear of something after death, the unknown which includes (we may construe) the possibility of eternal punishment, damnation."[151] All of this is a far cry from the turn-of-the-century insistence on the skeptical agnosticism of "To be, or not to be."

None of these writers explicitly addresses the Q1 version of "To be, or not to be"—not surprisingly, since, thanks to Duthie, the passage had become merely an amusing example of the damage that faulty memory could do to a beautiful soliloquy. As in the years immediately following Bunbury's discovery, the speech was no longer *read*, because it was no longer perceived as significantly *different*. But the silence itself is telling, since it depends entirely on the idea that Q1 is nothing but a bad attempt to reconstruct Shakespeare's *Hamlet*. And if Q1 is taken to be a memory of Q2/F, then perhaps the overt religiosity of the speech in Q1 has been allowed once again to influence readings of "To be, or not to be" in its familiar version. After all, despite these critics' insistence that Hamlet's "dread of something after death" involves infernal torments, there is no explicit discussion of heaven and hell, salvation and damnation in the speech—except in Q1. Belsey's parenthetical caveat—"the unknown which includes (*we may construe*) the possibility of eternal punishment, damnation"—indicates the need to read between Hamlet's lines to find this religious meaning. Similarly, Edwards notes somewhat uneasily: "Although I believe that *Hamlet* is primarily a religious play, and that Hamlet perpetually sees himself in a relationship with heaven and hell, yet it is noticeable that Hamlet voices very few really Christian sentiments"—at least not in the familiar text.[152] Earlier critics took this lack of "really Christian sentiments" to indicate Hamlet's Montaignean skepticism about the afterlife, specifically by contrast to Q1 Hamlet's consistent expressions of faith. But for Edwards it can only be a paradox, since "To be, or not to be" has become Christianized by its reference to *conscience* in the moral-religious sense.

As Duthie's *"Bad" Quarto* exorcised the specter of the *Ur-Hamlet* from Q1, so too faded the necessity of reading the familiar version of "To be, or not to be" in opposition to the religiosity of its Q1 doppelgänger. What returned, I am arguing, was a variant on the late nineteenth-century religious reading of the speech that imported into it the Christian soteriology of Q1. These Christian writers had understood Q1 as a Shakespearean rough draft that expressed somewhat disjointedly if forthrightly the same fundamentally Christian sentiments that they saw in the familiar version of the soliloquy. This understanding of the textual situation (essentially Knight's position) was already untenable among scholars at the turn of the century, and only more so after Duthie. But Duthie's theory of memorial reconstruction had precisely the same effect of allying rather than distinguishing Q1 and the familiar text of the play. Shakespeare cannot supersede the barbarism of Q1 in his final version, since Q1 simply *is* that final version, albeit very poorly remembered. Duthie's theory enables a more religious reading of "To be, or not to be" and of Hamlet's *conscience* in particular, because it now becomes easy to see Q1's frankly religious language as yet another example of the forgetful reporter making more explicit, quotidian, and jumbled what is nonetheless ultimately Shakespeare's text. Jenkins saw in the reporter a "characteristic tendency to be at the same time too vague and too explicit," and claimed (as we saw in Chapter 2) that in memorial reconstruction the genuine text "is often made crudely explicit." Although Jenkins argues that the reporter "muddles the whole conception" of Hamlet's soliloquy by "making death itself the dream," it is clear that he, like Hibbard and Edwards, sees the Q1 reporter as trying to capture essentially the same ideas as are expressed in the familiar version.[153] Once one accepts that position, "we may construe" the Last Judgment in the words of Q2/F and find religious meaning in Hamlet's speech despite the fact that this Hamlet "voices very few really Christian sentiments."

Duthie's memorial reconstruction theory, in other words, eliminates the crucial disintegrationist idea: that Shakespeare's *Hamlet* resulted from the layered revision of often recalcitrant material from the *Ur-Hamlet*, which could be inferred from Q1, *Brudermord*, and *The Spanish Tragedy*. In the roughly seventy years between the Clarendon edition and Duthie's *"Bad" Quarto*, the disintegrationist movement made available a view of Shakespeare's authorship that was far more radical than anything that had come before or that would follow—a radical vision that derives ultimately from Bunbury's discovery of Q1. In the hands of the disintegrationists, Shakespeare was located in a complex, stemmatic lineage of which he was only one part and which he could never fully overcome. This vision dominated turn-of-the-century criticism, resulting in a new historicizing of Shakespeare and his greatest play in the context of the Elizabethan theater in general and revenge tragedy in particular. That historicism, of course, has never disappeared. But once Duthie provided the solution to the problem of radical disintegration, historicist analysis did not require such anxious attempts to isolate in character development and philosophical subtlety Shakespeare's advance over earlier versions of the play. *Conscience* could return to meaning simply conscience. The perturbed spirit of Old *Hamlet* had once again been laid to rest.

The idea that Hamlet's *conscience* might signify *consciousness* has helped to obscure an important oddity about the soliloquy as it appears in the received text: the line does not truly make sense in its context. In all three texts of *Hamlet*, as I will show, *conscience* is decidedly unlikely to carry any meaning other than the religious one. Yet in its familiar version, "To be, or not to be" includes no religious language aside from this word, leaving *conscience* curiously unanchored. Indeed, the line seems almost to be imported from the Q1 version of the speech, where it fits perfectly. Perhaps Q2 "To be, or not to be" is a memorial reconstruction of Q1?

The word *conscience* appears seven other times in Q2 and F, in lines that are virtually identical in those two texts. In each case it clearly has a moral-religious meaning. When Hamlet says that he will "catch the conscience of the King" (Q2, sig. G1r), he means that he will use *The Mousetrap* to reveal the King's inner sense of guilt. Claudius's conscience is then revealed in an aside, as he responds to Polonius's comments on hypocrisy by confessing: "How smart a lash that speech doth giue my conscience!" (Q2, sig. G2r). Here for the first time, an audience can be certain that Claudius committed the crime, since his internal judge prompts this self-incriminating exclamation. When Laertes believes the King has also killed his own father, he cries, "To hell allegiance, vowes to the blackest deuill, / Conscience and grace, to the profoundest pit" (Q2, sig. L1v), signaling his willingness to revenge even if it runs counter to his own moral instincts and his hope of salvation. Claudius soon persuades him that Hamlet is responsible for his father's death, concluding: "Now must your conscience my acquittance seale" (Q2, sig. L3r); that is, if Laertes judges rightly, according to the dictates of his moral guide, he must admit that the King is not guilty. Laertes's desire for revenge then turns on the actual murderer of his father, and here too he refuses to be deterred by morality or religion: in the midst of the duel he admits that killing Hamlet "is almost against my conscience" (Q2, sig. N4v), but only *almost*.

Hamlet's own interest in the relation of conscience to revenge surfaces most clearly in the final act. Unlike Laertes, however, Hamlet sees vengeance as fully compatible with moral judgment. He excuses his killing of Rosencrantz and Guildenstern: "They are not neere my conscience" (Q2, sig. N2r)—they do not cause him any moral or spiritual qualms. And he asks Horatio, rhetorically, "i'st not perfect conscience" to kill Claudius (Q2, sig. N2r)? The moral-religious quality of *conscience* here is clear from the alternative that Hamlet immediately presents (in the Folio only): "And is't not to be damn'd / To let this Canker of our nature come / In further euill?" (F, sig. 2p6r). In each of these cases, there can be little doubt that the word carries its traditional religious meaning. Indeed, as we have seen, these uses are often explicitly contrasted with *conscience does make cowards of us all* by those editors and critics who argue that in that case (and only that case) the word signifies *consciousness*.

Q1 includes only three of these eight uses of *conscience*: Hamlet's line in "To be, or not to be," his rhyming couplet about catching the King's conscience, and Laertes's comment during the duel. But interestingly, Q1 adds two further references to *conscience*, both of which substitute for what is in the received text a more periphrastic reference. That is, Q1 clarifies or makes more concrete the moral stakes of Q2/F by reference to the familiar concept of Christian conscience. Thus while in the received text the Ghost urges Hamlet to leave his mother "to heauen / And to those thornes that in her bosome lodge / To prick and sting her" (Q2, sig. D3v), in Q1 he says more straightforwardly: "Leaue her to heauen, / And to the burthen that her conscience beares" (sig. C4v).[154] And when Claudius is attempting to pray, his speech begins in Q1 with the wish "that this wet that falles vpon my face / Would wash the crime cleere from my conscience!" (sig. G1v), a line that echoes but also specifies as a matter of conscience the penitential cleansing that he longs for in the traditional text: "what if this cursed hand / Were thicker than it selfe with brothers blood, / Is there not raine enough in the sweete Heauens / To wash it white as snowe" (Q2, sig. L1r). This is not to say that the word could never mean *knowledge* or *consciousness*, with no necessary religious connotation.[155] But throughout the three texts of *Hamlet*, *conscience* everywhere else carries a religious significance, so much so that it can substitute in Q1 as shorthand for more elaborate metaphorical discussions of right and wrong in the received text.

Even more important, the idea that "conscience does make cowards of us all" is an early modern commonplace that, like many of Hamlet's phrases in this speech, can be found in numerous other texts.[156] And in this sententious usage, the word *conscience* always has its familiar religious meaning. In Sidney's *Arcadia* (1590), we read that "the King (O the cowardise of a guiltie conscience) before any man set vpon him, fled away." The same idea appears in Edward Hall's *Union of the Two Noble and Illustrate Famelies of Lancastre & Yorke* (1548), when Richmond exhorts his army by telling them that that he expects Richard III's followers "being greued and compuncted with the pricke of ther corrupt consciences cowardely to flye and not abyde the battaill." And in Robert Cawdry's *Treasurie or Store-house of Similes* (1600), the second of twenty-eight similes under the heading "*Conscience good, or euill*" notes that a bad conscience is "cowardly, and vanquished, assoone as it is assayled." In numerous sermons and religious treatises, we are told that "An ill Conscience enfeebles vs, makes very cowards of vs"; "An euill Conscience makes vs dastards, and cowards"; "There is no coward to an ill Conscience"; an evil man's "conscience . . . turnes him into a very coward and weakling"; sinners "cannot abide the force and sting of their conscience, but fall downe coward-like"; "the cause that every wicked man is a coward, and will so conforme to the current of the time, is his ill conscience." The reason that conscience makes cowards is that evil men, knowing they are likely to be damned, fear death because of the divine judgment that will follow: "The conscience, wherin remains the memory of former violence & injustice, makes men Cowards, and afraid to grapple with death."[157]

As Nathanael Carpenter and many others explained, "the vsuall Prouerbe amongst profane Ruffians; that *conscience makes cowards*" was, as typically cited, imprecise and indeed blasphemous.[158] Only those with reason to believe they will be damned fear death, living "as *Damocles* at *Dionysius* Table," with "*Gods* fearfull iudgements, as a sword pendulous ouer their heads." The proper Christian perspective would make clear that it is not "a *good*, but an *euill* conscience which makes men cowards: Onely hee, who wants guilt, wants feare."[159] When the Hamlet of Q1 says, "O this conscience makes cowards *of vs all*," then, he may be using the proverb in a looser sense than strict theologians would have preferred. Nonetheless, in the fully Christian eschatology of the Q1 speech, Hamlet's line represents a perfect application of this commonplace to argue that the fear of hell makes sinners shrink from dangerous actions.

And in fact, the speech does imply something of Carpenter's distinction between a good and an evil conscience. Hamlet asks who would "indure" all of the tribulations of "this weary life, / When that he may his full *Quietus* make, / With a bare bodkin." Some people, he seems to suggest, endure these hardships because of the "hope of something after death": perhaps this is "hee, who wants guilt" and hence "wants feare" of what is to come after death. Of course, those with a clear conscience are also those least likely to commit the sin of suicide.[160] On the other hand, those with an evil conscience fear the "euilles . . . that we know not of," the hellish torments beyond human understanding, and these people refrain from killing themselves only because their consciences make them cowards.

In this way, Q1 Hamlet plays on two different meanings of the maxim. In the commonplace tradition, the idea that conscience makes us cowards could carry not only the straightforwardly religious meaning discussed above but also, less commonly, an ironic meaning. Shakespeare himself provides the most famous instance of the ironic usage, when the two murderers in *Richard III* discuss whether or not to kill Clarence. The second murderer feels some qualms of conscience but is persuaded by the first to ignore them; he concludes that he will "not meddle" with conscience, for "it is a dangerous thing, / It makes a man a coward: A man cannot steale, / But it accuseth him: he cannot sweare, but it checks him: / He cannot lie with his neighbors wife, but it detects / Him." Typically placed in the mouths of villains, this use of the commonplace treats cowardice ironically, as an ungodly misreading of conscience as a check on freedom of will: "euery / Man that meanes to liue wel, endeuors to trust / To himselfe, and to liue without it." Similarly, Richard III himself thinks of conscience as a Machiavellian strategy of control: "Let not our babling dreames affright our soules: / Conscience is but a word that cowards vse, / Deuisd at first to keepe the strong in awe." In his dream, however, he calls out to his "Coward conscience" and reveals that, beneath his ironic use of the commonplace, he in fact provides an instance of the more orthodox religious meaning: "My conscience hath a thousand seuerall tongues. . . . I shall dispaire."[161]

Q1 Hamlet deploys the maxim in a straightforward sense in relation to sinners, who have a cowardly fear of death. But since he refers to "us all," he also seems to be speaking ironically about the so-called cowardice of those who hope to be happy and smiling after death. What restrains these people from suicide is faith rather than fear, of course, but to the profane like Richard III it may appear merely cowardice in the face of death. Conscience makes cowards of sinners, and conscience makes "cowards" of the righteous. Whereas preachers tended to stress that it was only a *bad* conscience that produced cowardice, while "*the righteous are bold as a Lion*," Q1 Hamlet cleverly shows how both a good and a bad conscience could prevent action that would lead to death—but for very different reasons.[162] Far from being a "bad" version of the received text of "To be, or not to be," then, Q1 Hamlet's soliloquy shows a complex mastery of the commonplace tradition in its multilayered adaptation of the maxim that *conscience makes cowards* to its Christian vision of the afterlife. Q1 "To be, or not to be" is not without its syntactical and semantic difficulties, of course, but this reading of Hamlet's *conscience* fits both with the overall thrust of the soliloquy—its eschatological dichotomizing into heaven and hell, happy and accursed, smiling and damned, good and ill conscience—and with the commonplace tradition.

The familiar version of "To be, or not to be," by contrast, is difficult to reconcile with this tradition. Not only is there no mention of eternal judgment, the basic precondition for the commonplace in every other text in which it is used in the period, but the ensuing lines about the "Natiue hew of Resolution" becoming "sicklied o're, with the pale cast of Thought" and "enterprizes of great pith and moment" losing "the name of Action" (F, sig. 2o5r) shift the emphasis toward a generalized opposition between thought and action. This nonreligious opposition has no real presence in the commonplace tradition of *conscience makes cowards*. Indeed, these final lines tellingly do not appear in Q1, since they bear little relation to the Christian eschatology of that text. In Q2/F, we might say, Hamlet remembers a proverb that he has previously thought meet to set down in his tables, and he attempts to deploy it in a rhetorical set piece of his own invention. But he fails to integrate the sententia properly into his speech, as the commonplace tradition required. Q1 Hamlet is the better rhetorician.

Without this eschatological vision, the familiar version of "To be, or not to be" lacks the foundation necessary to the meaning of both the straightforward and the ironic use of the commonplace. Precisely because the line therefore appears out of place by comparison with the fully Christian version in Q1, once critics began to grapple with that new (old) version, Hamlet's *conscience* generated a large commentary tradition dedicated to explaining that its "true" meaning carried no religious significance. Before then, as I have shown, critics and editors seem largely to have assumed that *conscience* carried its traditional meaning. This raises the question: how did these earlier readers reconcile the explicitly Christian commonplace that *conscience makes cowards* with the complete absence of Christian theology from "To be, or not to be"?[163]

An intriguing clue emerges from the earliest evidence we have of someone actually reading the soliloquy. At Meisei University in Tokyo, a remarkable copy of the First Folio shows an early or mid-seventeenth-century reader actively engaged with Shakespeare's plays, marking up his or her copy with detailed marginal comments.[164] The reader made notes of key plot points but was at least as interested in extracting usable commonplaces from the text. This early Shakespeare enthusiast read, that is, according to two equally viable contemporary methods of engaging with printed drama: one that disregards the fictive world of the play in order to remove lines to make them available for later repurposing, and another that is invested precisely in that fictive world. In the first category are generalizing and abstracting comments such as "Madnesse by loue" (Polonius diagnosing Hamlet), "Mercie blots away offense" (Claudius's futile prayer), and "dissuasion to a woman from marriage" (the nunnery scene).[165] These notes indicate passages suitable for later transcription into a commonplace book under appropriate headings. They take little notice of the plot, for example disregarding that Polonius appears to be incorrect in his diagnosis of Hamlet's madness and that Claudius is in fact unable to find the mercy that might blot away his offence. Likewise, in this category of gloss, the reader eliminates character names so that they do not interfere with the abstraction required for the later reuse and application of the passages: Old Hamlet can become simply "a father," as can Polonius; Hamlet and Leartes are equally "a sonne," and Gertrude is "a mother." Elsewhere, however, the reader stays close to the plot, retaining character names and the particulars of the drama: "hamlet obiects to his mother the vilde / murther of his father and her / Incestuous mariage with his vncle."¹⁶⁶ This seventeenth-century reader appropriated Shakespeare flexibly, in other words, deploying diverse reading practices as occasion served.

All the more striking, therefore, is the reader's glossing of "To be, or not to be," which is entirely in the sententious mode of annotation. The reader clearly understood this speech primarily as a rhetorical set piece suitable for extraction and reuse rather than, like many critics, as a turning point in the plot or the development of Hamlet's character. In the top margin of the page on which the speech appears, he or she has written several glosses (Figure 25). Some generalize maxims from the dialogue preceding Hamlet's entry: "Our hipocrisie makes us surpasse the / deuill in Wickednesse" and "sting of conscience" commonplace Polonius's lines about how "pious Action" can "surge [sugar] o're / The diuell himselfe" and the King's subsequent guilty aside. The commonplacing impulse of these notes is continued with "To be, or not to be." The Meisei reader noted the speech as particularly rich in discussions of "doubt what befalles after death" and "Miseries and disgraces wherto we are subiect." But one line in particular apparently stood out, the only line actually quoted (or nearly quoted): "Conscience makes us cowards."¹⁶⁷ To this early commonplacer, Hamlet's line about conscience was the centerpiece of the speech, in part no doubt because it was already sententious.

What is most remarkable about the Meisei reader's handling of "To be, or not to be" is the "question" that he understood Hamlet to be debating: "whether we ought to ouercome our / selues and our passions by extreame patience / or die seeking desperat / reuenge."¹⁶⁸ As discussed above, in the critical history the decidedly minority position that the speech is not about suicide but rather about revenge was first advocated by Samuel Johnson about a century later, and then forcefully rejected by Malone. And this is precisely the view of the speech picked up by Belsey and Prosser in their influential arguments that Hamlet's *conscience* must be taken in the moral-religious sense. Like these revisionist critics, this early reader seems to link an interest in *conscience makes us cowards* to the belief that Hamlet is here debating whether to kill the King.

But there the similarity ends, because the underlying methods of reading differ fundamentally. For both Belsey and Prosser, Hamlet's use of the commonplace must be taken solely in the ironic sense. Hamlet's Christian conscience tells him not to revenge, not to give in to wrath, but "part of his

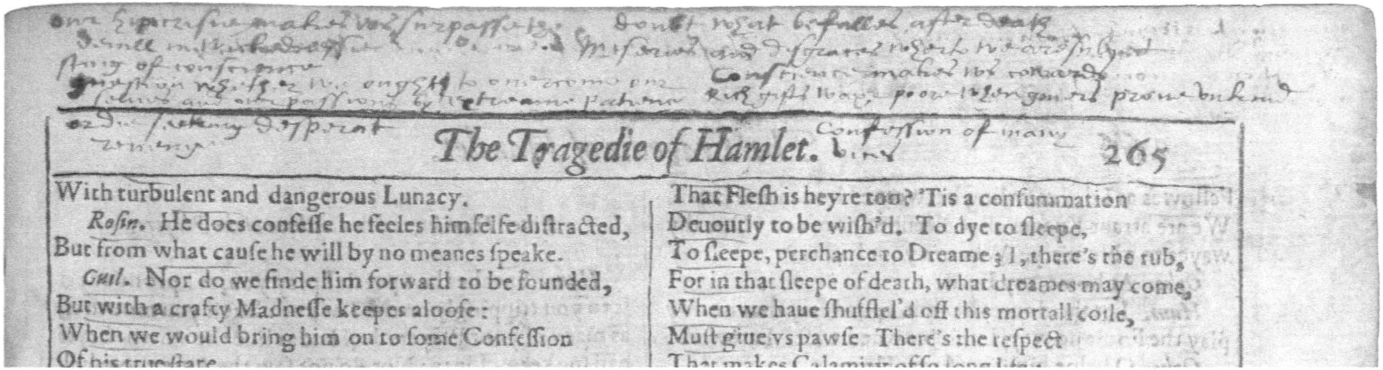

The Tragedie of Hamlet. 205

With turbulent and dangerous Lunacy.
Rosin. He does confesse he feeles himselfe distracted,
But from what cause he will by no meanes speake.
Guil. Nor do we finde him forward to be founded,
But with a crafty Madnesse keepes aloofe:
When we would bring him on to some Confession
Of his true state.

That Flesh is heyre too? 'Tis a consummation
Deuoutly to be wish'd. To dye to sleepe,
To sleepe, perchance to Dreame; I, there's the rub,
For in that sleepe of death, what dreames may come,
When we haue shufflel'd off this mortall coile,
Must giue vs pawse. There's the respect

Figure 25. A contemporary reader's annotations on *To be, or not to be* in the Meisei First Folio.

Reproduced by permission of Meisei University, shelf mark MR 774, sig. 2o5r.

nature is committed . . . to passionate, mindless vengeance," and he therefore "castigates himself with his own inaction and calls it unmanly cowardice."[169] As with Richard III and Clarence's murderers, in other words, Hamlet is wrong to say that his conscience makes him cowardly; he is mistaking Christian virtue for cowardice. The revisionist reading of the soliloquy therefore somewhat oddly requires Hamlet to speak of conscience like a typical villain. More important, even in its ironic version the commonplace that *conscience makes us cowards* requires a Christian framework to be understood, and yet the rest of this speech is not simply agnostic about the afterlife but is premised on an unknowing that actively *forgets* Christianity: the shock of Hamlet's comment that "no traveller returns" from death lies not so much in the frequently noted incongruity that he has just seen a ghost as it does in the blasphemous denial of Christ's resurrection. Given the gap between the thoroughly Christian commonplace and the non-Christian context of the soliloquy, readings like Belsey's and Prosser's—and indeed all recent critical attempts to read *conscience* as in one way or another equivalent to "fear of Hell"—fail to offer a coherent understanding of "To be, or not to be."

While the demise of the fin-de-siècle movement to read Hamlet's *conscience* as *consciousness* seemed to produce a simple return to earlier readings that understood *conscience* unproblematically in the Christian context, in fact that "return" involved a crucial transformation. The history of *Hamlet* after Q1 has obscured the meaning of Hamlet's line in its early editions, in fact, not simply because the discovery of Q1 led to a novel speculative-philosophical interpretation of the line but also because it encouraged later critics, in reaction, to imagine that the religious meaning of *conscience* was the commonsensical, straightforward reading. But it is not: such a reading leads to a basic contradiction in the speech. *Conscience* seems as if it must carry its fully Christian meaning, and yet the speech in which it occurs seems to rule out that meaning.

How does the reader of the Meisei First Folio differ from these twentieth-century critics and their supposed return to a more commonsense understanding of *conscience*? Unlike modern critics, the Meisei annotator makes no attempt at a holistic reading that can account for "To be, or not to be," or for the play more broadly, as a coherent statement on conscience, the afterlife, revenge, or suicide. Indeed, he or she typically does not read holistically at all, preferring a decontextualizing and fragmenting hermeneutic that was perfect for commonplacing. Alongside Polonius's speeches of advice to Laertes and Ophelia, for instance, the Meisei reader notes: "Wise precepts of a father to a sonne going to trauell In foraine countries" and "a fathers wise counsell to his doghter not to beleeue the promises and oathes of a young professed lover." At the same time, when Hamlet mocks Polonius by applying to him his reading about the "plentiful lack of wit" of old men, the Meisei reader glosses: "defects of old men."[170] The long-standing debate about whether Polonius should be taken as a wise councillor or a comically foolish old man does not obtain here: the Meisei reader understands Polonius's speeches as instances of rhetoric rather than insights into character, fragments of reusable material rather than parts of a continuous narrative. This is not to say that early modern readers could not read in a more unified manner, paying attention to character and plot; as we have seen, the Meisei reader noted key plot points for later reference. But they also had at their disposal this alternate mode of reading that is largely at odds with modern literary critical practice. And the Meisei reader turned to this commonplacing mode to read "To be, or not to be."

"To be, or not to be" thus becomes a speech "about"—that is, able to be transcribed into a commonplace book under headings associated with— whether we should "ouercome our / selues and our passions by extreame patience / or die seeking desperat / reuenge." And it is also a speech that includes the sententia "Conscience makes us cowards." What it is not, or does not have to be, is a speech in which this sententia forms part of a single, coherently logical statement. At one moment, Hamlet can voice a clearly non-Christian and skeptical perspective on the afterlife ("doubt what befalles after death"); at another, he speaks a commonplace about conscience that requires the audience to maintain precisely the Christian eschatology that the rest of the speech denies. When Samuel Johnson wrote that "this celebrated soliloquy" bursts from "a man distracted with contrariety of desires" and is therefore "connected rather in the speaker's mind, than on his tongue," he was reimagining in a characterological mode something that the Meisei reader understood in a textual mode: "To be, or not to be" is not a unified speech but rather a patchwork of maxims and meditations. (Similarly, the speech itself is a fragment within the larger play: as an impersonal set piece with no overt relation to any of the other characters or the plot, it can be "patched" in at various points in the play with no need to revise elsewhere, as shown by its alternative location in Q1.)

If we want a unified discussion of the "question"—or the "point"—we will find it only in Q1. Only in that text does the entire speech hang together, despite the occasional syntactical difficulty; only there does Hamlet's citation of the proverb that conscience makes us cowards participate in a seamless analysis of the relationship between this world and the next, death and the Last Judgment. In other words, the textual situation around this speech is precisely the opposite of how editors have traditionally presented it: while Q1 may be less philosophically adventurous, nonetheless it is far more coherent than Q2 or F. The repeated claim that Q1 "To be, or not to be" sounds like burlesque or parody simply derives from its discovery long after "every *English* Reader" already knew the "Beauties" of the familiar version, as George Stubbes wrote as early as 1736. But in fact it is Q1 that is "connected" not in the critically invented "mind" of Hamlet but "on his tongue"—that is, in the actual text of the play as we have it.

My suggestion that Q2 "To be, or not to be" is a memorial reconstruction of Q1—one that contains some of the right words, the memorably sententious remarks, but only disjointedly and out of their proper context—is of course tongue in cheek. But it is meant to raise a serious question: Why is this speech more coherent in Q1 than in Q2 or F, and why do those latter texts involve this strange disconnect between a Christian commonplace and a decidedly un-Christian meditation? If Q1 is in fact some kind of reported text, then we might apply a version of the editorial principle of *difficilior lectio* ("the more difficult reading" is the correct one) and conclude that Q1 shows the reporter's memory defaulting to what he already knew when faced with a more complex and theologically radical comment on death. Unconsciously erasing the disjunctures in the Q2/F version of the speech, the reporter remembered the commonplace about conscience and therefore "remembered" the orthodox Christian theology that ought to have surrounded it. This analysis not only conforms to traditional understandings of memorial reconstruction—in which the reporter is often thought to substitute the banal for the poetic or innovative—but also explains why Q1 "To be, or not to be" voices such a traditional vision of the "four final things."

But what this theory cannot explain is the oddity of the familiar version of the speech. In Q2/F, Hamlet's commonplace about conscience seems like a remainder, an errant line in search of its context, carried over from a version of the speech in which it would have been more appropriate. Maybe Shakespeare simply used the proverb without thinking too hard about whether it worked in its new context; given that he had already put it in the mouths of murderers in *Richard III*, perhaps it came to mind when he considered the "bare bodkin" as a (self-)murder weapon. Or else perhaps Shakespeare, like the Meisei reader, was less concerned with that fit than we are. But when we consider how much more religiously orthodox Q1 is than the received text—from "To be, or not to be" to Hamlet's dying words—the Christian underpinnings of *conscience does make cowards* suggests that Q2 and F have somehow been influenced by

Q1. Everything about twentieth-century bibliography, of course, tells us that such an influence is impossible. But once we see how our readings of this line have so thoroughly derived from the history of scholarly engagement with Q1, that influence becomes apparent, impossible or not. The impossibility itself is a residue of *Hamlet* after Q1.

Conclusion

Q1 in the Library at Babel

In 1825, Payne and Foss summarily told their readers that Q1 *Hamlet* represented the play "as originally written by Shakespeare, which he afterwards altered and enlarged." By 2006, that brief editorial statement of textual origins had expanded to hundreds of pages, as readers were offered the most extensive edition of Q1 to date. With the massive scholarly apparatus of the Arden Shakespeare, Ann Thompson and Neil Taylor present Q1 as part of a three-text edition: Q2 appears as "the Arden *Hamlet*" in one volume and "The Texts of 1603 and 1623" in a second.[1] Thompson and Taylor's *Hamlet* crystallizes the dominant postmodern approach to the Shakespearean text, just as Knight's and Collier's rival editions did for the Victorians, just as the Clarendon edition did for the fin-de-siècle and modernist periods after the waning of the Romantic opposition of Knight and Collier. And like Jenkins's New Bibliographic edition, its predecessor in the second series Arden Shakespeare, Thompson and Taylor's *Hamlet* serves as both the culmination and, I believe, the exhaustion of the dominant approach of its moment. Their edition therefore suggests that the study of *Hamlet* and the Shakespearean text after Q1 may once again be about to change.

On the question of authorship, Thompson and Taylor could not be further from the confident pronouncement of Payne and Foss. They too justify their edition by the name of Shakespeare, but this name is now thoroughly enmeshed in and formed by early modern print and theatrical culture: "Each of Q1, Q2 and F is a version of *Hamlet* which appeared either in, or soon after, Shakespeare's lifetime. Each includes a printed claim to be by him. Each has a case to be considered as 'authentic'."[2] Rather than rising singularly above his environment, as both the disintegrationists and their critics sought to demonstrate, this Shakespeare can only be invoked obliquely, by reference to the moment in which he lived ("Shakespeare's lifetime") or to the title-page attribution of his authorship ("a printed claim to be by him"). But even so, Thompson and Taylor cannot quite anchor Shakespeare to these three texts: they hedge the word "authentic" with scare quotes, suggesting the impossibility of assigning bibliographic value to the word; they must blur their biographical criterion to include a text (F) that was printed not "in" but only "soon after" Shakespeare's lifetime; and their appeal to the "printed claim to be by him" proves too much, as it justifies the inclusion in the Arden Shakespeare of not only Q1 but also plays like *The London Prodigal* and *A Yorkshire Tragedy* that do not in fact appear in the series.

Because "Shakespeare" can only hover around these texts rather than firmly endorse them, when Thompson and Taylor argue that Q1, Q2, and F are "three representations of Shakespeare's *Hamlet*," they must immediately qualify their claim: the concept of "'Shakespeare's *Hamlet*' . . . need[s] careful handling." Here the editors carefully disavow the kind of superior scholarly knowledge that, as we have seen, their predecessors generally proclaimed: "We are not assuming that William Shakespeare was necessarily the sole author of every word in those early seventeenth-century texts, nor that we know the degree to which any of them represent the author's or authors' intentions, nor how it was that they came to be in print."[3] Thompson and Taylor thus profess their ignorance on the very subjects that have most exercised critics and editors since Henry Bunbury discovered his copy of Q1, subjects discussed throughout the preceding chapters: authorship and revision, stenography and memorial reconstruction, the transmission of the text and its passage into print. These texts can now be said to be "Shakespeare's *Hamlet*" only in a highly attenuated sense.

So attenuated, in fact, that they ultimately seem to dissolve into an undifferentiated penumbra that we might call "*Hamlet*": "If by '*Hamlet*' we mean a public representation of a 'Hamlet' narrative—that is, a story involving a character called Hamlet who has some continuity of identity with the Amlodi figure of Nordic myth—then these three texts are just three 'expressions' of *Hamlet* out of the infinite number of *Hamlet*s which have or could have come into existence."[4] As Thompson and Taylor elaborate this theory of infinite *Hamlet*s—an odd inversion of the parable about the infinite typewriting monkeys with infinite time producing the singular *Hamlet*—the reader is left wondering if there is in fact any substantive content to the phrase "Shakespeare's *Hamlet*" beyond the fact that Shakespeare's name appears on the title page. But the mere fact of that title-page attribution, as we have seen, has never been enough to guarantee Shakespeare's authorship of Q1 from the depredations of pirates, dishonest publishers, and editors wielding theories of stenographic or memorial reconstruction.

In their editorial decision to "treat each text as an independent entity" rather than conflating them, and in their confession that "we do not, after working on the play for about ten years, have a new or sensational 'theory of *Hamlet*' to offer our readers," Thompson and Taylor follow a general trend in recent studies of Shakespeare's early texts, a "New Textualism" that emerges out of the ashes of the theory of memorial reconstruction.[5] By the end of the twentieth century, that New Bibliographic theory had been seriously undermined, if it has not yet quite collapsed as a result.[6] And a number of other aspects of the New Bibliography had likewise come under attack by proponents of the New Textualism, who have generally been more interested in "unediting" than in producing critical editions that purported to recover the lost authorial manuscript.[7]

This movement to unedit Shakespeare, to pry apart the traditionally conflated editions of multiple-text plays, began not with *Hamlet* but rather with arguments that the quarto and Folio texts of *King Lear* represent different stages in the play's history of authorial revision, a rethinking that ultimately led to the inclusion of two versions of the play in the Oxford Shakespeare. But Q *King Lear* had not formed part of the original group of bad quartos outlined by Pollard, and its reevaluation, while questioning the theory of memorial reconstruction, left Q1 *Hamlet* largely unaffected. Nor did the reevaluation of *Lear* do much to disrupt traditional notions of Shakespearean authorship. If anything, this trend may have reinforced such notions by locating Shakespeare as the origin of virtually all artistic difference between the two texts, as in Steven Urkowitz's summation: "All that is needed [to account for the variation between Q and F *Lear*] is Shakespeare, capable of preternatural brilliance, well within his observed capacity to strike us dumb with amazement."[8] Thus when the Oxford editors Stanley Wells and Gary Taylor expressed regret that they had not treated *Hamlet* in a similar way to *Lear*, this regret did not involve Q1: they had wanted to edit Q2 and F *Hamlet* as two distinct versions, with authorial revision again explaining the variation.[9] While this strand of the New Textualism challenged the New Bibliographic tenet that Shakespeare's multiple texts ultimately testified to a single, authorially intended version of the play, it often simply accepted the traditional twentieth-century understanding of Q1 *Hamlet* and Pollard's other bad quartos.[10]

When the New Textualism moved on to critique these aspects of the New

Bibliography, Q1 *Hamlet* again moved to the center of debate. It was the first play published in the Shakespearean Originals series, which sought to present lightly edited texts of early quartos that had been "modernized out of all recognition" by "editorial intervention."[11] The publication of Q1 *Hamlet* in the series prompted a lengthy exchange in the *Times Literary Supplement*, including Brian Vickers's memorable comment that Q1 was "*Hamlet* by Dogberry" and his reassertion of the dogma that Duthie's *"Bad" Quarto* had "irrefutably confirmed" that Q1 was a memorial reconstruction.[12] Theoretical and logical problems plagued the Shakespearean Originals series, but other early work on Q1 *Hamlet* was more rigorous and encouraged critics to engage with it "as an independent entity."

Some authors in the landmark collection of essays *The "Hamlet" First Published*, for instance, avoided theories of origin entirely and were "concerned primarily with Q1's characteristics . . . as such and in the broader historical context."[13] In this vein, Urkowitz urged that we study "the Q1 text of *Hamlet* . . . as a product of the same theatrical industry that generated the works of Marlowe, Shakespeare, and Jonson." Rather like the Arden editors who followed him, and diverging from his earlier insistence on Shakespeare as the agent who could best account for textual variation, Urkowitz compellingly argued that treating each text on its own would enable, rather than close off, comparisons among them: "If we can analyze the virtues of *Gorboduc* and *A Faire Quarrel*, there is no reason not to study Q1 *Hamlet* as a drama with characteristics interestingly contrasted to *Hamlet* Q2 and F."[14] But notice that the ontological status of Q1 *Hamlet* vacillates in Urkowitz's very syntax between being a separate play in itself, like *Gorboduc* or *A Faire Quarrel*, and being another version of the same play represented differently in Q2 and F *Hamlet*.

Like the Arden editors, in other words, Urkowitz seems unable to decide exactly what *Hamlet* is. His argument both depends on and yet ultimately dissolves the crucial bibliographic principle that Q1, Q2, and F are three editions of the same play and that they can therefore be productively related to each other in a textual stemma. Revisionist work on *Lear*, in the Oxford Shakespeare and elsewhere, had found this textual relationship between editions in Shakespeare himself, but as the New Textualism turned its attention to the three texts of *Hamlet*, it seemed to lose its faith in the stemma.

We can see the same uneasiness in Paul Werstine's foundational New Textualist essay "The Textual Mystery of *Hamlet*." Werstine initially lays out a persuasive argument against conflating Q2 and F *Hamlet* that is reminiscent of Wells and Taylor or Urkowitz on *King Lear*, but he turns in his final section to a powerful critique of theories like theirs: "According to the conventions of revisionist textual criticism, I should now rise in an *o altitudo* to invoke Shakespeare as necessarily the source of the divergent patterns in Q2 and F unearthed here." Instead, Werstine argues that the "purely aesthetic patterns" that seem to demarcate these two versions of *Hamlet* "can have no claim to historicity; they do not exist beyond this paper," products of the critic's inventive mind.[15] Like the Arden editors, Werstine urges us to reconsider the texts of *Hamlet* on their own terms, without conflating them, but he resists what would traditionally be the next step for bibliography and editing: an attempt to show how these different versions might have come about.[16] Thinking through the similarities and differences among Q1, Q2, and F *Hamlet* of course implies that they are three texts of the same work, and yet with little sense of the textual stemma that lies behind them, they remain stubbornly disjunct.

Much of the scholarship associated with the New Textualism more broadly, beyond *Hamlet,* follows the same pattern. What unites all of these studies is the combination of a close and rigorous attention to the materiality of Shakespeare's printed editions, a detailed examination of the texts in all their variation, and an insistent refusal to speculate about textual origins. Scholars have reexamined "as an independent entity" each of the plays in Pollard's group of bad quartos, as well as many others in the expanded canon of plays supposedly reconstructed by memory. These texts are now often seen, in Leah Marcus's words, as "different instead of debased."[17] Many critics have followed Urkowitz's call to "stop chasing this idealized shadow"—the authorially intended text—"and look instead at the extant legacy of theatrical treasure in the multiple texts."[18] As a result, as Gabriel Egan notes, the "bad quartos are now often put on an equal footing with the good editions and published as alternative versions of the same plays."[19] Hence in 2000, as the Arden editors would do with *Hamlet,* Jill L. Levenson produced edited texts of both Q1 and Q2 *Romeo and Juliet* for the Oxford Shakespeare, arguing that they represented "two different and legitimate kinds of witnesses" to what was a "mobile text."[20] But again, Egan's phrase "alternative versions of the same plays" masks a real logical problem: by declining to speculate on the bibliographic relationship between these "alternative versions," the New Textualism ultimately has no way to explain precisely how (or even *that*) they are "the same" play.

In this context, what is most innovative about the third series Arden *Hamlet* is not its decision to edit Q2 and F separately: this editorial choice simply puts into effect the belatedly expressed desire of Taylor and Wells. Nor is the

Arden the first to offer readers a carefully prepared, modernized text of Q1: Frank Hubbard had done so in 1920, Albert Weiner in 1962, and Kathleen Irace in 1998.[21] What is striking about the Arden *Hamlet*, rather, is how far this edition pushes the New Textualist tendency to resist editing. This editorial recusal makes the Arden emblematic of critical thought on the play after the refutation of Duthie's "irrefutable" argument and after the three great editions by Jenkins, Hibbard, and Edwards that were all based on Duthie's work. Precisely because Thompson and Taylor so brilliantly lay out the textual situation and editorial history of the play, while at the same time consistently declining to put their understanding into action in the usual way, the Arden *Hamlet* seems perfectly timed for its critical moment, when the New Bibliographic certainties no longer convince but neither do we have any persuasive new theories of Q1 and its relationship to Q2 and F.

Thompson and Taylor not only believe that the three texts are "remarkably distinct entities" with "sufficient merit to be read and studied" separately. They further suggest that it may simply be impossible to create the kind of textual stemma that, as I have shown, has underwritten scholarship on the play since the late nineteenth century and that has become an editorial requirement since the New Bibliography: "We do not feel that there is any clinching evidence to render definitive any of the competing theories," and the "temptation to deny that we have a theory for any one text, let alone all three, is almost overwhelming." While they recognize that in practice if one emends at all, some theory of the text must underlie one's choices, nonetheless their "disposition is agnostic."[22] That attitude comes through clearly as they repeatedly resort to hedging and balancing phrases: "there is no consensus here either," "But there are alternative interpretations . . . ," "But, alternatively . . . ," "There is some force to these parallels, but . . . ," "so much of the evidence is either contradictory or ambiguous."[23] For this reason, their essay on "The Nature of the Texts" reads less like the usual statement of editorial principles and bibliographic conclusions than like an editorial history, which neutrally explicates the major positions that have been taken on the problem. Even when they make their most forceful claims—and these are generally based on editorial consensus rather than a strong truth claim—they can see numerous objections: "Almost all editors think the printer's copy for Q2 was Shakespeare's foul papers. . . . It is worth noting, however, that some features of Q2 proposed as support for this position can be challenged."[24] And so forth.

After thirty pages of this balanced and patient summary of others' arguments, Thompson and Taylor do lay out their own theory of the texts. But this theory is just as tentative and deliberately narrow as their discussion of the phrase "Shakespeare's *Hamlet*." Since no theory of the texts "is proven (or, we imagine, finally provable) and none can be dismissed out of hand," their own "procedure has been to weigh the rival theories of transmission of the three texts and settle for the most probable." As they readily admit, this is not "a strong theory of the texts' transmission" but rather "a default position arrived at by eliminating what we are persuaded are the less likely options."[25] This "default position" is itself telling: ultimately, Thompson and Taylor revert to what is essentially a less confident version of the traditional twentieth-century theory that Q1 is a memorial reconstruction of a performance text recorded by F, with Q2 in some way derived from Shakespeare's manuscript. Nonetheless, they prefer to edit three separate texts of *Hamlet* so as to preserve their integrity as discrete versions. Here we can see the simultaneous culmination and exhaustion of the New Textualism: in the most extensive and rigorous scholarly edition of *Hamlet* to emerge from this revisionist bibliography, there is finally no way forward, only a "weak" regression to a familiar theory.

The Arden edition, and the New Textualism more broadly, thus seems "like a man to double busines bound" (Q2, sig. L1r), trapped between two alternatives, each of which it rejects. By refusing to conflate or even to present a "strong" theory of the relationships among the three texts, the Arden editors express a widely shared skepticism about the analytic tools of the New Bibliography. At the same time, they reject the extreme "unediting" toward which their own bibliographic agnosticism would seem to lead them: the idea "that it is impossible and unnecessary to determine the origins of the three texts known as Q1, Q2 and F in the ways in which other editors have attempted, that each is of equal authority, and that an editor's job is to reproduce them verbatim and without emendation."[26] Their reversion to a quite traditional theory of the texts, now merely hedged in a cautious tone, suggests the impossibility of finding any escape from this double bind within the terms of the New Textualism itself.

In fact, with the loss of faith in our ability to construct the kind of complex stemma characteristic of both disintegrationism and the New Bibliography, the New Textualism can only lightly adhere to *any* particular theory of textual origins. The diagram that Thompson and Taylor produce of their preferred theory resembles a stemma one would find in an edition like Jenkins's, but we must remember that here the connections between texts have become weakened shadows of their formerly definitive selves and should perhaps have been represented by dotted lines (Figure 26). Meanwhile, "unediting" leads to the conclusion that we cannot hope to reconstruct these textual relations, and hence Thompson and Taylor propose a diagram that is not quite a diagram (Figure 27).

These two diagrams offer the perfect representation of the quandary in which we now find ourselves. The old stemmatics seem no longer possible—or possible only in a ghostly, attenuated form—but the New Textualist "stemma" is self-contradictory at a fundamental level. If these disjunct texts cannot be linked to each other at all, why are all three located in the same diagram in the first place? Common sense tells us that these are three texts of the same play called *Hamlet*, and of course the blurb on the title page of Q2 itself claims a family relation with Q1 (although one that, as we have seen, may be more ambiguous than has generally been thought). But when, as Levenson writes of *Romeo and Juliet*, every "hypothetical stemma collapses under the weight of possibilities," we are left with no rigorous rationale for their interrelation.[27] Our bibliographic theory, in other words, pushes us in the opposite direction of common sense, toward the conclusion that these are three completely discrete plays. No wonder Thompson and Taylor shy away from the "unediting" position to which this diagram gestures, but they are left with nothing else to fall back on other than the hollowed-out shell of a familiar theory.

The gap between these two diagrams recalls Fredric Jameson's famous opposition of Van Gogh's painting of peasant's shoes and Andy Warhol's *Diamond Dust Shoes*. In the passage from the modernist to the postmodern artwork, what has been lost is a sense of depth, in both the hermeneutic and the historical sense. Unlike with Van Gogh's painting, Jameson writes, with Warhol's image there is "no way to complete the hermeneutic gesture and restore to these oddments that whole larger lived context" from which they emerge. A "crisis in historicity" leads to "a culture increasingly dominated by space and spatial logic" as opposed to "time, temporality and the syntagmatic"; the result is fragmentation and heterogeneity at the expense of coherent historical explanation.[28] The modernist (New Bibliographic) stemma organizes texts in spatial relation precisely so as to express the historical narrative of their coming-into-being. In the ironized postmodern "stemma," by contrast, the three texts of *Hamlet* are organized spatially but ahistorically. Q1, Q2, and F are forced into the same diagrammatic space, but with no underlying historical narrative that could provide the rationale for doing so. The postmodern stemma utterly resists any "hermeneutic gesture" that would seek to relate these texts and presents them simply as "oddments," three remnants of some putative "Shakespeare's *Hamlet*" that exists only hypothetically to provide the basis for their coexistence in the diagram.

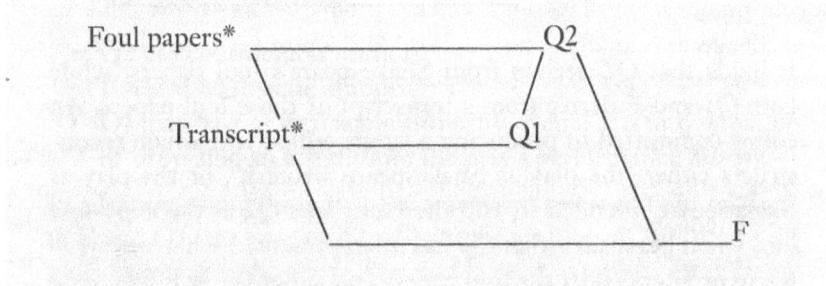

Figure 26. Editorial stemma of the texts of *Hamlet* (*Taylor-Thompson Q2*, 504).
Reproduced by permission of Bloomsbury Arden Shakespeare.

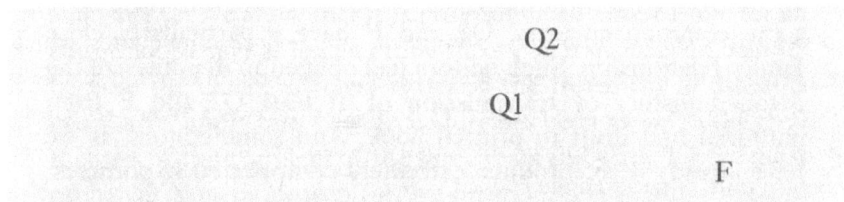

Figure 27. "Unedited" stemma of the texts of *Hamlet* (*Taylor-Thompson Q2*, 505).
Reproduced by permission of Bloomsbury Arden Shakespeare.

It is this logical conundrum—inevitable from within the New Textualist framework—that ultimately lies behind Thompson and Taylor's Borgesian image of an "infinite number of *Hamlet*s which have or could have come into existence." Likewise, in his foundational New Textualist essay "The Marriage of Good and Bad Quartos," Randall McLeod urges us to reject the "definitive" text in favor of "the *infinitive* text," defined as "a polymorphous set of all versions, some part of each of which has a claim to substantive status, and possibly presents, by whatever independent means of transmission, an element of Shakespearean dramaturgy."[29] But why limit ourselves, or rather how can we possibly limit ourselves under the theory of New Textualism, to "Shakespearean dramaturgy" when we cannot devise a stemma that in any way relates these texts under Shakespeare's authorship? How then can we define the boundaries of the "same" work such that it includes Q1 and Q2 *Romeo and Juliet* but not the German *Romeo und Julietta* or Arthur Brooke's poem, or the three texts of "Shakespeare's *Hamlet*" but not *Der bestrafte Brudermord* and *The Hystorie of Hamblet*? The infinitive text cannot historically organize this "polymorphous set of all versions" and so cannot offer us any real understanding of "Shakespearean dramaturgy." The Arden editors' echo of McLeod is not merely a verbal coincidence: the appeal to infinity allows for the evacuation of history.

Never has a major scholarly edition of *Hamlet* made such a serious, rigorous, and careful case for bibliographic agnosticism. With no firm basis for a textual stemma, we can see a concomitant erosion of the foundation for the kind of retrograde bibliography that Q1 prompted Collier to innovate and that has served, from Collier to Chambers to Pollard to Duthie, to justify the relegation of Q1 to historical oddity. The resultant editorial even-handedness enables us to read Q1 "on its own" (to the extent that is ever possible), but it simultaneously makes Q1 something of a diminished thing. With no way to determine its connection to the play as we have long known it, Q1 becomes an isolated "*Hamlet*," to borrow Thompson and Taylor's scare quotes, which can generate little of the urgency and critical pressure that motivated scholarly inquiry in the century and a half after Bunbury's discovery. What we gain in variety we lose in significance. The Library at Babel cannot account for Q1 as *Hamlet*, only as one possible *Hamlet*.

We can see the same impulse at work beyond textual studies, I think, in the repeated claims of recent critics, actors, and directors that, whatever bibliographers may think of its quality, Q1 makes for excellent theater. A nod toward the "theatricality" of Q1 seems by now almost obligatory in editorial introductions and essays on Q1, and actors themselves are especially prone to find an excitement and vitality in Q1 that the received text is said to lack.[30] This belief emerged in the nineteenth century as a polemical attempt to save Shakespeare's reputation, and it continues to be imbued with the desire to "prove" in the theater bibliographic arguments that, by their nature, cannot be so proven. The first major staging of Q1 after Bunbury's discovery was William Poel's 1881 production, designed in collaboration with Furnivall to demonstrate that Q1 was "Shakespeare's first draft of the play (though clumsily pirated as to language)." In this way, Furnivall and Poel hoped to fend off what they saw as the "flat burglary" committed by the Clarendon edition a decade earlier, and furthered by the disintegrationists, which would have given much of the credit for *Hamlet* to whoever wrote the pre-Shakespearean play.[31] The current interest in staging Q1 likewise derives from the desire to rehabilitate that text, although here the polemical opponent is the New Bibliography and its theories of memorial reconstruction and bad quartos. As a kind of experiment or laboratory of dramatic texts, performance can alert us to aspects of

Q1 that we did not recognize when reading it on the page, helping us to make sense of passages that had seemed merely garbled to more literary minded critics. But whether or not one can mount a successful production of Q1 in 1881 or 1991 or 2014 cannot ultimately tell us if that text is in fact a rough draft, a memorially or stenographically reported text of *Hamlet* as it was performed in the early seventeenth century, or something else entirely.[32]

Furthermore, as Janette Dillon trenchantly notes, the argument that Q1 has an exceptionally close connection to the early stage rests on a fundamental contradiction. On the one hand, the emphasis on the theatricality of Q1 is a remnant of the New Bibliographic view that the text is a memorial reconstruction and therefore provides privileged access to early stagings of *Hamlet*. For this reason, the major New Bibliographic editors of the later twentieth century share the belief that Q1 "throws light on the theatrical and textual history of the play" (Jenkins), yields "glimpses of an acting version of the tragedy current in the early seventeenth century" (Hibbard), and is the "one link we have with *Hamlet* as acted at the Globe theatre" (Edwards).[33] And yet, most recent advocates for the stage-worthiness of Q1 reject the theory of memorial reconstruction that underwrites this notion. We have still not fully grappled with Dillon's sharp critique of this contradiction and more broadly of the unexamined idea that Q1 and the other "bad quartos" are particularly theatrical.[34] This belief has such a hold on our imaginations, I think, because it allows us to isolate Q1 as an "independent entity" in the theater just as much as the Arden edition does on the page. Taking the New Bibliographic idea that Q1 is somehow more theatrical than Q2 or F, but rejecting the New Bibliographic stemma that would make Q1 wholly derivative of those other texts, this approach likewise yields a Q1 that is "different rather than debased," valuable on its own terms but only insofar as we decline to speculate on its possible relationship to other *Hamlets*. Both in editing and performance, close attention to the text of Q1 now seems possible only through a constitutive refusal to ask questions about its historical origins.

The decision of the Arden editors to offer a three-text *Hamlet* thus seems to me a stopgap measure that, for all the benefits of their excellent edition (and there are many), provides yet another way of allaying the ghost of old *Hamlet*. With Q1 now largely cut off from the received text, we need not fear any "flat burglary" of Shakespeare's originality, the danger that Shakespeare's *Hamlet* might turn out to be less Shakespeare's than we had thought. The epistemological openness that accepts Q1 as a distinct version rather than wholly derivative of Q2 and F can be salutary and productive; it has enabled far more critical attention to that text than was possible in the New Bibliographic moment. And yet it has also been less productive of new investigations than one would have thought; instead, we have generally been content with Q1 as a distinct "version," without looking too closely at the precise relations to Q2 and F that, after all, are the necessary precondition for the very idea of a "version." Such a viewpoint allows Q1 to be safely contained, certainly more worthy of critical study and performance but nonetheless cordoned off from the familiar text of *Hamlet* and in no danger of contaminating it.

Ironically, then, the Arden *Hamlet* represents the dialectical culmination of one of the very strands of the history of *Hamlet* after Q1 that the New Textualism sought to critique. By taking to its limit the isolation of Q1 from "Shakespeare's *Hamlet*"—positing a Borgesian *Hamlet* of infinite and hence ultimately free-floating, unmoored variation—the Arden editors find themselves in a fascinating paradox. Precisely because they want to accord Q1 the kind of attention it has not received from earlier scholars haunted by the risk that it might undermine Shakespeare's masterpiece, Thompson and Taylor unwittingly repeat that very quarantining. Just as the Clarendon edition revealed the exhaustion of the Romantic opposition of Knight and Collier, of revision and stenography, so too the paradox that hides within the Arden edition demonstrates the impossibility of going further in a purely New Textualist analysis of Q1 and *Hamlet*.

The final paradox in this book thus turns out to be my own. At the end of my genealogical investigation, I have come to believe that refusing the search for textual origins ultimately offers no solution to the problems posed by that search itself. It threatens rather to replicate them in an unexamined way. Ultimately some questions about *Hamlet*, about its text and its meaning, inevitably return us to the vexed textual issues that the New Textualism has profitably bracketed, that I have begun my own study by bracketing, that I *had* to bracket in order to begin this book. For some of the questions we want to ask, it simply does matter whether the text of Q1 was created before or after the text of Q2, whether it was a rough draft, some intermediate stage in Shakespeare's revision of an earlier play, a stenographic or memorial report of Shakespeare's version attested by Q2, or something else that we have not considered. Was *country matters* (intentionally or accidentally) altered to *contrary matters*, or vice versa? Was the word *closet* written out of the text of *Hamlet* or added to it? Does Q1 "To be, or not to be" badly remember the familiar version of the speech, or is it possible that the familiar version has somehow been influenced by the religiosity of Q1? I would not have been able to frame these questions had I not begun from a perspective broadly in line with the New Textualism. But they cannot be answered from within that perspective. If we are interested in *Hamlet*, rather than the metaphysical possibility of infinite *Hamlet*s, then the issue of textual origins can be productively deferred, but it will not ultimately be evaded.

Barring the miraculous discovery of yet another text of *Hamlet* in a closet or library somewhere, and perhaps even then, these origins seem destined to remain obscure—although this appearance of destiny is itself a condition of our New Textualist moment. If there is one thing that this genealogy makes absolutely clear, it is that the critical desire to know the origins of Q1 has never faded, only changed its aspect. I suspect that it is about to do so again. Indeed, the endurance of *Hamlet* as a central text, perhaps *the* central text, in the Western literary canon may owe less to the play's perfection—to what Harold Bloom calls the "competitive and triumphant power" of canonized works—than it does to the continual effort to reconstitute that text, to make whole and integral a play that has often seemed out of joint and out of time.[35] Our current New Textualist contentment with the texts as independent entities will yield to some new effort to understand how Q1 *Hamlet* relates to its Q2 and F doppelgängers, how Shakespeare the author is related to these multiple texts that seem in some way to be his, and how Shakespeare's play might have been informed by that other, lost *Hamlet* that has haunted us since the eighteenth century.

What will a bibliographic inquiry into the relationships among the multiple texts of *Hamlet* look like after the New Textualism—with *after* signifying not a rejection but an incorporation? How might we synthesize the historical investments of the New Bibliography with the critical attention to multiplicity and materiality of the New Textualism? How can we undertake the kinds of empirical investigation into the texts of Shakespeare that the New Bibliography promoted while maintaining the healthy skepticism of the New Textualism about our ability to know these facts?[36] Perhaps we can see some movement toward such a synthesis in recent scholarship on the material textuality of play scripts by Tiffany Stern, Paul Menzer, James Marino, and others, who bring together performance theory, theater history, and book history. Like the Oxford Shakespeare, this work avoids the internal contradictions of the "versioning" movement because it roots the variation among different texts of the same play in a textual stemma. Rather than finding the source of this variation in authorial revision, however, these scholars tend to locate it in the multiplicity of texts produced by theatrical production and revival.[37]

Partly based on this research into actors' parts and cues, Stern has recently advanced the theory that Q1 is a "noted" text, taken down by several spectators working together, although not necessarily or entirely in shorthand: a return, with key differences, to the revolutionary theory of retrograde bibliography developed by Collier immediately after Bunbury's discovery.[38] Such a return to older and discarded theories from a fresh perspective may yield important insight into Q1. Stylometric analysis, for example, has recently been advanced with more energy than at any time since Fleay and the disintegrationists used their metrical tests to pry apart Shakespeare's authorship into an abundance of collaboration. With the approaching digitization of virtually the entire surviving early modern textual corpus and the refinement of computer tests for authorship, we may find new methods for producing a stemma of the three early texts of *Hamlet*. Likewise, the primary archival materials that underlie our ideas about the performance and printing of early modern drama have been reexamined less often than we might think, and we will benefit from new investigations not only of older theories but of the documents themselves, as in Paul Werstine's recent comprehensive analysis of surviving playhouse manuscripts.[39] But while we may see some indications here of new directions, no coherent movement has yet emerged, and I suspect that New Textualist "versioning" will continue to be the dominant approach to Q1 and the other variant Shakespearean texts for some time to come.

This is not to say that our ideas about the Shakespearean text always change slowly. As F. J. Furnivall wrote, when the Clarendon edition appeared, it immediately revolutionized the study of Q1: "Till 1871, all critics were, I believe, agreed that . . . Shakspere was indebted to no one for his *Hamlet*," but Clark and Wright's edition suddenly opened completely new avenues of investigation. The important point, rather, is that we will generally be unable to predict when such sudden transformations will occur, or in what direction. As I hope to have shown, in each period of critical and editorial engagement with Q1 since 1823, certain assumptions about the nature of that text and about Shakespeare as an author have come to seem inevitable and have created scholarly blind spots that we are able to perceive only in hindsight. Before the Clarendon edition proposed that Q1 might incorporate aspects of the *Ur-Hamlet*—a text that itself had long been known to have existed—the Romantic consensus about Shakespearean authorship seems to have made this idea virtually unthinkable, even though it later came to seem like an obvious possibility. Doubtless our current editorial and textual theories about Q1 are constrained by blind spots of our own—some of which I have tried to explore in this book—that are preventing us from seeing alternatives. When some future incarnation of Clark and Wright's 1872 Clarendon edition appears, we will wonder how we could have failed to imagine them.

Whatever shape those future investigations take, however, they must reckon with the uncanny historicity of Q1, for the past and its engagements with the textual problems of *Hamlet* have thoroughly shaped our very perception of the object of study. For this reason, to grapple adequately with the mysteries of this text, we need an analysis that situates these questions of origin in dialectical relationship with the genealogy of *Hamlet* after Q1. From the moment it appeared in Henry Bunbury's closet, Q1 has challenged and transformed our views of *Hamlet*, Shakespeare, and the nature of the Shakespearean text. However often we try to forget it, in whatever ways we try to exorcise it, Q1 commands us to remember. Only by attending to its ghostly origins, its simultaneous apparition across two centuries of intervening time, can we hope to remember it properly.

NOTES

INTRODUCTION

1. Bunbury, *Correspondence*, 80. Here Bunbury dates the find to 1823. In his own copy of the Payne and Foss reprint, however, he wrote that the book "was found by me in the Library at Barton when it came into my possession in 1821" (Collection of Arthur and Janet Freeman, London; I am grateful to Janet Freeman for the transcription). (I infer that he may have been inventorying from his comment here that he found the book when Barton Hall "came into my possession.") For Dibdin's story about his influence on Bunbury's discovery, see Freeman and Freeman, "Did," 350n5. Bunbury described his discovery to Dibdin in a letter of October 19, 1824 (Folger Shakespeare Library Y.c.161[1]), indicating that he was prompted to write by Dibdin's account of the "extreme rarity of the first Edition of Hamlet (small 4to) which you date in 1604." In an inscribed copy at the Folger Shakespeare Library (PR2807 1825a copy6), Bunbury wrote that he found the book "in a closet of the Library at Barton," perhaps explaining the multiple possible locations. And in personal communication, Great Barton local historian Frank Holmes informs me that the library of Barton Hall "was built between 1766 and 1770" and that contemporary records describe its only entrance as "a dark closet or 'porte derobe' at the farther end of the dining room." Since a *porte dérobée* (derived from *dérober*, to hide, conceal, or steal) was generally a secret doorway or entranceway, the library seems to have been secluded by a kind of closet leading from the dining room. Bunbury likely found the book in this room.

2. I am grateful to Stephen Tabor at the Huntington Library for information regarding the provenance of their copy, which was purchased in 1914 already inlaid. Devonshire was following the practice of John Philip Kemble, whose collection of dramatic texts he acquired in 1820. The plays were then generally rebound into "volumes containing a half-dozen plays," and Huntington seems to have been responsible for taking these apart and individually rebinding the more valuable plays. Sherburn, "Huntington," 43; see also Davies, "Huntington," 54. On the disbinding of early *Sammelbände*, see Knight, *Bound*, esp. 21–53.

3. Bunbury, *Correspondence*, 80. Bunbury claimed that Devonshire paid £230, but Henry Foss reported that he and Payne had received £250 for it ("Our," *Athenaeum* 1512: 1277). A more contemporary notice indicated that "the Duke of Devonshire has purchased the first edition of *Hamlet* from Messrs. Payne and Foss, for nearly 200 guineas," or £210 (*Times* [31 March 1825]: 3).

4. "Hamlet," *Literary*, 59.

5. "Hamlet," *Literary*, 58.

6. "Hamlet," *Literary*, 59; Shakespeare, *First*, unnumbered prefatory page.

7. For the familiar version, see Shakespeare, *Comedies*, sig. 2o5r, from which I quote here; and Shakespeare, *Hamlet* (1604), sig. G2r, which differs only in capitalization. For the line in Q1, see

Shakespeare, *Hamlet* (1603), sig. D4v. Hereafter, I cite the early editions of *Hamlet* parenthetically in the text; unless the reference would be ambiguous, I cite Q1 only by signature, while including "Q2" or "F" before the signature for those texts.

8. "Hamlet," *Literary*, 58.

9. "Hamlet," *Literary*, 58. Dibdin also thought Hanmer had owned the book (*Library*, 2.813). In the inscribed copy of the 1825 reprint at the Folger, Bunbury explicitly rejected this suggestion, since Hanmer does not mention it in his edition, "nor in his autograph corrections of Theobald's Edition (which is in my possession)."

10. Nashe, "To the Gentlemen," sig. **3r. See Farmer, *Essay*, 85–86n.

11. Lodge, *Wits*, sig. H4v; black letter changed to roman and roman to italic. See Farmer, *Essay*, 75–76. For the other allusions, see Dekker, *Satiro-mastix*, sig. G3v; Smith, *Sir*, sig. K1r; and Rowlands, *Night-Raven*, sig. D2r.

12. Foakes, ed., *Henslowe's*, 21.

13. On the textual history of this copy, see Cohn, *Shakespeare*, 239–40 (the book is unusually paginated, with each page including an odd number for the left-hand column and an even for the right). "True original copy" alludes to the title page of F, "published according to the true Original Copies."

14. Stern, "'If.'"

15. Smith, "Ghost," 177. See also Erne, *Beyond*, 146–56.

16. *Malone 1790*, 1.1.308.

17. Malone, for example, wrote that the 1608 edition "undoubtedly was a republication" (*Malone 1790*, 9.183).

18. I am particularly influenced here by Leonard Barkan's discussion of the "specially elliptical quality" of the discovery of buried classical sculpture in the Renaissance in *Unearthing*, 7: "That the statue emerges from the ground, that it is to some extent deprived of physical and historical context, that it is imperfect—all these circumstances contribute to a sense that the image is in itself incomplete. The experience must be finished."

19. Browne, *Hydriotaphia*, sig. B7v.

20. Browne, *Hydriotaphia*, sigs. A2v, F4r–v.

21. Browne, *Hydriotaphia*, sig. A3r. On the urns merely as occasion for meditation, see Preston, *Thomas*, 130, 137.

22. Browne, *Hydriotaphia*, sig. B1v.

23. Browne, *Hydriotaphia*, sig. B7v.

24. "Literary," *Gentleman's*, 68.

25. Although Goethe did learn of its existence after writing *Wilhelm Meister*, in which are found his famous remarks on Hamlet's character; see my Chapter 3. I am not suggesting that *no one* in the intervening period was aware of the edition. Various people obviously owned the two extant copies of Q1—and perhaps others subsequently destroyed, or still lost. And, as discussed below, material evidence in Rooney's copy reveals that an early eighteenth-century owner was aware of what he had on his hands. My point is simply that, more broadly speaking, Q1 was "lost" to common knowledge quite early.

26. "Hamlet," *Literary*, 59.

27. Freud, "Uncanny." On this "temporal alterity," see also Freeman, "Time," 59. I am informed here by Derrida's "hauntology," which itself develops as a reading of *Hamlet* (see *Specters*). See also the discussion of Nietzsche's concept of the "untimely" in Garber, *Shakespeare's*, 209–12; and in Harris, *Untimely*, 10–13.

28. In "Rossencraft," Jeffrey Masten explored the variation in the naming of these two characters, noting in the process "the distinct possibility that the first quarto of *Hamlet* is in some sense punished for its belated appearance on the scene." Although he did not pursue this line of reasoning, his thinking about the belatedness of Q1 accords with my own in many respects. I am grateful to Masten for sharing this unpublished work with me.

29. Freud, "Uncanny," 220.

30. Garber, *Shakespeare's*, 173.

31. De Grazia, "Anachronism," 13. See also Aravamudan, "Return."

32. On Malone's innovation, see de Grazia, *Shakespeare*, 56–71. The New Bibliographic theory of textual authority is most forcefully elaborated in Greg, "Rationale."

33. Lesser, *Renaissance*, 21–22.

34. See Liu, "Power"; and Kastan, *Shakespeare After Theory*, 24. On this aspect of literary historicism more broadly, see Dimock, "Theory."

35. Foucault, "What," 159.

36. See Stern, *Rehearsal*; Stern, *Making*; Stern and Palfrey, *Shakespeare*; and Stern, *Documents*. See also Menzer, *Hamlets*; and Marino, *Owning*. These critics all draw on earlier scholarship about Shakespearean revision by scholars such as Gary Taylor, Michael Warren, and Steven Urkowitz, but with new insight deriving from the intersection of theater history, performance studies, and book history.

37. See Brayman Hackel, *Reading*; Sherman, *Used*; Smyth, "Shreds"; Knight, *Bound*; and the special issue of the *Journal of Medieval and Early Modern Studies* on "Renaissance collage," edited by Smyth, Sherman, and Juliet Fleming (forthcoming).

38. Berman, "Politics," 327.

39. See Harris, *Untimely*, 2; on the implications for book history, see St Clair, *Reading*, 2–4; Farmer and Lesser, "Canons."

40. Bristol, *Big-time*, 15, 13; Lanier, *Shakespeare*, 4. An important early touchstone for work in this field is Taylor, *Reinventing*.

41. The *Gentleman's Magazine* enthused that "not the slightest mention has ever been made" of it before, "the earliest [edition] which has ever obtained notice being that of 1604." The play "as it appears in this print of 1603" was "utterly unknown" to "the various able and laborious commentators of Shakspeare" ("Literary," *Gentleman's*, 68–69).

42. See Harris, *Untimely*; Stallybrass, "Worn"; and Jones and Stallybrass, *Renaissance*; on reprinting, see Stallybrass, "*Thrift*"; St Clair, *Reading*; and McGill, *American*; on presentism, see Grady and Hawkes, "Introduction." Recent work on "queer historicism" includes Dinshaw, "Temporalities"; Dinshaw, *How*; Freccero, *Queer*; Love, *Feeling*; Freeman, "Introduction"; Menon, *Unhistorical*; and Menon, ed., *Shakesqueer*. Interestingly, work in this field, as in recent studies of temporal dislocation more generally, returns again and again to *Hamlet*, frequently alluding to Hamlet's "the time is out of joint" (see Aravamudan, "Return," 347). Postcolonial critiques of "Western time" likewise turn to Hamlet's words, as in Dipesh Chakrabarty's foundational claim that "historical time is not integral, that it is out of joint with itself," and Jed Esty's recent comment that "colonial time is out of joint with national-historical time." Chakrabarty, *Provincializing*, 16; Esty, *Unseasonable*, 223n49.

43. Masten, *Queer*; Traub, "New."

44. Harris, *Untimely*, 5. I have also found important both Dimock's challenge to traditional historicism, in which "the task of the critic is to lock that context into place, by locating the historicity in the text and the text in history" ("Theory," 1061); and de Grazia's challenge to the "'cognitive distance' that is the very basis of our disciplinary knowledge," which prevents anachronism and establishes traditional historiography ("Anachronism," 31).

45. It is characteristic of this blind spot that one of the best recent books in the field opens with an impossible statement: "From the beginning of the Shakespeare editorial tradition in the eighteenth century, editors and textual critics have been particularly perplexed by five of these playtexts: Q1 *Romeo and Juliet* (1597), Q1 *Henry 5* (1600), Q1 *The Merry Wives of Windsor* (1602), Q1 *Hamlet* (1603), Q1 *Pericles* (1609)" (Maguire, *Shakespearean*, 3). Since Q1 *Hamlet* was unknown until the 1820s, it cannot have perplexed critics "in the eighteenth century." The paradox exemplifies the uncanny historicity of Q1 *Hamlet*.

46. Foucault, "Nietzsche," 139, 140, 142.

47. Foucault, "Nietzsche," 146.

48. Eliot, *Middlemarch*, 305.

49. Wilson, *Manuscript*, 18–20.

50. Fleay, "Neglected," 88.

51. De Grazia, "*Hamlet* Before Its Time," 367.

52. On plays as pamphlets, see Stallybrass and Chartier, "Reading."

53. See Rooney's account in *Hamlet*, 12. One wonders how it could have taken Rooney until the last page to notice any variations from the received text; his collation may not have been very thorough.

54. Rooney never mentions his purchase price, but rumors ranged from a shilling to two pounds (Freeman and Freeman, "Did," 353n17).

55. Rooney, Letter, 1191.

56. "Literary," *Eclectic*, 426. Freeman and Freeman ("Did," 350–52) provide a full discussion of the sale. As they show, Halliwell felt that *he* had been taken advantage of by Rooney.

57. Freeman and Freeman, "Did," 352.

58. Lactantius, *Divine*, 71.

59. Freeman and Freeman, "Did," 359n36. The information about interleaving in this paragraph derives from the Freemans' article.

60. Quoted in Freeman and Freeman, "Did," 361. I have expanded superscript abbreviations.

61. Stubbes, *Some*, 33. The essay is anonymous but now generally attributed to Stubbes.

62. "Our," *Athenaeum* 1508: 1168.

63. Shakespeare, *First*, unnumbered prefatory page.

64. Mommsen, "Hamlet," 182.

65. Wilhelm Bernhardi, "Shakespeare's *Hamlet*: Ein literarhistorisch-kritischer Bersuch," originally published in the 1857 edition of the *Hamburger literarisch-kritische Blätter*, quoted here in translation from Cohn, *Shakespeare*, cxx. *Furness 1877* (2.116) likewise gives the honor of this "first" to Bernhardi.

66. See Collier, *Memoirs*, 18; Collier's views on these questions were widely followed. Malone thought that the Globe had been built in 1596 and that the Chamberlain's Men were playing in the Blackfriars by 1604 (*Malone 1790*, 1.2.57, 1.2.325).

67. Collier, *New*, 10–11.

68. See Knight, ed., *Comedies*, 1.xiv; and Knight, *Old*, xiii. In 1856, Rooney likewise insisted that the initials stood for "Nich. Landure (not Nich. Ling as stated, upon what grounds I do not know)" (*Hamlet*, 5).

69. Browne, *Hydriotaphia*, sig. A2r.

70. Jeffrey Masten's "discovery" of a previously unknown copy of the first edition of Marlowe's *Edward II*—which, like Q1, had been on a library shelf all along—makes clear again that we have not yet found all we might find in the archives ("Bound"). Barbara Mowat explores the ultimate archival fantasy, the discovery of Shakespeare's dramatic manuscripts. She shows that, despite the recurring

wish of editors from Rowe to Fredson Bowers, "there is abundant evidence that, should manuscripts of Shakespeare's play come to light today, we would not thereby be guaranteed an unproblematic text" ("Problem," 134).

71. I thus disagree fundamentally with Clayton's concluding remarks in "Introduction": "Would it have made any difference if Q1 *Hamlet* had never returned? Obviously not, for we should never have suspected its existence and could hardly have recreated it by conjecture if we had" (46). As mentioned above, it is not true that "we should never have suspected its existence"; Malone correctly inferred the edition's existence from the blurb on the title page of the second quarto. More important, the history of *Hamlet* and of Shakespearean criticism more generally would have looked very different indeed had the edition not been found.

72. Browne, *Pseudodoxia*, sig. a3r.

73. Mary Bly prefers the word *bawdy* to *obscene* because it "brings with it connotations of humour, coming from roots in the Old French word *bauderie*, or gaiety," and hence "it stands for the precise kind of wordplay I am discussing" (*Queer*, 12). I use the word more interchangeably with *obscene*, which in the context of Q1 better conveys the long critical history of finding this pun more indecent than humorous.

74. The book also explores a period in the editorial history of Shakespeare that has been relatively neglected, compared to the great eighteenth-century editions and the New Bibliography of the early twentieth century. On this neglect of the nineteenth century, see Murphy, *Shakespeare in Print*, 5.

CHAPTER 1. AS ORIGINALLY WRITTEN BY SHAKESPEARE

1. "Shakspeare," *Circulator*, 60. In fact, this article called for "a republication of those eleven plays, precisely as the text stands in the volume they now occupy"; no such reprint ever appeared, unfortunately, making it more difficult now to reconstruct the *Sammelband*, or indeed even to locate the copies it once contained. Alan Galey shows that, because of its belated discovery as well, Q1 was the first book ever reproduced in photographic facsimile. The reproduction was overseen by Collier himself in 1858. See Galey, *Shakespearean*, ch. 4.

2. Shakespeare, *First*, unnumbered prefatory page.

3. "Literary," *Gentleman's*, 68.

4. "Diary," *Inspector*, 324. It is unclear if this is a genuine M.P. writing, or a literary impersonation.

5. See Shattuck, *Shakespeare*.

6. See Malone's chronology in *Steevens 1778*, 1.292–93.

7. *Singer 1826*, 10.152–53.

8. Caldecott, *Hamlet*, vi.

9. "Literary," *Gentleman's*, 69; *Times* (22 February 1825): 3. See also Taylor, "First," 555.

10. On this editorial pessimism, see Egan, *Struggle*, 12–37.

11. "Shakspeare's," *Gentleman's*, 336.

12. "Recovered," *United* (1 May 1825): 115; this reprints and adapts "Varieties," *Monthly*. But the final sentence does not appear in the earlier article.

13. Greg, ed., *Merry*. See Maguire, *Shakespearean*, 74–78.

14. Steevens, ed., *Twenty*, 7.

15. *Pope 1723*, 1.viii; *Theobald 1733*, 1.223; *Johnson 1765*, 2.557; Capell, *Notes*, 2.3.83, 2.3.73; *Malone 1790* 1.1.328.

16. *Pope 1723*, 6.247, emphasis reversed; Capell, *Notes*, 2.4.1, 2.4.14; *Malone 1790*, 1.1.328.

17. *Johnson 1765*, 6.88.

18. *Johnson 1765*, 4.394, 4.461; *Warburton 1747*, 1.[lxxvi].

19. *Theobald 1733*, 4.110.

20. *Warburton 1747*, 1.[lxxvi], on *Henry VI*; Capell, *Notes*, 2.4.40, on *Shrew*.

21. *Johnson 1765*, 4.22. *Richard II* was generally taken to have been revised, with the "parliament scene" a major addition; Capell seems to have been the first to claim that it instead testified to censorship (Capell, *Notes*, 2.3.169).

22. *Pope 1723*, 3.296, emphasis reversed; see also *Johnson 1765*, 4.265; *Warburton 1747*, 4.211.

23. Capell, *Notes*, 2.4.124.

24. Capell, *Notes*, 1.1.131; *Johnson 1765*, 8.282.

25. *Johnson 1765*, 8.357.

26. "Players trash" is one of Warburton's signature phrases (*Warburton 1747*, 6.70, 8.64, 8.362), but the sentiment was widespread.

27. Johnson's *Proposals for Printing by Subscription the Dramatic Works of William Shakespeare*, quoted in *Malone 1790*, 1.1.ii.

28. *Theobald 1733*, 1.xxxvii–xxxviii.

29. Malone likewise asserted that it "was a common practice to carry table-books to the theatre . . . and there is reason to believe that the imperfect and mutilated copies of one or two of Shakspeare's dramas, which are yet extant, were taken down by the ear or in short-hand during the exhibition" (*Malone 1790*, 1.2.122–23). But while vaguely alluding to "one or two" texts, he does not specify. Another passage in his preface suggests that he had in mind *Merry Wives* and *Henry V*, although he immediately qualifies his judgment about the former by raising "a doubt whether it is a first sketch or an imperfect copy" (*Malone 1790*, 1.1.x). And in this passage Malone imagines the "imperfect copy" not as a stenographic transcription of performance but rather as a compilation made from actors' parts. The vagueness of Malone's language, and the doubts he immediately raises each time that he brings up the question of shorthand or other kinds of "imperfect copy," indicate the ideological pressures of his larger editorial goal to assert the textual authority of the quartos.

30. Jeanne Addison Roberts comes to a similar conclusion, pointing to a comment attributed to James Boaden in Samuel Weller Singer's 1826 edition as "the first unequivocal statement of an alternative to the revision theory" ("*Merry*," 145). In the introduction to his edition, Capell identified several plays (*Henry V, King John, Merry Wives, Shrew, 2–3 Henry VI, Romeo and Juliet*) as a different category of quarto, since these were "no other than either first draughts, or mutilated and perhaps surreptitious impressions of those plays, but whether of the two is not easy to determine" (*Capell 1767*, 1.2). But when he comes to deal with each of these plays individually, Capell seems to be thinking mainly of authorial revision: see his comments on *King John* (*Capell 1767*, 1.2), *Merry Wives* (Capell, *Notes*, 2.3.73–74), *Romeo and Juliet* (*Notes*, 2.4.1, 2.4.14) *Shrew* (*Notes*, 2.4.40), and *2–3 Henry VI* (*Notes*, 1.2.39). He sees *Henry V* as "mangl'd" (*Notes*, 1.2.5) by performers and the need to suppress the Choruses after the fall of Essex; then, as with the *Henry VI* plays, "some scribe of profound ignorance, set to work by the printer," further deformed the text (*Notes*, 1.2.5).

31. *Johnson 1765*, 5.225.

32. *Malone 1790*, 6.396–97.

33. *Steevens 1778*, 1.Prefaces.305.

34. *Malone 1790*, 1.1.324. The Freemans are thus technically incorrect in saying that Collier was the first to discuss "stenographic shorthand, which, though well-known to have been employed by pirates of sermons and plays, had not hitherto been signalled in connection with specific Shakespearian texts" (Freeman and Freeman, *John*, 394). Malone deserves the honor, although he tellingly retracted the claim.

35. *Steevens 1778*, 1.Prefaces.305.
36. See Woodmansee, *Author*; Leader, *Revision*.
37. Quoted in Leader, *Revision*, 1.
38. Young, *Conjectures*, 12.
39. De Grazia, *Shakespeare*, 145; see also McMullan, *Shakespeare*, 128–36.
40. "Dramatic," *Drama*, 276; "Hamlet," *Literary*, 58; "Dramatic," *Drama*, 276.
41. Collier, *History*, 1.281.
42. *Boswell 1821*, 1.xiii. Boswell helpfully placed "the following mark (||)" next to variant passages, so "that the curious reader may learn how our author improved upon his first conceptions" (*Boswell 1821*, 6.4).
43. *Collier 1843*, 6.368–69. Lukas Erne recognizes Collier's innovation here as "the first to argue that Q1 basically derives from Q2," but he does not trace this innovation to its source, Collier's reading of Q1 *Hamlet* (Erne, ed., *First*, 7).
44. *White 1862*, 10.15.
45. *Cambridge 1866*, vii–viii.
46. *Collier 1843*, 4.461, 4.463.
47. *Collier 1843*, 1.173.
48. *Collier 1843*, 8.268, 267.
49. Pollard, *Shakespeare's Folios*, 64–80.
50. Collier, *Reasons*, 9.
51. *Collier 1843*, 7.191.
52. Freeman and Freeman, *John*, 389.
53. On Collier's feud with Dyce, see Freeman and Freeman, *John*, 384–86.
54. On these societies and their norms, see Hollingsworth, "Shakespeare." This deference helps to explain how Collier escaped detection for his forgeries for as long as he did: "It is remarkable how far all the sceptics of the 1830s and 1840s would go to avoid even hinting at a living perpetrator," most instead blaming George Steevens and imagining that Collier merely found these pre-forged documents (Freeman and Freeman, *John*, 442).
55. In his *Athenaeum* piece, Collier did give some minimal evidence for his claim—citing Horatio's variant line, "we did think it *writ down / right done* in our duty"—but here too he mainly draws on his personal reputation and honor to persuade readers: "I will adduce, at present, only one instance, and your readers may, perhaps, take my word for it, that proofs of the same fact might easily be multiplied" (Collier, "Edition," 1221).
56. See Freeman and Freeman, *John*, 355, 374.
57. Quoted in Foakes, ed., *Collier*, 15.
58. He takes pains, as well, to vindicate Coleridge "from the accusation that he had derived his ideas of Hamlet from Schlegel" (*Collier 1843*, 7.193).
59. Like his father, Collier had worked as a newspaperman, a profession that required knowledge of shorthand: "My father taught me at an early age the use of abbreviated characters, and I hardly know any species of instruction that . . . has stood me in greater stead" (Coleridge, *Seven*, v).
60. Coleridge, *Seven*, vii.
61. *Knight 1839, Doubtful*, 400.
62. *Knight 1839, Doubtful*, 400.
63. See Gray, *Charles*; and Prince, *Shakespeare*, 16–36. Prince writes that "Knight's theory was that by educating the working classes, publications such as the *Penny Magazine* could inoculate them against the radical notions fostered by ignorance" (24).

64. *Bent's Monthly Literary Advertiser* 407 (10 November 1838): 130.

65. Gray, *Charles*, 154; see also Murphy, *Shakespeare for the People*, 67.

66. Gray, *Charles*, 156.

67. *Bent's Monthly Literary Advertiser* 408 (10 December 1838): 147.

68. Prospectus quoted in Murphy, *Shakespeare in Print*, 189. In the revised edition of 1867, however, Knight did pay tribute to the work done in the interim by Collier, Dyce, Halliwell, and others for their "large additions to our means of appreciating and understanding 'the greatest in all literature'" (*Knight 1867, Comedies*, 1.vi).

69. "White's," *Hours*, 169. In *Hamlet*, for instance, Knight goes so far as to print passages that appear in Q2 but not in F in square brackets to indicate that they were likely cut by Shakespeare at some point—a strikingly modern editorial procedure.

70. *Knight 1867, Comedies*, 1.vi, emphasis added.

71. Prospectus quoted in Murphy, *Shakespeare in Print*, 190, 189.

72. *Knight 1839, Doubtful*, 387. Knight is speaking specifically of Richard Farmer, celebrated by so many earlier editors of Shakespeare: "He wrote 'An Essay on the Learning of Shakspeare,' which has not one passage of solid criticism from the first page to the last, and from which, if the name and the works of Shakspere were to perish, and one copy—an unique copy is the affectionate name for these things—could be miraculously preserved, the only inference from the book would be that William Shakspere was a very obscure and ignorant man, whom some misjudging admirers had been desirous to exalt into an ephemeral reputation, and that Richard Farmer was a very distinguished and learned man, who had stripped the mask off the pretender."

73. *Knight 1839, Doubtful*, 332.

74. *Knight 1839, Doubtful*, 389.

75. *Knight 1839, Doubtful*, 385.

76. See Freeman and Freeman, *John*, 340–42.

77. Collier's father was, at different times, a wool importer, a factory manager, and a journalist; Halliwell's was a wealthy draper. Collier worked as a journalist for much of this period, but he had also befriended Lord Francis Egerton (of the Bridgewater family) and become "a sort of librarian" to the Duke of Devonshire, as the duke himself put it; "his infatuation with the ducal aura . . . would fuel his hopes and fantasies for decades" (Freeman and Freeman, *John*, 218, 157). Halliwell married the daughter of the baronet Sir Thomas Phillipps, over the father's objections, and added her surname to his own.

78. As de Grazia shows (*Shakespeare*), this disciplinary formation can be traced to late eighteenth-century editors like Malone, but it grew more powerful in the early nineteenth century with the creation of the various scholarly societies such as the Camden and the Shakespeare. See Hollingsworth, "Shakespeare," 52–53.

79. In the inaugural list of Shakespeare Society members, for example, all three men sign themselves "Esq.," but Halliwell and Collier are able to add "F.S.A." (Fellow of the Society of Antiquaries), and Halliwell also "F.R.S." (Fellow of the Royal Society). *Gentleman's Magazine Literary Advertiser* (December 1840), 49. Knight was never accepted into the Society of Antiquaries, perhaps because it often "excluded on social grounds (trade connections, low birth)" those not worthy of their company, but perhaps because of his opposition to the "parade . . . of useless learning" (Freeman and Freeman, *John*, 160).

80. Collier, *Reasons*, 23n1. Freeman and Freeman, however, read the passage as expressing genuine approbation (*John*, 390). The line that Reed omitted and Boswell "restored" is "And each particular hair to stand an end"; it seems to have been left out of Reed's variorum text purely by accident. Knight had "pointed out" the missing line in his *Pictorial Edition*, adding, with his characteristic understanding of the printer's trade, that "We know no book more incorrectly printed that the booksellers'

stereotype edition of Shakspere in one volume. . . . And yet the typographical errors of the first folio, printed from a manuscript, are always visited by the commentators with the severest reprehension" (*Knight 1839, Comedies*, 1.310). What Collier takes as Knight's gratuitous swipe at Reed (since the text had long since been "restored"), is, in its original context, part of Knight's defense of the First Folio, a defense that was simultaneously a critique of the professional Shakespeare critics.

81. "Reviews," *Archaeologist*, 198. The review is unsigned but may well be by Halliwell himself; it includes one of Halliwell's works but consigns it to a brief final paragraph, perhaps indicating that he is reviewing his own book here. Halliwell was certainly not opposed to doing so: in 1841, he had published three separate reviews of his own work in the *Gentleman's Magazine*. See Spevack, *James*, 26–27. This review, however, does not appear in the bibliography.

82. See Thomas, "Poetry"; Thomas quotes the sonnet in full on 354.

83. Knight quoted in Freeman and Freeman, *John*, 382.

84. Collier, ed., *Fools*, ix. Knight responded in an open letter to the society. The occasion engendered a "long-term scholarly feud" (Freeman and Freeman, *John*, 374).

85. By modern editorial standards, Collier's collation is not as meticulous as he imagined. See Freeman and Freeman, *John*, for an even-handed evaluation (392–93) and for the approval of Collier's "painstaking collations" in contemporary reviews (417).

86. *Collier 1843*, 7.191; Young, *Conjectures*, 12.

87. *Bent's Monthly Literary Advertiser* 407 (10 November 1838): 130.

88. *Knight 1839, Doubtful*, 385.

89. Another way in which Knight differs from eighteenth-century views of revision is that Collier's brief mention of shorthand in 1831 already led him cautiously to add that this "sketch of the perfect Hamlet" may, "as Mr Collier says, have been . . . a corrupt copy of that sketch," even one deriving from "a short-hand copy" (*Knight 1839, Tragedies*, 1.87–88). Following the discovery of Q1 *Hamlet*, in other words, even the century's most energetic proponent of revision could no longer quite believe that Shakespeare's variant quartos might represent his rough drafts in any straightforward way.

90. *Malone 1790*, 1.1.305.

91. *Collier 1843*, 1.lxxxiv n4.

92. *Knight 1839, Tragedies*, 1.92. This argument was revived in the late twentieth century by Sams, "Taboo," which robustly challenges all aspects of the theory of memorial reconstruction to suggest that Shakespeare wrote the *Ur-Hamlet*, which is related to Q1, then later revised it into Q2 and F.

93. *Timon of Athens* was "the only exception," according to Knight (*Knight 1839, Doubtful*, 51).

94. *Knight 1839, Tragedies*, 1.91.

95. *Knight 1839, Histories*, 1.387.

96. Quoted in Leader, *Revision*, 25.

97. *Knight 1839, Tragedies*, 1.92.

98. *Collier 1843*, 1.cxiv, lxxxiv n4.

99. *Collier 1843*, 1.cxiv n9.

100. *Collier 1843*, 1.cxiv.

101. *Collier 1843*, 7.189.

102. *Collier 1843*, 7.190. As Marino writes, a "*Hamlet* open to revision as late as 1602 or 1604 (or 1623) leaves Shakespeare himself open to charges of imitation and influence"; by contrast, modern editors have indulged in the "fantasy of an *ur-Hamlet*, a text discarded and replaced completely after a single act of heroic composition" (*Owning*, 104, 105). Collier's rhetoric works to obviate just such charges and enact just such a fantasy. See also Marcus, *Unediting*, 135: twentieth-century editors "posited the Ur-*Hamlet* as unrecoverable and thereby created an unbridgeable gulf between it and

Shakespeare's version of the play," so that "Shakespeare's *Hamlet* magically achieved the status of a charismatic original independent of any forebears." Actually, as I show, this strategic move goes back as far as Collier.

103. Elwin, "Recent," 316.
104. *Knight 1839, Histories*, 1.309.
105. *Gentleman's Magazine Literary Advertiser* (December 1840), 49.
106. Greg, ed., *Merry*, xxiii.
107. See Maguire, *Shakespearean*, 26–38; and on the New Bibliographers' amnesia about their debt to Collier and other nineteenth-century scholars, see 62–63.
108. For instance, citing dissenters to the revision theory, Harold Jenkins acts as if Collier had never existed, instead beginning with Mommsen and moving to Richard Grant White and then Duthie (*Jenkins*, 18n4). In his Oxford edition, however, Hibbard does note Collier's foundational role (*Hibbard*, 75). For a more recent example of Mommsen occluding Collier, see Jowett, "Editing," 6.
109. Mommsen, "Hamlet," 182; for Mommsen and Collier's correspondence, see the Folger Shakespeare Library N.a.64. I am grateful to András Kisery for alerting me to this archive.
110. Mommsen, "Hamlet," 182.
111. One of the few recent critics to stress Mommsen's debt to Collier is Stewart in "Actor."
112. *Cambridge 1866*, 8.viii.
113. *Cambridge 1866*, 7.viii.
114. White, "Two," 468. It should be noted that White pays tribute to Knight as a "justly distinguished . . . venerable and enthusiastic editor" who "ingeniously advocated the alluring theory of a revision"—although, as with Collier's earlier tribute to him, we might detect some faint praise in "enthusiastic," "ingeniously," and "alluring" (470). On White's Shakespeare, see Falk, "Critical."
115. "Young," *All*, 138.
116. "Young," *All*, 141.
117. Elwin, "Recent," 315.
118. Marmion Savage, quoted in Freeman and Freeman, *John*, 418. There is no question which edition of Shakespeare the Victorian public preferred, however: Knight's enjoyed "unmatched circulation" in its own time (Freeman and Freeman, *John*, 383).
119. He argued furthermore that the variations in Q1 *Romeo and Juliet* were not "merely those of a piratical edition" but rather proved that "the author greatly improved and amplified the play subsequently to its original appearance on the stage" (Dyce, ed., *Works*, 7.101; *Dyce 1857*, 1.clxxx). In the first edition, Dyce's comments on Q1 *Hamlet* are more ambiguous, but he clarified his meaning in the second, admitting in a footnote that he had "expressed myself" poorly and was consequently misunderstood to be advocating a position close to Collier and Mommsen (Dyce, ed., *Works*, 7.100).
120. Hunter's *New* was the most important commentary on the different placement of "To be, or not to be" and the nunnery scene; Gervinus found Knight's view "indisputably more just" than Collier's and Mommsen's in part because of the different names of Polonius and Reynaldo (Gervinus, *Shakespeare*, 2.108); Delius pointed to these aspects and the new scene between Horatio and the Queen (see *Furness 1877*, 2.21).
121. *Collier 1843*, 7.191.
122. *Cambridge 1866*, 8.x.
123. *Clarendon 1872*, viii, x, viii.
124. *Clarendon 1872*, viii, x.
125. The term "New Textualism" was coined by de Grazia and Stallybrass in "Materiality," 276.
126. *Clarendon 1872*, x–xii.

127. *Collier 1843*, 7.189.

128. The term "*Ur-Hamlet*" itself entered into English scholarship from the German at the turn of the twentieth century. Smith is incorrect, however, in saying that the "suggestion that there was a *Hamlet* play before Shakespeare's *Hamlet* dates back to Edmond Malone's posthumously printed edition of Shakespeare's works of 1821" ("Ghost," 177). In fact, Malone came to this conclusion in his 1790 edition (*Malone 1790*, 9.183).

129. In Clark and Wright's description of Q1 as a "transition state," we can hear the influence of evolutionary science; on this strand in late nineteenth-century Shakespeare scholarship, see Chapter 4.

130. On the shift from neoclassicism to organic unity in *Hamlet* criticism, see Grady, "*Hamlet*," 147–50.

131. Halliwell-Phillipps, *Memoranda*, 5. By the 1850s Halliwell had begun to wonder about Collier, and he emphasized the need for his new Shakespeare edition by alluding ominously to "the ingenuity of some of the most skilful fabricators of modern times" (quoted in Freeman and Freeman, *John*, 647). Nonetheless, he never overtly accused Collier and instead suggested Collier may himself have been deceived by the forgeries of someone else.

132. Halliwell-Phillipps, *Memoranda*, 24.

133. Halliwell-Phillipps, *Memoranda*, 63–64.

134. Halliwell-Phillipps, *Memoranda*, 79; these remarks specifically address the second volume of *Furness 1877*. See the discussion in my Chapter 4 of the importance of the publication of the Variorum on this point.

135. See, for example, Robertson, "Upshot," 275–76; Robertson, *Hamlet*, 21.

136. Robertson, "Upshot," 143. Robertson doubted "whether Mr. Halliwell Phillipps quite saves himself in the eyes of devout Shakspereans by saying early in his *brochure* that 'the tragedy of "Hamlet" is unquestionably the highest effort of artistic literary power yet given to the world,'" when he had just indicated that it is filled with "perplexing inconsistencies" ("Upshot," 143).

137. Eliot, "Hamlet," 941, 940.

138. Eliot, "Hamlet," 940.

139. White, "Two," 470.

140. *Collier 1843*, 1.clxxvii, 1.ccxiii.

141. Wilson, *Manuscript*, 1.15.

142. Pollard, *Shakespeare's Fight*, 50, 53.

143. Pollard, *Shakespeare's Folios*, 80.

144. Wilson, *Manuscript*, 1.xxv.

145. Wilson, *Manuscript*, 1.92, 1.171.

146. Greg, *Editorial*, 17.

147. *Hibbard*, 69. Jenkins is only a bit more circumspect: the "Second Quarto . . . was evidently intended to supersede the First"; Q2 "comes from an authentic manuscript, and . . . it is usually held that this manuscript was the author's own foul papers" (*Jenkins*, 36–37).

148. *Thompson-Taylor Q2*, 12.

149. Honigmann, *Stability*, 190.

150. *Edwards*, 27.

151. Arber, *Transcript*, 3.212.

152. Pollard, *Shakespeare's Folios*, 74; *Edwards*, 9; *Jenkins*, 15.

153. Johnson, "Nicholas," 212. For an excellent recent discussion of the politics of Ling's publishing career, see Melnikoff, "Nicholas." He does not, however, address the economic dilemma that I argue Ling must have faced in publishing Q2.

154. Kastan, *Shakespeare and the Book*, 27–30. See also Terri Bourus ("Shakespeare," 216), who notes how busy Roberts was in this year, and also stresses the relationship between Ling and his old fellow apprentice Valentine Simmes. She speculates that "Ling asked Roberts, who appears not to have had the time to print *Hamlet*, if he would release the job to Simmes, who appears to have needed the work." Hirrell argues similarly in "Roberts," 726–28.

155. Erne, *Shakespeare*, 81.

156. We know that the edition appeared in bookshops after 19 May 1603, when the Lord Chamberlain's Men received their royal patent, because on the title page Shakespeare's acting company is called "his Highnesse seruants." It may well have appeared after Roberts's entry in July, in fact. Since Q2 is dated 1604 in some copies and 1605 in others, it was likely printed around the turn of the year, perhaps a bit earlier if Ling was dating ahead.

157. *Thompson-Taylor Q2*, 78. Bourus's explanation relies on a speculative narrative: Roberts and Ling are "skeptical about this second manuscript" of *Hamlet*, but someone from the theatrical company, "possibly Richard Burbage, may have convinced Roberts to read the text"; Roberts "would have recognized the revised *Hamlet*'s potential for sale to a reading public eager for pleasurable distractions" after the plague year of 1603, and now "Shakespeare's name was certainly recognizable and popular." To avoid competition with Q1, "all the copies of the Simmes printing would have to be recalled, or suppressed. The copies in Ling's (and any other shops) would have been rather easily recovered and destroyed. The only surviving first quartos were those that had been sold and were in private hands" ("Shakespeare," 218–19). Why Ling would have wanted to destroy his own books is a question Bourus never asks.

158. Taylor, "First," 556. "These parties" refers to Roberts and Ling, since at the time of this article, Roberts was thought to have printed Q1.

159. On reprinting as an index of popularity, see Farmer and Lesser, "Popularity."

160. Of the 86 first editions of professional plays during this period, three were reprinted in the same year (*1 Henry IV*, *The Two Angry Women of Abington*, and *Every Man out of His Humor*); three others were reprinted in the next calendar year (*Richard II*, *Richard III*, and *1–2 Edward IV*); and four more were reprinted in the subsequent calendar year (*The Spanish Tragedy*, *The Taming of A Shrew*, *Romeo and Juliet*, and *Henry V*). *Hamlet* might be considered to have been reprinted either in the next or the subsequent calendar year, depending on how we interpret the variant date of Q2. In any case, such plays were rare, and they consisted largely of Shakespearean drama.

161. My argument here elaborates on Lesser and Stallybrass, "First," 372–76.

162. See Greg, *Shakespeare*, 331–32.

163. As a comparison, another contemporary printer, Thomas Creede, looks far more like Roberts than like Simmes: Creede printed 305 editions, and only eight of these (2.6 percent) used the hanging indent for something other than biblical verses.

164. Two of the others derived indirectly from Simmes: Q2 *The Shoemaker's Holiday*, printed by George Eld for John Wright, followed Simmes's first quarto in its use of the hanging indent; Q2 *1 Sir John Oldcastle* similarly followed the first edition (printed by Simmes for Thomas Pavier), even though it was now printed by William Jaggard for Pavier, perhaps a deliberate attempt to mimic the earlier design as part of the "Pavier Quartos."

165. Reprint editions in general were conservative in their design, partly because simply reprinting a previous edition line by line saved time and expense. But Roberts's compositors were not, in fact, resetting the title page of Q1 in the usual way of reprinting; they were changing its text even while adhering to its unusual mise-en-page.

166. On the popularity of Shakespearean drama in print around the turn of the century, see Farmer and Lesser, "Popularity," 11.

167. Farmer, "Myth."

168. The 1599 edition of *The Spanish Tragedy* reads "former impression" instead of "first impression."

169. On sermons and note taking in relation to *Hamlet*, see Stern, "Sermons." Ling copublished the editions with John Busby. As with Q2 *Hamlet*, the title page for Smith's sermon does *not* completely denigrate the earlier edition, since the revised version also advertises that it is printed "according to the Coppie by Characterie, as he preached it" (Smith, *Affinitie*, title page). Note taking, in other words, does not conflict with a "corrected" edition.

170. In her Oxford Shakesepare edition of *Romeo and Juliet*, Jill L. Levenson argues similarly that while "scholars have assumed that Q2 replaces and/or repudiates Q1, it may simply be acknowledging a connection with a version of the play authorized by Shakespeare's company" (Levenson, ed., *Romeo*, 111–12).

171. I exclude *The Malcontent* (1604), which claims on its title page to have been "Augmented by Marston . . . With the Additions played by the Kings Maiesties servants." These comments appear only in the third edition, and since all three editions of the play were published in 1604 following a July entry in the Stationers' Register, I assume that Q3 appeared fairly late in the year, and thus is unlikely to have influenced Ling's title page for Q2 *Hamlet*.

172. Interesting, Kyd's *Solimon and Perseda*, the only other non-Shakespearean play before 1604 to advertise corrections, is linked to *The Spanish Tragedy*, since it deals with the same subject as Hieronimo's play-within-the-play. And so too is Q3 *The Malcontent* (1604), which refers to *The Spanish Tragedy* in its added Induction.

173. Here too printed sermons may provide a nondramatic parallel. The second edition of William Perkins's sermon, *The Combat betweene Christ and the Diuell displayed* (1606), which had been previously published from notes as *Satans Sophistrie Answered by Our Saviour Christ* (1604), claimed on its title page to be "much enlarged by a more perfect copie, at the request of *M. Perkins* Executors." But the revised edition did not seek to supersede or replace the earlier one, since it incorporates the dedication from Robert Hill that was included in the first edition, in which Hill indicates that he collated multiple texts taken down during the preaching. On this edition, see Stern, "Sermons."

174. Jonson, *Fovntaine*, sig. A4v.

175. Critics since Coleridge have suggested that Shakespeare wrote these passages, a theory that has recently been reinforced by stylometric analysis. See Vickers, "Identifying"; and Bruster, "Shakespearean."

176. On this aspect of the Q1 company attribution, see Lander, *Inventing*, 113. Nevertheless, as Paul Menzer has shown (*Hamlets*, 113), the chronology of the Q1 title page is itself ambiguous, since the claim to performance "in the Cittie of London" casts the play back into the earlier 1590s and "seems to fold in some of the fourteen-year performance history of the play."

177. I am grateful to Alan Farmer for pointing out the possible double meaning of *again* in the blurb.

178. Of all professional plays first published between 1576 and 1640, 21 of 317 (6.6 percent) reached a third edition in eight years or fewer.

CHAPTER 2. CONTRARY MATTERS

1. "Hamlet," *Literary*, 59.

2. "Hamlet," *Morning*, 3; "Shakspeare," *Kaleidoscope* (1 February 1825), 260–62; "Shakspeare," *Circulator*, 79–80, in truncated form; "Recovered," *United* (1 May 1825), and "Recovered," *United* (15 May 1825).

3. "Shakspeare," *Kaleidoscope* (25 January 1825), 254.

4. "Literary," *Gentleman's*, 69. A similar, but not verbatim, article appeared as "Shakspeare," *Circulator*, 60. These early responses probably underlie a later instance from 1875 recounted in Taylor and Thompson, "Obscenity," 491.

5. See also Boaden, *Memoirs of Mrs. Siddons*, 2.208: Hamlet "ought to have placed some guard upon his fancy when he forces a conversation with Ophelia; Hamlet is *gross*, at least in the original play" (2.208). For Boaden, "the original play" seems to mean the received text of Q2/F—*original* not because it is Shakespeare's first draft but rather because it is the original text with which the world was familiar. In other words, Boaden as well is expressing relief at the lack of indecency in the newly discovered version, but whether this refers to *contrary matters* or to the absence of the lines about "nothing" lying "between maids' legs" is impossible to determine.

6. Foucault, *History*.

7. Taylor and Thompson, "Obscenity."

8. *Jenkins*, 295; *Hibbard*, 254; *Bevington*, 1122. The coy gloss has become a cliché; see Timothy McBride's poem "Country Matters," which begins: "Our teacher pointed out the 'ugly pun' / in Hamlet's 'country,' but he never mouthed / the consummating 'cunt'" (McBride, "Country," 22).

9. Taylor and Thompson, "Obscenity," 493–97. They refer also to David Bevington's Bantam edition: "the coarse and bawdy things that country folk do (with a pun on the first syllable of *country*)" (Bevington, ed., *Hamlet*, 73); and Edwards's New Cambridge: "The sexual pun in 'country' is found also in the fifteenth century *Castle of Perseverance*" (*Edwards*, 157). See also Orgel and Braunmuller, eds., *Complete*, 1368: "rustic (with a bawdy pun on the first syllable: 'cunt-ry')."

10. *Thompson-Taylor Q1/F*, 117; *Thompson-Taylor Q2*, 305; *Norton*, 1710.

11. A street of the same name also once existed in York; both were later renamed. See "cunt, *n.*," *Oxford English Dictionary*, online edition, 1.

12. "cunt, *n.*," *Oxford English Dictionary*, online edition, 1. I have followed the Middle English Dictionary in altering "cunnig" to "cunni[n]g."

13. So the *Oxford English Dictionary* (online edition) surmises in its etymological note on "quaint, *n.1*": "either punningly after CUNT *n.* or as a euphemistic substitution for that word." It is difficult to determine to what extent *queynte* represents an alternate spelling of *conte*, and to what extent the distinct word equivalent to modern *quaint* was being used euphemistically or punningly. On this question, see the debate among Benson, "Queynte"; Fleming, "Quaint"; and Delany, "Anatomy." Dane argues against a pun in "Queynte"; as does Knapp, *Time-Bound*, 136. By the early modern period the word *quaint* could simply denote *vagina*, as in Florio's definition of *potta*, given later in this paragraph.

14. "Cunt," in Williams, *Dictionary*, 1.352, italics substituted for boldface; Florio, *Worlde*, sig. 2A6v.

15. See Knapp, *Time-Bound*, 139; and Williams, *Shakespeare's*, 87–88: such puns result from a "taboo evaded by disguise," and "dramatists smuggle [the word] in by such devices." See also Sheidlower, *F Word*, xii–xiii: "The demand for bawdy humor meant that in the past, as now, writers found ways to use certain words even if such words were prohibited by social conventions"; the example of *country matters* follows.

16. "Country," in Williams, *Dictionary*, 1.316–17. On *As You Like It*, see also Knapp, *Time-Bound*, 140. On Donne's usage, see Redpath, ed., *Songs*, lines quoted from 227, reference to *Hamlet* at 229; Braden, ed., *Sixteenth-Century*, 526. In personal communication, Lars Engle suggests that if *country* does not include a pun on *cunt* here, it may carry meanings connected with "bundling" or other "unschooled" sexual pleasures. A version that circulated in manuscript has the variant line, "sucked on

childish pleasures sillily," but such variants are common in manuscript circulation and therefore cannot be easily taken as bowdlerization.

17. At the end of Book 7 of *Actes and Monuments* (1583), for instance, after writing of events on the Continent, John Foxe noted that "it remayneth after this degresse, to returne and reduce our story againe, to our owne countrey matters, heere done and passed at home" (2.972); and in a 1628 translation of Virgil's *Eclogues*, the gloss notes that "*Thalia*, (that is the Muse which hath preheminence over the fields) did first daign to sport in *Theocritus* his verse, applying it selfe first to sing of Country matters" (Lathum, *Virgils*, sig. G3r).

18. Sidney, *Arcadia*, sigs. Q1r; Knapp, *Time-Bound*, 140.

19. Williams himself writes that the country "is a refuge for lovers," the "polar opposite to court or city as a place of innocent sexuality," and "an unending source of fresh young women to replace the jaded London whores" (*Dictionary*, 1.316), adducing examples from the drama. But it is hard to differentiate these examples, where he apparently sees no pun, from Hamlet's and Touchstone's lines, where he does.

20. Knapp, *Time-Bound*, 203n4.

21. Marlowe and Chapman, *Hero*, sig. N1v; Braunmuller, "Hot," 99.

22. *Homer*, sigs. G3r–v.

23. The spelling of the word as *cuntry* is sometimes understood as a similar attempt to draw attention to the pun, but this seems unlikely given the variability of spelling in general in the period. A reference in a Marprelate pamphlet to "cuntry Parsons & Fickers" may indeed carry the pun, since "ficken" was German slang for "fuck," but the spelling *cuntry* was also used by the Earl of Essex in a letter to Queen Elizabeth, where it was was hardly likely to involve an obscene pun. I am grateful to Kristen Poole for alerting me to the Marprelate reference (Marprelate, *Oh*, sig. G1r); for the Essex letter, see Doughtie, "Earl," 356.

24. The same is true of the story about the Restoration actress who flubbed her line: "Crying, O my Dear *Count*! She Inadvertently left out, O, in the pronuntiation of the Word *Count*! giving it a Vehement Accent, put the House into such a Laughter, that *London* Bridge at low Water was silence to it" (Downes, *Roscius*, 22). But this does not indicate that a pun on *cunt* was present in the word *count* (or *country*), as it has sometimes been read. Just the opposite: it shows that the word had to be accidentally pronounced differently in order for the obscenity to appear.

25. *Thompson-Taylor Q2*, 305.

26. On *eye*, see Williams, *Dictionary*, 1.453–56; Partridge, *Shakespeare's*, 130–31; Maguire, "Feminist," 70.

27. *Bevington*, vii. See Cordner's comment that "editors themselves generally remain silent about the principles or preferences that shape their style of annotation" ("Actors," 181). For a salient exception, see Hunter, "Social."

28. Small, "Editor," 189.

29. Battestin, "Rationale," 8. See also Walker, "Principles." Walker's essay is concerned only with annotation of vocabulary, but like Battestin's, it is based in a theory of meaning that is historical and strongly authorial.

30. Jack, "Novels," 323. Jansohn calls Jack's proposal "impossible" and "altogether quite naive, since one will never be able to recreate the authentic circumstances under which an earlier reader has encountered the text," but she still maintains a fundamentally historical understanding of the function of the gloss ("Annotation," 213–14). For an incisive discussion and critique of these issues, see Walsh, *Shakespeare*, ch. 1.

31. On this social function of wit, see Zucker, *Places*; and, in a later period, English, *Comic*.

32. I am influenced here by Small, "Editor," 206: "If, as I have suggested, appeals to an 'original' readership will not help, for not only must there have been in fact very diverse kinds of readers, but the novel itself seems to discriminate *between* kinds of readers, then the annotator's only recourse is to appeal to a notion of authorial intention."

33. See Small, "Editor," 203.

34. As Cordner points out, overconfident glossing "can detach words from their immediate dramatic context" and result in notes that "narrow down unacceptably the range of meaning those words can in practice carry on the lips of actors" ("Actors," 191, 193).

35. Delany, "Anatomy," 14. In this sense, I both agree and disagree with Delany's argument that "wordplay does the very opposite of tie up loose ends. In fact it creates them, and that, I suggest, is one source of discomfort for the scholarly tendency" to discount obscene puns. In the history I am tracing here, meaning is confined and loose ends are tied up through the repeated invocation of the pun, not its dismissal.

36. Thompson, "Feminist," 95, 99.

37. Maguire, "Feminist," 71.

38. Wells, *Looking*, 1, 18, 2 (emphasis added).

39. Harris, *Untimely*, 5.

40. Partridge, *Shakespeare's*, 110.

41. Holderness and Loughrey, eds., *Tragicall*, 121.

42. Legman, *Rationale*, 219.

43. Irace, ed., *First*, 105.

44. *Thompson-Taylor Q1/F*, 117.

45. Andrew Gurr skeptically concludes: "The pronunciation of most vowels is speculative, and indeed always variable, even from the same speaker. Moreover, since even the relatively brief historical period of speech recordings, since about 1890, speech and particularly RP [Received Pronunciation] can heard [*sic*] to have changed with recognisable thoroughness almost every decade, a retrieval process yearning all the way back to Shakespeare invites only despair" (Gurr, "Other," paragraph 2).

46. See Lopez, *Theatrical*, 40–41, 43.

47. Shakespeare, *Henry the fift*, sig. C3v.

48. The English word at issue here is actually *gown*, not *count* or *country*, and the vulgar pun is on the French *con*, not the English *cunt*. Could the Folio's spelling indicate some attempt, perhaps after the play's initial performance, to make the pun more evident to readers lacking French? If the pun is on *gown* and *con*, the quarto seems to indicate it better. It is just possible that the Folio's spelling is being affected by the English word *cunt*.

49. Rubinstein, *Dictionary*, 56. Williams's *Dictionary* likewise includes an entrance for *con* (1.289–90), and cross-references to this entry from numerous other words, although he too is silent on Q1's *contrary*.

50. Webb, *Shakespeare's*, 30.

51. *Edwards*, 157.

52. *Thompson-Taylor Q2*, 305.

53. Jonson, *Comicall*, sigs. I3r–v.

54. Ostovich, ed., *Every*, 239. The same problem occurs with references to Donne's "Good-Morrow": Redpath imagines that "there would . . . probably be an inevitable sexual overtone (cf. 'country matters' in *Hamlet*, III. ii. 117)," without noticing the contradiction between *probably* and *inevitable* (Redpath, ed., *Songs*, 229). And see also the reading of Raleigh's phrase "Guiana is a countrey that hath yet her maydenhead," in Montrose, "Work," 12: "His metaphor . . . activates the bawdy Elizabethan

pun on *countrey*," with a footnote only to Partridge's entries for *country* and *country matters*, themselves derived primarily from *Hamlet* and entirely from Shakespeare; and the reading of Raleigh in Sanford, *Maps*, 54: "The pun on the word 'country' to refer to women's genitals (as in Hamlet's 'country matters' [3.2.116]) is commonplace." Again and again, the pun is described as common or "Elizabethan," while the only other text mentioned is *Hamlet*.

55. Mowat reported by Billings, "Squashing," 434; de Grazia and Stallybrass made the same point about the modernization of *weyward* to *weird* in editions of *Macbeth* ("Materiality," 263).

56. Taylor and Thompson, "Obscenity," 494.

57. Similarly, it is difficult to interpret the other major variation between the Q1 text and those of Q2 and F, because that evidence also points both ways. The explicit exchange about the "fair thought to lie between maids' legs," which follows *country matters* in Q2 and F, does not appear in Q1. This "omission"—if that is indeed what it is, rather than being added later—might initially seem to lend support to the bowdlerization theory, on the theory that sexual references in the passage more broadly were removed or altered, including changing *country* to *contrary*. But it is difficult to draw conclusions from the absence of any specific passage in Q1, given how much shorter that text is overall. Indeed, the fifteen lines immediately following Hamlet's "Nothing" in Q2 and F, all apparently innocent, also do not appear in Q1, and so the entire section may well have been removed as unnecessary, in an attempt to speed up the action and get to the dumb show more quickly.

58. Folger STC 22274 Fo.2 no7. See Lee, "Shakespeare," 189. I am very grateful to David Kastan for alerting me to this copy of F2.

59. The attribution to Sankey was first proposed in a letter to the *Times* by Patrick Ryan (12 April 1922). See also the appendix in Frye, *Shakespeare*; Frye accepts the identification of Sankey.

60. Perhaps Sankey read the plays individually as requested, when students wanted to read or perform a particular one. It is clear that, like most early modern censors, Sankey did not "apply his principles with any strict uniformity, and much that one would expect to fall under either his dogmatic or his ethical ban escapes his attack" (Lee, "Shakespeare," 190).

61. See the digital edition of the promptbook by Evans.

62. Since the text derives ultimately from Q2, unlike the Folio-based Smock Alley promptbook, the earlier lines cut in Smock Alley—Hamlet's clarification of his question and Ophelia's "I, my Lord"—do not appear at all in the Players' Quartos.

63. Shakespeare, *Hamlet* (1676), sigs. G2r–v. Later editions follow the first at this point.

64. *Johnson 1765*, 8.218.

65. Richard Farmer argued that the passage had been added by actors, for Shakespeare "surely . . . would not have admitted such obscenity and nonsense" (*Essay*, 86). Farmer's explanation thus anticipates the reception of *contrary matters* after the discovery of Q1.

66. *Johnson 1765*, 2.153, 8.53.

67. Furthermore, the eighteenth-century debate about bawdiness and Ophelia was overwhelmingly concerned not with this exchange but with the songs that she sings in her mad scenes: see the comments of Jeremy Collier, Goethe, and Tieck in Farley-Hills, ed., *Critical*, 1.19, 2.28, 2.152.

68. *Malone 1790*, 9.306.

69. See, e.g., the introduction to Griffiths, ed., *Country*, xx; Birth and Hooper, eds., *Oxford*, 159. The Wikipedia entry on the play asserts simply that the "title itself contains a lewd pun" (accessed 5 July 2013).

70. A search through Eighteenth Century Collections Online reveals no glosses on the line in *Hamlet* prior to Johnson, other than Theobald's remarks discussed immediately following, and only a single usage of the phrase *country matters* in the obscene sense, also discussed in this chapter.

71. Theobald, *Shakespeare*, 86.

72. Stubbes also rebuked Shakespeare for the indecency of this dialogue: "I might also justly find Fault with the want of Decency in his Discourses to *Ophelia*, without being thought too severe" (*Remarks*, 39). But he is clearly referring to the scene as a whole, with no particular reference to *country matters*, and hence this comment cannot illuminate the question. Neither can George Steevens's gloss on the word *jig* in a line immediately following this dialogue: "A *jig* was . . . a ludicrous dialogue in metre, and of the lowest kind, like *Hamlet*'s conversation with *Ophelia*" (*Steevens 1778*, 10.292).

73. On the reasons for this change in method, see Stern, "I Do."

74. Theobald reproduced a number of notes from *Shakespeare Restored* in his edition, and so some of the text that Johnson quotes does appear there, but Johnson never cites anything from Theobald that is not also in his edition of the plays. Johnson apparently used Theobald's second edition of 1740, since his quotation of Theobald's note on "*A very very* Peacock" ends with several lines that Theobald added to the second edition. See *Johnson 1765*, 8.227; and compare *Theobald 1733*, 7.302, and Theobald, ed., *Works*, 8.169–70. Johnson also worked with Theobald's marked-up copy of the First Folio, later owned by George Steevens, and now in the British Library, shelf mark C.39.i.12.

75. *Yorick's*, 7.

76. Addison and Steele, *Spectator*, 4.70 (originally appeared in issue number 269). Aaron Hill provides another common, innocent use; when explaining "the Reason why the *Turks* neglect improving Lands," Hill writes that "this universal negligence in Country matters, may proceed from that inglorious and submissive Slavery wherein they live" (Hill, *Full*, 75).

77. Mason, *Comments*, 388. His allusion to the currency of the phrase "in common life" is intriguing, with its suggestion that the double entendre had never gone out of use but may have been forgotten in elevated circles—although he provides no documentation and, given the paucity of references in print, we may wonder whether he is merely trying to distance himself and his readers from the "common" people who might use such a phrase, just as Jenkins refers to "a popular pun" in his Arden edition two centuries later.

78. Pinkerton, "Conclusion," 312; the volume is pseudonymously attributed to Robert Heron.

79. Only a year earlier, the actress and sometime royal mistress Mary Robinson had anonymously published *The Memoirs of Perdita* (1784), a titillating roman-à-clef that includes a direct allusion to the passage: "For reasons known best to themselves, the happy assignation was to take place at Colnbrooke, near which place Florizel's constant companion St. L—— had taken a villa for the enjoyment of rural recreation, and perhaps also of such other *country matters* as Hamlet alludes to" (Robinson, *Memoirs*, 96). Robinson's paralleling of "rural recreation" and "*country matters*" indicates that while the phrase still retained its "innocent" signification, that meaning was becoming ironized as the sexual meaning became more available. (The ascription to Robinson is by no means assured.)

80. On stage as well, the line may have been cut not simply as part of a wholesale excision of the passage but specifically for its double entendre, although again the evidence is ambiguous. A reviewer saw Kemble's 1783 production twice, once on opening night when Kemble apparently retained the passage as a whole, and then again later when he removed it. The reviewer approved the deletion, exclaiming, "Oh, how glad I am to see that they have now left out that shocking indecency, when Hamlet talks to Ophelia about *country matters*!" As usual, *country matters* refers to sex here, but does the reviewer imply that it is a pun? The italics suggests that he is pointing directly to this phrase as the "shocking indecency," but on the other hand, if the phrase itself is so obscene, it is a little surprising that the reviewer uses it so casually. Quoted in Mills, *Hamlet*, 64, although Mills does not preserve the italics. (The review of Kemble actually appears in the 6 October 1783 issue of the *Morning Chronicle and London Advertiser*, not, as Mills reports, the 4 October issue.)

81. Steevens, ed., *Plays*, 15.183; Reed, ed., *Plays*, 18.195. Also in 1793, Joseph Rann glossed the phrase as "any thing indecent" (Rann, ed., *Dramatic*, 6.326); he had likely seen Malone's edition.

82. *Boswell 1821*, 1.viii.

83. "Découverte," *Bibliothèque*, 83.

84. Elze, *Shakespeare's*, 195. I am grateful to Bethany Wiggin and Simon Richter for translating the German and Dutch. The original note reads: "*I meant country matters?*] QA: I meant contrary matters.—Was Hamlet meint kann nicht zweifelhaft sein, allein woher kommt die Bezeichnung 'country matters'? Dergleichen 'erbauliche Dinge' wie Schlegel übersetzt hat, kommen doch in der Stadt eben so wohl vor, als auf dem Lande. Johnson hat 'country manners' vermuthet, worüber K. John I, 1 zu vergleichen ist. Am naivsten hat sich die holländische Übersetzung geholfen, wo es heisst: Dacht gy dan, dat ik als een Boer op uw schoot wilde zitten? Wir sind geneigt, in 'country' eine Verderbniss anzunehmen, zu deren Verbesserung QA den Weg zeigt."

85. Heussi, *Shakespeare's*, 215. I am grateful to Bethany Wiggin for translating the German. The original note reads: "QA.: contrary matters. Was Hamlet meint, ist nicht schwer zu errathen, aber wie dies durch country oder contrary matters bezeichnet werden kann, ist nicht abzusehen. Soll country matters die rechte Lesart sein, so musste man's deuten: robe, ungeschlachte Dinge, wie sie den ungebildeten Landbewohnern eigen sind. Ist es aber in den Städten in diesem Punkte besser? Es liegt wohl ein Schreib- oder Druckfehler zu Grunde. Contrary ist unsinnig."

86. *Singer 1826*, 10.251.

87. *Singer 1826*, 1.xviii.

88. *Singer 1826*, 10.210, 10.293.

89. *Steevens 1773*, 10.156; *Caldecott 1819*, notes to *Hamlet*, 14; *Boswell 1821*, 7.193.

90. *Singer 1826*, 10.168.

91. *Singer 1826*, 10.284.

92. *Singer 1826*, 10.152.

93. Marshall, *Study*, 141–42n, 81.

94. Singer, *Dramatic*, 9.233.

95. Taylor and Thompson, "Obscenity," 492–93. And if the continuation of the exchange as it stands in Q2 and F, with Hamlet's comment about what lies "between maids' legs," was indeed cut from Q1 for reasons of propriety, then again the preferred method was simply removal, not subtle changes of wording.

96. I have not, however, found anyone who actually discusses the variant in the context of an argument about memorial reconstruction. If the memorial reconstruction involved dictation at any point, then the situation starts to resemble Collier's theory, since the possibility of aural error is introduced.

97. *Jenkins*, 114.

98. Maguire, *Shakespearean*, 152.

99. "Contrary, *adj., n., adv., and prep.*," *Oxford English Dictionary*, online edition, 2b: "Opposite to the proper or right one; 'the wrong'." The definition is marked as obsolete and rare, but the two citations are to *Merchant of Venice* and *King John*.

100. Most modern editors explain Q2's lack of Hamlet's second question and Ophelia's response as a printing error caused by eye skip: the accidental omission of lines due to the immediate recurrence of similar lines in the manuscript. See, for example, *Jenkins*, 39; *Hibbard*, 93. This is possible, but it relies on numerous assumptions about the relationship of the three texts that I want to bracket here.

101. Editors routinely find a sexual innuendo in Hamlet's initial request to lie in Ophelia's lap, present in both Q2 and F. But they are almost invariably glossing the passage as it stands in F, since

that version of the passage is included even in editions (such as *Jenkins*) where the stated goal is to reconstruct Shakespeare's intentions as represented in the authorial manuscript believed to lie behind Q2. For this reason, the distinction between Q2 and F at this point has rarely been considered. Jenkins's gloss on "*lie in your lap*" exemplifies the problem: "Hamlet first implies, then (l. 113 [*I mean, my head upon your lap*]) affects not to have meant, an indecent meaning, which he returns to at l. 115 [*Do you think I meant country matters?*]" (*Jenkins*, 294). But in Q2, Hamlet has not "first" implied and "then" affected not to have meant anything: Hamlet here asks only the single question, *Lady shall I lie in your lap?*

102. Writing shortly after the publication of the Q1 reprint but possibly without having seen it, Henry Mercer Graves addressed this passage in his attempt to show that Hamlet was not truly mad. His reading shows that even at this stage in its critical history, *country matters* did not always take center stage in the analysis of sexual innuendo in the passage. Graves focuses entirely on the question "Lady, shall I lie in your lap?" which he takes as a masterful balance of politeness and wayward innuendo (Graves, *Essay*, 39–41).

103. Indeed, some twentieth-century productions of the traditional text have staged the scene in this way, although it is far more available in Q1. See Taylor and Thompson, "Obscenity," 488–89.

104. Williams, *Dictionary*, 652; Goddard, *Neaste*, sig. D2v; Marlowe, *All*, sig. E4r.

105. Shakespeare, *Troylus*, sig. H1v.

106. Florio, *Worlde*, sig. E6r. His definition of *capocchio* ("a doult, a noddie, a loggarhead, a foolish pate, a shallow skonce") follows immediately. See Rubinstein, *Dictionary*, 44. Malone uneasily referred readers to Florio: "The word in the old copy is *chipochia*, for which Mr. Theobald substituted *capocchio*, which he has rightly explained. *Capochia* may perhaps be used with propriety in the same sense, when applied to a *female*; but the word has also an entirely different meaning, not reconcileable to the context here, for which I choose to refer the reader to Florio's Italian Dictionary, 1598" (*Malone 1790*, 8.245). In his 1821 revision, Boswell silently removed the latter part of Malone's note, thereby avoiding a reference to obscenity that Malone had made available to his readers, much as he did with *country matters* (*Boswell 1821*, 8.365). Despite Malone's reluctance to acknowledge the applicability of Florio's definition to this passage, the interpretation seems easy enough and perfectly plausible.

107. If we consider Q1 Hamlet's question in full—"Lady will you giue me leaue, and so forth: / To lay my head in your lappe?"—the potential obscenity may be underscored further. Laurie Maguire has shown that "by Shakespeare's day *&c / etcetera* is not just a substitute for a bawdy verb or noun but is a bawdy term in itself." Hamlet's "and so forth" may serve a similar function here, substituting for some suggestive gesture or calling attention to the double meaning that follows. Maguire notes, however, that for "Shakespeare and his contemporaries, 'and so forth' seems to have the limited meaning that *etcetera* does for us today: it concludes lists." For this reason, she writes, Q1 Hamlet's use of the phrase is "unusual, untypical, unShakespearean." Maguire, "Typographical," 4, 27–28.

CHAPTER 3. ENTER THE GHOST IN HIS NIGHT GOWNE

1. A point also made by Stewart, "Actor," 9.
2. See Bourne, "Play."
3. *Pope 1723*, 1.xxii, 1.157, emphasis removed.
4. Hanmer, ed., *Works* 1.iii–iv.
5. *Theobald 1733*, 1.xxxviii.
6. Both quoted in Farley-Hills, ed., *Critical*, 2.xlviii.

7. Styan, *Shakespeare*, 235.
8. Wells and Taylor, et al., eds., *William*, xxxviii.
9. For Freud's initial suggestion, see his letter to Wilhelm Fliess, 15 October 1897, in Freud, *Complete*, 272–73. For Jones, see "Oedipus" and "Psycho-Analytic." The study was finally expanded into Jones, *Hamlet*.
10. Charney, "*Hamlet*," 469.
11. *Hibbard*, 176.
12. Andrews, "His," 164.
13. *Jenkins*, 318.
14. Dawson, ed., *Hamlet*, 9–10.
15. Halio, *Understanding*, 48.
16. See Worthen, *Shakespeare*. Halio explicitly wants to recover "'Shakespeare's' *Hamlet*"; while "we know that there is not one *Hamlet* but many *Hamlets*," he nonetheless seeks a "way through this subjectivism of 'interpretation'" back to the "essential" play (Halio, "Essential," 84).
17. Aebischer, *Shakespeare's*, 79.
18. Buhler, *Shakespeare*, 71.
19. Halio, "Essential," 93.
20. Wells, *Shakespeare*, 361.
21. Styan, *Shakespeare*, 162; Gielgud, "Hamlet," 64.
22. *Thompson-Taylor Q2*, 333–34.
23. Taylor, *Reinventing*, 261–62; Rosenberg, *Masks*, 646; Wells, *Looking*, 24.
24. Styan, *Shakespeare*, 162; see Wells, *Shakespeare*, 361.
25. Andrews, "His," 164; see also Rosenberg, *Masks*, 646. For Bradley's remarks, see *Shakespearean*, 119. Note that Bradley wrote before Jones popularized the theory in the Anglophone world; Cary DiPietro writes that "Freud may have consulted *Shakespearean Tragedy* between 1904 and 1913, when the revised comments on *Hamlet* appeared in the English translation of *The Interpretation of Dreams*, but the connection is probably less direct . . . rooted in the exchanges of Romanticism between England and Germany in the nineteenth century" (DiPietro, "A. C. Bradley," 44).
26. Stewart, "Early"; see also Jardine, *Reading*, 148–57.
27. Orlin, "Gertrude's," 63.
28. "Shakspeare," *Blackwood's*, 252.
29. Werder, *Heart*, 148; Werder's book originated as lectures given in 1859–60.
30. See Taranow's remarkable reconstruction of the production (focusing on the Paris debut, not the London staging) in *Bernhardt*. Taranow is one of the few scholars to recognize that the "use of a bed in this scene, which is generally considered modern, is actually older than realized" (*Bernhardt*, 162).
31. Morand and Schwob, eds. and trans., *Tragique*, 252. The emphasis is in the original.
32. Grein, *Premières*, 39; "Madame," *Times*, 7; Taranow also notes that "the bed . . . attracted only minimal attention" and refers to another unnamed reviewer, who called "the scene the 'bedchamber scene,'" but so nonchalant was his attitude towards the appearance of the bed that he names the scene only in connection with his praise of the treatment of the Ghost" (*Bernhardt*, 162).
33. On the release date of Freud's book, see Gay, *Freud*, 3.
34. See "Hamlet," *Literary*, 58–59; "Découverte," *Bibliothèque*, 82.
35. "Dramatic," *Drama*, 276.
36. "Record," *Dial*, 78–79.
37. Gunthio, "Running," 342. For the attribution to Collier, see Kliman, "At Sea."
38. Dibdin, *Bibliophobia*, 86n.

39. Bates, "Hamlet," 380.

40. Quoted from a review of Edwin Booth's 1864 production, in which the lines were cut as usual, in Shattuck, *Hamlet*, 55. Booth restored the lines in his 1870 production, but by this time opinion was beginning to shift: Irving was criticized by several reviewers for omitting the lines in 1874, and he restored them in his 1878 revival. See *Spectator* 47 (7 November 1874): 1395; "Mr.," *Graphic*, 463; "At the Play," *Theatre*, 48–49.

41. Voltaire, *Critical*, 155.

42. Elizabeth Montagu (1769), quoted in Farley-Hills, ed., *Critical*, 1.195.

43. Stubbes, *Some*, 42, 43–44.

44. Stubbes, *Some*, 13.

45. Stubbes, *Some*, 32.

46. *Steevens 1773*, 10.182. See also Boaden, *Memoirs of the Life*, 2.61. For a modern interpretation of the choice of costume, see Jones and Stallybrass, *Renaissance*, 245–68.

47. Reed, *Lectures*, 421.

48. See Roach, *Player's*, 111. On the passing down of the precise "action" of a role, see Stern, *Rehearsal*, 58. On the performance text of *Hamlet*, see Glick, "*Hamlet*."

49. Some commenters tried to define the meaning of *nightgown* so that it did not lead readers to imagine that the Ghost has just been roused from sleep. Instead, we are often told that the "night-gown in which the ghost appeared in this scene was what we call a dressing-gown, or *robe de chambre*," an article of clothing more suitable to the dignity of the Ghost. Such dressing gowns might be "furred" or trimmed with "gold lace," in fact, making them especially regal. Victorian writers were certain that a "night-gown, to be worn in bed, was a thing unknown, not only in Hamlet's time but in Shakespeare's," thereby eliminating at least part of the difficulty of the new stage direction. "Passage," *Galaxy*, 281–82. For similar comments, see "Young," *All*, 140; Rolfe, ed., *Shakespeare's*, 238; MacDonald, ed., *Tragedie*, 173; White, *Studies*, 93.

50. *Collier 1843*, 7.192.

51. Collier, *Notes*, 418.

52. On Ophelia, Collier writes: "The stage-direction in the quarto, 1603, is curiously minute: 'Enter Ophelia, playing on a lute, and her hair down, singing.' She therefore accompanied herself in her fragments of ballads" (*Collier 1843*, 7.304). His respect for the authority of the stage directions is completely at odds with his general scorn for the text of Q1.

53. The Victorian habit of redefining the nightgown has also stuck with us, no doubt because the stage direction still often seems, as W. W. Greg wrote in 1902, "impossible for a serious edition" ("Old," 422). Dover Wilson alerted the readers of *What Happens in Hamlet* to the historical difference in the meaning of this costume: "At that period, of course, 'night gown' meant what we should now call 'dressing-gown.'" (*What*, 250n3). Contemporary critics often do the same: "'Nightgown' . . . makes very good sense if one remembers that the Elizabethan nightgown was a warm, lined garment, usually with a fur collar, worn both indoors and out and roughly equivalent to our dressing gown" (Charney, "*Hamlet*," 468). See also Andrews, "His," 166n14; Braunmuller, ed., *Hamlet*, 91; *Hibbard*, 282. On this point, see McLuskie, "*Enter*," 4.

54. Jones and Stallybrass, *Renaissance*, 245; see also Bann, "Ghostly."

55. Stubbes, *Some*, 42; Boaden, *Memoirs of the Life*, 2.65. In *Brudermord*, Hamlet says: "I can readily believe that you see nothing, for you are no longer worthy to look on his form" (*Furness 1877*, 2.133).

56. "Passage," *Galaxy*, 281–82. These writers are likely influenced by Strachey's *Shakespeare's Hamlet*, which had famously (or infamously, to its many critics) argued that the Ghost is subjective

even in his first appearance, a claim which required some rather dexterous argumentation to explain why Horatio and the sentinels can see him. In the closet scene, Strachey argued, Hamlet's meditation on the picture of his father leads the Ghost to appear again "in his habit as he lived" (75–76), although Strachey does not explicitly invoke the nightgown as evidence.

57. White, *Studies*, 93; see also the note in White, ed., *Mr.*, 3.574.

58. "Minor," *Appletons'*. The review is dated 7 June 1873.

59. Hudson, ed., *Plays*, 1.592.

60. Bradley dismissed the subjective ghost theory vehemently (*Shakespearean*, 139–40). Nonetheless, twentieth-century stagings have often dematerialized the Ghost, choosing to represent him as a shaft of light, a vapor or smoke, Hamlet's own mirrored reflection, or a hologram (see Rosenberg, *Masks*, 21–22). The subjective theory may have helped to make such performance choices possible, as part of the long historical transformation from what Jones and Stallybrass call the "gross materiality" of ghosts on the early modern stage to the ethereal, invisible beings of a more modern age (Jones and Stallybrass, *Renaissance*, 248).

61. Quoted in Farley-Hills, ed., *Critical*, 2.40.

62. Goethe, "First," 190, 192–94.

63. Schlegel and Herder quoted in Arac, "Impact," 289, 287. See also de Grazia, Hamlet *without Hamlet*, 14–15.

64. Foakes, ed., *Coleridge's*, 53.

65. One writer reported in 1845 that some "scoffers asked him 'if the Ghost had a wardrobe?'" to which Tieck "boldly, and very properly, answered, 'Yes; a ghost has as many changes of dress as his errand needs'" (Horne, "On the Character," 356). I have not been able to determine the exact year of the production: Tieck was involved with the Court Theater in Dresden from 1825; he died in 1853.

66. "Shakespeare's," *Edinburgh*, 65; the essay was also publicized (with the nightgown providing the sole detail) in "Goethe's," *Foreign*, 109, which was reprinted the following year in the Boston periodical the *Select Journal of Foreign Periodical Literature*; see also "Shakspeare," *London*, 217.

67. Bucknill, *Mad*, 109.

68. At Tom Taylor's Crystal Palace production the previous year, the Ghost appeared in the closet scene "not in mail, but in royal robes, the copy of those in which he is pictured" in his portrait ("Minor," *Appleton's*, 763). The performance may have influenced Irving, but it was not a major production, many of the actors were considered amateurs, and no one seems to have connected these robes with the nightgown of the Q1 stage direction.

69. Archer, *Henry*, 89.

70. "Henry," *Illustrated*, 126.

71. Irving, "Actor's," 524.

72. Dawson, ed., *Hamlet*, 64.

73. Russell, *Irving*, 14, 11–12.

74. Cook, *Nights*, 376.

75. See Glick, "*Hamlet*"; and for the same trend in critical thinking about the play, de Grazia, Hamlet *without Hamlet*.

76. Dawson, ed., *Hamlet*, 64.

77. Irving, *Henry*, 221; see also Hughes, *Henry*, 10; and Mills, *Hamlet*, 156.

78. "Henry," *Illustrated*, 126; "Theatres," *Times*, 8; review by Joseph Knight in 1874, quoted in Mills, *Hamlet*, 156.

79. "Mr.," *Graphic*, 463.

80. "Mr.," *All*, 181.

81. Roach, *Player's*, 15.
82. "Bourgeois cordiality" quoted in Hapgood, ed., *Hamlet*, 42.
83. Dawson, ed., *Hamlet*, 59. One contemporary remarked: "There is probably no artistic institution in England which unites all classes as [the Lyceum] does" (quoted in Dawson, ed., *Hamlet*, 58).
84. Cook, *Nights*, 260; see also *Saturday Review* (4 January 1879), 18; "At the Play," *Theatre*, 48–49; Oliphant, "Hamlet," 478.
85. Oliphant, "Hamlet," 477.
86. Oliphant, "Hamlet," 478–79; on the costume change, see Hughes, *Henry*, 81. The revival began on 30 December 1878, and so of course ran into 1879.
87. Oliphant, "Hamlet," 477.
88. Oliphant, "Hamlet," 478.
89. Marshall, ed., *Hamlet*, vii–viii; see also *Saturday Review* (4 January 1879), 18; "At the Play," *Theatre*, 48.
90. Hughes, *Henry*, 32. In her study copy, Ellen Terry, who played Ophelia in the revival, wrote next to this line: "Working it up tremendously—excitedly—*The laws of Climax*," stressing this scene as the denouement of the entire play (Hughes, *Henry*, 65).
91. Dawson comes to the same conclusion (Dawson, ed., *Hamlet*, 65), following Hughes (*Henry*, 62).
92. Irving, "Actor's," 528.
93. Russell, *Irving*, 7.
94. Quoted in Hughes, *Henry*, 64.
95. Jardine, *Reading*, 145–46.
96. "New," *Macmillan's*, 237. On Irving, melodrama, and developing ideas of psychological realism, see Salter, "Henry."
97. Marshall, *Study*, 52. Marshall's comments in this book are not specifically referring to Irving's production, but his thinking about the play was heavily influenced by Irving; immediately preceding this comment, he singles out the Ghost's nightgown, noting that he is dressed "as if he were going to the bed that his wife had so cruelly dishonoured" (*Study*, 50).
98. Russell, *Irving*, 49.
99. Salter, "Henry," 167.
100. See Hughes, *Henry*, 62; and Dawson, ed., *Hamlet*, 66. I am drawing throughout on Hughes's painstaking reconstruction of the production.
101. Russell, *Irving*, 50.
102. Russell, *Irving*, 49; on earlier actors' refusal of the blessing, see Hughes, *Henry*, 66; and Dawson, ed., *Hamlet*, 54.
103. Indeed, the bit may have been too innovative for contemporary audiences, since Irving cut it from the revival.
104. "Theatres," *Times*, 8; and "Theatres," *Graphic*, 443. For modern comments on this moment, see Hughes, *Henry*, 65; Hapgood, *Hamlet*, 215; Dawson, ed., *Hamlet*, 65.
105. Hughes, *Henry*, 68; see also Dawson, ed., *Hamlet*, 66.
106. *Johnson 1765*, 8.311; Shakespeare, *Bell's*, 3.sig. O2r.
107. Goethe, *Wilhelm*, 2.87–89. Hegel's discussion of *Hamlet* follows along similar lines: the distinctive character of modern drama consists partly in its emphasis on psychology, rather than on external ethical dilemmas as in ancient tragedy, and Hamlet is therefore "bandied from pillar to post" in the final acts "and finally through his own procrastination and the external course of events meets his own doom" (Hegel, *Selections*, 324). On the relation of plot events to Hamlet's character as theorized by Coleridge and Hegel, see de Grazia, *Hamlet without Hamlet*, 13–19, 166.

108. Quoted in Farley-Hills, ed., *Critical*, 2.53, 2.58, 2.52.

109. Mayer, "Encountering," 159; see also Salter, "Henry," 162; Hughes, *Henry*, 243. On Manichaeism, see Brooks, *Melodramatic*, 43. Irving's melodrama moved away from the type of moral clarity of the early melodramas, in which hero and villain are clearly demarcated, and toward a hero internally divided or guilty.

110. Strachey, *Shakespeare's*, 93. See also Hermann Ulrici's similar argument, where, however, the influence of Hegel is also prominent, as shown by his comment that Hamlet "has thus acknowledged the internal necessity in the course of the historical events, from which he tried to escape" (Ulrici, *Shakespeare's*, 504).

111. Eliot, "Hamlet," 941. Jardine "find[s] it striking that . . . [Eliot's] psychoanalytic reading of the play is established before psychoanalytic theory is explicitly introduced into literary studies" (*Reading*, 170n19). My argument here suggests that it would be less striking if we understood this alternative genealogy of the closet scene.

112. Oliphant, "Hamlet," 477.

113. Sonnenchein, "Shakespeare," 107, emphasis added.

114. Indeed, even well before Irving's Lyceum production this connection between nightgown and bedroom could be made: the 1835 writer in *Blackwood's* who referred to "the bedroom of the Queen," did so in a discussion of Tieck's idea that the Ghost ought to appear in his nightgown, "in the dress most suited to the place, 'in his habit as he lived'" ("Shakspeare," *Blackwood's*, 252)

115. Marshall, *Study*, 50; Marshall, ed., *Hamlet*, viii.

116. "At the Play," *Theatre*, 48–49.

117. Bradley, *Shakespearean*, 119.

118. Bradley, *Shakespearean*, 138, 139.

119. As de Grazia notes, partly for this reason Bradley's language can sound quite Freudian at times (Hamlet *without Hamlet*, 167–68).

120. Bradley was in London during the run of Bernhardt's *Hamlet*; he went to the theater often during this time, including to the premiere of his friend Gilbert Murray's play *Carlyon Sahib*, and it seems unlikely he would have missed such an important Shakespearean production as Bernhardt's. See his letters during 1899 to Gilbert Murray and Lady Murray, now in the Bodleian Library (MSS Gilbert Murray, boxes 122, 546).

121. Taranow, *Bernhardt*, 53–54.

122. Morand and Schwob, eds. and trans., *Tragique*, 138. Irving had cut the speech short after "bed," while Bernhardt continued, "mijoter dans la pourriture, se becqueter de miel et d'amour au-dessus de l'étable à pores!"

123. Wilson, *What*, 250.

124. Marshall, *Study*, 52.

125. Wilson, *What*, vii (only in the third edition), 218 (in both the first and the third edition).

126. Kliman, "Bed."

127. See Mills, *Hamlet*, quoting "an old critic who, in the reign of George II, refused to see any great merit in the performance of a new Hamlet, declaring, 'He did not upset the chair, sir. . . . Now Mr. Betterton always upset the chair'" (15). The same story is told of Garrick, who later made the moment his own; when one actor tried Hamlet in the later eighteenth century, "the Garrick worshippers" disparaged him because "in his agitation in the famous closet scene he did not upset the chair as was the traditional custom. 'Mr. Garrick, sir, always overthrew the chair,' they said." Brereton, *Some*, 19.

128. Belleforest, *Cinquiesme*, 203. On the interpretation of *stramentum* and *loudier*, see *Furness 1877*, 2.89, summarizing Elze; Roosbroeck, "Hamlet," 234; *Jenkins*, 319; *Hibbard*, 7. In a 1989 RSC

production, directed by Ron Daniels, Polonius in fact hid under the bedcovers (Aebischer, *Shakespeare's*, 78).

129. See Dessen and Thomson, *Dictionary*, 24–25.

130. For the "as if" formulation, see the entry for "bed" in Dessen and Thomson, *Dictionary*, and the stage direction from *The White Devil*, discussed next.

131. By the time of Rowe's edition, the Q1 stage direction seems already to have been lost, since in both engravings the Ghost appears in armor. But since, in early staging, a bed and a nightgown were in some ways interchangeable properties, serving similar functions by different means, some memory of early performance may be preserved in the engraver's decision to include a bed.

132. In total, about 16 percent of plays in the period call for a bed, but the use of the prop increases significantly in the seventeenth century and is weighted toward indoor theater plays. See Thomson, "Beds"; I am very grateful to Professor Thomson for sharing her paper with me.

133. Thomson ("Beds") cites George Peele's *The Battle of Alcazar*, which calls for a bed in the printed quarto but lacks the prop in the surviving manuscript plot; John Fletcher's *The Tamer Tamed*, which calls for a bed in the 1647 folio text but substitutes a chair in the manuscript; and *The First Part of the Contention* (*2 Henry VI*), which includes a bed direction in the quarto but not the Folio, although at a later point in the same play, both texts call for the bed. The substitution of chair for bed in *The Tamer Tamed* is intriguing given the stage tradition going back to Betterton of using chairs for Hamlet and Gertrude in this scene. Other plays call for a chair where we might expect a bed: in Anthony Brewer's *The Countrie Girle* (1647), the wounded captain enters "*in his Night-gowne*" along with "*Doctor, Servants, Chaire and stooles*" (sig. K1v), as if the chair were a sickbed. Dessen writes: "Thrusting a bed onto and then off the Elizabethan stage may not have been appropriate for all situations, however, so a more flexible solution was to use a portable chair in which the sick figure could be carried in and out expeditiously" (*Recovering*, 114).

134. Menzer notes that "Q1 shows a tendency toward eliminating explicit reference to properties" in general, because "Q1 remembers in part a text that strives for maximum material economy" due to touring, although he sees Q1 as a literary *construction* rather than a memorial reconstruction (*Hamlets*, 168–69).

135. It is therefore strictly incorrect to write about "the Closet Scene in Q1" as do Erne (*Shakespeare*, 239) and *Thompson-Taylor Q2*, 358.

136. While the stage directions simply call them "*Lordes*," we know who they are from the speech prefixes for "*Gil.*" in this scene (Rossencraft does not speak).

137. Cohn, *Shakespeare*, 275–76, 259–60, 257–58.

138. On the sexualized confounding of Old Hamlet and Claudius, see Adelman, *Suffocating*, 11–37. Intriguingly, in the revival of his blockbuster production, Irving substituted "incestuous" for "enseamed" here (Marshall, ed., *Hamlet*, 58).

139. Jones and Stallybrass, *Renaissance*, 263.

140. Jones and Stallybrass, *Renaissance*, 263–64.

141. Kehler, "First," 407. On Q1's characterization of Gertred as primarily a mother and the consequent minimizing of her political power, see also Gerstell, "Trafficking."

142. Erne, *Shakespeare*, 241. See also Eggert, *Showing*, 128: "Ironically, it is the most corrupt—or, for Urkowitz, the most immature—version of the play, the 'bad' Q1, that most grants to Hamlet the queen he seems most to want."

143. Jardine, *Reading*, 147–48.

144. Closets were not exclusively aristocratic, as Orlin shows ("Gertrude's"), since the word could signify a variety of rooms, including the kinds of storage rooms that even modest houses might

contain. But Gertrude's closet is clearly the kind of private chamber used for prayer, study, or meditation in an aristocratic household.

145. Weir, *Henry*, 42–43; Harris, *English*, 215. Note that in *Brudermord*, the King tells the Queen, "You, dearest consort, shall I follow to *your* bed-chamber," not "*our* bed-chamber" (Cohn, *Shakespeare*, 257–58, emphasis added).

CHAPTER 4. CONSCIENCE MAKES COWARDS

1. "Hamlet," *Literary*, 59.
2. Taylor, "First," 559.
3. Gunthio, "Running," 340. Gunthio also writes that the first quartos of *Merry Wives, Romeo and Juliet*, and *Henry V* are "genuine copies of the author's rough sketches" (340). If this was indeed Collier writing, we can see how Q1 *Hamlet* provided the impetus for his entire theory of stenographic piracy and retrograde bibliography, for he soon changed his opinion of these other plays, as discussed in Chapter 1.
4. White, "Two," 474.
5. I am particularly influenced here by Marcus, *Unediting*, 143–45; Lander, *Inventing*, 128–29; and Serpieri, ed. and trans., *Primo*.
6. Donne, *Poems*, sig. F2v.
7. On Shakespeare's use of the "sentential relative," see Hope, *Shakespeare's*, 109–10, although not citing this instance. Thompson and Taylor attach "which" to the preceding question, but escape the seeming incongruity by glossing it as "the uncertainty of which" (*Thompson-Taylor Q1/F*, 94). This is a plausible interpretation, but it requires a stronger editorial intervention than my alternative.
8. Lander, *Inventing*, 129.
9. *Johnson 1765*, 8.207.
10. Goldsmith, "Metaphors," 2.202, 2.208.
11. Editors have explained the phrase by a parallel with the Celts, who, "rather than show fear by flight, would draw their swords and throw themselves into the tides as though to terrify them" (*Jenkins*, 490); Furness cites Clement Ingleby as the first to discover this parallel (*Furness 1877*, 1.209).
12. *Johnson 1765*, 8.208–9. He admittedly offered his emendation "not confidently" (209).
13. See *Furness 1877*, 1.213–14, for a selection of the voluminous commentary on this line.
14. *Johnson 1765*, 8.207.
15. *Malone 1790*, 9.286.
16. For a variety of early critics on this side of the debate, see Richards, "Meaning"; and, more recently, Prosser, *Hamlet*; Petronella, "Hamlet's"; Belsey, "Case"; and Bruster, *To Be*, 40.
17. Fletcher, *Scornful*, sig. C4r.
18. Stubbes, *Some*, 38; ten years earlier, Theobald called it a "noble Speech" (*Shakespeare*, 82); Johnson refers to "this celebrated soliloquy" (*Johnson 1765*, 8.207).
19. Quoted in Farley-Hills, ed., *Critical*, 2.77.
20. Kastan notes that "I there's the point" is "a perfectly uncorrupt Shakespearean line," appearing in *Othello* (*Shakespeare and the Book*, 27).
21. "Almost a parody": Barnet, ed., *Hamlet*, 145; "gibberish": *Hibbard*, 86; "likely to be greeted as parody" and "an apparent burlesque": Marcus, *Unediting*, 133; "edge of parody": Irace, "Origins," 90. It should be noted, however, that Marcus uses the language of parody and burlesque while making the more important point: "So deeply engrained in our cultural expectations is the established text of 'To be or not to be' that any deviation from it is likely to be greeted as parody" (*Unediting*, 133).

22. *Knight 1839, Tragedies,* 1.90.

23. Desclozeaux, "Comparaison," 58–59, my translation. I have rendered "la conscience" as "the awareness," since the meaning of the English word *conscience* is precisely the question in this chapter. On Desclozeaux's criticism of *Hamlet*, see Bailey, *Hamlet,* 64–67. Bailey notes that the "publication of the First Quarto in English in 1825 was an event of no little importance to the history of *Hamlet* in France." French critics appreciated its "relative shortness and greater simplicity" and saw "in it unquestionably Shakespeare's original draft and a priceless source of information on his predilection for the play, his manner of working over style and composition, his own intellectual evolution" (66).

24. Verity, ed., *Tragedy,* 192.

25. Verity, ed., *Hamlet,* 172.

26. Lowes, ed., *Hamlet,* xxv–xxvi, 208–9. The general editor was Wilbur Cross, a future editor of the Yale Shakespeare. The misquotation—"conscience *doth*" instead of "conscience *does*"—was, and remains, widespread. It seems to have been particularly common in religious writings of the period, perhaps because it made Shakespeare sound more biblical.

27. Ridley, ed., *Hamlet,* 186, 191.

28. "Goldsmith," *Crypt,* 38.

29. *Knight 1839, Biography,* 527.

30. Strachey, *Shakspeare's,* 60.

31. *Boswell 1821,* 7.328; for later reuses of the note before Furness, see *Singer 1826,* 10.241; *Clarendon 1872,* 170; Rolfe, ed., *Shakespeare's,* 218. The line receives no note, and the word does not appear in the glossary, in the following major editions (keyed to bibliographic numbers in Murphy, *Shakespeare in Print*): William Harness (London: Saunders and Otley, 1825; Murphy §476), A. J. Valpy (London: A. J. Valpy, 1832–34; Murphy §480), *Collier 1843,* Barry Cornwall (London: Robert Tyas, 1843; Murphy §486), Gulian C. Verplank (New York: Harper & Brothers, 1844–47; Murphy §488), William Hazlitt (London: Routledge, 1851–52, Murphy §492), *Hudson 1856, Dyce 1857,* Howard Staunton (London: Routledge, 1858–60; Murphy §500), *White 1862,* The Globe Shakespeare (Cambridge and London: Macmillan, 1864; Murphy §590), Thomas Keightley (London: Bell and Daldy, 1864; Murphy §591), *Cambridge 1866,* Charles and Mary Cowden Clarke (London: Cassell, Petter, and Galpin, 1864–69?; Murphy §595). The lone editorial exception other than Knight is Caldecott, who glosses the word as "A state of doubt and uncertainty, a conscious feeling or apprehension, a misgiving 'How our audit stands.'" (*Caldecott 1819,* text of *Hamlet,* 69). This comes close to the idea of consciousness or speculation that was later to dominate, but even here the moral sense is strongly present, since the "doubt" and "conscious feeling or apprehension" relate to the audit of our sins at the Last Judgment.

32. Furness, Jr., ed., *Tragedy,* 132–33.

33. Chambers, ed., *Hamlet,* 183, 237, italics substituted for boldface.

34. *Cone 1897,* 82 (a note added by Cone to White's Riverside edition); *Herford 1899,* 8.197; Neilson, ed., *Complete,* 1218; Lee, ed., *Complete,* 15.91; Wilson, ed., *Hamlet,* 192.

35. Bradley, *Shakespearean,* 98n1. Freud's interpretation of the line in his 1897 letter to Fliess retains the moral understanding but gives it a psychological turn that seems possibly indebted to the new reading of *conscience* as *consciousness*: "How does Hamlet the hysteric justify his words, 'Thus conscience does make cowards of us all'? . . . His conscience is his unconscious sense of guilt" (Freud, *Complete,* 272–73).

36. White et al., eds., *New,* 14.100; see *White 1862,* 11.178.

37. *Hudson 1856,* 10.276; Hudson, ed., *Complete,* 14.220; Black and George, eds., *Hamlet,* 107.

38. Schmidt, *Shakespeare-Lexicon,* 1.236. Likewise in 1868 James Russell Lowell compared a

passage in Dante to "a part of Hamlet's famous soliloquy:— / 'Thus conscience [*i.e. consciousness*] doth make cowards of us all" ("Shakespeare," 661); and in 1870, a correspondent to *Once a Week* wrote that the "true poetical signification" of the line has been "wrested by a literal interpretation to the present popular, but, I believe, corrupted meaning," since *conscience* here means not "the internal judge between right and wrong" but rather "consciousness, the knowledge that 'we know what we are, but we know not what we may be'" ("Correspondent," *Once*, 109). F. J. Furnivall also hinted at the new meaning in 1877: Hamlet's "reason for not killing himself is no longer God's canon against self-slaughter, but that the dread of something after death puzzles the will. And then he degrades conscience into identity with this same dread, and seems to offer it as the excuse of letting his resolution to sweep to his revenge, 'lose the name of action.'" A footnote on the word *conscience* in this passage reads, somewhat mysteriously: "See the text as against the meaning ordinarily given to the word and passage." Furnivall never makes explicit this "unordinary" meaning, and there is no gloss in the text, but his opposition to the "meaning ordinarily given to the word and passage" suggests that he intends something like "speculation." But he may simply mean that Hamlet "degrades conscience" into a crude dread, acting from the baser motive of the "fear of Hell" that C. S. Lewis would later find in the word, rather than from the virtuous desire for good. Furnivall, Introduction, lxxi.

39. Joseph, *Conscience*, 111, 116. G. Wilson Knight had earlier expressed the possibility that the word meant "conscience in the modern sense" but seemed to settle more on "excessive self-consciousness" (*Wheel*, 305–6).

40. Lewis, *Studies*, 207. Other contemporary critics were more hesitant, as prevailing opinion shifted: L. C. Knights refused to choose, deciding that "here both meanings are present" (*Some*, 221, citing D. G. James's *The Dream of Learning* [1951]), and Nicholas Brooke similarly had "doubts about the word 'conscience'. It has been confidently glossed 'consciousness' by most recent commentators," but Brooke insisted that it cannot "mean *only* that" and that "conscience must, at least in part, mean conscience" (Brooke, *Shakespeare's*, 195–96).

41. Prosser, *Hamlet*, 169.

42. Belsey, "Case," 127.

43. *Edwards*, 147.

44. *Hibbard*, 241.

45. *Jenkins*, 280, 493.

46. *The Norton Shakespeare* is typical in its even-handedness: "Both consciousness (introspective knowledge) and moral conscience" (*Norton*, 1706). See also Nigel Alexander's edition: "*a) consciousness, power of thought, b) power of distinguishing between good and evil*" (Alexander, ed., *Hamlet*, 144). The Folger *Hamlet* gives only "knowledge, consciousness" (Mowat and Werstine, eds., *Hamlet*, 128), while the Barnes & Noble *Hamlet* gives only "Knowledge of right and wrong" (Dolven, ed., *Hamlet*, 190).

47. Prosser, *Hamlet*, 169.

48. Belsey, "Case," 128–29. Jonathan Bate likewise sees the shift occurring as part of "a shift in emphasis from 'conscience' to 'consciousness' that occurred in the intellectual life of late-eighteenth-century Europe" (*Genius*, 258).

49. Coleridge, *Literary*, 2.205.

50. *Knight 1839*, *Tragedies*, 1.174.

51. Greenblatt, *Hamlet*, 208.

52. Foucault, "Nietzsche," 146.

53. Schlegel did, however, translate *conscience* as *Gewissen* here, which may have influenced and been influenced by German Romantic conceptions of Hamlet.

54. Coleridge, *Friend*, 100.

55. Schlegel, *Course*, 2.194.

56. Coleridge, *Notes*, 1.208; Hazlitt, *Characters*, 118.

57. Corson, "Hamlet," 344, 346; later reproduced in his *Introduction to the Study of Shakespeare* (Boston: D. C. Heath, 1893).

58. Mommsen, "Hamlet," 182.

59. Quoted in *Furness 1877*, 2.116; the original articles appear as "Shakespeare's *Hamlet*. Ein literar-historisch kitischer Versuch," in various issues of the 1857 *Hamburger literarisch-kritische Blätter*.

60. *Clarendon 1872*, xii.

61. Furnivall, "Is," 101.

62. Fleay thought that Q1 was a touring script, "an example of Shakespeare's hurried revision of the work of an earlier writer [Kyd], but it must be remembered in a most mutilated form," while Q2 represented "the full working out of his own conception, in the shape fittest for private reading," and F "his practical adaptation of it to the requirements of the stage" (Fleay, *Chronicle*, 233–34).

63. See Grady, *Modernist*, 57–61; Taylor, *Reinventing*, 281–83; de Grazia, "Essential," 79–80.

64. Grady stresses Fleay's metrical tests as the sine qua non of disintegrationism, its "particular methodology" (*Modernist*, 63). He also separates Stoll into his own category, but contemporaries, as I will show, consistently aligned him and Schücking with Robertson.

65. Schücking, *Character*, 147, 26.

66. Abercrombie, "Plea," 247. Abercrombie was hostile to the movement, but his summary here of its basic assumptions is accurate.

67. Hence Robertson wrote that *The Problem of "Hamlet"* "reviews and attempts to resolve the most interesting and the most extensive debate relating to any of" Shakespeare's plays, and serves "as an illustration of what is claimed to be the proper method of investigating all" (*Problem*, 8).

68. Fleay, "Neglected," 87–88.

69. Robertson, "Upshot," 357; Robertson is here quoting and endorsing the judgment of Halliwell-Phillips. In "Upshot," we can see already the basic method that Robertson would later employ in his books on *Hamlet*.

70. For Robertson's biography, see Freedon, "Robertson."

71. Robertson, *Hamlet*, 6–7.

72. Robertson, "Upshot," 357–58.

73. Lewis, *Genesis*, iii, 64.

74. Lewis, *Genesis*, 46.

75. Robertson, *Hamlet*, 57, 71; Robertson, *Problem*, 76. On these paleontological metaphors, see also Smith, "Ghost," 183.

76. Robertson, "Upshot," 214.

77. Stoll, *Hamlet*, 1; Stoll advertises Robertson's "forthcoming monograph on the '*Problem of Hamlet*'" in a note on the first page.

78. Stoll, *Hamlet*, 1–2.

79. Schücking, *Character*, 147.

80. Schücking, *Character*, 8; Wilson, *What*, 15; the grouping became conventional, not least because all three published important monographs in 1919. See Babcock, "Modern"; and Routh, review.

81. Robertson, *Problem*, 11.

82. Boas, ed., *Works*, liv. The attribution to Kyd was made by Gregor Sarrazin in *Thomas Kyd und sein Kreis* (1895) and immediately accepted as proving the case "beyond reasonable doubt," as John Corbin wrote (*Elizabethan*, 31). For Boas's view of Q1 and the *Ur-Hamlet*, see also Boas, *Shakespeare*,

384–85. Malone had earlier suggested Kyd as the author (*Malone 1790*, 9.183), but Robertson makes the point that Malone's inference "now rests more definitely on (*a*) the actual survivals of Kyd's phraseology in the First Quarto and (*b*) on the nature of the gibes by Nashe . . . in his preface to Greene's MENAPHON in 1589" (Robertson, *Hamlet*, 125). The first of these was of course unavailable to Malone and his contemporaries.

83. Eliot, "Hamlet," 941. The essay was later expanded in *The Sacred Wood*, and reference was added to Stoll's book as well.

84. On the inferential method of the disintegrationists, see Robertson, *Hamlet*, 156n1; and Smith, "Ghost," 179.

85. Roberston, *Problem*, 67, 74; Boas, ed., *Works*, xlvi; Corbin, *Elizabethan*, 3.

86. Crawford, *Hamlet*, 77, 26; Crawford's own theory is idiosyncratic, but his method here reveals the influence of disintegrationism.

87. Robertson, *Problem*, 85.

88. Lewis, *Genesis*, 129.

89. Corbin, *Elizabethan*, 49; see also Robertson, *Hamlet*, 156–57. Charles Knight had argued similarly that "Hamlet is fully conceived in the original play, whenever he is in action. . . . It is the contemplative part of his nature which is elaborated in the perfect copy," but for Knight, "the original play" meant Shakespeare's first draft as attested by Q1, which had no discernible connection to any earlier play (*Knight 1839, Tragedies*, 1.89).

90. Bradley, *Shakespearean*, 89, 90. Bradley also wrote that the different placement of "To be, or not to be" in Q2 and F provided "a notable instance of the truth that 'inspiration' is by no means confined to a poet's first conceptions" (112–13n3).

91. Robertson, *Hamlet*, 71; Robertson, *Problem*, 67. Stoll makes the same point in *Hamlet*, 3–4.

92. Lewis, *Genesis*, 71, 82, 83, 133. Stubbes had earlier noted Shakespeare's "injudicious" decision to retain Hamlet's madness from "the Ground-work of his Plot," linking this choice to the "Absurdity" of Hamlet's delay, but he did not integrate this analysis into a full-blown study of the play in the characteristic manner of the disintegrationist critics (*Some*, 33).

93. Robertson, *Hamlet*, 157.

94. Robertson, *Problem*, 73, 18, 73, 77, 74.

95. Stoll, *Hamlet*, 13.

96. Stoll, *Hamlet*, 64, 68.

97. Schücking, *Character*, 162, 167. Stoll did acknowledge that the "Elizabethan 'humor' of melancholy . . . predominates in his temperament" but denied that this was a "pathological condition" that undermined his heroism or led to his delay (*Hamlet*, 72).

98. Stoll, *Hamlet*, 30. While he claims that Shakespeare "elevated the character not only of Hamlet but of the King and Queen" (*Hamlet*, 70), Stoll is unique among the disintegrationists in that he never claims the philosophical and meditative aspects of Hamlet's character as Shakespeare's signal contribution to the drama.

99. Schücking, *Character*, 169.

100. On this connection, see de Grazia, "Essential," 80; and DiPietro, "Shakespeare," 147.

101. Greg, review of Robertson, 337, 339.

102. Greg, review of Schücking, 228. So too Pollard's foundational *Shakespeare's Folios and Quartos* followed the Clarendon edition and the disintegrationists on the origins of *Hamlet*: "That the quarto of 1603 is a bad piracy is generally admitted, as also that it represents the play in an intermediate stage between the lost *Hamlet* [of Kyd?] and the fully Shakespearian *Hamlet* of the Folio and the second and subsequent quartos" (74).

103. Chambers, "Disintegration." On Q1, see also Chambers, *William*, 1.415–25.

104. Wilson, "Copy," 183, 181, 180. On Wilson's theory, see Egan, *Struggle*, 101–2, although he does not note the resemblance to the disintegrationist theory.

105. The theory of "continuous copy" is that the authorial draft of a play would then frequently become the theatrical promptbook, which would then undergo various revisions and alterations over time, all without being retranscribed, thereby yielding a palimpsestic manuscript.

106. Wilson, *What*, 14–15.

107. Wilson, *What*, 16. On the New Bibliographic resistance to revision and adherence to ideals of "wholeness and integrity," see also Egan, *Struggle*, 114.

108. Stoll, "Anachronism," 557. Even the historicist scholars, he noted, "seem often to keep their antiquarian knowledge and their criticism in separate compartments" when they come to interpret the play. Thus Chambers follows the traditional Romantic reading that, in doubting the Ghost and sparing Claudius at prayer, Hamlet is merely "covering his weakness with unreal reasons," even though, with his wealth of historical knowledge, Chambers "surely knows that *per se* the Prince's doubt of the Ghost and his reason for sparing the King were, for a revenge-play, very real" (Stoll, *Hamlet*, 47n4, quoting Chambers's Warwick edition of *Hamlet*).

109. *Cone 1897*, 172.

110. Kittredge, ed., *Hamlet*, xv. Kittredge thought Q1 was "merely a bad copy of an abridged version of Shakespeare's HAMLET" (x), hardly a disintegrationist view.

111. Houston, "There's," 48.

112. Robertson, *Montaigne*, 177–78.

113. Schücking, *Meaning*, 69; see Stoll, *Hamlet*, 30, for similar comments about Shakespeare's transcendence of Kyd.

114. Lewis, *Genesis*, 26–28. So too Robertson saw "anomalies" in the religious outlook of the play: Hamlet "philosophises with Montaigne and yet delays his revenge in the spirit of the Christianized savage who fears to send the praying murderer to heaven" (*Montaigne*, 179).

115. Robertson, *Montaigne*, 177.

116. Lewis, *Genesis*, 101.

117. Robertson, *Shakespeare*, 1.190. The analysis here is very similar to that of Furness Jr., in his Variorum *Richard III*, and may have been influenced by it. For the rejection of religious motivation, see Robertson, *Problem*, 73n2.

118. Robertson, *Montaigne*, 192–93. Robertson compares Shakespeare's agnostic transformation of *Hamlet* to the Duke's consolation speech to Claudio in *Measure for Measure*, which "contains not a word of Christian doctrine . . . of sin and salvation, of forgiveness and absolution" (*Montaigne*, 191).

119. As early as 1845, Joseph Hunter had discussed the earlier placement of the soliloquy in Q1, and throughout the second half of the nineteenth century, writers occasionally debated Hunter's claim that "the play is greatly injured by the change" in positioning. But the text itself continued to receive little notice, and even Hunter never actually interpreted the Q1 version of the speech, simply dismissing it as corrupt (Hunter, *New*, 2.237; see 2.239).

120. *Herford 1899*, 8.197, 8.118, 8.121, 8.127.

121. Robertson, "Upshot," 213; Chambers, "Disintegration," 32.

122. Robertson, *Hamlet*, 33, 23, 33.

123. Chambers, "Disintegration," 32.

124. *Herford 1899*, 8.125.

125. On this genre of Shakespearean piety, see LaPorte, "Bard."

126. Dyer, "Proverb," 683.

127. Hood, *World*, 264–65; Lightfoot, *Cambridge*, 167–68 (from a sermon preached in 1870); Hoyt, "Prayer-Meeting," 155; Garvie, *Guide*, 128, and see the preface for the origin of the text in a class for lay preachers.

128. MacDonald, ed., *Hamlet*, 124–25, viii. See Sadler, "MacDonald."

129. Blackmore, *Riddles*, 235, 245, 248, 244.

130. See, for example, Bowden, *Religion*, 295.

131. Blackmore, *Riddles*, 242.

132. Others had made this argument before, of course, and it was made increasingly in the early twentieth century, most influentially by Chambers and by H. D. Gray, who identified the actor who played Marcellus as the culprit ("First," 178–79). But as I will show, Duthie's argument was more powerful in explaining Q1. For Chambers's role, see Erne, *First*, 6.

133. See *Hibbard*, 76.

134. Bowers, *Elizabethan*, vii, 91, 90, 278. Bowers cites Charlton Lewis and Stoll on occasion but makes no mention of Robertson, no doubt because he had by then been discredited by the extremes of his authorship attributions.

135. Bowers, *Elizabethan*, ix.

136. Duthie, *Bad*, x; for this argument about Kyd, see 43.

137. Duthie, *Bad*, 196, 195. The disintegrationists had noted the verbal resemblance of the Queen's lines to *The Spanish Tragedy*, but they had taken this correspondence to mean that Kyd had recycled lines from his own play while writing the *Ur-Hamlet*.

138. Duthie, *Bad*, 151, 155. Steven Urkowitz later used this scene to undermine the theory of memorial reconstruction, since it is close to the source material and it is difficult to imagine faulty memory bringing the play more in line with its prose sources ("Well-sayd," 48). The power of Duthie's theory, however, is that it can imagine actors doing precisely this: poorly reconstructing a play by drawing on a variety of possible texts, including earlier versions, sources, and other plays in repertory.

139. Duthie, *Bad*, 213. Duthie acknowledges that the care with which the new sequence was managed suggests a deliberate alteration, "postulating behind Q1 a stage-version in which this sequential change has been made of set purpose," but crucially this stage version postdates Q2 as well (218).

140. Duthie, *Bad*, 258. The echoes of both Q1 and Q2 in *Brudermord* are handily explained by supposing "that one or more of this group had taken part in a version which had been illicitly compiled for performance by a company in the English provinces (the Q1 text)," while others provided "what they could remember of the full Shakespearian text" (259).

141. *Collier 1843*, 7.189.

142. Duthie, *Bad*, 253.

143. Duthie, *Bad*, 203, 205.

144. Duthie, *Bad*, 191.

145. *Edwards*, 25.

146. *Jenkins*, 117. On this editorial banishment of Q1, see Marcus, *Unediting*, 134.

147. *Hibbard*, 378.

148. *Jenkins*, 120.

149. *Jenkins*, 489, 492.

150. *Edwards*, 147, 48.

151. Belsey, "Case," 128.

152. *Edwards*, 50.

153. *Jenkins*, 34, 114, 24. Laurie Maguire shows that overexplicitness is often imagined to be a characteristic flaw of reported texts (*Shakespearean*, 106, 202–3).

154. In the *thorns* that *prick* and *sting* Gertrude, many editors see an allusion to "the nightingale's wakefulness" (*Thompson-Taylor Q2*, 218), but the testimony of Q1 suggests a more straightforward echo of the phrase, "prick of conscience," already cliché by 1603. The reader of the Meisei folio, discussed later in this chapter, glossed these lines exactly as Q1 does: "exhortation to take Iust vengeance but to forbeare it against his mother and Leaue her to heauens punishment and her owne conscience" (sig. 2o1v). The copy has been digitized with full transcriptions of the marginalia, available at http://shakes.meisei-u.ac.jp/ (cited hereafter as "Meisei First Folio"). See also Yamada, *First*.

155. See the various examples cited in "conscience, *n.*," *Oxford English Dictionary*, online edition, II.7.a.

156. On Shakespeare's use of commonplaces in "To be, or not to be," see Stallybrass, "Against"; he does not, however, discuss this line. See also Honigmann, "To Be."

157. Sidney, *Arcadia*, sig. T1v; Hall, *Vnion*, sigs. 2K1v–2K2r; Cawdry, *Treasurie*, sig. O2v; Parr, *Plaine*, sigs. H3v, K8v; Powell, *Tom*, sig. E2v; Rogers, *Commentary*, sig. Z1v; Bolton, *Two*, sig. K3r; Bland, *Souldiers*, sigs. C3r–v.

158. Carpenter, *Geographie*, sig. 2S6v.

159. Carpenter, *Achitophel*, sig. D3r.

160. As Lander argues, Q1 seems far more committed than the received text to the Calvinist theory of "'experimental predestination,' the belief that experience and the searching of one's conscience could provide evidence of election" (*Inventing*, 130).

161. Shakespeare, *Richard the Third*, sigs. D1v (I have silently deleted the accidental duplication in "trust to / To himselfe"), M2v, L4v–M1r.

162. Bolton, *Two*, sig. K3r.

163. Lander argues that, by contrast with Q1, the familiar "To be, or not to be" is suffused with "a newly revived Pyrrhonism," a "classical skepticism" that "finds an especially condensed expression in the word *conscience*." Lander's reading depends on holding in tension both the religious and the speculative meaning of *conscience*, refusing to separate "morality from epistemology." In this way, he writes, Q2 undermines the kind of epistemological certainty about salvation, or "experimental predestination," that the Q1 version more fully endorses: "Q2 consistently raises questions that seem designed to undermine any such assurance" (*Inventing*, 129–30). The problem with this reading, within the genealogy of *Hamlet* after Q1, is that the speculative-philosophical understanding of Hamlet's *conscience* was almost entirely unknown before Bunbury's discovery.

164. My discussion of the Meisei First Folio is also informed by Hsy, "Analysis."

165. Meisei First Folio, sigs. 2o3r, 2p1v, 2o5v.

166. Meisei First Folio, sig. 2p1v. For examples of the generic descriptions of these characters, see sigs. 2N5v, 2N6v.

167. Meisei First Folio, sig. 2o5r.

168. The reader originally wrote *oughth* but then struck through the final *h*.

169. Belsey, "Case," 139–40.

170. Meisei First Folio, sigs. 2N6v, 2o3r.

CONCLUSION

1. *Thompson-Taylor Q1/F*, 2.
2. *Thompson-Taylor Q2*, 91.
3. *Thompson-Taylor Q2*, 93.

4. *Thompson-Taylor Q2*, 93.

5. *Thompson-Taylor Q2*, 92, 137.

6. Maguire was careful to point out that her critique did not require the conclusion that memorial reconstruction *never* occurred. She allowed that a "strong case" or a "case" could be made for the memorial reconstruction of several plays, including (in the latter group) Q1 *Hamlet* (*Shakespearean*, 324–25). On the critique of memorial reconstruction more generally, see Egan, *Struggle*, 100–128.

7. "Unediting" is the term promulgated by McLeod in "UN *Editing*."

8. Urkowitz, *Shakespeare's*, 149. Because this group continued to favor more traditional analytic bibliographic methods, Egan distinguishes them from the New Textualists, describing them as "new" New Bibliographers (*Struggle*, 42). See Taylor, "Renaissance."

9. Wells and Taylor, "Oxford," 16–17.

10. Similarly, Ioppolo accepts that "Duthie established in 1941 that Quarto 1 was a reported text of an acting version." She does believe that "several significant and stunning variants in characterization, plot, structure, and theme between the reported Quarto and Quarto 2/Folio" are due to revision (*Revising*, 134, 136). These are the traditional "problem" aspects of the play for the theory of stenographic or memorial piracy: Gertred's characterization, the scene between Horatio and Gertred, and so on. Ioppolo's argument thus represents a transition between the initial revisionist arguments that focused on *Lear* and Q2/F *Hamlet* and later, fuller critiques of the theory of bad quartos.

11. Holderness and Loughrey, "Text," 190, 183.

12. Vickers, "*Hamlet*."

13. Clayton, "Introduction," 28. On the theoretical difference of this strand from the Oxford Shakespeare revisionism, see Jowett, "Editing," 16.

14. Urkowitz, "Back," 288.

15. Werstine, "Textual," 23, 24. See also Mowat, "Forms."

16. In his recent, magisterial book on theatrical manuscripts, Werstine seems to modify this position somewhat; he now seeks a renewed "empirical editing of Shakespeare" that still attempts to discern the "printer's copy for the plays of Shakespeare and his contemporaries" but is "more constrained by empirical evidence" and more humble in its epistemological claims, "respecting the limits of the documentary evidence in hand" (Werstine, *Early*, 221, 10, 231).

17. Marcus, "Levelling," 168. Two of the most important critiques of the theory of bad quartos were by Werstine: "Narratives" and "Century." Another crucial essay was Cloud, "Marriage."

18. Urkowitz, "Well-sayd," 69.

19. Egan, *Struggle*, 127. See also Jowett, "Editing," 9.

20. Levenson, ed., *Romeo*, 127. Levenson notes that a set of "critical unknowns" in the bibliographic evidence "leads to an impasse which blocks the search for copy and a stemma" (117).

21. Hubbard, ed., *First*; Weiner, ed., *Hamlet*; Irace, ed., *First*. See also Serpieri, ed. and trans., *Primo*.

22. *Thompson-Taylor Q2*, 92, 11, 507.

23. *Thompson-Taylor Q2*, 477, 81, 481; *Taylor-Thompson Q1/F*, 9.

24. *Thompson-Taylor Q2*, 501.

25. *Thompson-Taylor Q2*, 507, 509.

26. *Thompson-Taylor Q2*, 505. Lander offers a similar critique when he writes that an overinvestment in the "integrity" of each of the three texts can "merely celebrate difference by venerating the material book in all its splendid idiosyncrasy," and yet "the effort to see through these versions in order to discern the ideal text (or texts) intended by the author often leads to a neglect of the specificities of the various printings" (*Inventing*, 123). See also Levenson, ed., *Romeo*, 104; and Dawson, "Correct," 31–47, 40–41.

27. Levenson, ed., *Romeo*, 124. As Taylor comments, editing is based on intertextual proximity:

"Editing can be defined as the effort to establish a proximate text . . . proximate to something we value," whether "the individualized authorial text," for instance, or "the socialized collaborative text" ("Renaissance," 129). See also Edward Pechter's argument that "since [in New Textualist theory] there is no way to sort out the textual markings deposited by the many diverse agents who may have 'penetrated and altered' them, this respect [for the diversity of textual documents] leaves us with nothing to say" (Pechter, *Shakespeare*, 135).

28. Jameson, *Postmodernism*, 8–9, 25. See also, from a specifically editorial perspective, Greetham, "Editorial."

29. Cloud, "Marriage," 422. He writes that the "infinitive text is of particular interest to historically-minded scholars," which is true in the sense that the early printings are historical documents that provide evidence we cannot access in modern editions; but it is false in another important sense of "history," the historical relationships among these variant texts.

30. See the various comments in Loughrey, "Q1," 125; and *Thompson-Taylor Q1/F*, 22–37. Marcus, *Unediting*, 152–55, offers a theoretical analysis of comments like these that to some extent reduplicates them.

31. Poel quoted in Rosenberg, "First," 242.

32. For a critique of this implied argument, see Dillon, "Is," 82; and Worthen, *Shakespeare*, 5, 155–91. In fact, as Dillon also points out (83), modern productions of Q1 often "cheat" in one way or another, either by occasionally importing lines from the received text, by emending the text, or by ingenious staging choices that can explain away what would otherwise appear as problems in the Q1 text. Poel emended the text for his 1881 production.

33. *Jenkins*, 36; *Hibbard*, 89; *Edwards*, 24; all quoted and discussed in Dillon, "Is," 80–81.

34. Based on an examination of actors' cues, Menzer argues that Q1 may in fact be "not the most theatrical but the most *literary* of the three earliest printed texts of *Hamlet* in that it was designed for a reader, not for any practical theatrical use" (*Hamlets*, 62–63). Peter Stallybrass and I have made a similar argument based on the appearance of printed commonplace markers in Q1 (Lesser and Stallybrass, "First"). Another important exception is Marino's chapter on *Hamlet*, which sees more continuity than disjuncture between the pre-Shakespearean *Hamlet*, Q1, Q2, and F (*Owning*). From a very different perspective, Erne argues that Q1, and the first quartos of *Henry V* and *Romeo and Juliet*, "reflect, or at least dimly reflect, what Shakespeare and his fellows performed in London and elsewhere" (*Shakespeare*, 219), but he does so with a fully revised theory of textual transmission, thereby avoiding the contradiction Dillon points out.

35. I am here following Dimock, who quotes Bloom in this context; her "theory of resonance inverts the Bloomian hypothesis, by linking literary endurance not to the persistent integrity of the text but to its persistent unraveling, not to the text's timeless strength but to something like its *timeful* unwieldiness" (Dimock, "Theory," 1061–62).

36. As Werstine rightly notes: "Only by presenting evidence from these documents according to the established practice of New Bibliography from the time of Pollard is it possible to demonstrate that New Bibliography's most enduring editorial categories are invalid." He therefore describes his study as "an extended essay in New Bibliography" despite its thorough critique of some of the key conclusions of that movement (*Early*, 4, 1).

37. See Stern, *Documents*; Stern and Palfrey, *Shakespeare*; Menzer, *Hamlets*; and Marino, *Owning*.

38. Stern rejects the memorial reconstruction hypothesis because Marcellus "misremembers his own cues" ("Sermons," 2) and because other aspects of the text do not reflect early modern performance practices. See also Davidson, *Shakespeare*, which offers a stenographic theory that differs in important respect from Stern's new hypothesis.

39. Werstine, *Early*.

BIBLIOGRAPHY

FREQUENTLY CITED SHAKESPEARE EDITIONS

These editions, cited in notes by the following abbreviations, are listed chronologically. For multi-volume works, I use the format "volume.page" or, if a volume contains multiple parts, "volume.part.page." If the volumes have multiple imprint dates, the abbreviation takes the date of the volume containing *Hamlet*. If the edition appears in Murphy, *Shakespeare in Print*, I provide the reference number.

Pope 1723	Pope, Alexander, ed. *The Works of Shakespeare*. 6 vols. London: J. Tonson, 1723–25. Murphy §194.
Theobald 1733	Theobald, Lewis, ed. *The Works of Shakespeare*. 7 vols. London: A. Bettesworth and C. Hitch, J. Tonson, F. Clay, W. Feales, and R. Wellington, 1733. Murphy §206.
Warburton 1747	Warburton, William, ed. *The Works of Shakespear*. 8 vols. London: J. and P. Knapton et al., 1747. Murphy §231.
Johnson 1765	Johnson, Samuel, ed. *The Plays of William Shakespeare*. 8 vols. London: J. and R. Tonson et al., 1765. Murphy §283.
Capell 1767	Capell, Edward, ed. *Mr William Shakespeare his comedies, histories, and tragedies*. 10 vols. London: J. and R. Tonson, 1767–68. Murphy §304.
Capell, *Notes*	Capell, Edward. *Notes and Various Readings of Shakespeare*. 2 vols. London: For the author, 1779.
Steevens 1773	Steevens, George, with Samuel Johnson, eds. *The Plays of William Shakespeare*. 10 vols. London: C. Bathurst et al., 1773. Murphy §332.
Steevens 1778	Steevens, George, with Samuel Johnson and Isaac Reed, eds. *The Plays of William Shakspeare*. 10 vols. and 2 supplementary vols. London: C. Bathurst et al., 1778–80. Murphy §343–44.
Malone 1790	Malone, Edmond, ed. *The Plays and Poems of William Shakspeare*. 10 vols. London: J. Rivington and Sons et al., 1790. Murphy §357.
Steevens 1793	Steevens, George, with Samuel Johnson and Isaac Reed, eds. *The Plays of William Shakspeare*. 15 vols. London: T. Longman et al., 1793. Murphy §375.
Caldecott 1819	Caldecott, Thomas, ed. *Hamlet and As You Like It. A Specimen of an Edition of Shakespeare*. London: John Murray, 1819. Murphy §456. Irregularly paginated: I cite the "text of *Hamlet*" or "notes to *Hamlet*."
Boswell 1821	Boswell, James, ed. *The Plays and Poems of William Shakspeare*. 21 vols. London: F. C. and J. Rivington et al., 1821. Murphy §470.

Singer 1826	Singer, Samuel Weller, ed. *The Dramatic Works of William Shakspeare.* 10 vols. Chiswick: Charles Whittingham, 1826. Murphy §478.
Knight 1839	Knight, Charles, ed. *The Pictorial Edition of the Works of Shakspere.* 8 vols. London: Charles Knight, 1838–43. Murphy §483. Volumes irregularly numbered: I cite each genre (*Comedies, Histories, Tragedies*) according to its two volumes, plus *Doubtful* plays and *Biography*.
Collier 1843	Collier, John Payne, ed. *The Works of William Shakespeare.* 8 vols. London: Whittaker, 1842–44. Murphy §484.
Hudson 1856	Hudson, Henry Norman, ed. *The Works of William Shakespeare.* 11 vols. Boston: James Munroe, 1851–56. Murphy §493.
Dyce 1857	Dyce, Alexander, ed. *The Works of William Shakespeare.* 6 vols. London: Edward Moxon, 1857. Murphy §501.
White 1862	White, Richard Grant, ed. *The Works of William Shakespeare.* 12 vols. Boston: Little, Brown, 1857–66. Murphy §502.
Cambridge 1866	Clark, William George, John Glover, and William Aldis Wright, eds. *The Works of William Shakespeare.* Cambridge Shakespeare. 9 vols. Cambridge and London: Macmillan, 1863–66. Murphy §587.
Knight 1867	Knight, Charles, ed. *The Pictorial Edition of the Works of Shakespeare.* 2nd ed. 8 vols. London: Routledge, 1867. Murphy §598. Volumes cited as with *Knight 1839*.
Clarendon 1872	Clark, William George, and William Aldis Wright, eds. *Hamlet, Prince of Denmark.* Clarendon Shakespeare—Select Plays. Oxford: Clarendon, 1872. Murphy §603.
Furness 1877	Furness, Horace H., ed. *Hamlet.* Variorum Shakespeare. 2 vols. Philadelphia: J. B. Lippincott, 1877. Murphy §623.
Cone 1897	Cone, Helen Gray, ed. *Hamlet . . . from the Riverside Edition Edited by Richard Grant White.* Boston: Houghton, Mifflin, 1897.
Herford 1899	Herford, C. H., ed. *The Works of Shakespeare.* Eversley Edition. 10 vols. London: Macmillan, 1899. Murphy §872.
Jenkins	Jenkins, Harold, ed. *Hamlet.* Arden Shakespeare. London: Methuen, 1982. Murphy §1339.
Edwards	Edwards, Philip, ed. *Hamlet.* New Cambridge Shakespeare. Cambridge: Cambridge University Press, 1985. Murphy §1568.
Hibbard	Hibbard, G. R., ed. *Hamlet.* Oxford Shakespeare. Oxford: Clarendon, 1987. Murphy §1533.
Norton	Greenblatt, Stephen, Walter Cohen, Jean E. Howard, and Katharine Eisaman Maus, eds. *The Norton Shakespeare: Based on the Oxford Edition.* New York: Norton, 1997. Murphy §1706.
Bevington	Bevington, David, ed. *The Complete Works of Shakespeare.* 5th ed. New York: Pearson Longman, 2004.
Thompson-Taylor Q2	Thompson, Ann, and Neil Taylor, eds. *Hamlet.* Arden Shakespeare. London: Arden Shakespeare, 2006.
Thompson-Taylor Q1/F	Thompson, Ann, and Neil Taylor, eds. *Hamlet: The Texts of 1603 and 1623.* Arden Shakespeare. London: Arden Shakespeare, 2006.

OTHER WORKS

Abercrombie, Lascelles. "A Plea for the Liberty of Interpreting." In Mackail, ed., *Aspects.* 227–54.
Addison, Joseph, and Richard Steele. *Spectator.* 4th ed. 8 vols. London: J. Tonson, 1718.
Adelman, Janet. *Suffocating Mothers: Fantasies of Maternal Origin in Shakespeare's Plays, Hamlet to The Tempest.* New York: Routledge, 1992.
Aebischer, Pascale. *Shakespeare's Violated Bodies: Stage and Screen Performance.* Cambridge: Cambridge University Press, 2004.
Alexander, Nigel, ed. *Hamlet.* Macmillan Shakespeare. London: Macmillan, 1973.
Andrews, Michael Cameron. "His Mother's Closet: A Note on *Hamlet.*" *Modern Philology* 80 (1982): 164–66.
Arac, Jonathan. "The Impact of Shakespeare." In *The Cambridge History of Literary Criticism, Volume 5: Romanticism.* Ed. Marshall Brown. Cambridge: Cambridge University Press, 2000. 272–95.
Aravamudan, Srinivas. "The Return of Anachronism." *Modern Language Quarterly* 62 (2001): 331–53.
Arber, Edward. *A Transcript of the Registers of the Company of Stationers of London, 1554–1640 A.D.* 5 vols. London: Privately printed, 1875–77.
Archer, William. *Henry Irving, Actor and Manager: A Critical Study.* London: Field and Tuer, 1883.
Armin, Robert. *The History of the two Maids of More-clacke.* London: Thomas Archer, 1609.
"At the Play. In London." *Theatre* (1 February 1879): 48–49.
Babcock, R. W. "Modern Sceptical Criticism of Shakespeare: Elmer Edgar Stoll." *Sewanee Review* 35.1 (1927): 15–31.
Bailey, Helen Phelps. *Hamlet in France: From Voltaire to Laforgue.* Geneva: Librairie-Droz, 1964.
Bann, Jennifer. "Ghostly Hands and Ghostly Agency: The Changing Figure of the Nineteenth-Century Specter." *Victorian Studies* 51 (2009): 664–85.
Barkan, Leonard. *Unearthing the Past: Archaeology and Aesthetics in the Making of Renaissance Culture.* New Haven: Yale University Press, 1999.
Barnet, Sylvan, ed. *Hamlet.* 2nd ed. Signet Classic Shakespeare. New York: Penguin, 1998.
Bate, Jonathan. *The Genius of Shakespeare.* London: Picador, 1997.
Bates, William. "'Hamlet' Bibliography." *Notes and Queries*, 2nd ser. 9 (19 May 1860): 378–80.
Battestin, Martin C. "A Rationale of Literary Annotation: The Example of Fielding's Novels." *Studies in Bibliography* 34 (1981): 1–22.
Belleforest, François de. *Le cinquiesme tome des histoires tragiques.* Lyon: Les heritiers de Benoist Rigaud, 1551.
Belsey, Catherine. "The Case of Hamlet's Conscience." *Studies in Philology* 76 (1979): 127–48.
Benson, Larry D. "The 'Queynte' Punnings of Chaucer's Critics." *Studies in the Age of Chaucer* 1 (1985): 23–47.
Bevington, David, ed. *Hamlet.* New York: Bantam, 1987.
Berman, Russell A. "Politics: Divide and Rule." *Modern Language Quarterly* 62 (2001): 317–30.
Billings, Timothy. "Squashing the 'shard-borne Beetle' Crux: A Hard Case with a Few Pat Readings." *Shakespeare Quarterly* 56 (2005): 434–47.
Birth, Dinah, and Katy Hooper, eds. *The Oxford Concise Companion to English Literature.* 4th ed. Oxford: Oxford University Press, 2012.
Black, Ebenezer C., Henry Norman Hudson, and Andrew Jackson George, eds. *Hamlet.* New Hudson Shakespeare. Boston: Ginn, 1909.
Blackmore, Simon Augustine. *The Riddles of Hamlet and the Newest Answers.* Boston: Stratford, 1917.
Bland, Francis. *The Souldiers March to Salvation.* York: s.n., 1647.

Bly, Mary. *Queer Virgins and Virgin Queans on the Early Modern Stage*. Oxford: Oxford University Press, 2000.
Boaden, James. *Memoirs of Mrs. Siddons, Interspersed with Anecdotes of Authors and Actors*. 2 vols. London: Henry Colburn, 1827.
———. *Memoirs of the Life of John Philip Kemble*. 2 vols. London: Longman, Hurst, Rees, Orme, Brown and Green, 1825.
Boas, Frederick S. *Shakspere and his Predecessors*. New York: Scribner's, 1896.
———, ed. *The Works of Thomas Kyd*. Oxford: Clarendon, 1901.
Bolton, Robert. *Two Sermons Preached at Northampton*. London: George Miller, 1635.
Bornstein, George, and Ralph G. Williams, ed. *Palimpsest: Editorial Theory in the Humanities*. Ann Arbor: University of Michigan Press, 1993.
Bourne, Claire M. L. "A Play and No Play: Printing the Performance in Early Modern England." Ph.D. diss. University of Pennsylvania, 2013.
Bourus, Terri. "Shakespeare and the London Publishing Environment: The Publisher and Printers of Q1 and Q2 *Hamlet*." *AEB: Analytical and Enumerative Bibliography* 12 (2001): 206–26.
Bowden, Henry Sebastian. *The Religion of Shakespeare, Chiefly from the Writings of the Late Mr. Richard Simpson, M.A.* London: Burns and Oates, 1899.
Bowdler, Thomas, and Henrietta Maria Bowdler, eds. *The Family Shakespeare*. 6 vols. London: Longman, Brown, Green, Longmans, and Roberts, 1860–65.
Bowers, Fredson Thayer. *Elizabethan Revenge Tragedy, 1587–1642*. Rev. ed. Gloucester, MA: Peter Smith, 1959.
Braden, Gordon, ed. *Sixteenth-Century Poetry: The Annotated Anthology*. Oxford: Blackwell, 2005.
Bradley, A. C. *Shakespearean Tragedy: Lectures on Hamlet, Othello, King Lear, Macbeth*. London: Macmillan, 1904.
Braunmuller, Albert R. "The 'Hot Low Countries' in Chapman's *Hero and Leander*." *English Language Notes* 8.2 (1970): 97–99.
———, ed. *Hamlet*. Pelican Shakespeare. New York: Penguin, 2001.
Brayman Hackel, Heidi. *Reading Material in Early Modern England: Print, Gender, and Literacy*. Cambridge: Cambridge University Press, 2005.
Brereton, Austin. *Some Famous Hamlets, from Burbage to Fechter*. London: David Bogue, 1884.
Brewer, Anthony. *The Countrie Girle*. London: A. R., 1647.
Bristol, Michael D. *Big-time Shakespeare*. London: Routledge, 1996.
Brooke, Nicholas. *Shakespeare's Early Tragedies*. London: Methuen, 1968.
Brooks, Peter. *The Melodramatic Imagination: Balzac, Henry James, Melodrama, and the Mode of Excess*. New Haven: Yale University Press, 1976.
Browne, Thomas. *Hydriotaphia, Urne-Buriall*. London: Henry Brome, 1658.
———. *Pseudodoxia Epidemica*. London: Edward Dod, 1646.
Bruster, Douglas. "Shakespearean Spellings and Handwriting in the Additional Passages Printed in the 1602 *Spanish Tragedy*." *Notes and Queries* n.s. 60 (2013): 420–24.
———. *To Be or Not to Be*. London: Continuum, 2007.
Bucknill, John Charles. *The Mad Folk of Shakespeare: Psychological Essays*. London: Macmillan, 1967.
Buhler, Stephen M. *Shakespeare in the Cinema: Ocular Proof*. Albany: SUNY Press, 2001.
Bunbury, Henry. *The Correspondence of Sir Thomas Hanmer, Bart, Speaker of the House of Commons, with a Memoir of his Life*. London: Edward Moxon, 1838.
Caldecott, Thomas. *Hamlet and As You Like It. A Specimen of an Edition of Shakespeare*. London: For the editor, 1832.

Carpenter, Nathanael. *Achitophel, or, The Picture of a Wicked Politician.* London: Michael Sparke, 1629.
———. *Geographie Delineated.* London: Henry Cripps, to be sold by Henry Curteyne, 1635.
Cawdry, Robert. *A Treasurie or Store-House of Similies.* London: Thomas Creede, 1600.
Chakrabarty, Dipesh. *Provincializing Europe: Postcolonial Thought and Historical Difference.* Princeton: Princeton University Press, 2000.
Chambers, E. K. "The Disintegration of Shakespeare." In Mackail, ed., *Aspects.* 23–48.
———. *William Shakespeare: A Study of Facts and Problems.* 2 vols. Oxford: Clarendon, 1930.
———, ed. *Hamlet.* Warwick Shakespeare. London and Glasgow: Blackie and Son, 1893.
Charney, Maurice. "*Hamlet* without Words." *ELH* 32 (1965): 457–77.
Clayton, Thomas. "Introduction: *Hamlet*'s Ghost." In Clayton, ed., *Hamlet.* 21–52.
———, ed. *The* Hamlet *First Published (Q1, 1603): Origins, Form, Intertextualities.* Newark: University of Delaware Press, 1992.
Cloud, Random [Randall McLeod, pseud.]. "The Marriage of Good and Bad Quartos." *Shakespeare Quarterly* 33 (1982): 421–31.
Cohn, Albert. *Shakespeare in Germany in the Sixteenth and Seventeenth Centuries.* London: Asher, 1865.
Coleridge, Samuel Taylor. *The Friend; a Series of Essays.* London: Gale and Curtis, 1812.
———. *The Literary Remains of Samuel Taylor Coleridge.* Ed. H. N. Coleridge. 4 vols. London: William Pickering, 1836.
———. *Notes and Lectures upon Shakespeare and Some of the Old Poets and Dramatists with Other Literary Remains of S. T. Coleridge.* Ed. H. N. Coleridge. 2 vols. London: William Pickering, 1849.
———. *Seven Lectures on Shakespeare and Milton . . . [with] A List of All the Emendations in Mr. Collier's Folio, 1632; and an Introductory Preface by J. Payne Collier, Esq.* London: Chapman and Hall, 1856.
Collier, John Payne. "The Edition of 'Hamlet' in 1603." *Athenaeum* 1510 (4 October 1856): 1220–21.
———. *The History of English Dramatic Poetry to the Time of Shakespeare: and Annals of the Stage to the Restoration.* 3 vols. London: John Murray, 1831.
———. *Memoirs of the Principal Actors in the Plays of Shakespeare.* London: Shakespeare Society, 1846.
———. *New Facts Regarding the Life of Shakespeare.* London: Thomas Rodd, 1835.
———. *Notes and Emendations to the Text of Shakespeare's Plays, from Early Manuscript Corrections in a Copy of the Folio, 1632.* London: Whittaker, 1853.
———. *Reasons for a New Edition of Shakespeare's Works.* London: Whittaker, 1841.
———, ed. *Fools and Jesters; with a Reprint of Robert Armin's Nest of Ninnies. 1608. With an Introduction and Notes.* London: Shakespeare Society, 1842.
Cook, Dutton. *Nights at the Play: A View of the English Stage.* London: Chatto and Windus, 1883.
Corbin, John. *The Elizabethan Hamlet: A Study of the Sources, and of Shakspere's Environment, to show that the Mad Scenes had a Comic Aspect now Ignored.* New York: Scribner's, 1895.
Cordner, Michael. "Actors, Editors, and the Annotation of Shakespearian Playscripts." *Shakespeare Survey* 55 (2002): 181–98.
"A Correspondent." *Once a Week* (5 March 1870): 108–9.
Corson, Hiram. "Hamlet." *Shakespeariana* 32 (August 1886): 337–52.
Crawford, Alexander Wellington. *Hamlet, an Ideal Prince.* Boston: Richard G. Badger, 1916.
Dane, Joseph. "'Queynte': Some Rime and Some Reason on a Chaucer[ian] Pun." *Journal of English and Germanic Philology* 95 (1996): 497–514.
Davidson, Adele. *Shakespeare in Shorthand: The Textual Mystery of King Lear.* Newark: University of Delaware Press, 2009.
Davies, Godfrey. "The Huntington Library." *Shakespeare Survey* 6 (1953): 53–63.

Dawson, Anthony B. "Correct Impressions: Editing and Evidence in the Wake of Post-Modernism." In Thompson and McMullan, eds., *In Arden.* 31–47.
———, ed. *Hamlet.* Shakespeare in Performance. Manchester: Manchester University Press, 1995.
"Découverte d'une ancienne edition de douze pièces de Shakespeare. (Literary Gazette No. 418, p. 58)." *Bibliothèque Universelle des Sciences, Belles-Lettres, et Arts* 29 (1825): 80–84.
de Grazia, Margreta. "Anachronism." In *Cultural Reformations: Medieval and Renaissance in Literary History.* Ed. Brian Cummings and James Simpson. Oxford: Oxford University Press, 2010. 13–32.
———. "The Essential Shakespeare and the Material Book." *Textual Practice* 2 (1988): 69–86.
———. "*Hamlet* Before Its Time." *Modern Language Quarterly* 62 (2001): 355–75.
———. Hamlet *without Hamlet.* Cambridge: Cambridge University Press, 2007.
———. *Shakespeare Verbatim: The Reproduction of Authenticity and the 1790 Apparatus.* Oxford: Clarendon, 1991.
de Grazia, Margreta, and Peter Stallybrass. "The Materiality of the Shakespearean Text." *Shakespeare Quarterly* 44 (1993): 255–83.
Dekker, Thomas. *Satiro-mastix.* London: Edward White, 1602.
Delany, Sheila. "Anatomy of the Resisting Reader: Some Implications of Resistance to Sexual Wordplay in Medieval Literature." *Exemplaria* 4 (1992): 7–34.
Derrida, Jacques. *Specters of Marx: The State of the Debt, the Work of Mourning, and the New International.* Trans. Peggy Kamuf. New York: Routledge, 1994.
Desclozeaux, Ernest. "Comparaison entre l'édition actuelle d'Hamlet et celle de 1603." *Le Globe* 4.12 (9 September 1826): 57–59.
Dessen, Alan C. *Recovering Shakespeare's Theatrical Vocabulary.* Cambridge: Cambridge University Press, 1995.
Dessen, Alan C., and Leslie Thomson. *A Dictionary of Stage Directions in English Drama, 1580–1642.* Cambridge: Cambridge University Press, 1999.
"Diary of an M.P." *The Inspector, Literary Magazine and Review* (January 1827): 318–28.
Dibdin, Thomas Frognall. *Bibliophobia: Remarks on the Present Languid and Depressed State of Literature and the Book Trade.* London: Henry Bohn, 1832.
———. *The Library Companion; Or, The Young Man's Guide, and the Old Man's Comfort, in the Choice of a Library.* 2 vols. London: Harding, Triphook, Lepard, and J. Major, 1825.
Dillon, Janette. "Is There a Performance in This Text?" *Shakespeare Quarterly* 45 (1994): 74–86.
Dimock, Wai Chee. "A Theory of Resonance." *PMLA* 112 (1997): 1060–71.
Dinshaw, Carolyn. *How Soon Is Now? Medieval Texts, Amateur Readers, and the Queerness of Time.* Durham: Duke University Press, 2012.
———. "Temporalities." In *Middle English.* Ed. Paul Strohm. Oxford: Oxford University Press, 2007. 107–23.
DiPietro, Cary. "A. C. Bradley (26 March 1851–2 September 1935)." In *Great Shakespeareans: Bradley, Greg, Folger.* Ed. Cary DiPietro. London: Continuum, 2011. 8–67.
———. "The Shakespeare Edition in Industrial Capitalism." *Shakespeare Survey* 59 (2006): 147–56.
Dolven, Jeffrey, ed. *Hamlet.* New York: Barnes and Noble, 2007.
Donne, John. *Poems, By J. D. with Elegies on the Authors Death.* London: John Marriot, 1633.
Doughtie, Edward. "The Earl of Essex and Occasions for Contemplative Verse." *English Literary Renaissance* 9 (1979): 355–63.
Downes, John. *Roscius Anglicanus, or an Historical Review of the Stage.* London: Henry Playford, 1708.
"Dramatic Discovery." *The Drama; or Theatrical Pocket Magazine* 7.6 (March 1825): 276.

Duthie, George Ian. *The "Bad" Quarto of* Hamlet: *A Critical Study*. Cambridge: Cambridge University Press, 1941.
Dyce, Alexander. ed. *The Works of William Shakespeare*. 2nd ed. 9 vols. London: Chapman and Hall, 1864–67.
Dyer, T. F. Thiselton. "Proverb Lore." *The Sunday at Home: A Family Magazine for Sabbath Reading* 1487 (28 October 1882): 683–85.
Egan, Gabriel. *The Struggle for Shakespeare's Text: Twentieth-Century Editorial Theory and Practice*. Cambridge: Cambridge University Press, 2010.
Eggert, Katherine. *Showing Like a Queen: Female Authority and Literary Experiment in Spenser, Shakespeare, and Milton*. Philadelphia: University of Pennsylvania Press, 2000.
Eliot, George. *Middlemarch: A Study of Provincial Life*. Edinburgh and London: William Blackwood and Sons, 1874.
Eliot, T. S. "Hamlet and His Problems." *Athenaeum* 4665 (26 September 1919): 940–41.
[Elwin, Whitwell]. "Recent Editions of Shakespeare." *Quarterly Review* 79 (1846–47): 310–35.
Elze, Karl. *Shakespeare's Hamlet*. Leipzig: Gustav Mayer, 1857.
English, James F. *Comic Transactions: Literature, Humor, and the Politics of Community in Twentieth-Century Britain*. Ithaca: Cornell University Press, 1994.
Erne, Lukas. *Beyond "The Spanish Tragedy": A Study of the Works of Thomas Kyd*. Manchester: Manchester University Press, 2001.
———. *Shakespeare as Literary Dramatist*. Cambridge: Cambridge University Press, 2003.
———, ed. *The First Quarto of Romeo and Juliet*. New Cambridge Shakespeare: The Early Quartos. Cambridge: Cambridge University Press, 2007.
Esty, Jed. *Unseasonable Youth: Modernism, Colonialism, and the Fiction of Development*. Oxford: Oxford University Press, 2012.
Evans, G. Blakemore, ed. Digital edition of the Smock Alley Promptbook of *Hamlet*. http://etext.lib.virginia.edu/bsuva/promptbook/ShaHamP.html. Accessed 26 October 2012.
Falk, Robert P. "Critical Tendencies in Richard Grant White's Shakespeare Commentary." *American Literature* 20 (1948): 144–54.
Farley-Hills, David, ed. *Critical Responses to Hamlet, 1600–1900*. 4 vols. New York: AMS Press, 1996–2006.
Farmer, Alan B. "The Myth of Shakespeare's Indifference to Print, or Shakespeare the Obsessive Reviser." Paper presented to the European Shakespeare Research Association biennial conference. Montpellier, France. 27 June 2013.
Farmer, Alan B., and Zachary Lesser. "Canons and Classics: Publishing Drama in Caroline England." In *Localizing Caroline Drama: Politics and Economics of the Early Modern English Stage, 1625–1642*. Ed. Alan B. Farmer and Adam Zucker. New York: Palgrave, 2006. 17–41.
Farmer, Alan B., and Zachary Lesser. "The Popularity of Playbooks Revisited." *Shakespeare Quarterly* 56 (2005): 1–32.
Farmer, Richard. *An Essay on the Learning of Shakespeare*. 2nd edn. Cambridge: W. Thurlbourn and J. Woodyer, to be sold by J. Beecroft, J. Dodsley, and T. Cadell, 1767.
Fleay, F. G. *A Chronicle History of the Life and Work of William Shakespeare: Player, Poet, and Playmaker*. London: John C. Nimmo, 1886.
———. "Neglected Facts on Hamlet." *Englische Studien*. Heilbronn: Gebr. Henninger, 1883. 87–93.
Fleming, John V. "Quaint Light in Troy." In *Classical Imitation and Interpretation in Chaucer's Troilus*. Lincoln: University of Nebraska Press, 1990. 1–44.

Fletcher, John. *The Scornful Ladie*. London: Miles Partrich, 1616.
Florio, John. *A Worlde of Wordes*. London: Edward Blount, 1598.
Foakes, R. A., ed. *Coleridge's Criticism of Shakespeare: A Selection*. London: Athlone Press, 1989.
———. *Collier on Coleridge: The Text of the Lectures, 1811–12*. Charlottesville: Folger Shakespeare Library and the University Press of Virginia, 1971.
———. *Henslowe's Diary*. 2nd ed. Cambridge: Cambridge University Press, 2002.
Foucault, Michel. *A History of Sexuality, Volume 1: An Introduction*. Trans. Robert Hurley. New York: Vintage, 1990.
———. "Nietzsche, Genealogy, History." In *Language, Counter-Memory, Practice: Selected Essays and Interviews*. Ed. Donald F. Bouchard. Trans. Donald F. Bouchard and Sherry Simon. Ithaca: Cornell University Press, 1977. 139–64.
———. "What Is an Author?" In *Textual Strategies: Perspectives in Post-Structuralist Criticism*. Ed. Josué V. Harari. Ithaca: Cornell University Press, 1979. 141–60.
Foxe, John. *Actes and Monuments of matters most speciall and memorable, happenyng in the Church*. 2 vols. London: John Day, 1583.
Freccero, Carla. *Queer/Early/Modern*. Durham: Duke University Press, 2006.
Freedon, Michael. "Robertson, John Mackinnon (1856–1933)." *Oxford Dictionary of National Biography*. Oxford: Oxford University Press, 2004. Online edition, May 2006. http://www.oxforddnb.com/view/article/35783. Accessed 18 December 2012.
Freeman, Arthur, and Janet Ing Freeman. "Did Halliwell Steal and Mutilate the First Quarto of *Hamlet*?" *Library* 2 (2001): 349–63.
Freeman, Arthur, and Janet Ing Freeman. *John Payne Collier: Scholarship and Forgery in the Nineteenth Century*. New Haven: Yale University Press, 2004.
Freeman, Elizabeth. "Introduction." *GLQ: A Journal of Lesbian and Gay Studies* 13 (2007): 159–76.
———. "Time Binds, or, Erotohistoriography." *Social Text* 23.3–4 (2005): 57–68.
Freud, Sigmund. *The Complete Letters of Sigmund Freud to Wilhelm Fliess, 1887–1904*. Ed. and trans. J. Moussaieff Masson. Cambridge, MA: Harvard University Press, 1985.
———. "The Uncanny." In *The Standard Edition of the Complete Psychological Works of Sigmund Freud, Volume XVII (1917–1919): An Infantile Neurosis and Other Works*. Ed. and trans. James Strachey et al. London: Hogarth Press and the Institute of Psycho-Analysis, 1955. 218–52.
Frye, Roland Mushat. *Shakespeare and Christian Doctrine*. Princeton: Princeton University Press, 1963.
Furness, Horace Howard, Jr., ed. *The Tragedy of Richard the Third*. Variorum Shakespeare. Philadelphia: J. B. Lippincott, 1908.
Furnivall, F. J. Introduction to *The Leopold Shakespeare. The Poet's Works in Chronological Order, from the text of Professor Delius*. London: Cassell, Petter, Galpin, [1877]. vii–cxxxvi.
———. "Is the Character of Hamlet Shakspere's Creation or Not?" *Academy* 431 (7 August 1880): 101.
Galey, Alan. *The Shakespearean Archive: Experiments in New Media from the Renaissance to Postmodernity*. Cambridge: Cambridge University Press, 2014.
Garber, Marjorie. *Shakespeare's Ghost Writers: Literature as Uncanny Causality, With a New Preface by the Author*. Rev. ed. New York: Routledge, 2010.
Garvie, Alfred E. *A Guide to Preachers*. New York: George H. Doran, 1906.
Gay, Peter. *Freud: A Life for Our Time*. 1988; New York: Norton, 1998.
Gerstell, Emily. "Trafficking Women: Gender, Economics and the Politics of Marriage in Early Modern English Drama." Ph.D. diss. University of Pennsylvania, 2014.
Gervinus, Georg Gottfried. *Shakespeare Commentaries*. Trans. F. E. Burnett. 2 vols. London: Smith, Elder, 1863.

Gielgud, John. "The Hamlet Tradition: Notes on Costume, Scenery and Stage Business." In *John Gielgud's* Hamlet: *A Record of Performance*. Ed. Rosamond Gilder. London: Methuen, 1937. 29–81.
Glick, Claris. "*Hamlet* in the English Theater—Acting Texts from Betterton (1676) to Olivier (1963)." *Shakespeare Quarterly* 20 (1969): 17–35.
Goddard, William. *A Neaste of Waspes*. Dort: s.n., 1615.
Goethe, J. W. von. "The First Edition of *Hamlet*." Trans. Randolph S. Bourne. In *Goethe's Literary Essays*. Ed. J. E. Spingarn. New York: Harcourt, Brace, 1921. 190–94.
———. *Wilhelm Meister's Apprenticeship*. Trans. Thomas Carlyle. 3 vols. Edinburgh: Oliver and Boyd; London: G. and W. B. Whittaker, 1824.
"Goethe's Posthumous Works." *Foreign Quarterly Review* 12.23 (1833): 81–109.
Goldsmith, Oliver. "Metaphors." In *Essays and Criticisms*. 3 vols. London: J. Johnson, 1798. 2.197–223.
"Goldsmith *versus* Shakspeare." *The Crypt, or, Receptacle for Things Past: An Antiquarian, Literary, and Miscellaneous Journal* 2 (1828): 34–39.
Grady, Hugh. "*Hamlet* and the Present: Notes on the Moving Aesthetic 'Now'." In Grady and Hawkes, eds., *Presentist*. 141–63.
———. *The Modernist Shakespeare: Critical Texts in a Material World*. Oxford: Clarendon, 1991.
Grady, Hugh, and Terence Hawkes. "Introduction: Presenting Presentism." In Grady and Hawkes, eds., *Presentist*. 1–5.
Grady, Hugh, and Terence Hawkes, eds. *Presentist Shakespeares*. London: Routledge, 2007.
Graves, Henry Mercer. *An Essay on the Genius of Shakespeare*. London: James Bigg, 1826.
Gray, H. D. "The First Quarto 'Hamlet'." *Modern Language Review* 10 (1915): 171–80.
Gray, Valerie. *Charles Knight: Educator, Publisher, Writer*. Aldershot: Ashgate, 2006.
Greenblatt, Stephen. *Hamlet in Purgatory*. Princeton: Princeton University Press, 2001.
Greetham, D. C. "Editorial and Critical Theory: From Modernism to Postmodernism." In Bornstein and Williams, eds., *Palimpsest*. 9–28.
Greg, W. W. *The Editorial Problem in Shakespeare: A Survey of the Foundations of the Text*. Oxford: Clarendon, 1942.
———. "Old Plays and New Editions." *Library*, 2nd ser. 3 (1902): 408–26.
———. "The Rationale of Copy-Text." *Studies in Bibliography* 3 (1950–51): 19–36.
———. Review of J. M. Robertson, *Did Shakespeare Write "Titus Andronicus"? Modern Language Review* 1 (1906): 337–41.
———. Review of L. L. Schücking, *Zum Problem der Überlieferung des Hamlet-Textes. Review of English Studies* 8 (1932): 228–31.
———. *The Shakespeare First Folio: Its Bibliographical and Textual History*. Oxford: Clarendon, 1955.
———, ed. *The Merry Wives of Windsor, 1602*. Oxford: Clarendon, 1910.
Grein, J. T. *Premières of the Year*. London: John Macqueen, 1900.
Griffiths, Trevor R., ed. *The Country Wife*. By William Wycherley. London: Nick Hern, 2001.
Gunthio, Ambrose [John Payne Collier?]. "A Running Commentary on the Hamlet of 1603." *European Magazine, and London Review* 1.4 (December 1825): 339–47.
Gurr, Andrew. "Other Accents: Some Problems with Identifying Elizabethan Pronunciation." *Early Modern Literary Studies* 7.1 / Special Issue 8 (May 2001). http://extra.shu.ac.uk/emls/07-1/gurrothe.htm.
Halio, Jay L. "Essential *Hamlet*." *College Literature* 1.2 (1974): 83–99.
———. *Understanding Shakespeare's Plays in Performance*. Manchester: Manchester University Press, 1988.
Hall, Edward. *The Vnion of the two noble and illustrate famelies of Lancastre & Yorke*. London: Richard Grafton, 1548.

Halliwell-Phillipps, James Orchard. *Memoranda on the Tragedy of Hamlet*. London: James Evan Adlard, 1879.
"Hamlet—Edition of 1603." *Morning Chronicle* (24 January 1825): 3.
"Hamlet: Edition of 1603." *Literary Gazette, and Journal of Belles Lettres, Arts, Sciences, &c.* 418 (22 January 1825): 58–59.
Hanmer, Thomas, ed. *The Works of Shakespear*. 6 vols. Oxford: Oxford University Press, 1743–44.
Hapgood, Robert, ed. *Hamlet*. Shakespeare in Production. Cambridge: Cambridge University Press, 1999.
Harris, Barbara J. *English Aristocratic Women, 1450–1550: Marriage and Family, Property and Careers*. Oxford: Oxford University Press, 2002.
Harris, Jonathan Gil. *Untimely Matter in the Time of Shakespeare*. Philadelphia: University of Pennsylvania Press, 2009.
Hazlitt, William. *Characters of Shakespeare's Plays*. Boston: Wells and Lilly, 1818.
Hegel, G. W. F. Selections from *The Philosophy of Fine Art* (1835). Trans. F. P. B. Osmaston. In *Theatre/Theory/Theatre: The Major Critical Texts from Aristotle and Zeami to Soyinka and Havel*. Ed. Daniel Gerould. New York: Applause, 2000. 314–26.
"Henry Irving: Actor and 'Hamlet'." *Illustrated Sporting and Dramatic News* (7 November 1874): 126.
Heussi, Jacob. *Shakespeare's Hamlet*. Parchim: J. Heussi, 1868.
Heywood, Thomas. *A Woman Kilde with Kindnesse*. London: William Jaggard, to be sold by John Hodgets, 1607.
Hill, Aaron. *A Full and Just Account of the Present State of the Ottoman Empire*. London: For the author, to be sold by John Mayo, 1709.
Hirrell, Michael. "The Roberts Memoranda: A Solution." *Review of English Studies* 61 (2010): 711–28.
Holderness, Graham, and Bryan Loughrey. "Text and Stage: Shakespeare, Bibliography, and Performance Studies." *New Theatre Quarterly* 9 (1993): 179–91.
Holderness, Graham, and Bryan Loughrey, eds. *The Tragicall Historie of Hamlet Prince of Denmark*. Shakespearean Originals. Hemel Hempstead: Harvester Wheatsheaf, 1992.
Hollingsworth, Mark. "Shakespeare Criticism." In *Shakespeare in the Nineteenth Century*. Ed. Gail Marshall. Cambridge: Cambridge University Press, 2012. 39–59.
Homer Alamode, the Second Part, in English Burlesque. Or, A Mock-Poem upon the Ninth Book of Iliads. London: Dorman Newman, 1681.
Honigmann, E. A. J. *The Stability of Shakespeare's Text*. Lincoln: University of Nebraska Press, 1965.
———. "To Be or Not to Be." In Thompson and McMullan, eds., *In Arden*. 209–10.
Hood, Edwin Paxton. *The World of Proverb and Parable*. London: Hodder and Stoughton, 1885.
Hope, Jonathan. *Shakespeare's Grammar*. London: Thomson Learning, 2003.
Horne, R. H. [writing as Prof. Grabstein]. "On the Character of the Ghost in 'Hamlet'." *Fraser's Magazine* 32.184 (September 1845): 250–56.
Houston, Percy H. "There's Nothing Either Good or Bad but Thinking Makes It So." *Shakespeare Association Bulletin* 24 (1949): 48–53.
Hoyt, Wayland. "Prayer-Meeting Service." *Homiletic Review* 49.2 (February 1905): 154–56.
Hsy, Jonathan. "An Analysis of Marginalia in Two Editions of Shakespeare's First Folio." Unpublished paper. University of Pennsylvania, 2002.
Hubbard, Frank G., ed. *The First Quarto Edition of Shakespeare's Hamlet*. Madison: University of Wisconsin Press, 1920.
Hudson, Henry Norman, ed. *The Complete Works of William Shakespeare*. Harvard Shakespeare. 20 vols. Boston: Ginn and Heath, 1880–81.

———, ed. *Plays of Shakespeare, Selected and Prepared for Use in Schools, Clubs, Classes, and Families*. 3 vols. Boston: Ginn Brothers, 1870.
Hughes, Alan. *Henry Irving, Shakespearean*. Cambridge: Cambridge University Press, 1981.
Hunter, G. K. "The Social Function of Annotation." In Thompson and McMullan, eds., *In Arden*. 177–93.
Hunter, Joseph. *New Illustrations of the Life, Studies, and Writings of Shakespeare*. 2 vols. London: J. B. Nichols and Son, 1845.
Huret, Jules. *Sarah Bernhardt*. Trans. G. A. Raper. London: Chapman and Hall, 1899.
Ioppolo, Grace. *Revising Shakespeare*. Cambridge, MA: Harvard University Press, 1991.
Irace, Kathleen. "Origins and Agents of Q1 *Hamlet*." In Clayton, ed., *Hamlet*. 90–122.
———, ed. *The First Quarto of Hamlet*. New Cambridge Shakespeare: The Early Quartos. Cambridge: Cambridge University Press, 1998.
Irving, Henry. "An Actor's Notes on Shakspeare. No. 2. Hamlet and Ophelia." *Nineteenth Century* 1 (May 1877): 524–30.
Irving, Laurence. *Henry Irving: The Actor and His World*. New York: Macmillan, 1951.
Jack, Ian. "Novels and Those 'Necessary Evils': Annotating the Brontës." *Essays in Criticism* 32 (1982): 321–37.
Jameson, Fredric. *Postmodernism: Or, The Cultural Logic of Late Capitalism*. Durham: Duke University Press, 1991.
Jansohn, Christa. "Annotation as Cultural Activity or, Re-constructing the Past for the Present." In *Problems of Editing*. Ed. Christa Jansohn. Tübingen: Max Niemeyer, 1999. 211–23.
Jardine, Lisa. *Reading Shakespeare Historically*. New York: Routledge, 1996.
Johnson, Gerald. "Nicholas Ling, Publisher 1580–1607." *Studies in Bibliography* 38 (1985): 203–14.
Jones, Ann Rosalind, and Peter Stallybrass. *Renaissance Clothing and the Materials of Memory*. Cambridge: Cambridge University Press, 2000.
Jones, Ernest. *Hamlet and Oedipus*. London: Gollancz, 1949.
———. "The Oedipus-Complex as an Explanation of Hamlet's Mystery: A Study in Motive." *American Journal of Psychology* 21 (1910): 72–113.
———. "A Psycho-Analytic Study of Hamlet." In *Essays in Applied Psycho-Analysis*. London: International Psycho-Analytical Press, 1923. 1–98.
Jonson, Ben. *The Comicall Satyre of Every Man out of His Humor*. London: William Holme, 1600.
———. *The Fovntaine of Selfe-Love. Or Cynthias Revels*. London: Walter Burre, 1601.
Joseph, Bertram. *Conscience and the King: A Study of "Hamlet."* London: Chatto and Windus, 1953.
Jowett, John. "Editing Shakespeare's Plays in the Twentieth Century." *Shakespeare Survey* 59 (2006): 1–19.
Kastan, David Scott. *Shakespeare After Theory*. New York: Routledge, 1999.
———. *Shakespeare and the Book*. Cambridge: Cambridge University Press, 2001.
Kehler, Dorothy. "The First Quarto of *Hamlet*: Reforming Widow Gertred." *Shakespeare Quarterly* 46 (1995): 398–413.
Kittredge, George Lyman, ed. *Hamlet*. Boston: Ginn, 1939.
Kliman, Bernice. "At Sea about *Hamlet* at Sea: A Detective Story." *Shakespeare Quarterly* 62 (2011): 180–204.
———. "The Bed in HAMLET's Closet Scene: Rowe 1709 and 1714." *Shakespeare Newsletter* 43.1 (1993): 8–9.
Knapp, Peggy. *Time-Bound Words: Semantic and Social Economies from Chaucer's England to Shakespeare's*. New York: St. Martin's Press, 2000.

Knight, Charles. *Old Lamps, or New? A Plea for the Original Editions of the Text of Shakspere.* London: Charles Knight, 1853.
———, ed. *The Comedies, Histories, Tragedies, and Poems of William Shakspere.* 2nd ed. 12 vols. London: Charles Knight, 1842.
Knight, G. Wilson. *The Wheel of Fire.* 1930; London: Methuen, 1970.
Knight, Jeffrey Todd. *Bound to Read: Compilations, Collections, and the Making of Renaissance Literature.* Philadelphia: University of Pennsylvania Press, 2013.
Knights, L. C. *Some Shakespearean Themes and An Approach to "Hamlet."* Palo Alto: Stanford University Press, 1966.
Kyd, Thomas. *The Spanish Tragedie.* London: Edward White, [1592].
———. *The Spanish Tragedie.* London: Edward White, 1594.
———. *The Spanish Tragedie.* London: William White, 1599.
———. *The Spanish Tragedie.* London: Thomas Pavier, 1602.
———. *The Spanish Tragedie.* London: Thomas Pavier, 1603.
———. *The Tragedie of Solimon and Perseda.* London: Edward White, 1599.
L[athum], W[illiam]. *Virgils Eclogues Translated into English.* London: William Jones, 1628.
Lactantius. *Divine Institutes.* Trans. Anthony Bowen and Peter Garnsey. Liverpool: Liverpool University Press, 2003.
Lander, Jesse M. *Inventing Polemic: Religion, Print, and Literary Culture in Early Modern England.* Cambridge: Cambridge University Press, 2006.
Lanier, Douglas. *Shakespeare and Modern Popular Culture.* Oxford: Oxford University Press, 2002.
LaPorte, Charles. "The Bard, the Bible, and the Victorian Shakespeare Question." *ELH* 74 (2007): 609–28.
Leader, Zachary. *Revision and Romantic Authorship.* Oxford: Clarendon, 1996.
Lee, Sidney. "Shakespeare and the Inquisition: A Spanish Second Folio." In *Elizabethan and Other Essays, by Sir Sidney Lee.* Ed. Frederick S. Boas. Oxford: Clarendon, 1929. 184–95.
———, ed. *The Complete Works of Shakespeare.* 20 vols. New York: Harper Brothers; Cambridge: Cambridge University Press, 1906–8.
Legman, G. *Rationale of the Dirty Joke: An Analysis of Sexual Humor, Volume 1.* 1968; New York: Simon and Schuster, 2006.
Lesser, Zachary. *Renaissance Drama and the Politics of Publication: Readings in the English Book Trade.* Cambridge: Cambridge University Press, 2004.
Lesser, Zachary, and Peter Stallybrass. "The First Literary *Hamlet* and the Commonplacing of Professional Plays." *Shakespeare Quarterly* 59 (2008): 371–420.
Levenson, Jill L., ed. *Romeo and Juliet.* Oxford Shakespeare. Oxford: Oxford University Press, 2000.
Lewis, C. S. *Studies in Words.* Cambridge: Cambridge University Press, 1960.
Lewis, Charlton M. *The Genesis of Hamlet.* New York: Henry Holt, 1907.
Lightfoot, Joseph Barber. *Cambridge Sermons.* London: Macmillan, 1890.
"Literary Intelligence—Shakspeare." *Gentleman's Magazine* (January 1825): 68–69.
"Literary Miscellanies." *Eclectic Magazine of Foreign Literature, Science, and Art* (November 1856): 426.
Liu, Alan. "The Power of Formalism: The New Historicism." *ELH* 56 (1989): 721–71.
Lodge, Thomas. *Wits Miserie.* London: Adam Islip, to be sold by Cuthbert Burby, 1596.
Lopez, Jeremy. *Theatrical Convention and Audience Response in Early Modern Drama.* Cambridge: Cambridge University Press, 2003.
Loughrey, Bryan. "Q1 in Recent Performance: An Interview." In Clayton, ed., *Hamlet.* 123–36.
Love, Heather. *Feeling Backward: Loss and the Politics of Queer History.* Cambridge, MA: Harvard University Press, 2007.

Lowell, James Russell. "Shakespeare Once More." *North American Review* 219 (April 1868): 629–70.
Lowes, John Livingston, ed. *Hamlet*. New York: Henry Holt, 1914.
MacDonald, George, ed. *The Tragedie of Hamlet, Prince of Denmarke*. London: Longmans, Green, 1885.
Mackail, J. W., ed. *Aspects of Shakespeare: Being British Academy Lectures*. Oxford: Clarendon, 1933.
"Madame Bernhardt's Hamlet." *Times* (13 June 1899): 7.
Maguire, Laurie E. "Feminist Editing and the Body of the Text." In *A Feminist Companion to Shakespeare*. Ed. Dympna Callaghan. Oxford: Blackwell, 2000. 59–79.
———. *Shakespearean Suspect Texts: The "Bad" Quartos and Their Contexts*. Cambridge: Cambridge University Press, 1996.
———. "Typographical Embodiment: The Case of *etcetera*." In *The Oxford Handbook on Shakespeare and Embodiment*. Ed. Valerie Traub. Oxford: Oxford University Press, forthcoming. Unpublished typescript.
Marcus, Leah. "Levelling Shakespeare: Local Customs and Local Texts." *Shakespeare Quarterly* 42 (1991): 168–78.
———. *Unediting the Renaissance: Shakespeare, Marlowe, Milton*. New York: Routledge, 1996.
Marino, James J. *Owning William Shakespeare: The King's Men and Their Intellectual Property*. Philadelphia: University of Pennsylvania Press, 2011.
Marlowe, Christopher. *All Ouids Elegies: 3 Bookes. By C. M. Epigrames by J. D.* London: s.n., 1603?
Marlowe, Christopher, and George Chapman. *Hero and Leander: Begun by Christopher Marloe; and finished by George Chapman*. London: Paul Linley, 1598.
Marprelate, Martin. *Oh read ouer D. Iohn Bridges, for it is a worthy worke*. Fawsley, Northants.: s.n., 1588.
Marshall, Frank. *A Study of Hamlet*. London: Longmans, Green, 1875.
———, ed. *Hamlet, a Tragedy in Five Acts . . . as Arranged for the Stage by Henry Irving*. Rev. ed. London: Chiswick Press, 1879.
Marston, John. *The Malcontent*. London: William Aspley, 1604.
Mason, John Monck. *Comments on the Last Edition of Shakespeare's Plays*. Dublin: P. Byrne, 1785.
Masten, Jeffrey. "Bound for Germany: Heresy, Sodomy, and a New Copy of Marlowe's *Edward II*." *TLS: The Times Literary Supplement* (21/28 December 2012): 17–19.
———. "Rossencraft and Gilderstone Are Dead." Paper delivered to the Shakespeare Division of the Modern Language Association. 1991.
———. *Queer Philologies*. Philadelphia: University of Pennsylvania Press, forthcoming.
Mayer, David. "Encountering Melodrama." In *The Cambridge Companion to Victorian and Edwardian Theatre*. Ed. Kerry Powell. Cambridge: Cambridge University Press, 2004. 145–63.
McBride, Timothy. "Country Matters." In *The Manageable Cold: Poems*. Evanston: Northwestern University Press, 2010. 22–23.
McGill, Meredith L. *American Literature and the Culture of Reprinting, 1834–1853*. Philadelphia: University of Pennsylvania Press, 2003.
McLeod, Randall. "UN *Editing* Shak-speare." *Sub-stance* 10, no. 4–11, no. 1 (1981–82): 26–55.
McLuskie, Kathleen. "'*Enter the ghost in his night gowne*': The Corpus of Shakespeare Now." *Shakespeare Studies* (Japan) 44 (2006): 1–16.
McMullan, Gordon. *Shakespeare and the Idea of Late Writing: Authorship in the Proximity of Death*. Cambridge: Cambridge University Press, 2008.
Melnikoff, Kirk. "Nicholas Ling's Republican *Hamlet* (1603)." In *Shakespeare's Stationers: Studies in Cultural Bibliography*. Ed. Marta Straznicky. Philadelphia: University of Pennsylvania Press, 2013. 95–111.

Menon, Madhavi. *Unhistorical Shakespeare: Queer Theory in Shakespearean Literature and Film*. New York: Palgrave, 2008.

———, ed. *Shakesqueer: A Queer Companion to the Complete Works of Shakespeare*. Durham: Duke University Press, 2011.

Menzer, Paul. *The Hamlets: Cues, Qs, and Remembered Texts*. Newark: University of Delaware Press, 2008.

Mills, John A. *Hamlet on Stage: The Great Tradition*. Westport, CT: Greenwood Press, 1985.

"Minor Mention." *Appletons' Journal of Literature, Science, and Art* 9 (1873): 763–64.

Mommsen, Tycho. "'Hamlet,' 1603; and 'Romeo and Juliet,' 1597." *Athenaeum* 1528 (7 February 1857): 182–83.

Montrose, Louis. "The Work of Gender in the Discourse of Discovery." *Representations* 33 (1991): 1–41.

Morand, Eugène, and Marcel Schwob, eds. and trans. *La Tragique Histoire d'Hamlet, Prince de Danemark*. Paris: Libr. Charpentier et Fasquelle, 1900.

Mowat, Barbara. "The Forms of *Hamlet*'s Fortunes." *Renaissance Drama* 19 (1988): 97–126.

———. "The Problem of Shakespeare's Text(s)." In *Textual Formations and Reformations*. Ed. Laurie E. Maguire and Thomas L. Berger. Newark: University of Delaware Press, 1998. 131–48.

Mowat, Barbara, and Paul Werstine, eds. *Hamlet*. Folger Shakespeare. New York: Simon and Schuster, 1992.

"Mr. Irving as Hamlet." *Graphic* 259 (14 November 1874): 463.

"Mr. Irving's Hamlet." *All the Year Round* n.s. 13 (5 December 1874): 179–82.

Murphy, Andrew. *Shakespeare for the People: Working-Class Readers, 1800–1900*. Cambridge: Cambridge University Press, 2008.

———. *Shakespeare in Print: A History and Chronology of Shakespeare Publishing*. Cambridge: Cambridge University Press, 2003.

Nashe, Thomas. "To the Gentlemen Students *of both Uniuersities*." In *Menaphon*. By Robert Greene. London: Sampson Clarke, 1589. Sigs. 2*1r–A3r.

Neilson, William Allan, ed. *The Complete Dramatic and Poetic Works of William Shakespeare*. Boston and New York: Houghton Mifflin and The Riverside Press, 1906.

"The New Hamlet and His Critics." *Macmillan's* 31.183 (January 1875): 236–41.

[Oliphant, Margaret]. "Hamlet." *Blackwood's* 125 (April 1879): 462–81.

Orgel, Stephen, and A. R. Braunmuller, eds. *The Complete Pelican Shakespeare*. New York: Penguin, 2002.

Orlin, Lena Cowen. "Gertrude's Closet." *Shakespeare Jahrbuch* 134 (1998): 44–67.

Ostovich, Helen, ed. *Every Man out of His Humor*. By Ben Jonson. Revels Plays. Manchester: Manchester University Press, 2001.

"Our Weekly Gossip." *Athenaeum* 1508 (20 September 1856): 1168.

"Our Weekly Gossip." *Athenaeum* 1512 (18 October 1856): 1277.

Parr, Elnathan. *A Plaine Exposition vpon the Whole 8. 9. 10. 11. Chapters of the Epistle of Saint Paul to the Romans*. London: Samuel Man, 1618.

Partridge, Eric. *Shakespeare's Bawdy*. 1947; New York: Routledge, 2001.

"A Passage in Macbeth." *Galaxy* 6 (August 1868): 281–82.

Pechter, Edward. *Shakespeare Studies Today: Romanticism Lost*. New York: Palgrave Macmillan, 2011.

Perkins, William. *The Combat betweene Christ and the Diuell displayed*. London: Eleazer Edgar, to be sold by Cuthbert Burby, 1606.

Petronella, Vincent F. "Hamlet's 'To Be or Not to Be' Soliloquy: Once More unto the Breach." *Studies in Philology* 71 (1974): 72–88.

Pinkerton, John. "Conclusion of the remarks on the last edition of Shakspere 1778." In *Letters of Literature*. London: G. G. J. and J. Robinson, 1785. 301–15.
Pollard, Alfred W. *Shakespeare's Fight with the Pirates and the Problem of the Transmission of His Texts*. Cambridge: Cambridge University Press, 1920.
———. *Shakespeare's Folios and Quartos: A Study in the Bibliography of Shakespeare's Plays 1594–1685*. London: Methuen, 1909.
Powell, Thomas. *Tom of All Trades*. London: Benjamin Fisher, 1631.
Preston, Claire. *Thomas Browne and the Writing of Early Modern Science*. Cambridge: Cambridge University Press, 2005.
Prince, Kathryn. *Shakespeare in the Victorian Periodicals*. New York: Routledge, 2008.
Prosser, Eleanor. *Hamlet and Revenge*. Palo Alto: Stanford University Press, 1968.
Rann, Joseph, ed. *The Dramatic Works of Shakspeare*. 6 vols. Oxford: Clarendon, 1786–93.
"A Record of Impressions Produced by the Exhibition of Mr. Allston's Pictures in the Summer of 1839." *Dial: A Magazine for Literature, Philosophy, and Religion* 1.1 (July 1840): 73–82.
"Recovered Edition of Shakspeare." *United States Literary Gazette* (1 May 1825): 115–16.
"Recovered Edition of Shakspeare. [Concluded.]" *United States Literary Gazette* (15 May 1825): 152–56.
Redpath, Theodore, ed. *The Songs and Sonnets of John Donne*. 2nd ed. Cambridge, MA: Harvard University Press, 2009.
Reed, Henry Hope. *Lectures on English History and Tragic Poetry*. London: John F. Shaw, 1856.
Reed, Isaac, ed. *The Plays of William Shakspeare*. 21 vols. London: J. Johnson et al., 1803.
"Reviews of Recent Antiquarian Works. SHAKESPEARIAN LITERATURE." *Archaeologist, and Journal of Antiquarian Science* 5 (January 1842): 193–202.
Richards, Irving T. "The Meaning of Hamlet's Soliloquy." *PMLA* 48 (1933): 741–66.
Ridley, M. R., ed. *Hamlet*. New Temple Shakespeare. London: J. M. Dent and Sons; New York: E. P. Dutton, 1934.
Roach, Joseph R. *The Player's Passion: Studies in the Science of Acting*. Newark: University of Delaware Press, 1985.
Roberts, Jeanne Addison. "*The Merry Wives* Q and F: The Vagaries of Progress." *Shakespeare Studies* 8 (1975): 143–75.
Robertson, J. M. *"Hamlet" Once More*. London: Richard Cobden-Sanderson, 1923.
———. *Montaigne and Shakespeare, and Other Essays on Cognate Questions*. London: Adam and Charles Black, 1909.
———. *The Problem of "Hamlet."* London: George Allen and Unwin, 1919.
———. *The Shakespeare Canon*. 4 vols. London: George Routledge and Sons, 1922.
——— [writing as Arthur Gigadibs]. "The Upshot of *Hamlet*." *Our Corner* 5 (1885): 142–49 (part I), 212–20 (part II), 275–83 (part III), 353–60 (part IV).
[Robinson, Mary?]. *The Memoirs of Perdita*. London: G. Lister, 1784.
Rogers, Richard. *A Commentary upon the Whole Booke of Iudges*. London: Thomas Man, 1615.
Rolfe, William J., ed. *Shakespeare's Tragedy of Hamlet, Prince of Denmark*. New York: American Book Company, 1878.
Rooney, M. W. *Hamlet, First Edition (1603). The Last Leaf of the Lately Discovered Copy, Carefully Reprinted, with a Narrative of its Discovery*. Dublin: M. W. Rooney, 1856.
——— [misattributed as C. W. W. Rooney]. Letter. *Athenaeum* 1509 (27 September 1856): 1191.
Roosbroeck, Gustave L. van. "Hamlet in France in 1663." *PMLA* 37 (1922): 228–42.
Rosenberg, Marvin. "The First Modern English Staging of *Hamlet* Q1." In Clayton, ed., *Hamlet*. 241–48.

———. *The Masks of Hamlet*. Newark: University of Delaware Press, 1992.
Routh, H. V. Review of Levin L. Schücking, *Die Characterprobleme bei Shakespeare. Eine Einführung in das Verständnis des Dramatikers*. *Modern Language Review* 16 (1921): 78–87.
Rowe, Nicholas, ed. *The Works of Mr. William Shakespear*. 6 vols. London: Jacob Tonson, 1709.
———. *The Works of Mr. William Shakespear*. 9 vols. London: Jacob Tonson, 1714.
Rowlands, Samuel. *The Night-Raven*. London: John Deane and Thomas Bailey, 1620.
Rubinstein, Frankie. *A Dictionary of Shakespeare's Sexual Puns and Their Significance*. 2nd ed. London: Macmillan, 1989.
Russell, Edward R. *Irving as Hamlet*. London: Henry S. King, 1875.
S., W. *The Lamentable Tragedie of Locrine*. London: Thomas Creede, 1595.
Sadler, Glenn Edward. "MacDonald, George (1824–1905)." *Oxford Dictionary of National Biography*. Oxford: Oxford University Press, 2004. Online edition, May 2006. http://www.oxforddnb.com/view/article/35783. Accessed 24 July 2012.
Salter, Dennis. "Henry Irving, the 'Dr Freud' of Melodrama." In *Melodrama*. Ed. James Redmond. Cambridge: Cambridge University Press, 1992. 161–82.
Sams, Eric. "Taboo or Not Taboo? The Text, Dating and Authorship of *Hamlet*, 1589–1623." *Hamlet Studies* 10 (1988): 12–46.
Sanford, Rhonda Lemke. *Maps and Memory in Early Modern England: A Sense of Place*. New York: Palgrave Macmillan, 2002.
Schlegel, August Wilhelm von. *A Course of Lectures on Dramatic Art and Literature*. Trans. John Black. 2 vols. London: Baldwin, Cradock, and Joy, 1815.
Schmidt, Alexander. *Shakespeare-Lexicon: A Complete Dictionary of all the English Words, Phrases and Constructions in the Works of the Poet*. 2 vols. Berlin: Georg Reimer; London: Williams and Norgate, 1874.
Schücking, Levin L. *Character Problems in Shakespeare's Plays: A Guide to the Better Understanding of the Dramatist*. English trans. London: George H. Harrup, 1922.
———. *The Meaning of Hamlet*. Trans. Graham Rawson. 1937; New York: Barnes and Noble, 1966.
Serpieri, Alessandro, ed. and trans. *Il primo Amleto*. Venice: Marsilio, 1997.
"Shakspeare in Germany. Part I. Shakspeare's Tragedies.—Hamlet." *Blackwood's Edinburgh Magazine* 37.231 (February 1835): 236–55.
"Shakspeare." *The Circulator of Useful Knowledge*. London: Thomas Boys, 1825. 60.
"Shakspeare." *The Circulator of Useful Knowledge*. London: Thomas Boys, 1825. 79–80.
"Shakspeare." *Kaleidoscope* (25 January 1825): 254–55.
"Shakspeare." *Kaleidoscope* (1 February 1825): 260–62.
"Shakspeare." *London Quarterly Review* 22 (1864): 201–34.
"Shakspeare's *Tragedy of* Hamlet, *reprinted (verbatim) from the recently discovered Edition of* 1603." *Gentleman's Magazine* 95 (April 1825): 335–36.
Shakespeare, William. *Bell's Edition of Shakespeare's Plays As they are performed at the Theatres Royal in London*. 5 vols. London: John Bell and C. Etherington, 1774.
———. *Comedies, Histories, & Tragedies*. London: Isaac Jaggard, William Jaggard, Edward Blount, John Smethwick, and William Aspley, 1623. (F).
———. *Comedies, Histories, & Tragedies*. London: Robert Allot, William Aspley, Richard Hawkins, Richard Meighen, and John Smethwick, 1632. (F2).
———. *The Cronicle History of Henry the fift*. London: Thomas Millington and John Busby, 1600.
———. *The First Edition of the Tragedy of Hamlet*. London: Payne and Foss, 1825.

———. *Hamlet, Prince of Denmark. A Tragedy. As it is now Acted by his Majesty's Servants.* London: M. Wellington, 1718.
———. *The Historie of Troylus and Cresseida.* London: Richard Bonian and Henry Walley, 1609.
———. *The History of Henrie the Fourth.* London: Andrew Wise, 1599.
———. *The Most Excellent and lamentable Tragedie, of Romeo and Iuliet.* London: Cuthbert Burby, 1599.
———. *A Pleasant Conceited Comedie called, Loues labors lost.* London: Cuthbert Burby, 1598.
———. *The Tragedy of Hamlet Prince of Denmark. As it is now Acted at his Highness the Duke of* York's *Theatre.* London: John Martyn and Henry Herringman, 1676.
———. *The Tragedy of King Richard the Third.* London: Andrew Wise, 1597.
———. *The Tragicall Historie of Hamlet Prince of Denmarke.* London: Nicholas Ling and John Trundle, 1603. (Q1).
———. *The Tragicall Historie of Hamlet, Prince of Denmarke.* London: Nicholas Ling, 1604. (Q2).
———. *The Tragœdy of Othello, The Moore of Venice.* London: Thomas Walkley, 1622.
"Shakespeare's Critics: English and Foreign." *Edinburgh Review or Critical Journal* 182 (1849): 39–77.
Shattuck, Charles H. *The Hamlet of Edwin Booth.* Urbana: University of Illinois Press, 1969.
———. *The Shakespeare Promptbooks: A Descriptive Catalogue.* Urbana: University of Illinois Press, 1965.
Sheidlower, Jesse. *The F Word.* 3rd ed. New York: Oxford University Press, 2009.
Sherburn, George. "Huntington Library Collections." *Huntington Library Bulletin* 1 (1931): 33–106.
Sherman, William H. *Used Books: Marking Readers in Renaissance England.* Philadelphia: University of Pennsylvania Press, 2008.
Sidney, Philip. *The Countesse of Pembrokes Arcadia.* London: William Ponsonby, 1590.
Singer, Samuel Weller. *The Dramatic Works of William Shakespeare, the Text Carefully Revised with Notes.* London: Bell and Daldy, 1856.
Small, Ian. "The Editor as Annotator as Ideal Reader." In *The Theory and Practice of Text-Editing: Essays in Honour of James T. Boulton.* Ed. Ian Small and Marcus Walsh. Cambridge: Cambridge University Press, 1991. 186–209.
Smith, Emma. "Ghost Writing: *Hamlet* and the Ur-Hamlet." In *The Renaissance Text: Theory, Editing, Textuality.* Ed. Andrew Murphy. Manchester: Manchester University Press, 2000. 177–90.
Smith, Henry. *The Affinitie of the faithfull.* London: Nicholas Ling and John Busby, 1591.
Smith, Thomas. *Sir Thomas Smithes Voiage and Entertainment in Rushia.* London: Nathaniel Butter, 1605.
Smyth, Adam. "'Shreds of Holinesse': George Herbert, Little Gidding, and Cutting Up Texts in Early Modern England." *ELR* 42 (2012): 452–81.
Sonnenchein, E. A. "Shakespeare on the German Stage." *Academy* 431 (7 August 1880): 106–7.
Spevack, Marvin. *James Orchard Halliwell-Phillipps: A Classified Bibliography.* New York: Georg Olms, 1997.
St. Clair, William. *The Reading Nation in the Romantic Period.* Cambridge: Cambridge University Press, 2004.
Stallybrass, Peter. "Against Thinking." *PMLA* 122 (2007): 1580–87.
———. "*Thrift, Horatio, Thrift*: Recycling Woodblocks and the Printing of Books." Lecture delivered at the Rare Book School. University of Virginia. 30 July 2008.
———. "Worn Worlds: Clothes, Mourning, and the Life of Things." *Yale Review* 81.2 (1993): 35–50.
Stallybrass, Peter, and Roger Chartier. "Reading and Authorship: The Circulation of Shakespeare

1590–1619." In *A Concise Companion to Shakespeare and the Text*. Ed. Andrew Murphy. Oxford: Blackwell, 2010. 35–56.

Steevens, George, ed. *The Plays of William Shakspeare*. 15 vols. London: T. Longman et al., 1793.

———. *Twenty of the Plays of Shakespeare, Being the whole Number printed in Quarto During his Life-Time*. 4 vols. London: J. and R. Tonson, T. Payne, and W. Richardson, 1766.

Stern, Tiffany. *Documents of Performance in Early Modern England*. Cambridge: Cambridge University Press, 2009.

———. "'I Do Wish That You Had Mentioned Garrick': The Absence of Garrick in Johnson's Shakespeare." In *Comparative Excellence: New Essays on Johnson and Shakespeare*. Ed. Eric Rasmussen and Aaron Santesso. New York: AMS Press, 2007. 71–96.

———. "'If I Could See the Puppets Dallying': *Der Bestrafte Brudermord* and Hamlet's Encounters with the Puppets." *Shakespeare Bulletin* 31 (2013): 337–52.

———. *Making Shakespeare: From Stage to Page*. London: Routledge, 2004.

———. *Rehearsal from Shakespeare to Sheridan*. Oxford: Clarendon, 2000.

———. "Sermons, Plays and Note-Takers: *Hamlet* Q1 as a 'Noted' Text." *Shakespeare Survey* 66 (2013): 1–23.

Stern, Tiffany, and Simon Palfrey. *Shakespeare in Parts*. Oxford: Oxford University Press, 2007.

Stewart, Alan. "The Actor and the Bad Poet: The Memorial Reconstruction of Shakespeare." Paper delivered to the annual meeting of the Shakespeare Association of America. Bellevue, Washington. 8 April 2011.

———. "The Early Modern Closet Discovered." *Representations* 50 (1995): 76–100.

Stoll, E. E. "Anachronism in Shakespeare Criticism." *Modern Philology* 7 (1910): 557–75.

———. *Hamlet: An Historical and Comparative Study*. Minneapolis: University of Minnesota Press, 1919.

Strachey, Edward. *Shakespeare's Hamlet: An Attempt to Find the Key to a Great Moral Problem*. London: J. W. Parker, 1848.

[Stubbes, George]. *Some Remarks on the Tragedy of Hamlet Prince of Denmark*. London: W. Wilkins, 1736.

Styan, J. L. *The Shakespeare Revolution*. Cambridge: Cambridge University Press, 1977.

Taranow, Gerda. *The Bernhardt Hamlet: Culture and Context*. New York: Peter Lang, 1996.

Taylor, Gary. *Reinventing Shakespeare: A Cultural History, From the Restoration to the Present*. New York: Weidenfeld and Nicolson, 1989.

———. "The Renaissance and the End of Editing." In Bornstein and Williams, eds., *Palimpsest*. 121–50.

[Taylor], J[ohn]. "The First Edition of Hamlet." *London Magazine* n.s. 1.4 (April 1825): 555–64.

Taylor, Neil, and Ann Thompson. "Obscenity in *Hamlet* III.ii; 'Country Matters'." *Textus* 9.2 (1996): 485–500.

"Theatres." *Graphic* (7 November 1874): 443.

"The Theatres—Lyceum." *Times* (12 November 1874): 8.

Theobald, Lewis. *Shakespeare restored*. London: R. Franklin and T. Woodman, Charles Davis, and S. Chapman, 1726.

———, ed. *The Works of Shakespeare*. 8 vols. London: H. Lintott, C. Hitch, J. and R. Tonson, C. Corbet, R. and B. Wellington, J. Brindley, and E. New, 1740.

Thomas, Sophie. "Poetry and Illustration: 'Amicable Strife'." In *A Companion to Romantic Poetry*. Ed. Charles Mahoney. Oxford: Blackwell, 2011. 354–72.

Thompson, Ann. "Feminist Theory and the Editing of Shakespeare: *The Taming of the Shrew* Revisited."

In *The Margins of the Text*. Ed. D. C. Greetham. Ann Arbor: University of Michigan Press, 1997. 83–103.
Thompson, Ann, and Gordon McMullan, eds. *In Arden: Editing Shakespeare: Essays in Honour of Richard Proudfoot*. London: Thomson Learning, 2003.
Thomson, Leslie. "Beds on the Early Modern Stage." Paper presented to the annual meeting of the Shakespeare Association of America. New Orleans. April 2004.
Traub, Valerie. "The New Unhistoricism in Queer Studies." *PMLA* 128 (2013): 21–39.
Ulrici, Hermann. *Shakespeare's Dramatic Art*. Trans. L. Dora Schmitz. London: George Bell and Sons, 1876.
Urkowitz, Steven. "Back to Basics: Thinking about the *Hamlet* First Quarto." In Clayton, ed., *Hamlet*. 257–91.
———. *Shakespeare's Revision of* King Lear. Princeton: Princeton University Press, 1980.
———. "'Well-sayd Olde Mole': Burying Three *Hamlets* in Modern Editions." In *Shakespeare Study Today: The Horace Howard Furness Memorial Lectures*. Ed. Georgianna Ziegler. New York: AMS Press, 1986. 37–70.
"Varieties, Literary and Miscellaneous." *Monthly Magazine, or British Register* (1 February 1825): 72–73.
Verity, Arthur Wilson, ed. *Hamlet*. Pitt Press Shakespeare for Schools. Cambridge: Cambridge University Press, 1926.
———. *The Tragedy of Hamlet Edited for the Use of Students*. Students' Shakespeare. Cambridge: Cambridge University Press, 1904.
Vickers, Brian. "*Hamlet* by Dogberry." *TLS: The Times Literary Supplement* 4734 (24 December 1993): 5–6.
———. "Identifying Shakespeare's Additions to *The Spanish Tragedy* (1602): A New(er) Approach." *Shakespeare* 8 (2012): 13–43.
Voltaire. *Critical Essays on Dramatic Poetry*. Glasgow: Robert Urie, 1761.
Walker, Alice. "Principles of Annotation: Some Suggestions for Editors of Shakespeare." *Studies in Bibliography* 9 (1957): 95–105.
Walsh, Marcus. *Shakespeare, Milton, and Eighteenth-Century Literary Editing: The Beginnings of Interpretative Scholarship*. Cambridge: Cambridge University Press, 1997.
Webb, J. Barry. *Shakespeare's Erotic Word Usage: The Body, Its Parts, Analogue and Images*. Hastings: Cornwallis Press, 1989.
Webster, John. *The White Divel*. London: Thomas Archer, 1612.
Weiner, Albert B., ed. *Hamlet: The First Quarto, 1603*. New York: Barron's Educational Series, 1962.
Weir, Alison. *Henry VIII*. New York: Ballantine, 2001.
Wells, Stanley. *Looking for Sex in Shakespeare*. Cambridge: Cambridge University Press, 2004.
———. *Shakespeare for All Time*. 2002; Oxford: Oxford University Press, 2003.
Wells, Stanley, and Gary Taylor. "The Oxford Shakespeare Re-Viewed by the General Editors." *AEB: Analytic and Enumerative Bibliography* n.s. 4 (1990): 6–20.
Wells, Stanley, and Gary Taylor, with John Jowett and William Montgomery, eds. *William Shakespeare: The Complete Works*. Oxford Shakespeare. Oxford: Clarendon, 1986.
Werder, Karl. *The Heart of Hamlet's Mystery*. 1875. Trans. Elizabeth Wilder. New York: Putnam's, 1907.
Werstine, Paul. "A Century of 'Bad' Shakespeare Quartos." *Shakespeare Quarterly* 50 (1999): 310–33.
———. *Early Modern Playhouse Manuscripts and the Editing of Shakespeare*. Cambridge: Cambridge University Press, 2013.
———. "Narratives About Printed Shakespeare Texts: 'Foul Papers' and 'Bad' Quartos." *Shakespeare Quarterly* 41 (1990): 65–86.

———. "The Textual Mystery of *Hamlet*." *Shakespeare Quarterly* 39 (1988): 1–26.
White, Richard Grant. *Studies in Shakespeare*. Boston: Houghton, Mifflin, 1886.
———. "The Two Hamlets." *Atlantic Monthly* 48.288 (1881): 467–79.
———, ed. *Mr. William Shakespeare's Comedies, Histories, Tragedies, and Poems*. Riverside Shakespeare. 3 vols. Boston: Houghton, Mifflin, 1883.
White, Richard Grant, William P. Trent, Benjamin W. Wells, and John B. Henneman, eds. *The New Grant White Shakespeare: The Comedies, Histories, Tragedies, and Poems of William Shakespeare*. 18 vols. Boston: Little, Brown, 1912.
"White's Shakespeare." *Hours at Home, A Popular Monthly, Devoted to Religious and Useful Literature* 2 (November–April 1866): 166–73.
Williams, Gordon. *A Dictionary of Sexual Language and Imagery in Shakespearean and Stuart Literature*. 3 vols. London: Athlone Press, 1994.
———. *Shakespeare's Sexual Language: A Glossary*. 1997; New York: Continuum, 2006.
Wilson, John Dover. "The Copy for 'Hamlet,' 1603." *Library*, 3rd ser. 9 (1918): 153–85.
———. *The Manuscript of Shakespeare's* Hamlet *and the Problems of Its Transmission: An Essay in Critical Bibliography*. Cambridge: Cambridge University Press, 1963.
———. *What Happens in Hamlet*. Cambridge: Cambridge University Press, 1935.
———. *What Happens in Hamlet*. 3rd edn. Cambridge: Cambridge University Press, 1951.
———, ed. *Hamlet*. Cambridge Shakespeare. Cambridge: Cambridge University Press, 1934.
Winter, William, ed. *Edwin Booth's Prompt-Book of Hamlet*. With manuscript notes by J. R. Pitman, c. 1884. New York: William Winter, 1879.
Woodmansee, Martha. *The Author, Art, and the Market: Rereading the History of Aesthetics*. New York: Columbia University Press, 1994.
Worthen, W. B. *Shakespeare and the Authority of Performance*. Cambridge: Cambridge University Press, 1997.
Yamada, Akihiro. *The First Folio of Shakespeare: A Transcript of Contemporary Marginalia in a Copy of the Kodama Memorial Library of Meisei University*. Tokyo: Yushodo Press, 1998.
Yorick's Meditations upon Various Interesting and Important Subjects. Dublin: James Hunter, 1760.
Young, Edward. *Conjectures on Original Composition*. London: A. Millar and R. and J. Dodsley, 1759.
"Young Shakespeare's Hamlet." *All the Year Round* n.s. 22 (25 January 1879): 138–41.
Zucker, Adam. *The Places of Wit in Early Modern English Comedy*. Cambridge: Cambridge University Press, 2011.

INDEX

Academy, 140
Adelphi Theatre, 143
Aebischer, Pascale, 117
Affinitie of the Faithfull, The (Henry Smith), 69
All the Year Round, 51–52
anachronism, 11–14, 18, 20, 21, 83, 156, 179
Andrews, Michael Cameron, 117
Arcadia, The (Sidney), 77, 197
Archaeologist, 43, 49
Armin, Robert, 44
As You Like It (Shakespeare), 77, 123
Athenaeum, 19, 40, 50

"Bad" Quarto of "Hamlet," The (Duthie), 189–95
bad quartos, 27, 29, 37, 39, 61–63, 65–66, 68, 108, 209–11, 217–18. *See also* New Bibliography; New Textualism
Bardolatry, 29, 184–85
Barkan, Leonard, 224n18
Barrymore, John, 118
Barton Hall, 1, 3, 8, 10, 23, 223n1
Bate, Jonathan, 251n48
Battestin, Martin, 80
Beaumont, Francis, 104
Belleforest, François de, 8, 145, 169, 175, 173, 178
Belsey, Catherine, 168, 169, 170, 171, 193, 194, 201–3
Berman, Russell, 12–13
Bernhardt, Sarah, 120–22; 121 (fig.), 123, 142 (fig.), 143, 153, 247n120, 247n122
Bernhardy, William, 172
Der bestrafte Brudermord (*Fratricide Punished*): closet scene in, 145, 152–53, 244n55; described, 6; as memorial reconstruction, 190–91, 195, 255n140; relation to *Ur–Hamlet*, 19, 172, 174, 176–78, 180, 188–92, 215

Betterton, Thomas, 126, 134, 145, 247n127, 238n133
Bevington, David, 76, 80
Bibliothèque Universelle des Sciences, Belles-Lettres, et Arts, 99
Blackfriars theater, 19, 47, 226n66
Blackmore, Simon Augustine, 187, 188
Blackwood's Magazine, 41, 120, 247n114
Blakeway, John Brickdale, 166
Bloom, Harold, 219, 258n35
Bly, Mary, 227n73
Boas, Frederick S., 176, 181
Boaz, Raphael, 226n12
Boone, T. and W., 16, 18
Booth, Edwin, 128 (fig.), 135–36, 244n40
Boswell, James, 6, 10, 43, 72, 99, 166, 229n42
Bourus, Terri, 234n154, 234n157
Bowden, Henry, 187, 188
bowdlerization, 75, 85–86, 88–89, 92, 105, 107–8, 110–12, 127 (fig.)
Bowers, Fredson, 189–90, 255n134
Bradley, A. C: on closet scene, 119, 120, 123, 124, 137, 141, 156, 245n60, 247n120; on "conscience," 167; on Hamlet's character, 141–43, 156, 177–79, 247n119; on Shakespeare's revision of *Hamlet*, 253n90
Braunmuller, A. R., 77
Bristol, Michael, 13
British Museum, 16
British Working-Man's Almanac, The, 41
Browne, Thomas, 8–10, 14, 15, 19–20
Bucknill, John Charles, 133
Buhler, Stephen M., 117–18
Bunbury, Henry, 1–5, 13, 15–16, 18, 23, 25, 58, 223n1, 223n3, 224n9
Bunbury, William, 3, 16
Burbage, Richard, 79, 107, 234n154
Butter, Nathaniel, 38

Caldecott, Thomas, 28, 103, 250n31
Cambridge Shakespeare. *See Works of William Shakespeare, The* (ed. Clark and Wright)
Canterbury Tales, The (Chaucer), 76
Capell, Edward, 29, 30, 166, 228n21, 228n30
Captain, The (Beaumont and Fletcher), 104
Carpenter, Nathanael, 198
Castle of Perseverance, The, 87
Cawdry, Robert, 197
Chakrabarty, Dipesh, 225n42
Chamberlain's Men, 19, 150, 226n66
Chambers, E. K., 166–67, 171, 180–81, 184–85, 254n108, 255n132
Chapman, George, 77–78
Charney, Maurice, 116–17, 244n53
Chaucer, Geoffrey, 76
Chiswick edition. *See Dramatic Works of William Shakespeare*
Chronicles of England, Scotland, and Ireland (Holinshed), 8
Cinthio (Giovanni Battista Giraldi), 8
Circulator of Useful Knowledge, The, 74
Clark, William George, 51, 54–57, 172, 173, 176, 220–21. *See also Hamlet*, Clarendon edition; *Works of William Shakespeare, The* (ed. Clark and Wright)
Claudius (character): in *Der bestrafte Brudermord*, 178; closet scene and, 103–4, 140, 143, 150–54; "conscience" and, 164, 187, 196; guilt of, 196, 201; killing of, 162, 168, 181–82, 187, 196; marriage of, 137, 138, 154; prayer scene and, 191–92, 197, 200; suspicions of, 178; in *Ur-Hamlet*, 178, 189
Clayton, Thomas, 227n71
clowns, 114–15
Cohn, Albert, 172
Coleridge, Samuel Taylor: "conscience" and, 171, 177; on *Hamlet*, 115, 132–33, 139, 162, 170, 246n107; on Kean, 133; as Shakespeare critic, 10, 18, 40–41, 45, 58, 140, 171, 175; on "To be, or not to be" soliloquy, 163. *See also* Romanticism
Collier, John Payne: as "Ambrose Gunthio," 157, 249n3; closet scene and, 123, 127–29; on Coleridge, 40–41; "country matters" and, 106; and Duke of Devonshire, 39; engraving of, 32 (fig.); forgeries of, 40, 47, 50, 51, 128–29 (fig.), 229n54, 233n131; Halliwell's friendship with, 57, 58, 230n77, 230n79, 233n131; *Hamlet* edition

(1843) of, 39–41, 56; on *Henry V*, 38; influence of, 50–51, 58, 112; Knight opposed by, 34, 40, 42–45, 47–49, 51–58, 73, 105, 106, 207, 218, 232n114; on *The Merry Wives of Windsor*, 38; Mommsen and, 50, 51, 54; New Bibliographical forgetting of, 50; on *Pericles*, 38; retrograde bibliography created by 37, 38, 50, 53, 189, 193, 216, 230, 249n3; scholarly societies and, 40, 43–45, 49, 57; on Shakespeare's authorship, 47–50, 56–57, 60–62, 128–29, 191, 231n89, 231–32n102; stenography and, 31, 34–45, 50–51, 53–54, 58, 60, 105, 106, 228n34, 229n59
Comédie-Française, 143
Comedy of Errors, The (Shakespeare), 77–78
Condell, Henry, 26, 30
Conjectures on Original Composition (Young), 34, 48
"conscience," 22, 193–206, 250n23, 251n46, 256n163; as "consciousness," 164–65, 167–71, 185–86, 195–97, 203, 250n31, 250n35, 250–51n38, 251n40, 251n46; as moral faculty, 164–72, 182–88, 193–95, 200–201, 203–6
continuous copy, 180, 254n105
"contrary matters." *See* "country matters" vs. "contrary matters"
"Copy for 'Hamlet,' 1603, The" (Wilson), 180
Corbin, John, 177
Corson, Hiram, 171
Country Girl, The (Garrick) 95
"country matters" vs. "contrary matters," 21, 72–102, 104–13, 157, 163, 164, 218, 236n13, 236n15, 237n23, 237n24, 238n48, 239n57, 239n70, 240n72, 240n79, 240n80, 242n102
Country Wife, The (Wycherley) 95
Coverley, Roger de, 97–98
Crypt, or, Receptacle for Things Past, The, 165
Cynthia's Revels (Jonson) 70

Daniel, P. A., 50
Dawson, Anthony, 117
Defence of Poetry, A (Shelley), 34
de Grazia, Margreta, 11, 14, 15, 34, 225n44, 230n78, 232n125
Delany, Sheila, 82
Delius, Nicholas, 53
Dessen, Alan C., 149

Devonshire, Duke of, 1, 3, 16, 39, 45, 223n2, 223n3
Diamond Dust Shoes (Warhol), 214
Dibdin, Thomas Frognall, 1, 123–25, 223n1, 224n9
Dickens, Charles, 51, 52
Dictionary of Sexual Language and Imagery in Shakespearean and Stuart Literature, A (Williams), 76
Dictionary of Shakespeare's Sexual Puns and Their Significance, A (Rubinstein), 86
Dillon, Janette, 217, 258n32
Dimock, Wai Chee, 14, 225n44
Dinshaw, Carolyn, 14
disintegrationism, 171–88, 189, 195, 207–8, 213, 216, 220, 253n86, 253n92, 255n137
Donne, John, 77, 238–39n54
Drama, 36, 123
Dramatic Works of William Shakespeare, The (ed. Singer, 1826), 73, 101–7; 102 (fig.).
Dulwich College, 6
Duthie, G. I., 189–95, 210, 212, 232n108, 255n132, 255n139, 257n10
Dyce, Alexander, 40, 53, 106, 232n119, 250n31

Early English Books Online (EEBO), 77
Edinburgh Review, 41, 133
Edward II (Marlowe), 226–27n70
Edwards, Philip, 87, 168–69, 193–95, 212, 217
Egan, Gabriel, 211, 257n8
Eighteenth Century Collections Online (ECCO), 97, 239n70
Eliot, George, 15
Eliot, T. S., 58, 140, 176, 247n111
Elizabethan Revenge Tragedy (Bowers), 189
Elze, Karl, 100–101, 104
Erne, Lukas, 64, 154, 229n43, 248n135, 255n132, 258n34
Essays (Montaigne), 184
Essex, Earl of, 33
Esty, Jed, 225n42
Every Man Out of His Humor (Jonson), 87

Family Shakespeare (ed. Bowdler and Bowdler, 1860–65), 107, 127 (fig.)
Farmer, Alan B., 68, 69, 235n117
Farmer, Richard, 5–6, 45, 104, 230n72
"First Edition of *Hamlet*, The" (John Taylor), 131–32

First Quarto. *See Hamlet*, Q1
Fleay, F. G., 173, 174, 220, 252n62
Fletcher, John, 104, 162, 248n133
Florio, John, 76, 110, 184, 242n106
Fortinbras (character), 27, 134
Foucault, Michel, 14, 75, 83, 170, 174
Foxe, John, 237n17
Fratricide Punished. See Der bestrafte Brudermord
Freccero, Carla, 14
Free Review, 175
Freud, Sigmund, 10, 11, 21, 243n25, 250n35; Oedipal reading of *Hamlet* by, 116–23, 131, 140, 141, 144, 145, 153–54, 156, 178–79
Furness, Horace Howard, 106, 166, 167, 172, 174–75, 250n31
Furness, Horace Howard, Jr., 166, 254n117
Furnivall, F. J., 172–73, 176, 185, 191, 216, 220, 250–51n38

Galaxy, 130
Galey, Alan, 227n1
Garber, Marjorie, 11
Garrick, David, 18, 95, 117, 125, 136, 247n127
Garvie, Alfred E., 186
genealogy: glossing and, 112–13; search for origins opposed to, 14–15, 170, 218–21
Genesis of Hamlet, The (Charlton Lewis) 175
Gentleman's Magazine, 10, 28, 74, 75, 79, 105, 106, 225n41
Gertrude (character), 3–5, 53, 103; as "Gertred" in Q1 *Hamlet*, 3, 151, 153, 154, 200; in closet scene, 116–26, 128, 129 (fig.), 130–56, 164, 188, 190, 197, 247n114, 248nn131–33, 248–49n144; degradation of, 178; illustrations of, 127 (fig.), 146 (fig.), 147 (fig.), 148 (fig.); in Meisei First Folio, 256n154
Gervinus, Gerog Gottfried, 53, 232n120
Gesta Danorum (Saxo), 8
Ghost (character): in closet scene, 122–50, 152–56, 177–78, 183, 200, 244n49, 245n60, 245n65, 245n68, 247n114; illustrations of, 146 (fig.), 147 (fig.), 148 (fig.); 149–50; nightgown costume of, 157, 163, 173, 197, 244n49, 244n53, 244n65, 247n114, 248n131
Gielgud, John, 117, 118, 120
Globe, Le, 163
Globe theater, 19, 61, 86, 149, 226n66

Goddard, William, 110
Goethe, J. W. von, 10, 28, 58, 123, 170, 171, 173, 175; on Q1 *Hamlet*, 131–33, 224n25; *Wilhelm Meister*, 131, 133, 139, 224n25. *See also* Romanticism
Goldsmith, Oliver, 159, 165
"Good Morrow, The" (Donne), 77, 238–39n54
Grady, Hugh, 14
Graphic, 135
Greenblatt, Stephen, 170
Greg, W. W., 29, 50, 61, 180–81, 190, 244n53
Guide to Preachers, A (Garvie), 186
Guildenstern (character), 103, 150, 164, 177, 179, 196; as "Gilderstone" in Q1 *Hamlet*, 151, 191
Gunthio, Ambrose, 157, 249n3
Guthrie, Tyrone, 118, 120

Halio, Jay L., 117
Hall, Edward, 197
Halliwell(-Phillipps), James Orchard, 16, 18, 43–44, 49, 57–58, 226n56, 230n77, 233n131, 233n136, 252n69
Hamlet (Shakespeare): Booth promptbook of, 128 (fig.); Christian interpretations of, 186–88, 193–95, 254n114; closet scene in, 21–22, 116–26, 127 (fig.), 128, 129 (fig.), 130–45, 146 (fig.), 147 (fig.), 148 (fig.), 149–56, 218; development out of earlier versions of, 172–81, 207–8, 210–14, 218–20, 253n102, 255n137; as generic revenge tragedy, 179, 181–82, 195; glossing of, 21, 75–78, 80–88, 94–101, 164–71, 182–88, 193–94, 200–201, 203–4, 239n70, 240n72, 251n46, 256n154; lack of tragic decorum in, 125–26, 132; as masterpiece, 15, 18, 30, 34, 115, 162–63, 185, 195, 218, 219; *The Mousetrap* in, 72, 93, 103, 196; obscenity in, 72–101, 104–12, 227n73, 242n107; Oedipal reading of, 116–23, 131, 140, 141, 144, 145, 153–54; postmodern approaches to, 207–9, 214–16; "problems" of, 176–82, 189, 257n10; "Smock Alley" promptbook of, 92–93 (fig.); textual stemma of, 190, 191–97, 199–214, 215 (fig.), 216–21, 241–42n101, 253n102, 258n34; "To be, or not to be" soliloquy in, 157–71, 174, 182–87, 190, 195–96, 198–205, 218, 232n120; versions of, 29, 30, 36, 48, 53, 55–58, 65–88, 92–103, 145, 150–56, 164–67, 176–205, 208–20. *See also specific editions*
Hamlet, Arden edition: 2nd series (ed. Jenkins, 1982), 75, 117, 169, 207; 3rd series (ed. Ann Thompson and Neil Taylor, 2006), 22, 55, 61, 75–76, 85, 118, 193, 207–14, 215 (fig.), 216–18
Hamlet, Clarendon edition (ed. Clark and Wright, 1872), 54–56, 172, 173, 180, 189, 191, 195, 216, 218, 220–21, 253n102
Hamlet, F (1623), 10, 11, 36, 37, 42, 44–45, 49, 56–57, 85–86, 164; "country matters" variant in, 109–12, 114–15; paratextual material in, 26, 30–31; Q1 *Hamlet* compared with, 84, 85, 86, 88–89, 101, 150–51, 153, 154, 159, 172–73, 242n106; Q2 *Hamlet* compared with, 72, 84–86, 88–89, 103–4, 109–12; "To be, or not to be" soliloquy in, 200–203. *See also* Inquisition Folio; Meisei First Folio; Perkins folio
Hamlet, New Cambridge edition (ed. Edwards, 1985), 87, 168–69, 192
Hamlet, Players' Duodecimo edition (1718), 17, 145, 148 (fig.)
Hamlet, Players' Quarto editions, 93–94, 239n62
Hamlet, Q1 (1603): as anachronistic, 11–14, 18, 20–23, 83; Bunbury copy of, 17–19; closet scene in, 123–32, 134, 135, 140–41, 144, 149–56, 157, 163, 173, 197, 244n49, 244n53, 244n65, 247n114, 248n131–33, 248–49n144; "contrary matters" variant in, 72–102, 104–12, 163, 164, 218, 239n57, 239n70, 240n72, 240n79, 240n80, 242n102; as corrupted, 28, 36, 47, 50–51, 53–55, 60, 61, 67–71, 115, 163, 180, 192, 194; discovery of, 1–6, 10, 13–15, 18–22, 25, 30–31, 64, 73–75, 83–84, 89, 99–101, 107, 157, 163–64, 171–72, 193–95, 223n1; ending of play in, 26–27; F *Hamlet* compared with, 72–75, 79, 84–86, 88–89, 101, 103–4, 107–12, 150–51, 153, 154, 159, 164, 172–73; ghostliness of, 11, 13, 15, 60, 214, 217, 219, 221; history of the book of, 1–6, 2 (fig.), 4 (fig.), 8, 14–19; journalism on, 26, 28, 34, 36, 73–75, 79, 104, 105, 210; as memorial reconstruction, 60, 62, 63, 74–75, 85, 129, 172, 189–95, 205, 208–10, 213, 216–18; monetary value of, 16–17, 83, 223n3, 226n54; as "new (old) Play,"

10, 18, 26; as "noted" text, 220, 235n169; origins of, 14–15, 22–23, 112, 129, 217–19, 221; publication of, 21, 29, 61, 63–69, 234n157; Q2 *Hamlet* compared with, 28, 30, 36, 54, 55–57, 60–75, 79, 84–86, 88–89, 101, 103–4, 107–12, 114–15, 150–51, 154, 153, 159, 164, 172–73, 183–84; reaction to, 27–28, 73–75, 79, 89, 101, 157, 159, 184–87, 216; Rooney copy of, 16–19, 171–72, 224n25; as rough draft, 106, 172, 173, 176–77, 180, 184, 186–87, 194, 216, 253n89; stage directions in, 248n131; theatricality of, 216–17; title page of, 2 (fig.), 66–68, 235n176; "To be, or not to be" soliloquy in, 157–71, 174, 183–84, 187, 188, 193–99, 200, 203–5, 218, 254n119, 256n163; "uncanny historicity" of, 10–11, 14–15, 21, 26, 39, 75, 88, 101, 112, 221, 226n45

Hamlet, Q2 (1604), 6, 7 (fig.), 10, 11, 20; "country matters" variant in, 72–87, 88–93, 101–2, 105, 107–11; 89–92 (figs.); F *Hamlet* compared with, 72, 84–86, 88–89, 103–4, 109–12; printing of, 21, 60, 61–71; Q2 *Hamlet* compared with, 28, 30, 36, 54–57, 60–71, 72–75, 84–86, 88–89, 103–4, 107–12, 114–15, 150–51, 153, 154, 159, 164, 172–73, 183–84; *The Spanish Tragedy* compared with, 69–70; title page of, 7 (fig.), 27, 28, 58–62, 66–71, 235n171; "To be, or not to be" soliloquy in, 195, 196, 199–200, 203, 205, 56n163

Hamlet, Shakespeare in Performance edition (ed. Dawson, 1995), 117

Hamlet, Students' Shakespeare edition (ed. Verity, 1904), 164–65

Hamlet (character): in closet scene, 116–26, 127 (fig.), 128, 129 (fig.), 130–45, 146 (fig.), 147 (fig.), 148 (fig.), 149–56; as Elizabethan, 178–79, 183, 253n93; madness of, 177–79, 189, 200–201, 242n102, 253n92; in Meisei First Folio, 203–4; obscenity and, 72–77, 79, 92–94, 96–97, 100–102, 107–12; on performance, 114–15; as philosophical, 177, 189, 193, 253n98; as psychological, 178–79, 183, 186–87, 246n107, 253n98; revenge of, 181–83, 186–87, 189, 196, 201–3, 254n108; versions of, 3–5, 53

"Hamlet and His Problems" (T. S. Eliot), 58

Hamlet and Oedipus (Ernest Jones), 144

Hamlet and Revenge (Prosser), 168

"*Hamlet" First Published, The* (ed. Clayton), 210

Hamlet in Purgatory (Greenblatt), 170

Hanmer, Thomas, 5, 96, 115, 166, 224n9

Harris, Jonathan Gil, 14, 83

Hathaway, Anne, 52

Hawkes, Terence, 14

Hazlitt, William, 10, 115, 170, 171, 250n31

Hecatommithi, Gli (Cinthio), 8

Hegel, G. W. F., 246n107, 247n110

Heminges, John, 26, 30

Henry IV, Part 1 (Shakespeare), 68

Henry IV, Part 2 (Shakespeare), 30, 33

Henry V (Shakespeare): language lesson in, 85–86, 88, 94, 115; rehabilitation of quarto edition of, 33–34, 47; as revised, 30–33, 46, 258n34; stenography and, 38, 228n30

Henry VI, Parts 1–3 (Shakespeare), 8, 29–33, 36, 46, 228n30, 248n133

Henry VIII, King of England, 155

Henry VIII (Shakespeare), 90

Henslowe, Philip, 6, 19, 70

Herder, Johann Gottfried von, 133

Herford, C. H., 167, 184, 185

Hero and Leander (Marlowe and Chapman), 77

Heussi, Jacob, 100–101, 104

Hibbard, G. R., 61, 76, 107, 117–19, 169, 192, 195, 212, 217, 232n108

historicism: 10–14, 17, 20–22, 195, 254n108; disintegrationism as a form of, 174–76, 179–81; in glossing, 80–81, 83, 113, 164–65, 188; as ideology of expertise, 43, 164–65, 188; performance in relation to, 116, 119–20

History of English Dramatic Poetry, The (Collier), 36

Holderness, Graham, 84, 88, 108

Holinshed, Raphael, 8

Holmes, Frank, 223n1

Homer Alamode, the Second Part, 78–79

Homiletic Review, 186

Honigmann, E. A. J., 62

Horatio (character), 3–5, 27, 53, 134, 139, 152, 154, 190, 191

Houston, Percy H., 182

Hubbard, Frank G., 212

Hudson, Henry Norman, 131, 167, 250n31

Hunter, Joseph, 53, 232n120, 254n119

Hydriotaphia, Urne–Buriall (Browne), 8–10

Hystorie of Hamblet, The, 8, 145, 215

"Illustrated Books and Newspapers" (Wordsworth), 44
"infinitive text," 215, 258n29
Inquisition Folio, 89–95, 98
Interpretation of Dreams, The (Freud), 116, 121–23, 141, 235n25, 243n25
Ioppolo, Grace, 257n10
Irace, Kathleen, 84–86, 89, 105, 212, 249n21
Irving, Henry, 123, 124 (fig.), 133–44, 149, 153, 156, 244n40, 245n68, 246n97, 246n103, 247n109, 247n114, 248n138

Jack, Ian, 81
Jameson, Fredric, 214
Jansohn, Christa, 81
Jardine, Lisa, 137, 155, 247n111
Jenkins, Harold, 75–76, 117, 169, 192–95, 207, 212, 213, 217, 232n108, 233n147, 241–42n100
Johnson, Gerald, 63
Johnson, Samuel, 10, 18, 240n74; on "country matters," 94–100, 104; on *Hamlet*, 30, 94, 99, 103, 139, 159, 162, 201, 204; on *Henry V*, 30, 32, 33, 36; on *Henry VI* plays, 32–33, 36; on *King Lear*, 30; on *The Merry Wives of Windsor*, 29; on *Richard II*, 30; on Shakespeare's authorship, 30–33
Jones, Ann Rosalind, 14, 130, 245n60
Jones, Ernest, 21, 116, 119, 122, 141, 144, 153–54, 156, 178–79
Jonson, Ben, 26, 28, 34, 70, 87, 210
Joseph, Bertram, 168

Kaleidoscope, 74
Kastan, David Scott, 63–64, 249n20
Kean, Edmund, 133, 136
Kehler, Dorothy, 154
Kemble, John Philip, 223n2, 240n80
King Hamlet. *See* Ghost (character)
King John (Shakespeare), 29, 30, 90, 100
King Lear (Shakespeare), 30, 185, 209–11
King's Men, 61–66
Kisery, András, 232n109
Kittredge, George Lyman, 181–82
Kliman, Bernice, 144–45
Knapp, Peggy, 77
Knight, Charles: biography of, 40, 43–44, 230n79; on Coleridge, 40–41; Collier opposed by, 34, 40, 42–45, 47–49, 51–58, 73, 105, 106, 207, 218, 232n114; on "conscience," 165, 166, 185–86; "Foliolatry" of, 42, 44–45; as popularizer of Shakespeare, 41–44, 232n118; portrait of, 35 (fig.); Romanticism of, 43–44; on Shakespeare's authorship, 40–50, 56–58, 60, 73, 170, 172–73, 230n69, 231n89, 253n89; on "To be, or not to be" soliloquy, 163
Kyd, Thomas, 176–79, 190, 235n172, 253n102, 252–53n82, 255n137

Lactantius, 16–17
Laertes (character), 139, 196, 200, 203–4
Lander, Jesse M., 159, 256n160, 256n163, 257n26
Lanier, Douglas, 13
Lee, Sidney, 167
Legman, G., 84, 88
Levenson, Jill L., 211, 214, 235n170
Lewis, Charlton M., 175, 177–78, 183, 189, 193, 255n134
Lewis, C. S., 168, 250–51n38
Library Companion, The (Dibdin), 1
Lightfoot, Joseph Barber, 186
Ling, Nicholas, 14, 20, 61–71, 234n154, 234n157, 235n169
Literary Gazette (London), 3–5, 10, 36, 73–74, 99–100, 157
Literary Gazette (United States), 74
Locrine, 68
Lodge, Thomas, 5, 6, 15, 45, 47, 70
London Magazine, 157
London Prodigal, The, 208
Looking for Sex in Shakespeare (Wells), 82–83
Loughrey, Bryan, 84, 88, 108
Love, Heather, 14
Love's Labour's Lost (Shakespeare), 61, 68, 69; punning in, 89–91, 94, 90 (fig.), 94
Lowes, John Livingston, 165, 188
Lyceum Theatre, 134, 136, 139, 140, 143, 247n114

Macbeth (Shakespeare), 149, 185
MacDonald, George, 186, 187
Maguire, Laurie E., 82, 108, 242n107, 255n153, 257n6
Malone, Edmond: *Der bestrafte Brudermord* ignored by, 6; "country matters" and, 95, 98–100, 242n106; discovery of Henslowe's Diary by, 6, 19; on Globe theater, 28–29, 226n66; influence of, 98–100, 102, 104, 106, 181, 230n78; on nightgown in Q1 *Hamlet*, 127; on Q2 *Hamlet*, 6, 28–29, 60,

66, 104, 227n71; as Shakespearean editor, 10, 12, 18, 20, 42, 44, 181; on Shakespearean revision, 28–30, 33–34, 45, 46, 224n17; stenography and, 31–34, 228n29, 228n34; on textual stemma, 28–30, 33, 233n128, 253n82; on "To be, or not to be" soliloquy, 162, 165–66, 201; Shakespeare variorum edition (1790) of, 6, 95, 98–100, 102, 104, 106, 233n128. *See also* stenography; *Ur-Hamlet*
Manuscript of Shakespeare's Hamlet, The (Wilson), 61
Marcus, Leah, 211, 249n21
Marino, James J., 219, 231–32n102, 258n34
Marlowe, Christopher, 77, 110, 184, 210, 226–27n70
"Marriage of Good and Bad Quartos, The" (McLeod), 215
Marshall, Frank, 106, 137, 141
Mason, John Monck, 98
Masten, Jeffrey, 14, 225n28, 226–27n70
Mathews, Charles, 157
McLeod, Randall, 215, 216, 257n7, 258n29
Measure for Measure (Shakespeare), 90, 254n118
Meisei First Folio, 200–201, 202 (fig.), 203–5, 256n154
melodrama, 137–41, 182, 247n109. *See also* Irving, Henry
Memoranda on the Tragedy of Hamlet (Halliwell), 57
memorial reconstruction: *Der bestrafte Brudermord* as, 190–91; challenges to, 209, 213, 216–17, 231n92, 255n138, 257n6, 257n10, 258n38; "country matters" and, 108–9, 241n96; Duthie on, 189–91, 193–95, 210, 255n138, 257n10; *The Merry Wives of Windsor* as, 29; Q1 *Hamlet* as, 60, 62, 63, 74–75, 85, 129, 172, 189–95, 205, 208–10, 213, 216–18; retrograde bibliography and, 37, 38, 50, 193, 216; theatricality and, 217; "To be, or not to be" soliloquy as, 195, 205
Menzer, Paul, 219, 248n134, 235n176, 258n34
Merchant of Venice, The (Shakespeare), 1, 91 (fig.)
Meres, Francis, 54
Merry Wives of Windsor, The (Shakespeare), 29–30, 38, 50, 105, 159
Midsummer Night's Dream, A (Shakespeare), 1

Milton, John, 26, 28
modernism, 58, 140, 173–74, 178, 207, 214. *See also* disintegrationism; Romanticism; New Bibliography; postmodernism
Mommsen, Tycho, 19, 50–51, 54, 172, 192, 232n108
Montaigne, Michel de, 183, 184, 194, 254n114
Montaigne and Shakespeare (Robertson), 183
Morning Chronicle, 74
Mowat, Barbara, 88, 226–27n70

Nashe, Thomas, 5, 6, 15, 45, 47, 70
Neilson, William Allan, 167
Nest of Ninnies, A (Armin), 44
New Bibliography: challenges to, 209, 213, 216, 258n36; Collier forgotten by, 50; disintegrationism compared with, 180–81, 213; as modern, 27, 55, 164, 180, 219; Q2 *Hamlet* and, 60; theatricality and, 216. *See also* Greg, W. W.; Pollard, A. W.; Wilson, John Dover
New Grant White Shakespeare, The (ed. White et al., 1912), 167
New Textualism, 209–16, 218–20; "infinitive text" and, 215, 258n29; retrograde bibliography eroded by, 216; unediting and, 22–23, 209, 213–14, 215 (fig.), 219–20, 257n7, 257n26, 257–58n27. *See also* postmodernism
Norton Shakespeare, The (ed. Greenblatt et al., 1997), 76, 251n46
Notes and Queries, 125

Old Hamlet. *See* Ghost (character)
Oliphant, Margaret, 136–37, 140, 156
Olivier, Laurence, 117, 118, 120
Ophelia (character), 3, 137, 139, 173, 177, 239n67; in Meisei First Folio, 203–4; obscenity and, 21, 72–75, 79, 92–93, 96, 101–2, 108–12, 241–42n101; in Oedipal interpretations, 141; as "Ofelia" in Q1 *Hamlet*, 107, 150–51; stage directions and, 129, 244n52
Orlin, Lena Cowen, 119
Ostovich, Helen, 87
Othello (Shakespeare), 30, 149
Oxford Shakespeare. *See William Shakespeare: The Complete Works*
Oxford English Dictionary, 76, 88, 109, 118, 165

Partridge, Eric, 84, 108
Pauncefort, Georgina, 136, 138
Pavier, Thomas, 69, 234n164
Payne and Foss: editorial indifference of, 18, 26–27; Q1 *Hamlet* reprinted by (1825), 3, 4 (fig.), 25–28, 36, 46, 99, 102–3, 207, 223n3. *See also* Henry Bunbury
Penny Magazine, 41
performance: changing scholarly views of, 30, 114–20; "country matters" variant and, 81, 83–89, 111–12; of closet scene, 120, 121 (fig.), 125–53; cutting of *Hamlet* in, 81, 92–94, 122, 134–35, 137, 139, 155, 240n80, 241n95, 244n40, 246n103, 247n122; glossing and, 80; of Henry Irving's *Hamlet*, 133–44, 156, 246n103, 247n122; historicism in relation to, 116, 119–20; of Q1 *Hamlet*, 216–17, 258n32, 258n34. *See also* memorial reconstruction; stenography
Pericles (Shakespeare), 38, 50
Perkins Folio, 128–29 (fig.)
Pictorial Edition of the Works of Shakspere, The (ed. Knight, 1838–43), 40–45, 49, 165, 166
Pictorial History of Greece, The (Knight), 42, 49
Pictorial History of Palestine, The (Knight), 42, 49
Pictorial History of Rome, The (Knight), 42, 49
Pinkerton, John, 98
piracy. *See* memorial reconstruction; stenography
Plays and Poems of William Shakspeare, The (ed. Malone, 1790), 6, 95, 98–100, 102, 104, 106, 233n128
Poel, William, 216, 258n32
Pollard, A. W., 39, 60–61, 63, 209, 211, 253n102, 258n36
Polonius (character): in closet scene, 120, 125, 134, 145, 150, 151, 155, 177, 179, 196, 200, 247–48n128; as "Corambis" in Q1 *Hamlet*, 5, 16, 53–54, 145, 150, 151, 201; as "Corambus" in *Der bestrafte Brudermord*, 6; in Meisei First Folio, 201, 203–4
Poole, Kristen, 237n23
Pope, Alexander, 29, 30, 51, 96, 115, 162, 166
postmodernism, 207–9; crisis of historicity in, 214–16. *See also* modernism; New Textualism; Romanticism

Problem of "Hamlet," The (Robertson), 58, 176, 252n67
Prosser, Eleanor, 168, 169, 201–3
Proverbs of Hendyng, 76
Pseudodoxia Epidemica (Browne), 19

Rationale of the Dirty Joke (Legman), 84
Reasons for a New Edition of Shakespeare's Works (Collier), 43–44
Reed, Henry Hope, 126, 166
Reed, Isaac, 6, 43, 99
Religious Tract Society, 186
Reynaldo (character), 5, 53–54
Richard II (Shakespeare), 30, 228n21
Richard III (Shakespeare), 69, 166, 167, 183–84, 198, 203, 205, 254n117
Ridley, M. R., 165
Riverside Shakespeare, 130, 167, 181
Roach, Joseph R., 135
Roberts, James, 61–67, 234n154, 234n157, 234n165
Roberts, Jeanne Addison, 228n30
Robertson, John Mackinnon, 58, 59 (fig.), 173–85, 189, 233n136, 252n64, 254n114. *See also* disintegrationism
Robinson, Mary, 240n79
Romanticism: authorship and, 34–35, 44; challenges to, 54, 56–58, 139–40, 143, 171–75, 179–80, 182; closet scene and, 132–33; "conscience" and, 169–72, 185–87; *Hamlet* and, 34–35, 46–49, 137, 139–40, 169–72, 254n108; national culture and, 43; Shakespeare criticism and, 34–35, 40–41, 43, 44, 46–49; theatricality and, 115. *See also* Collier, John Payne; disintegrationism; Knight, Charles; modernism; New Bibliography; postmodernism
Romeo and Juliet (Shakespeare), 1, 29, 30, 37–38, 50, 68, 69, 94; first quarto of, 37, 51, 102, 104, 159, 172, 211, 215, 258n34; second quarto of, 61, 211, 215; textual stemma of, 214
Romeo und Julietta, 215
Rooney, M. W., 16, 172, 224n25, 226n53, 226n54, 226n56, 226n68
Rosenberg, Marvin, 118, 245n60
Rosencrantz (character), 103, 150, 164, 177, 179, 196; as "Rossencraft" in Q1 *Hamlet*, 151, 191, 225n28, 248n136
Rowe, Nicholas, 10, 72, 96, 144–45, 146 (fig.), 147 (fig.), 248n131

Royal Shakespeare Company, 117
Rubinstein, Frankie, 86
"Running Commentary on the Hamlet of 1603, A" (Gunthio), 123, 157

Sanchæum, Guilielmum. *See* William Sankey
Sankey, William, 90–92 (figs.), 94, 239n60. *See also* Inquisition Folio
Saxo Grammaticus, 8, 145
Schlegel, August Wilhelm von: 10, 45, 132–33, 229n58; on *Hamlet*, 100, 139, 162, 170–71, 183, 251n53; modernist criticism and, 173, 175. *See also* Romanticism
Schmidt, Alexander, 167
Schücking, Levin L., 173, 176, 179, 182–83, 189, 252n64
Scornful Lady, The (Fletcher), 162
Second Folio (Shakespeare), 26, 114. *See also* Inquisition Folio; Perkins folio
Second Quarto. *See Hamlet*, Q2
Seneca, Lucius Annaeus, 5, 70, 177
Shakespeare, Hamnet, 52
Shakespeare, William: as author, 26–39, 45–71, 74–75, 83–84, 98–99, 104–8, 110, 112–3, 115–20, 170–95, 205–21; as genius, 26–29, 45–48, 57, 58, 182, 209; authorial intentions of, 30, 74, 80–83, 98–99, 116–18, 127–28, 175–76, 189–90, 208–9, 238n32, 241–42n101; popularization of, 40–45, 51–52; as reviser, 8, 12, 26, 28–37, 45–58, 73–75, 105–6, 173, 175–92, 195, 208–11, 218–20, 231n89, 231–32n102
Shakespearean Originals, 210
Shakespearean Tragedy (Bradley), 141–43, 178
Shakespeare for All Time (Wells), 118
Shakespeare in Germany (Cohn), 172
Shakespeare in the Cinema: Ocular Proof (Buhler), 117–18
Shakespeare-Lexicon (Schmidt), 167
Shakespeare Restored (Theobald), 17, 96–97
Shakespeare's Bawdy (Partridge), 84
Shakespeare's Erotic Word Usage (Webb), 86–87
Shakespeare's Fight with the Pirates (Pollard), 61
Shakespeare's Folios and Quartos (Pollard), 60–61, 253n102
Shakespeare Society, 40, 43, 44, 49, 52, 57, 230n79

Shelley, Percy Bysshe, 34
shorthand. *See* stenography
Sidney, Philip, 77, 197
Simmes, Valentine, 63, 64, 66–67, 234n154, 234n164
Singer, Samuel Weller, 73, 101–7. *See also Dramatic Works of William Shakespeare*
Small, Ian, 80
Smith, Emma, 6
Smith, Henry, 69
Society for the Distribution of Useful Knowledge (SDUK), 41, 42
Solimon and Perseda (Kyd), 68
Some Remarks on the Tragedy of Hamlet (Stubbes), 18, 125–26
Spanish Tragedy, The (Kyd), 68–70, 176–77, 190, 195, 235n172, 255n137
Spectator, 97–98
Stallybrass, Peter, 14, 130, 153–54, 232n125, 245n60, 256n156, 258n34
Stationers' Register, 62–63, 235n171
Staunton, Howard, 106, 250n31
Steevens, George, 29, 42, 51, 98, 99, 102, 127, 162, 166, 181, 240n72
stenography, 31–39, 44, 49–51, 60–62, 105–6, 127, 129, 180, 208–9, 217, 218, 228n29, 228n34, 249n3, 253n102, 257n10, 258n38
Stern, Tiffany, 219, 258n38
Sterne, Laurence, 97
Stewart, Alan, 119
Stoll, E. E., 119, 173, 175–76, 179, 181–83, 185, 252n64, 253n83, 253n93, 253n97–98, 255n132
Strachey, Edward, 165
Stubbes, George, 18, 125–26, 130, 138, 163, 205, 240n72, 253n92
Studies in Words (C. S. Lewis), 168
Study of Hamlet, A (Marshall), 106
Styan, J. L., 115, 118–20
stylometrics, 174, 220, 235n175
Sunday at Home Family Magazine for Sabbath Reading, 186

Tabor, Stephen, 223n2
Tamer Tamed, The (Fletcher), 248n133
Taming of the Shrew, The (Shakespeare), 30, 82
Taranow, Gerda, 143
Taylor, Gary, 116, 118, 209–12, 225n36, 257–58n27

Taylor, Neil: on closet scene, 118, 151, 248n135, 256n154; on obscenity, 75, 76, 79, 81, 85–88, 107, 236n4, 236n9; postmodern approach of, 207–9, 212–18; on printing of Q2 *Hamlet*, 61, 64; on "To be, or not to be" soliloquy, 249n7. *See also* New Textualism

Terry, Ellen, 246n90

"Textual Mystery of *Hamlet*, The" (Werstine), 210–11

Theobold, Lewis, 17, 18, 29–31, 96–97, 115, 162, 166, 240n74

Third Folio (Shakespeare), 92–93

Thompson, Ann: on closet scene, 118, 151, 248n135, 256n154; on obscenity, 75, 76, 79, 81, 82, 85–88, 107, 236n4, 236n9; postmodern approach of, 207–9, 212–18; on printing of Q2 *Hamlet*, 61, 64; on "To be, or not to be" soliloquy, 249n7. *See also* New Textualism

Thomson, Leslie, 149, 248n133

Tieck, Ludwig, 133, 245n65, 247n114

Times Literary Supplement, 210

Titus Andronicus (Shakespeare), 180

Touchstone (character), 77, 91

Traub, Valerie, 14

Traumdeutung, Die. See Interpretation of Dreams, The

Treasurie or Store-house of Similes, A (Cawdry), 197

Tristram Shandy (Sterne), 97

Troilus and Cressida (Shakespeare), 30, 90, 110

Trundle, John, 14, 61, 63–64

Twenty of the Plays of Shakespeare (ed. Steevens, 1766), 29

Two Maids of More-clacke, The (Armin), 149, 155

Ulrici, Hermann, 170–71, 247n110

uncanny, the, 10–11, 156

uncanny historicity. *See Hamlet*, Q1

Understanding Shakespeare's Plays in Performance (Halio), 117

unediting. *See* New Textualism

Union of the Two Noble and Illustrate Fameles of Lancastre & Yorke (Hall), 197

Ur-Hamlet: Der bestrafte Brudermord in relation to, 172, 174, 178, 188–93, 195; description of, 6–8, 177, 233n128; development of theory of, 55–57, 172–78, 180, 182–83, 185, 187–95, 220, 231n92, 231n102, 255n137. *See also* disintegrationism; New Bibliography

Urkowitz, Steven, 209, 210–11, 225n36, 248n142

Urn Burial (Browne), 8–10

Valpy, A. J., 106, 250n31

Van Gogh, Vincent, 214

Verity, Arthur Wilson, 164–65

Verplank, G. C., 106, 250n31

versioning. *See* New Textualism

Vickers, Brian, 210

Voltaire, 125, 132, 133

Voltemand (character), 103

Warburton, William, 30, 96, 162, 166

Warhol, Andy, 214

Warren, Michael, 225n36

Webb, J. Barry, 86–87, 88

Webster, John, 149

Weiner, Albert B., 212

Wells, Stanley, 82–83, 116, 118–19, 209–12

Werder, Karl, 120

Werstine, Paul, 210–11, 220, 257n16, 258n36

What Happens in Hamlet (Wilson), 119, 144, 180–81

White, Richard Grant, 37, 51, 54–57, 60, 130, 232n108, 250n31; on "To be, or not to be" soliloquy, 157–58, 163

White Devil, The (Webster), 149, 248n10

Wilhelm Meister's Apprenticeship (Goethe), 131, 133, 139, 224n25

Williams, Gordon, 76, 77, 110

William Shakespeare: The Complete Works (ed. Wells and Taylor, 1986), 116, 209, 210, 219, 257n13

Wilson, John Dover, 15, 61, 119, 120, 123, 144, 156, 167, 176, 180–81, 244n53

Woman Killed with Kindness, A (Heywood), 149, 155

Wordsworth, William, 44, 47

Working-Man's Companion, The, 41

Works of Mr. William Shakespear, The (ed. Rowe, 1709), 144–45, 146 (fig.), 147 (fig.)

Works of Thomas Kyd, The (ed. Boas, 1901), 181

Works of William Shakespeare, The (ed. Clark and Wright, 1863–66), 51, 53–54

Works of William Shakespeare, The (ed. Collier, 1842–44), 39–41, 56

Works of William Shakespeare, The (ed. Dyce, 1864–67), 37, 49, 167
World of Proverb and Parable, The (Hood), 186
World of Words, A (Florio), 110
Wright, William Aldis, 51, 54–57, 172, 173, 176, 220–21. *See also Hamlet*, Clarendon edition; *Works of William Shakespeare, The* (ed. Clark and Wright)

Wycherley, William, 95

Yorick's Meditations upon Various Interesting and Important Subjects, 97
Yorkshire Tragedy, A, 208
Young, Edward, 34, 44, 48

Zucker, Adam, 237n31

ACKNOWLEDGMENTS

Hamlet After Q1 grew out of two presentations that I gave in 2011 on Bunbury's discovery. The first was at the Centre for Renaissance and Early Modern Studies at the University of York, and I remain grateful to Bill Sherman for the invitation, and to everyone who participated for their valuable feedback on how to develop the project. The second was at L'Associazione Culturale Italo Britannica in Bologna, generously organized by its director, Valeria Sarti, and by Keir Elam of the Dipartimento di Lingue, Letterature e Culture Moderne. Without these two invitations, and the impetus they gave me to continue to think about Q1, the book would not have been written.

I want also to thank Ralph Cohen, Paul Menzer, and the rest of the organizing committee of the 2011 Blackfriars Conference for inviting me to present a talk on *country matters*; Colin Macdonald and Michael Plunkett of the Early Modern Interdisciplinary Group at the CUNY Graduate Center, and Peter Stallybrass of the Seminar in the History of Material Texts at Penn, for invitations to speak about the Ghost's nightgown; and Jonathan Lamb, David Bergeron, Geraldo Sousa, Richard Hardin, and Byron Caminero-Santangelo for bringing me to the University of Kansas to give the annual American and British Lecture on "To be, or not to be."

Numerous colleagues read portions of the manuscript, offered important critiques and suggestions, told me things I didn't know, and generally helped me think through the issues raised by Bunbury's discovery. I am indebted to Claire Bourne, Heidi Brayman Hackel, Claire Busse, Alice Dailey, Margreta de Grazia, Alan Dessen, Mario DiGangi, Lars Engle, Jed Esty, Alan Farmer, Emily Gerstell, Jim Green, Jane Hedley, Jonathan Hope, Janet Ing Freeman, David Kastan, Andràs Kisery, Bernice Kliman, Jeff Knight, Matt Kozusko, Ania Loomba, Heather Love, Ivan Lupić, Jack Lynch, Laurie Maguire, Sonia Massai, Jeff Masten, Cary Mazer, Russ McDonald, Gordon McMullan, Paul Menzer, Nichole Miller, Shannon Miller, Dianne Mitchell, Lucy Munro, Marissa Nicosia, Vimala Pasupathi, Kristen Poole, Aaron Pratt, Ben Robinson, Jessica

Rosenberg, Kathy Rowe, Melissa Sanchez, Lauren Shohet, Jerry Singerman, Adam Smyth, Eric Song, Peter Stallybrass, Alan Stewart, Marta Straznicky, Gary Taylor, Simran Thadani, Leslie Thomson, Dan Traister, Elly Truitt, Steve Urkowitz, Bronwyn Wallace, and Liliane Weissberg. I am particularly grateful to Douglas Bruster, Tiffany Stern, and Adam Zucker, who carefully read the entire manuscript and improved it immensely.

I have also benefited from the expertise and generosity of librarians and bibliographers at a number of research libraries, including Steve Galbraith, Goran Proot, Sarah Werner, and Heather Wolfe of the Folger Shakespeare Library; John Pollack and Lynn Farrington of the Kislak Center at Penn; Stephen Tabor of the Huntington Library; Jim Green and Connie King of the Library Company of Philadelphia; Katie Vaughan and Victoria Goodwin of the Bury St. Edmunds Record Office; and the local historian of Great Barton, Frank Holmes.

Finally, I am constantly grateful for the wonderful Laura Freeman, Vanetta Britt, and Chiara Bonafede, without whom I could never have found the time to write this book; for my parents, Mary and David Lesser, who have loved me and my work even when at times both seemed incomprehensible; and for my father-in-law, Gabe Silverman, who was in my life too briefly and who still inspires me to be more curious.